Arthur Young, Matilda Betham-Edwards

Arthur Young's Travels in France

During the Years 1787, 1788, 1789

Arthur Young, Matilda Betham-Edwards

Arthur Young's Travels in France
During the Years 1787, 1788, 1789

ISBN/EAN: 9783337211363

Printed in Europe, USA, Canada, Australia, Japan

Cover: Foto ©Andreas Hilbeck / pixelio.de

More available books at **www.hansebooks.com**

ARTHUR YOUNG'S TRAVELS IN FRANCE.

DURING THE YEARS 1787, 1788, 1789,

WITH

AN INTRODUCTION, BIOGRAPHICAL SKETCH, AND NOTES.

EDITED BY

MISS BETHAM-EDWARDS,

Officier de l'Instruction Publique de France.
Author of " The Roof of France,"
etc., etc.

FOURTH EDITION, CORRECTED AND REVISED.

LONDON:
GEORGE BELL & SONS, YORK ST., COVENT GARDEN,
AND NEW YORK.
1892.

in the Rotunda of the British Museum or by the library fireside, but after Arthur Young's own fashion—the fruit of investigations as laboriously and lovingly pursued as those of my great predecessor. I have now followed in his footsteps for upwards of fifteen years, visiting and revisiting various parts of the country described by him so graphically on the eve of the Revolution. Let us glance at the contrasted picture of France under the ancien régime and under the Third Republic.

His earliest journey takes him in a south-westerly direction, through the Orleannais and the Berri, where for the first time he meets with métayage—"a miserable system," he writes, "that perpetuates poverty and excludes instruction;" and he goes on to describe the fields as "scenes of pitiable management, and the houses, of misery."

Throughout the entire work we find métayage, or farming on half profits, condemned in the strongest terms, yet nothing has done more to improve the condition of the peasant and of husbandry within the last fifty years.[1] Métayage, indeed, which is but another name for co-operative agriculture, forms the stepping-stone from the status of hired labourer to that of capitalist; and whilst the métayer raises himself in the social scale, extensive wastes are by his agency brought under cultivation. So popular is "la culture à mi-fruits," that, according to the census of 1872, 11,182,000 hectares were in the hands of métayers, and 9,360,000 in those of peasant owners. In 1880 a diminution is seen—18 per cent. of métayage to set against 21 per cent. of proprietorship. Some parts of France are far more favourable to agricultural partnerships than others. We find 27,484 métairies in the department of the Landes, 24,893 in the Dordogne, 11,632 in the Allier, 11,568 in the Gironde, whilst in the Haute Savoie and the Lozère they may be counted by the hundred, the last-named numbering 325 only. In most cases, be it remembered, the métayer owns a bit of land. Two conditions are necessary to success: in the first place, the fermier-général, or farm bailiff, must be dispensed with; in the second, a good understanding is necessary between the two contracting

---

[1] See, for full information, the contribution of M. H. Baudrillart of the Institut to the "Revue des Deux Mondes," 1st Oct., 1885, "Le Métayage en France et son avenir."

parties—the one supplying land, stock, and implements, the other, manual labour, all produce being equally shared. From fifty to a hundred and fifty acres is found to be the most favourable size of a métairie.

We will now consider the present state of things in the Berri, a region about which Arthur Young has nothing to say, except that the husbandry was poor and the people miserable. As all readers of Georges Sand know well, it is a land of heaths and wastes, but the extent of uncultivated tracts is being reduced year by year. So rapid is the progress that the great novelist herself would hardly recognize certain portions of the country she has described so inimitably. What, then, must be the changes wrought in a hundred years? The transformation is partly realized by inspecting a pre-Revolutionary hovel. Here and there may be seen one of these bare, windowless cabins, now used as an out-house, and, in juxtaposition, the neat, airy, solid dwellings the peasant owners have built for themselves.

Four years ago I was the guest of a country gentleman near Châteauroux, chef-lieu of the department of the Indre, formed from the ancient Berri. Formerly owner of an entire commune, my host had gradually reduced his estate by selling small parcels of land to his day-labourers. He informed me that, whilst partly actuated by philanthropic motives, he was commercially a gainer. The expense of cultivating such large occupations was very great, and he could not hope for anything like the returns of the small freeholder. We visited many of these newly-made farms, with their spick-and-span buildings, the whole having the appearance of a little settlement in the Far West. The holdings varied in extent from six to thirty acres, their owners being capitalists to the amount of from two or three hundred to a thousand pounds. In each case the purchaser had built himself a small but commodious dwelling, and suitable out-houses. The land was well stocked and cultivated, the people were neatly and appropriately dressed, and the signs of general contentment and well-being delightful to contemplate. We next visited a métairie of nearly four hundred acres, and here the farmstead was on a large scale; the métayer employed several labourers who were boarded in the house, as was formerly the custom in certain parts of England, besides two or three dairymaids.

Artificial manures and machinery had here come into use; and if the culture could hardly be described as high farming, the land was clean and very productive. The cordial relations of "bailleur" and "preneur," or owner and métayer, testified to the satisfactoriness of the arrangement.

Not to be outdone by their rustic neighbours, the artizans of the Berrichon capital have, with few exceptions, become freeholders also. Suburban Châteauroux has, indeed, been appropriated by this class: the brand-new cottages and semi-detached villas on the outskirts of the town representing the thrift of the mechanic—an instance of self-help and sobriety hardly equalled throughout France. The houses were not only built for, but by their owners, in spare moments—another fact illustrating the innate economy of the French working man.

In purely agricultural districts of the Indre, land has quadrupled in value within the last forty or fifty years; near the towns, of course, the rise has been much higher.

Poitou is described by Arthur Young as "an unimproved, poor, and ugly country. It seems to want communication, demand and activity of all kinds." The ancient province of Poitou comprises La Vendée; but if we turn to the three carefully drawn maps appended to the original edition of the French Travels, we find the very name, so conspicuous a few years later, omitted altogether. Such a blank need not astonish us. "Who had so much as heard of La Vendée before 1793?" asks a French historian of the Vendean war. "Was it a province, a river, a mountain? Was it in Anjou, Brittany, or Poitou?" Nobody knew, and, till the outbreak of the insurrection, nobody cared to inquire. Only one road traversed the entire country—that from Nantes to La Rochelle—and on the creation of a department, it was found absolutely necessary to build a town as chef-lieu, none of sufficient importance existing. Waste, brushwood, heath and morass, with here and there patches of rye and buckwheat, occupied the place of the fertile fields and rich pastures that now rejoice the eye of the traveller in Bas Poitou. The transformation of recent years is startling enough. On the occasion of my first visit to this province fifteen years ago, many towns of the Vendean plain and Bocage were only accessible by diligence; since that period, railways have intersected the country in all directions—even the out of-the-way little town of Fontenay-le-Comte, so precious to the archæologist, has its branch line, whilst schools, railway stations, and other buildings of public utility have risen in all directions. Niort, chef-lieu of the Deux Sèvres, part of the ancient Bocage, and scene of the most terrible guerilla warfare of the Blancs and the Bleus, now possesses a railway station worthy of a capital. It may be briefly described as a town of 22,000 and odd souls, without a beggar. No rags, dirt, or vagrancy meet the eye in these clean, wide, airy streets. The Vendean costume still prevails, and whilst all is primitive, rustic, and provincial, evidences are here of immense and rapid progress. The immediate entourage of the town is one vast fruit and vegetable garden, the property of peasant owners. Melons, tomatoes, and peaches ripen in the sun, purple grapes cluster yellow walls, and luxuriant vegetation on all sides testifies to a highly favoured climate and soil. The produce of these market gardens is renowned throughout France. Two hundred acres are given up to the culture of the onion only.

La Vendée is a region of large tenant farms, and one visited by me in the neighbourhood of Niort may be accepted as a fair sample of the rest. The occupation consisted of four hundred and fifty acres, let on lease precisely as in England. For sixty-five years it had been held by members of the same family—a fact speaking volumes for both owner and tenant. It had consisted in part of waste, let at a nominal rent to begin with, the sum being raised as the land increased in value. Mule-rearing for Spain is one of the chief resources of La Vendée, and we were shown upwards of forty young mules of great beauty, varying in value from £30 to £80. The entire stock of the farm numbered seventy head of mules, horses, cows, and oxen, sixty sheep, besides pigs and poultry. Vineyards cover a tract of 30,000 hectares in this department, but here, as in many other places, the phylloxera had wrought entire ruin, only the blackened stocks remaining. The tenant farmer I name, as is almost universally the case, owned a small portion of land. Very likely, had inquiry gone back a generation or two, we should have found métayage the beginning of this prosperous family, their stepping-stone from the condition of day-labourer to that of capitalist.

Much larger holdings than the one just described exist in this part of France, and if the traveller takes a south-westerly direction from Niort to the sea coast, he will see a succession of large walled-in farmsteads recalling the moated granges of the Isle of Wight, the size and extent of the buildings attesting the importance of the occupation.

Of Languedoc Arthur Young writes in a very different strain. The picture, indeed, drawn by him of peasant owners round about Sauve and Ganges, in the department of the Gard, may well bear comparison with the traveller's experiences to-day.

" An activity has been here," he writes, " that has swept away all difficulties before it, and has clothed the very rocks with verdure. It would be an insult to common sense to ask the cause. The enjoyment of property *must* have done it. Give a man the secure possession of a black rock and he will turn it into a garden."

Here it is necessary to put in a word of explanation. Our author sets down one-third of French territory as belonging to the peasant at the time he wrote. This is one of the few errors of a very exact writer. In reality only a fourth of the soil belonged to the people before the Revolution, their little holdings having been acquired by means of incredible laboriousness and privation. The origin and development of peasant property throughout France can only be touched upon here. We must go very far back, farther even than the enfranchisement of the serfs by Louis le Hutin, in order to trace the progressive transfer of land.[1]

The Crusades, especially that of St. Bernard, brought about a veritable revolution in the matter of land tenure. The seigneurs, impoverished by all kinds of extravagance, then sold portions of property, not only to rich bourgeois and ecclesiastics, but to their own serfs, for the purpose of furnishing the necessary equipment. Many nobles thus succeeded in procuring ransom, forfeiting patrimony for their soul's good. The small owner by little and little contrived to better his position, and in the Etats Généraux of 1481, summoned by the great Anne of France, for the first time we find free peasants taking part in a legislative assembly. The Tiers Etat as a political body already existed.

---

[1] See H. Martin's " Histoire de France," vol. iii., p. 268, *et seq.*, " Les Serfs transformés en roturiers," and vol. vii., p. 190, " Etats Généraux."

In the words of a living authority lately quoted,[1] peasant property, far from being a device invented all of a piece and carried by force of law, dates from a period long anterior to the Revolution. In some places the number of small parcels of land has hardly changed from early times. The sale of church lands had by no means the effects attributed to it. About one-third of these consisted of forest, which was added to the state, another third consisted of buildings and town property, the remaining third, consisting of land, was sold in the lots actually existing without being divided at all, and the purchasers were for the most part well-to-do bourgeois.

These observations have seemed appropriate, as much confusion still exists on the subject among ourselves. That peasant property is the direct creation of the Revolution appears to be the generally accepted theory in England. Had Arthur Young's travels been read here with the attention paid to them by our French neighbours, such an error would have been cleared up long ago.

The Gard, of which our traveller gives so glowing a description, is by no means one of the most favoured departments. The phylloxera and the silkworm pest have greatly affected the prosperity of both town and country, yet the stranger halting at Le Vigan, or making his way thence to Millau in the Aveyron, finds himself amid a condition of things usually regarded as Utopian—a cheerful, well-dressed, self-supporting population, vagrancy unknown, and a distribution of well-being perhaps without a parallel in any part of Europe. Again and again will occur to his mind the famous passage with which Virgil concludes his second Georgic, that beautiful picture of pastoral happiness, which if imaginary in old Roman days, is so often realized in the rural France of our own.

Next Arthur Young visits the Landes on his way to Bordeaux. Here extraordinary changes have taken place within the last twenty years; what then must be the transformation wrought during the course of a century? Plantations, the sinking of wells, drainage, and irrigation, are fast fixing the unstable sands, making fruitful the marsh, and creating a healthful climate and fertile soil. Early in the present century the land

[1] M. H. Baudrillart, "Contemporary Review," May, 1886.

here was sold "au son de la voix;"[1] in other words, the accepted standard of measurement was the compass of human lungs. The stretch of ground reached by a man's voice sold for a few francs. Crops are now replacing the scant herbage of the salt marsh, and the familiar characteristic of the landscape, the shepherd's stilts, are already almost a thing of the past. The *échasse*, or in patois, *chanque*, a word dating from the English occupation, and derived by some authorities from "shank," is naturally discarded as the morass is transformed into solid ground. Six hundred thousand hectares of Landes planted with sea-pines produce resin to the annual value of fifteen million francs.

This noble tree, the *pinus maritima*, is here achieving a climatic revolution similar to the changes effected by the febrifugal Eucalyptus in the once fever-stricken plains of Algeria. The cork-tree, or chêne-liège, has proved equally effective. Many arid tracts are now covered with magnificent forests of recent growth, not only affording a source of revenue, but transforming the aspect and climatic conditions of the country. Only an inconsiderable proportion of the Landes remains in its former state.

Arthur Young's second journey takes him through Brittany and Anjou. Here also advance has been so rapid within our own time that the traveller revisiting these provinces finds his notes of ten or fifteen years ago utterly at fault.

"Landes—landes—landes" (wastes, wastes, wastes), "a country possessing nothing but privilege and poverty," such is the verdict passed by the Suffolk squire on Brittany in 1788. The privileges were swept away with a stroke of the pen twelve months later; the poverty, though an evil not to be so summarily dealt with, has gradually given way to a happier state of things Of no French province can the economist now write more hopefully.

Were I to renew my acquaintance with the friendly tenant farmers of Nozay in the Loire Inférieure, described by me elsewhere, or the hospitable freeholders of Hennebont in the Morbihan, I should without doubt find many changes for the better. The *sabots* into which the bare feet of both master and men, mistress and maids, were thrust a few years ago, have been

[1] See E. Réclus, "Géographie de la France."

replaced by shoes and stockings. Wheaten bread and butcher's meat find their way to many a farmhouse table. Cookery has improved. Wages have risen. Dwellings are built on a more wholesome plan.[1] Intellectual progress, whilst hardly keeping pace with the spread of material well-being, is yet satisfactory in the extreme. When interrogated by travellers of our own day in French, the Breton peasant would shake his head and pass on. Only the ebbing generation now remains ignorant of its mother tongue.

One curious omission must have struck most readers of the French travels. This quick and accurate observer who takes note of every object that meets his eye, who traverses the three historic highroads, diverging to the right and to the left in quest of information, never by any chance whatever mentions a village school. Had such schools existed we may be sure that he would have visited them, bequeathing us in a few graphic sentences an outline of their plan and working. The education of the people was a dead letter in France at the time he wrote. Here and there the curé or frères Ignorantins would get the children together and teach them to recite the catechism or spell a credo and paternoster. Writing, arithmetic, much less the teaching of French, were deemed unnecessary. The Convention during its short régime (1792-1796) decreed a comprehensive scheme of primary instruction, lay, gratuitous and obligatory, but the initiative was not followed up, and the first law on the subject carried into effect was that of 1833. How slowly matters advanced in Brittany may be gathered from an isolated fact. So late as 1872 two-thirds of the inhabitants of the Ille and Vilaine could neither read nor write. It remained for the Third Republic to remove this stigma, and within the last eighteen years schools have sprung up in all directions. The department just named numbered in 1884 between seven and eight hundred alone.[2]

[1] See M. H. Baudrillart, "Revue des Deux Mondes," 15th Oct. and 15th Nov., 1884.

[2] During the year spent by the present writer in Western France (1875-6), the following announcement often met the eye at Nantes: "Ecrivain publique, 10 centimes par lettre." Women servants who could read, much less write, were then an exception. The free night-schools opened by the municipal council rendered infinite service before

INTRODUCTION.

Agricultural progress has been more rapid. Rotation crops and four-course farming have long superseded the ruinous method of sowing the same crops, generally buckwheat or oats, for several years in succession, followed by an equally long period of fallow. Arthur Young's corner-stone of good farming, a fine piece of turnips, may now be seen here as at his native Bradfield. Artificial manures and machinery are used instead of the dried leaves and antiquated implements once in vogue. Upper Brittany has won for itself the name of the granary of western France, from its abundance of corn. The Breton breed of horses and cattle is second to none throughout the country. Between the years 1840 and 1880 upwards of 400,000 hectares of wastes have been brought under cultivation, and the process of clearing goes steadily on.

To many causes are due this transformation of a region so long stationary. Foremost stands the great agricultural college of Grand Jouan, near Nozay, in the Loire Inférieure, founded in 1830. Our Suffolk farmer sighed for such an institution, and predicted the advantages that would accrue generally from training schools of practical and theoretic agriculture. Such schools, alike on a large or modest scale, the latter called ferme-école, are now scattered all over France, Grand Jouan, precursor of the rest, still retaining pre-eminence. Its object is twofold: firstly, to form good farmers, gardeners, land-surveyors, and agricultural chemists; secondly, to develop the progress of agriculture by the introduction of the newest machinery and the most improved methods, by farming high, in fact, for the benefit of outsiders. The curriculum occupies two years and a half; day students, many of whom belong to the peasant class, are received at a cost of two hundred francs yearly.

"It is Grand Jouan that teaches us to farm," remarked a tenant farmer of the neighbourhood to the present writer in 1875, when showing, with no little pride, a field of turnips grown upon a layer of bone phosphate.

The spread of railways, the creation of roads and other facilities of communication, must be taken into account, also the

---

the passing of the great educational act of 1886. At the School Board election, Hastings, 1889, many voters could neither read nor write!

great advantages enjoyed by Brittany in respect of climate. Magnolias and camellias flourish out of doors all the year round at Nantes, and arrived at St. Pol de Léon (Finistère) in November, the tourist finds the soft air and warm sunshine of the south. The fruit and vegetables of Roscoff and other equally favoured spots produce sums that would have appeared fabulous a few years ago, much more in Arthur Young's time.[1] The strawberries of Plougastel alone bring an annual return of half a million francs. These market gardens, varying in extent from two or three to twenty-five hectares, are the property of peasant owners, but here as elsewhere a great variety of land tenure is found.

Métayage, whilst existing in the Côtes du Nord and the Loire Inférieure, is not regarded with much favour by the Breton. Tenant farming and ownership are more congenial to his somewhat uncompromising temperament. The *domaine congéable*,[2] a contract dating from the twelfth century, and of universal acceptance fifty years ago, is now found only in Finistère and the Morbihan. Nothing could be simpler than this arrangement—the owner handing over his land in return for a small rent, the farmer becoming possessor of outbuildings, if erected at his expense, stock and crops, both parties being at liberty to separate under certain conditions, one of which was the reimbursement of outlay. It will easily be seen that such a system would work well whilst the land possessed little value and capital was scarce. Nevertheless, the *domaine congéable* is still to be found in what we may well call a land of survivals. Two of these unfortunately form a serious stumbling-block to progress, and seem likely to outlast the picturesque costumes, the old-world traditions, even the ancient speech of the French Bretagne. Beggary and intemperance, from time immemorial, have degraded a population characterized by many sterling qualities. So far back as 1536[3] we find severe edicts against

---

[1] Nevertheless, in the space of five or six years the Revolution had quadrupled the resources of civilization and enormously developed material progress throughout the country.—Mignet, vol. ii., p. 179.

[2] "Congéable. Tenure à domaine congéable, tenure avec faculté pour le bailleur de congédier à volonté le preneur, en lui remboursant son amélioration."—Littré.

[3] See H. Martin, vol. viii., p. 273.

drunkenness in Brittany, comprised in the celebrated judicial reforms of François I. and his legists. According to this Draconian code, for the first offence the punishment was a term of bread and water diet in prison; for the second, flogging; in case of incorrigibility, loss of ears and banishment.

Orphanages, industrial schools, benefit societies, and other philanthropic measures are combating the first evil. The second, it is to be hoped, will disappear with the gradual spread of education and material well-being.

Great is the change that awaits the traveller in sunny, light-hearted, dance-loving Anjou. The Breton peasant, taciturn, reserved, yet hospitable, will set before his guest the best his larder affords—cyder, rye-bread baked weeks before, hard cheese, curds and whey; in Anjou the housewife brings out a white loaf, fresh butter and jam, wine, even liqueur. A lady tourist unaccompanied may safely entrust herself to a Breton driver. Throughout the long day's journey across solitary regions he will never once open his lips unless interrogated. But the English visitor in an Angevin country-house is soon regarded as a friend by all the neighbours. Many and many a time, the labours in the field over, the merry supper taken out of doors ended, have I been invited to join the peasant folk in the joyous round. Accompanied only by the sound of their own voices, and needing no other stimulus, for ball-room a stretch of sward, for illumination the stars, young and old forget the long day's toil and the cares of life in these innocent Bacchanalia. Ofttimes the dance would be prolonged till near midnight, the presence of a stranger apparently adding zest to the festivity; but no matter how hilarious the mirth, how open-hearted the sense of fellowship, no unseemly jest, no indecorous word, jars our ears.

"Maine and Anjou," writes our traveller, "have the appearance of deserts," and he goes on to note one feature of the country which even in our own time is apt to convey an idea of poverty. Throughout the department of the Maine and Loire, formed from the ancient Anjou, may still be seen those cave-dwellings or Troglodyte villages which astonished Arthur Young a century ago, ready-made habitations hollowed out of the tufa or yellow calcareous rock abounding in the department. Sometimes in our walks and drives we have the backs of the houses towards us, and see only their tall chimneys rising from behind the hedges. Elsewhere we come upon a vast cave, in shape like an amphitheatre, containing half-a-dozen cottages or human burrows, crops and fruit-trees flourishing overhead. But already in 1875 the darkest and most comfortless subterranean chambers had been abandoned, and on revisiting the country fourteen years later, I found neat, new dwellings everywhere springing up, the homes of peasant farmers built by themselves. In the commune of St. Georges des Sept Voies I visited several new houses constructed at a cost varying from £80 to £250, in every case most of the work being achieved by the owner. One well-to-do peasant was building for himself an eight-roomed house, or what in England would even be called a villa, with flower-garden in front, parlour, kitchen, and offices on the ground flour, above, four airy bedrooms.

In the Maine and Loire the land is much divided, very few farms consist of a hundred hectares, by far the larger proportion of three or four only, or *closeries*. Yet between the years 1833 and 1870 [1] the value of land showed a rise of 50 per cent., and since that period progress has been far more rapid. The creation of roads and railways, the use of artificial manures and machinery, the cross-breeding of stock, had in 1862 given the Maine and Loire the fourth rank among French departments, whilst in 1880 it stood first as a corn-producing country. Wine, corn, and fruit are largely exported, and the slate quarries of Angers, the linen manufactories of Cholet, employ thousands of hands, and bring in vast revenues, the latter in 1869 reaching the total of fifteen million francs.

The desert that saddened Arthur Young's eyes may now be described as a land of Goshen, overflowing with milk and honey. The peasant wastes nothing and spends little; he possesses stores of home-spun linen, home-made remedies, oil, vinegar, honey, cyder, wine of his own producing. So splendid the climate, so rich the soil, that the poorest eats asparagus, green peas, and strawberries every day when in season, and, as everyone owns crops, nobody pilfers his neighbour. The absolute security of unguarded possessions is one advantage of peasant

---

[1] See "Mémoires de la Société Industrielle de Maine et Loire," also E. Réclus, "Géographie de la France."

property, the absence of pauperism, another. Each commune charges itself with the maintenance of its sick or aged poor, provided no members of their own family are able to undertake the duty. The hatefulness of dependence and the strong inducements to thrift held out by secure possession of the land, render these public burdens comparatively light. As a rule only intemperance or an accumulation of misfortunes reduce the French peasant to accept alms.

The third journey covers an enormous area, and takes our traveller into regions widely divergent both in respect of scenery, population, and resources. He begins with Champagne, traverses Alsace-Lorraine, as the forfeited departments of the Upper and Lower Rhine are now called, makes his way through the Jura, Burgundy, the Bourbonnais, Auvergne, obtains a glimpse of the Rhône valley, visits the Papal state of Avignon and the Comté de Nice, familiar in these days as the Riviera, at the time he wrote, an appanage of Savoy.

It is curious that, although fully recognizing the existence of peasant owners and, as has been seen, rendering ample justice to their thrift and laboriousness, he never seems to have inspected any of the tiny holdings passed on the road. Probably the poor people, humiliated by want and all kinds of wretchedness, would have resented such an intrusion, feeling, in Scriptural phrase, "Verily to see the poverty of the land art thou come." In our own day nothing flatters the flourishing farming folk of the Seine and Marne more than the visit of an inquiring stranger. They are never too busy to be courteous, and the curious in agriculture need not hesitate to put a string of questions. What a contrast is presented by that recorded conversation with a peasant woman of Mars-la-Tour (Meurthe and Moselle) and chance acquaintance made with a housewife of eastern France at the present time!

Arthur Young describes his interlocutor as miserably clad, bent with toil, and although youthful, wearing a look of age, whilst the story she poured out, was one of hopeless struggle and unmitigated hardship. The farmeress of the rich cheese-making country of Brie en Champagne still works hard, drives to market with her eggs and butter, and even upon occasions lends a hand in the harvest field. But on Sundays and holidays her neat cotton dress is exchanged for a fashionable toilette;

her children receive a liberal education; when her daughters marry, they have a dowry of several thousand pounds.[1] With beaming satisfaction and genuine hospitality she welcomes an English visitor, offering new milk or cordials, delighted to show her household stores of linen, her dairy and poultry yard. Upon one occasion, after a long ramble amid the cornfields and vineyards near Couilly (Seine and Marne), I entered the shop of a village baker, and asked for a roll. The mistress very kindly invited me into her back parlour, brought out excellent bread, Brie cheese, the pleasant wine of the country, refusing payment. Hospitable instincts are fostered by prevailing ease and well-being. The little towns of this department all possess public baths, personal cleanliness is a noteworthy feature, and beggary is nil. Here, however, we have under consideration one of the wealthiest agricultural populations of France—the sale of cheese alone at the Meaux market reaches the sum of six or seven million francs yearly. Fruit and vegetables are largely exported, the village curé, as well as his parishioners, adding to income by the sale of pears and greengages. "You have come only just in time, ladies," said the vicaire of one of these villages to myself and friends, bent on making a purchase, during the summer of 1878; "almost all my greengages are ordered for the English market. Ah! those English, those English, they monopolize everything: our best fruit, and the island of Cyprus."

The rich red rose, erroneously called Provence rose, was in reality introduced here by the Crusaders, but no longer forms an article of commerce. Provins, ancient capital of La Brie, from which the rose derived its name, is as picturesque a town as any in the country.

The popularity enjoyed by Arthur Young on the other side of La Manche need not astonish us. Yet one passage of these Travels can but raise painful reflection in every conscientious and patriotic mind. Nothing can be more painful to ardent sympathizers with France and French character than a sojourn in Alsace-Lorraine. The sorrowful, indeed agonized clinging of born Alsatians to the mother-country, once witnessed, can never

---

[1] I have heard of one rich farmer's daughter of this district receiving a million of francs, £40,000, as her marriage portion.

be forgotten. But who is able to read the following passage by an English traveller in the Rhine provinces just a hundred years ago, without some change of feeling?—

"In Saverne," writes Arthur Young in 1789, " I found myself to all appearances in Germany. Looking at a map of France and reading histories of Louis XIV. never threw his conquest or seizure of Alsace into the light which travelling into it did; to cross a great range of mountains; to enter a level plain inhabited by a people totally distinct and different from that of France, with manners, language, ideas, prejudices and habits all different, made an impression of the injustice and ambition of such a conduct much more forcible than ever reading had done; so much more powerful are things than words." Nowa-days, if you question a blue-eyed, fair-haired, square-built peasant girl of Alsace-Lorraine as to her origin, she will glance round shyly to assure herself that there are no unfriendly listeners, and proudly reply in the tongue of her primitive ancestors, recently the conquerors of the fatherland, "Ich bin Französisch geboren" (I am French by birth). When spending an autumn in Alsace-Lorraine five years ago, I found Mulhouse still a French town in every respect but name. "Nous sommes plus Français que les Français" (we are more French than the French themselves) was the universal sentiment of rich and poor expressed without reserve in English hearing. A system of repression only to be compared to the Russian rule in Poland, and wholesale immigration of born Prussians, is gradually forcing a hated nationality upon this population so susceptible and so warm-hearted, uniting the graces of the French character with the sturdy qualities of the Teuton.

Thrice unhappy Alsace! In the position of a beautiful and richly-dowered orphan—alike the darling and the prey of one jealous foster-parent after another—the ill-fated country seems doomed to perpetual disenchantment and betrayal; her affections no sooner firmly implanted than they are torn up by the bleeding roots.

Of Franche-Comté not much is seen, the traveller's plans being disarranged by local disturbances. He does, however, pass through the departments of the Doubs and the Jura, formed from the ancient domain of Mary of Burgundy. Here, again, we who know every inch of the road are struck by what at first appears an unaccountable omission. No reference is made to the numerous village industries which now characterize the country, not only from the economist's point of view, but also adding peculiar features to the landscape. In the remotest valley of the Jura, breaking the solitude of pine forests, mingling their din with the roar of mountain torrents, is now heard the sound of mill-wheels and steam hammers, tall factory chimneys not a little detracting from scenery inimitably described by Ruskin. Whilst the majority of the inhabitants lead a pastoral life, and cheese-making is carried on everywhere, hardly a hamlet but possesses its special manufactory or handicraft. Turnery and wood-carving at St. Claude, gem polishing at Septmoncel and Oyonnax, clock and spectacle making at Morez,[1] employ thousands of hands; whilst among exports of lesser importance figure wadding, gum, clock cases, bottles, and baskets. Many of these trades are pursued by the craftsman at home and on his own account. Hours alike both pleasant and profitable have I spent in these cottage ateliers, chatting with my hosts as they worked, the clean little room opening on to a tiny garden, the baby and the kitten sporting in the sun.

The wood-carvers are veritable artists, and their elegantly carved pipe-stems find their way to the remotest corners of the earth.

Diamond polishing and turnery were carried on in the Jura several centuries ago. For the most part, however, village industries, as well as village schools, were ignored by Arthur Young, because they did not exist. When, in 1789, he passed within a few miles of the marvellously placed little cathedral city of St. Claude, the all-puissant count-bishop, inheritor of the rich abbey and its seigneurial dependencies, had only just been compelled to enfranchise his forty thousand serfs. These bondservants of a Christian prelate, whose cause the so-called atheist Voltaire had pleaded magnanimously in vain, were up to that time mainmortable—that is to say, if childless, they had no power to bequeath their property, which accrued to the seigneur.

[1] This *lunetterie* resolves itself into a scientific study of noses!—a long-nosed nation requiring one kind of spectacles, a short-nosed people another, and so on. A pair of spectacles can be made here for three halfpence.

The country was not without resources, but its revenues did not enrich the tiller of the soil. From early times the white wines of the Jura were celebrated throughout France. "I have some wine of Arbois in my cellar," wrote the gay Gascon, Henry IV., to the Duke de Mayenne on their reconciliation, "and I send you two bottles which I think you will not dislike."

The pretty little town of Arbois is worth visiting, not only for the sake of tasting its matchless wine, but also for its scenery—the valley of the Cuisance is indeed a corner of Eden. The soil is poor and the land minutely subdivided in the Jura, yet the condition of the peasant is now one of comparative ease and entire independence. Both morally and intellectually these mountaineers rank high among the rural population of France. An excellent notion of the mental capacities of the small landowners may be obtained by attending a sitting of the Juge de Paix. The skill and readiness with which they state their cause and act the part of their own advocate are remarkable. For the most part the quarrels among neighbours arise from contested boundaries; the judge, after patiently hearing both sides of the question, settles matters for once and for all by visiting the spot, and in person fixing the landmarks.

The villages of the Doubs, especially Ornans, home of the painter Courbet, so picturesquely placed, are also active centres of industry: kirsch, fabricated from cherries of local renown, absinthe, tiles, nails, wire, are largely manufactured, to say nothing of the Gruyère cheese, the staple product of Franche Comté. The Revolution in a few years metamorphosed entire regions. From this period dates the famous watch-making commerce of Besançon. Introduced by the Convention in 1793, it is now carried on so extensively that out of every hundred watches manufactured in France, eighty-six come from the chef-lieu of the Doubs. In 1880 the number of hands thus employed reached a total of 46,000. The Bisontin watchmaker often works on his own account; and here, as at Châteauroux in the Indre, is witnessed a striking example of thrift among the artizan class. Many of these working watchmakers contrive by dint of extreme laboriousness and economy to purchase a vineyard or garden in the suburbs. They build a summer-house, or even châlet, and with wives and children there spend Sundays and holidays amid their fruit and flowers.

From Franche Comté our traveller reaches Burgundy and the Bourbonnais. In the neighbourhood of Autun (Saône and Loire) he tells us that he looked for fat farmers, and found only starving métayers. The department is neither pre-eminent in the matter of agriculture nor of social advance, yet it is a sight now-a-days to see "the fat farmers" at the September fair of Autun. From early morning they pour into the town, some in gigs or hooded carriages, with wife and children, others on foot, and the greater number driving their cattle—the splendid white oxen known as the Morvan breed. These peasant farmers wear under the blue blouse shining broad cloth, and betake themselves at midday to the first hotel in the place, there to enjoy the table d'hôte breakfast; but no sooner is business over, without losing a moment, untempted by fireworks and other entertainments, all set off homewards. Such experiences enable us to understand the stability and solid wealth of the French farmer. He is not above work, and does not disdain the uniform of labour.

The same strict attention to daily concerns is seen on the occasion of a general election. Just before attending one of these cattle fairs of Autun I happened to be staying at St. Honoré-les-Bains, in the adjoining department of the Nièvre, when an election took place. The peasant farmers, although the day was Sunday, performed their electoral duties with the utmost despatch, and returned to their homes.

Much of the scenery of this part of France has an English look. We see fields set round with lofty hedges, winding lanes, sweeps of gorse and heather, alternately recalling Devonshire and Sussex. Here are found tenant farms, large properties cultivated by their owners, small holdings parcelled out among the peasants and métairies.

It was inevitable that a traveller in Arthur Young's time should miss many objects of striking interest on the way. The first itineraries of France seem to have been inspired by the Englishman's example—I allude to the voluminous works of Millin and Vaysse de Villiers published in the early part of the present century; the departmental system had not as yet created a French map, or, in the strict acceptance of the word, French geography. Archæology was a dead letter, and very little interest was felt, even by educated people, in the scenery or curiosities of their native land. Thus he halted at Auray, and there was no one to point out the great stone avenues of Carnac and the dolmens of Locmariaker; he passed through Alsace, ignoring the famous shrine and grandiose site of St. Odille, extolled by Goethe in his poetic reminiscences. Arrived at Autun, he was within easy reach of Avallon, so nobly towering over the beautiful valley of the Cousin, and of the abbey church of Vézélay, unique in splendour and of unique renown. Here, too, he was on the threshold of the little Celtic kingdom of the Morvan, where village communism, as existing among patriarchal tribes, remained in force till our own day, and where the stalwart husbandman still throws over his shoulder the Gallic sagum, or short cloak, worn by the contemporaries of Vercingetorix. The last village commune was broken up in 1848. The inhabitants of this most picturesque, but unproductive, country depend largely on industrial earnings, many migrating to Paris and other towns, and there pursuing various trades during part of the year. The curious "flottage à bûches perdues," or floating of loose logs, a speciality of the Morvan, gives work to thousands of men, women, and children at certain seasons.

A wretched village occupied the site of the world-famous iron-foundries of Le Creusot, when Arthur Young journeyed from Autun to Nevers in 1789. These works, now covering a superficies of three hundred acres, and employing ten thousand hands, have developed into a town almost tripling the respective populations of the above-mentioned towns, chefs-lieux of the Saône and Loire and the Nièvre.

From "the mild, healthy, and pleasant plains of the Bourbonnais," he passed into Auvergne, obtaining a glimpse of "the rich Limagne," of which Mr. Barham Zincke has given us an exhaustive account. The Velay is rapidly traversed, and the château of Polignac visited, already deserted by its owners, the thankless protégés of Louis XVI. and Marie Antoinette. From its ruined battlements and prison towers, the tourist now beholds a heart-quickening scene of rural ease and smiling fertility; far and wide the beautifully cultivated plain, with its varied crops, not one inch of land wasted, the whole forming a brilliant patchwork of green fields and yellow corn, whilst dotted here and there are neat little homesteads and pasturing flocks and herds.

From Le Puy, chef-lieu of the Haute-Loire, in spite of wretched inns and troublous times, Montélimar on the Rhône is reached, at that time belonging to Dauphiné, in our own, chef-lieu of the Drôme. Here he describes "mountains covered with chestnuts and various articles of cultivation, which in districts not waste or volcanic, are waste, or in a great measure useless." Until the ravages of the phylloxera, the choicer vineyards of the Drôme sold at the rate of 60,000 francs the hectare; but the manufactures of Crest and Romans now constitute the chief wealth of this department.

Next he visits Avignon and the country of Venaissin, described as "one of the richest districts in the kingdom," and followed by a picture of Vaucluse no traveller has as yet surpassed. It was not till two years later, be it remembered, that the Papal state of Avignon and the little Comté Venaissin were incorporated into French territory at the request of the inhabitants, forming, with the principality of Orange and a portion of Provence, the department of Vaucluse. The supersession of madder by chemical dyes, and the phylloxera have of late years greatly diminished the revenues of this wealthy region, which, if visited in summer, almost persuades the stranger that he is in the East. Nothing can be more Oriental than the veteran fig-trees, the peach orchards, the olive groves, all veiled with finest white dust beneath a burning blue sky.

Here may be said to end Arthur Young's survey of France on the eve of the Revolution, an enterprise altogether original, and carried out under extraordinary circumstances. We need not feel astonishment at the great popularity enjoyed by his work on the other side of the Channel. Whilst many fairly educated English folk have never so much as heard the author's name, it is familiar to every schoolboy in France. The Suffolk squire's scathing summing-up of the ancien régime, "Whenever you stumble upon a grand seigneur, even one that is worth millions, you are sure to find his property desert," is cited in the elementary histories for public schools approved by the minister of education. Whilst, moreover, English students have been hitherto compelled to resort to the British Museum or wait long and patiently for an expensive copy of these Travels to turn up at a secondhand bookseller's, unabridged edition after edition has appeared in Paris.[1]

Arthur Young did not hesitate to tell his French readers some blunt home-truths, apparently taken in excellent temper; his journal must be described, for all that, as one long, graceful acknowledgment of courtesies and hospitalities, recorded in an age when anything like international friendship was rare indeed.

The book has greater claims upon French sympathy. In spite of certain reservations, it is a vindication of peasant property and the Revolution, the two cardinal points of French belief. From the first page to the last, he sets down the abject wretchedness of the people and the stagnant condition of trade and commerce to bad government. But another adage of our "wise and honest traveller," his famous axiom, "The magic of property turns sands to gold," equally with improved administration, must account for the contrasted picture that now meets our view. By the light of after-events he was led to modify his ideas concerning the establishment of a democracy in France. But he had already given his experiences to the world; he could not undo the effect of his published work, and the observations summed up in his final chapter, to quote a great living critic, were "a luminous criticism of the most important side of the Revolution, worth a hundred times more than Burke, Paine, and Macintosh all put together. Young afterwards became panic-stricken, but his book remained. There the writer enumerates without trope or invective the intolerable burdens under which the great mass of the French people had for long years been groaning. It was the removal of those burdens that made the very heart's core of the Revolution, and gave to France that new life which so soon astonished and terrified Europe."[2]

Into Arthur Young's services to agriculture we have no space

[1] Twenty thousand copies were printed by order of the Convention, and distributed gratuitously in every commune. "Ce que," dit le Ministre de l'Intérieur, Garat, "contribua rapidement et sensiblement à métamorphoser les cailloux des collines en vignes fécondes, et les plaines abandonnées à la tourte en gros pâturages."—Garat, Mémoires, sur la Révolution, Paris, 1794.

[2] "Burke," by John Morley ("English Men of Letters"), p. 162.

to enter here. They have been briefly indicated by the brilliant, but all too rapid, historian of the English people. "The numerous enclosure bills," writes Mr. Green, "which began with the reign of George the Second, and especially marked that of his successor, changed the whole face of the country. Ten thousand square miles of untilled land have been added, under their operation, to the area of cultivation, while in the tilled land itself the production had been more than doubled by the advance of agriculture, which began with the travels and treatises of Mr. Arthur Young."

His claims are not only those of a foremost agriculturist, an indefatigable promoter of the arts of peace, a citizen of the world in the widest acceptation of the name. He had pondered long and deeply on those social and political problems that occupy thinkers of our own day. Eminently practical, he yet indulged from time to time in the loftiest idealism. "Why may not the time come," he writes in an early work, "when the whole world shall be in a state of knowledge, elegance, and peace?" Scattered throughout his writings we find, side by side with a statesmanlike grasp of facts, veritable flashes of inspiration, a deep philosophical insight into the possibilities of human progress.[1]

[1] In one of his private note-books Arthur Young writes that the manuscript of the French Travels went through a most careful process of excision before being submitted to the printer. He adds, "I am strongly of opinion that if nine-tenths of other writers would do the same thing, their performance would be so much the better, for one reads very few quartos that would not be improved by reducing to octavo."

Another interesting fact recorded is the item of expenditure. The first journey, lasting just upon six months, cost £118 15s. 2d. The second journey, of eighty-eight days, cost just £61, or at the rate of fourteen shillings a day, about the sum an economical traveller would spend in France at the present time, obtaining naturally much more comfort for his money.

Readers of Arthur Young will do well to consult the reports of the Administration of Agriculture in France, 1785-7, recently published with notes by MM. Pigeonneau and De Foville, whilst the work of the latter on the subdivision of land, "Le Morcellement," Paris, 1885, is a mine of information conveyed in a most interesting manner.

My warm thanks are due to Mr. and Mrs. Arthur Young, grandson and granddaughter-in-law of the great agriculturist, without whose kind assistance the following memoir could not have been written. The materials were placed at my disposal whilst enjoying the hospitality of Bradfield Hall, the modern mansion occupying the site of Arthur Young's old home.

I also beg to express my indebtedness to M. Paul Joanne, and other obliging correspondents, French and English.

BIOGRAPHICAL SKETCH.

ARTHUR YOUNG was born Sept. 11, 1741, at Whitehall, but this accident of birthplace does not deprive Suffolk of a distinguished son. His home from the first, as it remained throughout the greater part of his life, was Bradfield Hall, of Bradfield-Combust, near Bury St. Edmunds, a property held by the Young family since 1620. He was the youngest son of the Reverend Dr. Arthur Young, Prebendary of Canterbury Cathedral, chaplain to Arthur Onslow, Speaker of the House of Commons, and rector of Bradfield, and of Lucretia, born, de Coussmaker, a lady of Dutch extraction, whose family accompanied William III. to England. Mr. Speaker Onslow and the Bishop of Bristol stood sponsors for the boy, appropriate inauguration of a life destined to be spent in the best company. From his father, an extremely handsome man six feet in stature, and the author of a learned work commended by Voltaire, he inherited good looks, a striking presence, and literary facility; from his mother, an inordinate craving for knowledge, and conversational powers of a high order. He describes her as very amiable and cheerful, fond of conversation, for which she had a talent, and a great reader on a variety of subjects. She brought her husband a very large dowry, and no inconsiderable portion of this handsome jointure seems to have been swallowed up in the speculations of her son, one of the greatest agriculturists and least successful practical farmers who ever lived.

We can easily understand Arthur Young's love of rural life and keen appreciation of scenery, after a visit to Bradfield, reached from Mark's Tey on the Great Eastern Railway. It is a sweet spot, in the near neighbourhood of much of the beautiful country with which Gainsborough has familiarized us. Alighting at the quiet little station of Whelnetham, we follow a winding road overhung with lofty elms, that leads to the village; or in summer, knee-deep in wild flowers and waving grasses, we may take a traverse through the meadows, their lofty hedges a tangle of eglantine and honeysuckle, on every side stretches of rich pasture, cornfields, and woods. The place has a very old-world look; here and there, between the trees, peeps a whitewashed cottage, with overhanging thatched roof, or a farmhouse of equally rustic appearance, very little modernization having taken place in these regions.

The Suffolk farmer, as Arthur Young modestly calls himself, was in reality a country squire. His old home has been replaced by a Gothic mansion, but nothing can be more squirarchal than the well-wooded park, ornamental water with its swans, Queen Anne's garden and stately avenues, leading to church and lodge, which remain as they were in his own time. Opposite the gates of Bradfield Hall stands the village ale-house, no quainter, more antiquated hostelry in rural England. Between park and village, consisting of church, rectory-house, and a dozen cottages, lies the broad, elm-bordered road leading to the railway station. This is the old London coach road followed by our traveller when setting forth on his French travels a hundred years ago, enterprises regarded by his family mad as those of Don Quixote himself.

Entrancing as were these adventuresome journeys, we can fancy with what pleasure he hailed the first glimpse of Bradfield on returning home safe and sound from one expedition after another.

As happens with so many men of genius, Arthur Young owed little to schools or schoolmasters. He was first sent to the grammar school at Lavenham—that exquisitely clean, picturesque village, with its noble cathedral—no other name befits the church—lying between Sudbury and Whelnetham.

"I was sent to this school," he writes, "in order to learn the Latin and Greek languages, with the addition of receiving instruction in writing and arithmetic, taught by a man who attended every day for that purpose; but whether from my being a favourite of his, or having my attention too much affected by frequent visits to Bradfield, I afterwards found myself so ill-grounded in those languages, that for some time before leaving school I found it necessary to give much attention to recover lost time. My mother soon bought me a little white pony, which was sent every Saturday to bring me home, and though the plan was that of returning every Monday morning, yet the weather or some other circumstance would often occasion delays, not a little injurious. The latter part of the time I had a pointer and a gun, and went out with the master. I had also a room to myself and a neat collection of books, and I remember beginning to write a history of England, thinking that I could make a good one out of several others. How early began my literary follies! I seemed to have a natural propensity to writing books." Pretty well this for a boy of nine or ten! All readers of the "Travels in France" will remember Arthur Young's love of music and the drama. His diary shows at what an early age those tastes were fostered. In his thirteenth year, he tells us, he is taken to London, sees Garrick in tragedy, and hears the Messiah. Another characteristic, equally familiar to us, is his deep admiration of personal beauty, and his delight in the society of graceful, attractive women. This, too, we find a feature of his somewhat precocious boyhood.

"What commanded more of my attention," he writes, "was a branch of learning very different from Greek: it was the lessons I received from a dancing-master, who came over once a week from Colchester to teach the boys, and also some young ladies. Two of these in succession made terrible havoc with my heart. The first was a Miss Betsey Harrington, a Lavenham grocer's daughter, who was admitted by all who saw her to be truly beautiful."

On quitting Lavenham, his destiny remained for a moment undecided. His father wished him to be sent to Eton, and thence to one of the Universities. His mother opposed the scheme, and he was apprenticed, with a premium of £600, to a mercantile firm at Lynn. He wrote of this resolve in a strain of regret those who come after him cannot share. Had paternal influence prevailed, he tells us, his life might have been very different. Originality is nowhere more refreshing than in the Church. It is pleasant to fancy Arthur Young a bishop. But what other pen would have given us that inimitable picture of rural France on the eve of the great Revolution? Who else would have fought so valiantly the cause of the farmer at home?

Greenwich party. Talking of happiness, sensibility, and a total want of feeling, my mamma said, turning to me, ' Here's a girl will never be happy, never whilst she lives, for she possesses, perhaps, as feeling a heart as ever girl had.' Some time after, when we were near the end of our journey, ' And so,' said Mr. Young, ' my friend Fanny possesses a very feeling heart?' He harped on this some little time, till at last he said he would call me *feeling* Fanny; it was characteristic, he said, and a good deal more nonsense, that put me out of all patience, which same virtue I have not yet sufficiently recovered to recount any more of our conversation, charming as it was."

In the meantime he was making one disastrous attempt at practical farming after another, like a desperate gamester doubling the stakes with every loss. For a year or two after his marriage he remained at Bradfield, farming a copyhold of twenty acres, his sole fortune, and eighty more, the property of his mother.

This experiment proving a failure, he next hired an occupation of three times the size in Essex, which he was glad to be rid of in five years' time, paying a premium of £100 to the incoming tenant. His successor, a practical farmer, made a good deal of money out of the concern, probably as much as Arthur Young had lost by it, so hampering to worldly success is the possession of original ideas!

One of his farms he describes as " a devouring wolf," an epithet that need not surprise us when we consider that he made 3,000 experiments on his Suffolk holding alone.

The superstitious might see in the pertinacity with which Mrs. Young encouraged her son's ventures some preternatural foreshadowing of his career. Again and again she advertised for a farm for him, and nothing better offering itself, he hired some land in Hertfordshire, which ere long he anathematized as a "hungry vitriolic gravel, a Nabob's fortune would sink in the attempt to raise good, arable crops to any extent in such a country."

One of the most curious incidents in a career that detractors might well call Quixotic, is the origin of the famous English Tours. Will it be believed that just as Cervantes' half-mad hero set out in search of chivalrous adventure, and Dr. Syntax in search of the picturesque, this thrice-ruined farmer determined to explore the entire country till he could find land that would pay? Whenever he put pen to paper he was successful. Whenever he turned to experimental farming he almost ruined himself. These narratives of home travel from an agricultural point of view were a novelty, and also supplied an actual want. Not only did he give a succinct picture of farming as carried on at that time in various parts of England, but much information valuable to the general reader. The three works were largely sold, yet the author grew poorer and poorer.

In 1770 Fanny Burney gives a vivacious, jaunty picture of her uncle, as she used to call him. She describes him as most absurdly dressed for a common visit, being in light blue, embroidered with silver, having a bag and sword, and walking in the rain. "He was grown all airs and affectation," she adds, "yet I believe this was put on, for what purpose I cannot tell, unless it were to let us see what a power of transformation he possessed."

A year later we have a very different account. "Mr. and Mrs. Young have been in town for a few days," scribbled the girl-diarist. "They are in a situation that quite afflicts me. Mr. Young, whose study and dependence is agriculture, has half undone himself by experiments. His writings upon this subject have been amazingly well received by the public, and in his tours through England he has been caressed and assisted almost universally. Indeed, his conversation and appearance must ever secure him welcome and admiration. But, of late, some of his facts have been disputed, and though I believe it to be only by envious and malignant people, yet reports of that kind are fatal to an author, whose sole credit must subsist on his veracity. In short, by slow but sure degrees, his fame has been sported with and his fortune destroyed. . . . His children, happily, have their mother's jointure settled upon them. He has some thoughts of going abroad, but his wife is averse to it." A few weeks later she adds, "Mr. Young is not well, and appears almost overcome with the horrors of his situation; in fact, he is almost destitute. This is a dreadful trial for him, yet I am persuaded he will still find some means of extricating himself from his distresses, at least if genius, spirit, and enterprise can avail."

His own diary for this year contains the following entry:

"The same unremitting industry, the same anxiety, the same vain hopes, the same perpetual disappointment, no happiness, nor anything like it." He had indeed reached one of the acutest crises of his much-tried life; ruin stared him in the face.

But three months after that last sorrowful mention of her favourite, Fanny Burney once more strikes a cheerful note. Mr. Young had dined with her sister and herself, she wrote. Fortune, she hoped, smiled on him again, for he again smiled on the world. The originator of three thousand unsuccessful experiments was hardly the man to lose faith in himself. If occasional fits of dejection overtook him, he was ready an hour after to enter upon a history of agriculture throughout all ages and in all countries, make gigantic schemes in the interest of English husbandry, or to hire four thousand acres of Yorkshire moorland with the intention of turning the wilderness into a garden. His powers of work, of hoping against hope, of throwing heart and soul into new interests and undertakings, were phenomenal.

Of the year 1778 he writes: "Labour and sorrow, folly and infatuation: here began a new career of industry, new hopes, and never-failing disappointment." And once more the careless, yet inimitable pen of Fanny Burney gives us, in a few lines, the catastrophe that had wellnigh shipwrecked his life: "I have had lately a very long and very strange conversation with Mr. Young. We happened to be alone in the parlour, and either from confidence in my prudence, or from an entire and unaccountable carelessness of consequences, he told me that he was the most miserable fellow breathing, and almost *directly* said that his connexions made him so, and most vehemently added that if he was to begin the world again, no earthly thing should prevail with him to marry! That now he was never easy but when he was in a plow-cart, but that happy he could never be. I am very sorry for him, but cannot wonder."

In June, 1776, after a passage of twenty-four hours, he landed in Ireland. His stay did not extend over three years, and during a part of the time he was occupied in managing Lord Kingsbury's estate in County Cork. The result, nevertheless, was a survey of the country, and an inquiry into the condition of the people, which for accuracy, fulness of detail, and acuteness of observation, render it invaluable to this day. "Arthur

Young's Tour in Ireland," wrote Lord Lonsdale to Croker in 1849, "has given me the idea that his views of Ireland were nearer the truth than any other work."

An accession of fame does not always mean an increase of fortune, and the future was as hard a problem to the popular author, now in the prime of life and the fulness of powers, as to the ambitious stripling of twenty. On his return from Ireland he wrote, "I arrived at Bradfield on the first of January, and had then full time to reflect upon what should be the pursuit of my life, and upon what plan I could devise for that fresh establishment of myself which should at the same time prevent any relapse into those odious dependencies and uncertainties which from 1771 to 1778 had been the perpetual torment of my life. Whilst I was hesitating what plan to follow, an emigration to America crossed my mind, and much occupied my thoughts." This project was prevented by his mother's advanced years, and instead he took up leases on her estate, gradually increasing his occupation to four hundred acres. Henceforth his home was Bradfield, of which a few years later he became owner.

"My father," he tells us, "inherited Bradfield from his father Bartholomew Young, Esq., called Captain from a command in the militia, and it is remarkable that with only a part of the present estate he lived genteelly, and drove a coach and four on a property which would in the present time only maintain the establishment of a wheelbarrow."

Four children had been born to him, two daughters and a son, and after an interval of thirteen years, his youngest and best-beloved child, the little girl familiar to readers of the French Travels. Whilst he appears to have been an affectionate and conscientious father, all the passionate depth and tenderness of his nature were lavished on this latest born, his "darling child," his "lovely Bobbin." Her name was Martha, but her bright, quick ways, rosy complexion, and dark, vivacious eyes, had won for her the pet name of Robin, afterwards changed to Bobbin, and these mentions of Bobbin in private diaries, little notes written to her from France, and letters to others concerning her welfare, show his character in a new and touching light. This exquisite child—for the adoring praise of her father is amply substantiated by others—was the supreme joy and consolation of a life often steeped in uncommon bitterness, and when she died, there went forth a wail from an utterly desolated heart, that moves us to tears after the long lapse of years. This awful shadow is as yet far off. The existence of his darling corresponded to the most brilliant years of Arthur Young's career.

Glancing at the entries made between 1780 and 1787, that is to say, between the Irish and French journeys, we find many a stirring episode, and much evidence of indefatigable, even colossal labours, undertaken in a hopeful spirit. Some of these memoranda are passing humorous: he tells us, for instance, how whilst at Petworth, on a visit to Lord Egremont, he went into a bath at four o'clock a.m., the thermometer standing below zero, and on coming out walked straight into a shrubbery, and rubbed himself in the snow to see the effect of cold upon the body. It had none, he complacently adds, except that of increasing strength and activity. From another note we learn that he had been busy on stanzas to a lady.

The year 1783 opens with the project of the "Annals of Agriculture," which he calls, as well he might do, one of the greatest speculations of his life. Literary contributions were invited from all sides, and the work was launched under royal patronage. Arthur Young not only acted as editor, but wrote voluminously for its pages. The "Annals" consist of forty-five quarto volumes, and although much of the information therein contained has been superseded, they form, in the words of a competent authority, " a noble addition to any library. It is here, as a statesman, that Arthur Young stands pre-eminent. On questions of home or international trade, on commerce, or prices, on monopolies, on religious bigotry, on class arrogance and insolence, on endowed charities, on the poor laws, on the law of settlement, on taxation direct and indirect, on bounties and drawbacks, he knew as much as Cobden, and has written as wisely. That which his great contemporary Adam Smith reasoned out, Arthur Young seems to have reached with electric despatch by instinct."[1]

The "Annals" made a noise in the world; even Dr. Burney

---

[1] H. Pell, Esq., M.P. See "Arthur Young, agriculturist, author, and statesman," ' The Farmers' Club,' W. Johnson, Salisbury Square.

wrote enthusiastically about them. Would he were ten years younger, he said, he would take Arthur Young's white house and as much land as he could spare, and enter himself as his scholar. From far and near came testimonies equally flattering, and from remote quarters of Europe, flocked disciples and pupils to sit at the feet of the modern Varro. Among those who found their way to Bradfield were three young Russians, sent by the Empress Catherine to study farming under his care. He gives an amusing account of their examination. One of the three was so much awed that he resolutely refused to open his lips, for which offence, adds the narrator, I sincerely hope he was not sent to Siberia. Later came the nephew of the Polish ambassador, "a heavy, dull man, with a Tartar countenance; his intention was to learn agriculture, but he made poor progress." The Duke de Liancourt, that amiable champion of the Revolution, the President of the Dijon Parliament—and other distinguished personages familiar to readers of the French Travels—also visited Bradfield.

In the midst of these multifarious and engrossing occupations the scheme of an agricultural survey of France was gradually taking shape in his mind. Whilst contributing largely to the "Annals," making a variety of experiments with the aid of Priestley, holding what may be called a professorial chair in his own home, he was full of new projects.

In 1784 he had crossed to Calais with his son Arthur, "just to say that he had been in France." In 1787 his friends, the Duke de Liancourt and Lazonski, invited him to join them in a Pyrenean tour, and the invitation was accepted.

"This was touching a string tremulous to vibrate," he writes; "I had long wished for an opportunity to examine France. My darling child, my lovely Bobbin, I left in perfect health, the rest of my family well and provided for in every respect as they had themselves chalked out, the 'Annals' lodged in the hand of a man on whose friendship and abilities I could entirely confide." In spite of vehement remonstrances and agonized entreaties, he set out. "I implore you to give up this mad scheme. Think of your wife and children," his brother had written, and much more in the same strain, working himself up into a veritable frenzy of panic. An expedition to Patagonia, or a journey round the world, could hardly have inspired this timid counsellor with livelier terrors. He certainly never expected to see the foolhardy traveller again.

Arthur Young's mother had died two years before, and the event is thus noted in his journal: "My ever dear and venerated mother died. Happy, happy spirit." During her lifetime, as we have seen, he shrank from the notion of quitting England.

It is a curious and interesting fact that these French journeys exactly realized a plan of travel laid down in an early work. If we turn to the last chapter of that well-written and characteristic little book, "The Farmer's Letters to the People of England" (second edition, 1768), we shall find his own agricultural survey of France anticipated in every point. The nobility and men of large fortune travel, he writes, but no farmers; unfortunately those who have this peculiar and distinguishing advantage, the noble opportunity of benefitting themselves and their country, seldom inquire or even think about agriculture. Then follows the sketch of a farmer's tour in routes laid down for his imaginary traveller, being precisely those he was himself to follow a decade later. French Flanders must be visited, Lorraine and the adjoining provinces, Champagne and Burgundy. Then the tour of Franche Comté and of the Lyonnais should be made; next that of Normandy, Brittany, Orleannais, and Anjou. All the noble improvements of the Marquis de Turbilly in that province ought to be viewed with the most attentive eyes. From Anjou the traveller should journey through Guienne and Languedoc; next examine Provence—then enter Dauphiné, Gascony, and examine the heaths of Bordeaux; thence make his way to Spain, and travel towards Galicia.

To few of us is granted in middle age such entire fulfilment of the worthiest aspirations of youth. Little, perhaps, did the writer foresee that he was himself to be "that wise and honest traveller," who should describe rural France on the eve of the Revolution, not only for his own countrymen and his own epoch, but for all Europe and generations to come. We are gratified to find him at Turbilly, warmly received by its noble owner, and inspecting his farm, as he begged to be allowed to do, with the oldest surviving labourer of the late marquis.

He had left no anxieties behind him when setting out for France, but his heart is ever with his adored child. The fond letters he wrote to her in his large, clear, enviable handwriting have all been preserved. From Moulins, August 7, 1787, he writes, Bobbin being then four years old: "I think it high time to inquire how you do, pass your time, how the Mag (magpie) does, and the four kittens. I hope you have taken care of them, and remembered your papa wants cats. Do the flowers grow in your garden? Are you a better gardener than you used to be? The Marquis de Guerchy's little girls have a little house on a little hill, and on one side a little flower garden, on the other side a little kitchen garden, which they manage themselves and keep very clean from weeds. Bobbin would much like to see it." From Bagnères de Luchon he writes to his eldest daughter: "Do not forget to let me know how Bobbin does. God send her well and free from accidents. I hope she does not go alone near hedges for fear of snakes." From Limoges he sends many kisses to his dear little Bobbin, and her sister Mary is to say that he will be sure to bring her a French doll.

We must pass briefly over these rich, happy, dazzling years. The French Travels obtained all the éclat of a brilliant invention, which indeed, in a literary sense, they may be described. No one had done the same thing before, and now it was done to perfection. The author's name was soon in everybody's mouth. He received invitations to half-a-dozen courts. All the learned societies of Europe and America enrolled him as a member. His work was translated into a score of languages, and princes, statesmen, political economists, wits—not only of his own nationality, but from various parts of the world—paid a visit to Bradfield. Among his correspondents and guests were Washington, Pitt, Burke, Wilberforce, La Fayette, Priestley, Jeremy Bentham, that eccentric yet admirable philanthropist, Berchtold, and the Duc de Liancourt. Never, perhaps, had been seen in Suffolk such distinguished international gatherings.

The Burneys were, of course, frequent visitors at the pleasant country house described in "Camilla." Occasionally the too hospitable host—for although now owner of the maternal estate, Arthur Young was far from rich—would give a fête champêtre. At an early hour the guests arrived. The fishponds in the park were dragged, and after a long animated and perhaps the only work of the kind ever produced by a single pen.

Meantime honours and distinctions continued to pour in. The Empress Catherine sent him a magnificent gold snuff-box, with two rich ermine cloaks for his wife and eldest daughter. From her representative at Moscow came a second snuff-box, set with diamonds, and inscribed with the words in Russian, "From a pupil to his master." The Society of Arts adjudged him the honorary gold medal. The Salford Agricultural Society offered a special medal, on which was engraved, "for his services to his country."

And Fanny Burney paid him her prettiest compliments, which very likely he valued far more than gold snuff-boxes or medals. In a letter preserved at Bradfield occurs the following:—"P.S. Will Honeycomb says, if you would know anything of a lady's meaning, (always provided she has any) when she writes to you, look at the postscript. Now, pray, dear Sir, how came you ever to imagine what you are pleased to blazon to the world with all the confidence of self-belief that you think farming the only thing worth manly attention? You who, if taste, rather than circumstances, had been your guide, might have found wreaths and flowers almost any way you had turned, as fragrant as those of Ceres."

The enforced residence in London had many attractions. He dined out, he tells us, from twenty-five to thirty times in one month, and had received during the same period, "forty invitations from people of the highest rank and consequence." He mentions the fact of having had two interviews with the king, and what interests us in a far greater degree, a dinner in company of Hannah More. I was very eager, he writes, in listening to every word that fell from her lips, though not nearly so much so as I should have been many years after; an allusion explained by the last pages of this memoir. In 1796 he visited Burke, and this entry is too interesting to be passed by. The pair had corresponded on agriculture and had met before. Burke was naturally delighted with Arthur Young's recantation, "The Example of France." He had not seen, he wrote, anything in this controversy which stood better bottomed. It was a "most able, useful, and reasonable pamphlet." "I reached Mr. Burke's before breakfast," writes Young, "and had every reason to be pleased with my reception. 'Why, Mr. Young,' said Burke, 'it is many years since I saw you, and to the best of my recollection you have not suffered the smallest change. You look as young as you did sixteen years ago. You must be very strong. You have no belly. Your form shows lightness. You have an elastic mind.' I wish I could have returned anything like the compliment, but I was shocked to see him so broken, so low, and with such expressions of melancholy. I almost thought that I had come to see the greatest genius of the age in vain. The conversation was remarkably desultory, a broken mixture of agricultural observations, French madness, price of provisions, the death of his son, the absurdity of regulating labour, the mischief of our poor laws, the difficulty of our cottagers keeping cows, an argumentative discussion of any opinion seemed to distress him, and I therefore avoided it. Speaking on public affairs he said: 'I never read a newspaper, but if anything happens to occur which they think will interest me, I am told of it.' I observed there was strength of mind in the resolution. 'Oh, no,' he replied; 'it is mere weakness of mind.' It was evident that he would not publish on the subject that had brought me to Gregory's (here Arthur Young alludes to a project mooted in parliament for regulating the price of labour), but he declared himself absolutely inimical to any regulation whatever by law, that all such interference was not only unnecessary but mischievous. He observed that the supposed scarcity was extremely ill understood, and that the consumption of the people was clear proof of it. This in his neighbourhood was not lessened, as he had learned by a very careful examination of many bakers, butchers, and excisemen, nor had the poor been distressed further than what resulted immediately from that improvidence which was occasioned by the poor laws. After breakfast he took me a sauntering walk for five hours over his farm, and to a cottage where a scrap of land had been stolen from the waste. I was glad to find his farm in good order, and doubly so to hear that it was his only amusement except the attention he paid to a school for sixty children of noble French emigrants.

"Mrs. Crewe arrived just before dinner, and though she exerted herself with that brilliance of imagination which renders her conversation so interesting, it was not sufficient to raise the drooping spirits of Mr. Burke. . . . . Yet he tried once or twice to rally, and once even to pun. Mrs. Crewe observing that Thelwel was to stand for Norwich, observed that it would be horrid for Mr. Wyndham to be turned out by such a man. 'Aye,' Mr. Burke replied, 'that would not *tell well*.' She laughed at him in the style of condemning a bad pun. Somebody said it was a fair one. Burke said, 'It was neither very bad nor very good.' My visit on the whole," adds Arthur Young, "was interesting. I am glad once more to have seen and conversed with the man who I hold to possess the greatest and most brilliant parts of any person of the age he lived in. But to behold so great a genius so depressed with melancholy, stooping with infirmity of body, feeling the anguish of a lacerated mind, and sinking into the grave under accumulated misery—to see all this in a character I venerate, and apparently without resource or comfort, wounded every feeling of my soul, and I left him next day almost as low-spirited as himself."

The clouds were already gathering about his own horizon. A year later, and he too was a grief-stricken, desolated, prematurely aged man.

His second daughter Elizabeth, married to a son of Hoole, the translator of Ariosto, had died of consumption in 1794. Signs of the same terrible disease now began to show themselves in his bright, his adored Bobbin. In the midst of his engrossing occupations we find him constantly thinking of her, writing long letters, fulfilling her childish commissions. Bobbin has expressed a wish for a workbox, and he bestows as much attention on the purchase as if he were in treaty for 4,000 acres of moorland. He had looked at a good many, he wrote, but could find none under twenty-five shillings, or at still higher prices; he hears, however, that good ones are to be had at a lower figure, and will continue his researches. He shows the most painful eagerness about her health. She is to tell him every particular as to appetite, sleep, pulse, thirst. One of these letters ends thus: "I cannot read half your mother's letter, but enough to see that she is very angry with me for I know not what." He sends strict orders concerning her. Miss Patty is to ride out in the chaise or on double horse when Bonnet (a bailiff) is not obliged to be absent from the farm. If he is at market, when the days are long and Miss Patty rises early, she can have a ride before breakfast. Bonnet is to pay Miss Patty a shilling a week. In another note he reasons with the little patient on the childishness of demurring at medicines. She is ordered steel, and only takes it under protest. He urges her by the love she bears her father to follow out the doctor's orders in every particular. Change of air was tried, but the precious life could not be saved. She died about twelve months after his visit to Burke. "On Friday morning, June 19, at twelve minutes past one," he writes, "my dear, angelic child breathed her last." In a note below follows a later entry, "Here was my call to God. Oh! may it prove effective."

He never recovered from the blow. In his overpowering grief he could not bear to part with the mortal remains of his darling. When, at last, he consented to interment, the coffin was placed under the family pew, her heart lying where he knelt in prayer. He wept himself blind; the terrible calamity that now gradually overtook him being indeed imputed to excess of weeping.

Sorrow mastered, unmanned a nature singularly hopeful and elastic. He became a prey to morbid introspection, to the gloomiest views of human life. He fell at last into the mood that incites men to write or read such works as "Baxter's Saints' Rest," or in our own day, to join the Salvation Army. The blindness came on by slow degrees, and for some time he remained at his post.

"In London, I am alone and therefore at peace," he writes significantly in 1798. "I rise at four or five, and go to bed at nine or ten. I go to no amusements, and read some Scripture every day. I never lay aside my good books but for business."

He still continues to see old friends, however, and his former interest in public affairs does not wholly desert him. During the same year he visits Pitt several times at Holwood, and throws heart and soul into new enterprises. The loss of his child has awakened pity for suffering childhood. In one month alone we find seven dinners given to about forty-eight poor children each time. Another entry is to this effect: "Dinner to fifteen poor children, eleven shillings, another dinner, do., do., another to thirty-seven poor children, sixteen shillings and sixpence," and so on, and so on. Perhaps the following note may have something to do with these charities. "1798. Sold copyright of my travels for 280 guineas." What travels these were he does not say.

The business of the Board was still carried on as laboriously as before, but in 1808 he writes that his sight is so indifferent he is afraid of writing at all, and further on, " My eyes grow worse and worse. For me to read a letter of two sheets and a half would be a vain attempt. I pick out as much as they will let me."

Three years later he was operated upon for cataract, and from a curious and interesting letter written by his wife, we learn the cause, or supposed cause, of failure. All seemed going on well with the somewhat intractable patient, and the oculists held out good hope of recovery on one condition. He must remain calm. Weeping would be fatal. Wilberforce paid him a visit as he sat bandaged in a dark room. The visitor had been cautioned on no account whatever to agitate him, but either underrating his friend's susceptibility or his own, he began in his soft gentle voice, "The Duke of Grafton is dead," and went on to speak of the duke's death so touchingly that the other burst into tears. The mischief was done past recall. The last twelve years of life were spent by Arthur Young in total blindness. They were busier for all that than those of many men in the meridian. He was now chiefly at Bradfield, where the indefatigable veteran severely taxed the energies of his comparatively youthful associates. Besides his secretary, M. de St. Croix, he often enjoyed the friendly services of a granddaughter of Dr. Burney's, Miss Francis by name, a lady who, like Mezzofanti, was " a monster of languages, a Briareus of parts of speech, a walking polyglot." It was a definite understanding that this linguistic knowledge—to what special uses it was put we are not informed—should be kept up. Every day Miss Francis enjoyed an hour or more for the purpose of reading a little Latin, Greek, Hebrew, Spanish, Italian, Dutch, and so on. In a letter to her brother, Mary Young, the only surviving daughter, amusingly describes one of these long, well-filled days. When at Bradfield, she tells us, Miss Francis slept over the servant's hall with a packthread round her wrist, this packthread passing through the keyhole communicated with Arthur Young's room, and when he wanted to awake her, which was generally between four or five o'clock in the morning, he pulled it, on which she immediately rose. The pair would then sally forth for a two hours' walk on the turnpike road, stopping at some farmhouse to take milk, and afterwards distributing religious tracts at the cottages by the way, Miss Francis questioning the people upon their principles, reading to them, and catechizing the children. "At half-past eight[1] they return," writes Miss Young, "as that is the hour M. St. Croix gets up, who finds it quite enough to read and write for two hours and a half before breakfast. After breakfast the three adjourn to the library till one, when Mr. St. Croix takes his walk for an hour, Miss Francis and my father read, write, or walk till three o'clock. He puts children to school at Bradfield, Cockfield, and Stanningfield, and every Sunday they meet and are catechized. Every Sunday night a hundred meet, when Mr. St. Croix reads a sermon and chapter, and my father explains for an hour, after which a prayer dismisses them. Last Sunday they (Arthur Young and the linguist) went to church at Acton. Every Sunday they go to Acton or Ampton, each church ten miles out and ten home, besides teaching the schools and the meeting in the hall." She adds, "My father has taken out a license for the hall (*i.e.* Bradfield), as there is an assembly of people which would have been liable to information." This letter bears date May 13, 1814.

The Sunday evening services made a deep impression on the country folks. The villagers of Bradfield and the neighbourhood still talk of the blind old Squire who was a great preacher. They know little or nothing of his literary fame. The achievement by which he will be remembered is to them a sealed book. But he lives in local memory as a second Wesley, a wonderful stirrer-up of men's consciences, an unrivalled expounder of the Gospel. There is still living at Bury St. Edmunds (1889) a nonagenarian who has a vivid recollection of Arthur Young's sermons. In his vehemence the orator would move to and fro till he gradually had his back turned to the congregation, whereupon his daughter or secretary would gently place their hands upon his shoulders and restore him to the proper position.

It is a touching figure we now take leave of, that blind, fervid, silver-haired preacher, a hundred eager faces fixed upon

---

[1] There seems some confusion here, surely six must be meant.

his own, the rapt silence of the crowded meeting-place only broken by his trembling, impassioned tones. For the story of Arthur Young's life is mainly told. The world had not yet lost sight of him. He was from time to time pleasantly reminded of the conspicuous part he had played in it. He tells us how, in 1815, when breakfasting with Wilberforce, he met General Macaulay, who, recently travelling from Geneva to Lyons, had visited a French farm, where he found everything "in the highest style of management, and so much superior to all the rest of the country, that he inquired into the origin of such superiority. The answer of the owner was, ' My cultivation is entirely that of Monsieur Arthur Young, whose recommendations I have carried into practice with the success you see.'" For the most part the remaining years were uneventful. He bore his privations and infirmities with resignation, and retained full possession of his faculties to the last. He died at Sackville Street on the 20th April, 1820, and was buried at Bradfield. The handsome tomb in the form of a sarcophagus erected to his memory stands close to the roadside, over against the entrance to his old home. Passers-by may read the somewhat stilted yet veracious inscription on the outer slab :—

> "Let every real patriot shed a tear,
> For genius, talent, worth, lie buried here."

In France such a man would have had his statue long ago. Perhaps this more modest tribute were more to his taste. That a native of his beloved Suffolk, herself a frequent wayfarer throughout the length and breadth of France, should edit his French Travels a hundred years after they were written, would surely have pleased Arthur Young well.

Of his children two survived him, his daughter Mary, who died unmarried, and his son Arthur, whose son, the present owner of Bradfield, is the last of Arthur Young's race and name.

BIBLIOGRAPHY.

A Six Weeks' Tour through the Southern Counties of England and Wales. London, 1768. 8vo. Second edition, enlarged, 1769. 8vo. Third edition, 1772. 8vo.

A Six Months' Tour through the North of England, containing an account of the present state of Agriculture, Manufactures, and Population in several counties of this kingdom. London, 1771. 8vo. 4 vols. Plates.

The Farmer's Tour through the East of England; being a Register of a Journey through various counties, to inquire into the state of Agriculture, Manufactures, and Population. London, 1770 71. 8vo. 4 vols.

Tour in Ireland; with general observations on the present state of that kingdom in 1776-7-8. Dublin, 1780. 8vo. 2 vols. London, 1780. 8vo. 2 vols.

Travels during the years 1787, 1788, 1789, and 1790, undertaken more particularly with a view of ascertaining the Cultivation, Wealth, Resources, and National Prosperity of the Kingdom of France. Bury St. Edmunds, 1794. 4to. 2 vols. Vol. I. is a second edition, the first edition having been published in 1792. Reprinted, Dublin, 1798. 8vo. 2 vols.

The Farmer's Letters to the People of England; containing the sentiments of a practical Husbandman on the present condition of Husbandry, &c. London, 1768, 1771. 8vo. 2 vols.

The Farmer's Guide in Hiring and Stocking Farms. London, 1770. 8vo. 2 vols. With plans.

Rural Economy, or Essays on the Practical Part of Husbandry. London, 1770. 8vo.

A Course of Experimental Agriculture. London, 1770. 4to. 2 vols.

Political Arithmetic, or Observations on the present state of Great Britain, and the principles of her policy in the Encouragement of Agriculture. London, 1774.

The Farmer's Kalendar. London, 1800. 8vo. 1808. 8vo. 25th edition. Edited and extended by J. C. Morton. London, Routledge, 1862, bds., 10s. 6d.

Essays on Manures. London, 1804. 8vo.

Advantages which have resulted from the Board of Agriculture. London, 1809. 8vo.

Inquiry into the progressive value of money, as marked by the price of Agricultural Products. London, 1812.

Agricultural Surveys. Published by the Board of Agriculture.
Essex. 2 vols. 1807. 8vo.
Hertfordshire. 1804. 8vo.
Lincolnshire. 1798. 8vo.
Norfolk. 1804. 8vo.
Oxfordshire. 1809 or 1813. 8vo.
Suffolk. 1794. 4to. 1798, 1804. 8vo.
Sussex. 1703, 1808. 4to.
Hampshire. 1794.

Baxteriana; a selection from the works of Richard Baxter. 1815.

Oweniana. Select Passages from the Writings of John Owen, D.D. 1817.

Tracts and Pamphlets (in British Museum) as follows:—

On the Husbandry of three celebrated Farmers, Bakewell, Arbuthnot, and Duckett. 1811.

The Expediency of a Free Exportation of Corn at this time. 1770.

An Idea of the Present State of France. 1798.

Letter concerning the Present State of France. 1769.

Observations on the Waste Lands of Great Britain. 1773.

Proposals to the Legislature for numbering the People. 1771.

The question of Wool truly stated. 1788.

On the Size of Farms (contributed to Hunter's "Georgical Essays"). 1803.

On Summer Fallowing, in Hunter's "Georgical Essays." 1803.

Letters on Agriculture to General Washington. 1813.

An Address. 1793.

The Constitution safe without Reform. 1795.

An Inquiry into the state of the public mind among the Lower Classes. 1798.

An Essay on the management of Hogs. 1769.

The Example of France. 1793. (Numerous editions.)

Peace and Reform. 1799.

An Inquiry into the propriety of applying Wastes to the better maintenance of the Poor. 1801.

"The Annals of Agriculture" contain many contributions of Arthur Young not reprinted elsewhere.

PREFACE.

IT is a question whether modern history has anything more curious to offer to the attention of the politician, than the progress and rivalship of the French and English empires, from the ministry of Colbert to the revolution in France. In the course of those 130 years, both have figured with a degree of splendour that has attracted the admiration of mankind.

In proportion to the power, the wealth, and the resources of these nations, is the interest which the world in general takes in the maxims of political œconomy by which they have been governed. To examine how far the system of that œconomy has influenced agriculture, manufactures, commerce, and public felicity, is certainly an inquiry of no slight importance; and so many books have been composed on the *theory* of these, that the public can hardly think that time misemployed which attempts to give THE PRACTICE.

The survey which I made, some years past, of the agriculture of England and Ireland (the minutes of which I published under the title of *Tours*), was such a step towards understanding the state of our husbandry as I shall not presume to characterise; there are but few of the European nations that do not read these Tours in their own language; and, notwithstanding all their faults and deficiencies, it has been often regretted, that no similar description of France could be resorted to, either by the farmer or the politician. Indeed it could not but be lamented, that this vast kingdom, which has so much figured in history, were likely to remain another century unknown, with respect to those circumstances that are the objects of my enquiries. An hundred and thirty years have passed, including one of the most active and conspicuous reigns upon record, in which the French power and resources though much overstrained, were formidable to Europe. How far were that power and those resources founded on the permanent basis of an enlightened agriculture? How far on the more insecure support of manufactures and commerce? How far have wealth and power and exterior splendour, from whatever cause they may have arisen, reflected back upon the people the prosperity they implied? Very curious inquiries; yet resolved insufficiently by those whose political reveries are spun by their firesides, or caught flying as they are whirled through Europe in post-chaises. A man who is not practically acquainted with agriculture, knows not how to make those inquiries; he scarcely knows how to discriminate the circumstances productive of misery, from those which generate the felicity of a people; an assertion that will not appear paradoxical, to those who have attended closely to these subjects. At the same time, the mere agriculturist, who makes such journies, sees little or nothing of the connection between the practice in the fields, and the resources of the empire; of combinations that take place between operations apparently unimportant, and the general interest of the state; combinations so curious, as to convert, in some cases, well cultivated fields into scenes of misery, and accuracy of husbandry into the parent of national weakness. These are subjects that never will be understood from the speculations of the mere farmer, or the mere politician; they demand a mixture of both; and the investigation of a mind free from prejudice, particularly national prejudice; from the love of system, and of the vain theories that are to be found in the closets of speculators alone. God forbid that I should be guilty of the vanity of supposing myself thus endowed! I know too well the contrary; and have no other pretension to undertake so arduous a work, than that of having reported the agriculture of England with some little success. Twenty years experience, since that attempt, may make me hope to be not less qualified for similar exertions at present.

The clouds that, for four or five years past, have indicated a change in the political sky of the French hemisphere, and which have since gathered to so singular a storm, have rendered it yet more interesting, to know what France was previously to any change. It would indeed have been matter of astonishment, if monarchy had risen, and had set in that region, without the kingdom having had any examination professedly agricultural.

The candid reader will not expect, from the registers of a traveller, that minute analysis of common practice, which a man is enabled to give, who resides some months, or years, confined to one spot; twenty men, employed during twenty years, would not effect it; and supposing it done, not one thousandth part of their labours would be worth a perusal. Some singularly enlightened districts merit such attention; but the number of them, in any country, is inconsiderable; and the practices that deserve such a study, perhaps, still fewer: to know that unenlightened practices exist, and want improvement, is the chief knowledge that is of use to convey; and this rather for the statesman than the farmer. No reader, if he knows anything of my situation, will expect, in this work, what the advantages of rank and fortune are necessary to produce—of such I had none to exert, and could combat difficulties with no other arms than unremitted attention, and unabating industry. Had my aims been seconded by that success in life, which gives energy to effort, and vigour to pursuit, the work would have been more worthy of the public eye; but such success must, in this kingdom, be sooner looked for in any other path than in that of the plough; the *non ullus aratro dignus honos*, was not more applicable to a period of confusion and bloodshed at Rome, than one of peace and luxury in England.

One circumstance I may be allowed to mention, because it will shew, that whatever faults the ensuing pages contain, they do not flow from any presumptive expectation of success: a feeling that belongs to writers only, much more popular than myself: when the publisher agreed to run the hazard of printing these papers, and some progress being made in the journal, the whole MS. was put into the compositor's hand to be examined, if there were a sufficiency for a volume of sixty sheets; he found enough prepared for the press to fill 140: and I assure the reader, that the successive employment of striking out and mutilating more than the half of what I had written, was executed with more indifference than regret, even though it obliged me to exclude several chapters, upon which I had taken considerable pains. The publisher would have printed the whole; but whatever faults may be found with the author, he ought at least to be exempted from the imputation of an undue confidence in the public favour; since, to expunge was undertaken as readily as to compose.—So much depended in the second part of the work on accurate figures, that I did not care to trust to myself, but employed a schoolmaster, who has the reputation of being a good arithmetician, for examining the calculations, and I hope he has not let any material errors escape him.

The revolution in France was a hazardous and critical subject, but too important to be neglected; the details I have given, and the reflections I have ventured, will, I trust, be received with candour, by those who consider how many authors, of no inconsiderable ability and reputation, have failed on that difficult theme: the course I have steered is so removed from extremes, that I can hardly hope for the approbation of more than a few; and I may apply to myself, in this instance, the words of Swift:—" I have the ambition, common with other reasoners, to wish at least that both parties may think me *in the right*; but if that is not to be hoped for, my next wish should be, that both might think me *in the wrong*; which I would understand as an ample justification of myself, and a sure ground to believe that I have proceeded at least with impartiality, and perhaps with truth."

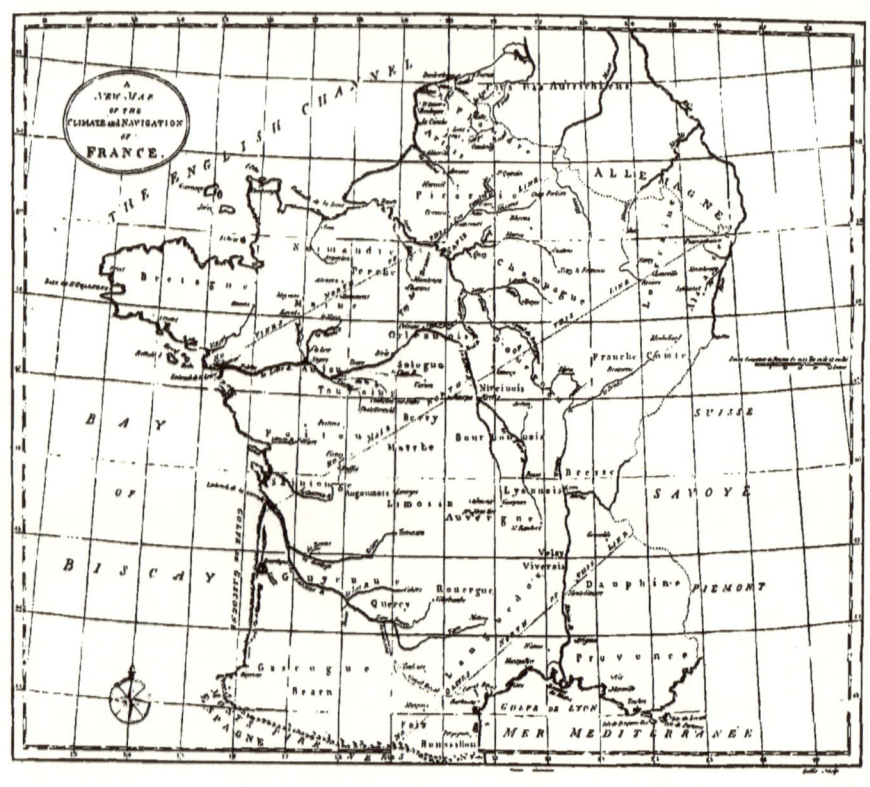

TRAVELS DURING THE YEARS
1787, 1788, AND 1789.

THERE are two methods of writing travels; to register the journey itself, or the result of it. In the former case, it is a diary, under which head are to be classed all those books of travels written in the form of letters. The latter usually falls into the shape of essays on distinct subjects. Of the former method of composing, almost every book of modern travels is an example. Of the latter, the admirable essays of my valuable friend Mr. Professor Symonds, upon Italian agriculture,[1] are the most perfect specimens.

It is of very little importance what form is adopted by a man of real genius; he will make any form useful, and any information interesting. But for persons of more moderate talents, it is of consequence to consider the circumstances for and against both these modes.

The journal form hath the advantage of carrying with it a greater degree of credibility; and, of course, more weight. A traveller who thus registers his observations is detected the moment he writes of things he has not seen. He is precluded from giving studied or elaborate remarks upon insufficient foundations: If he sees little, he must register little: if he has few good opportunities, of being well informed, the reader is enabled to observe it, and will be induced to give no more credit to his relations than the sources of them appear to deserve: If he passes so rapidly through a country as necessarily to be no judge of what he sees, the reader knows it: if he dwells long in places of

---

[1] See "Annals of Agriculture," vol. iii.
[All foot-notes are by the Editor unless it is stated otherwise.]

little or no moment with private views or for private business, the circumstance is seen; and thus the reader has the satisfaction of being as safe from imposition either designed or involuntary, as the nature of the case will admit: all which advantages are wanted in the other method.

But to balance them, there are on the other hand some weighty inconveniences; among these the principal is, the prolixity to which a diary generally leads; the very mode of writing almost making it inevitable. It necessarily causes repetitions of the same subjects and the same ideas; and that surely must be deemed no inconsiderable fault, when one employs many words to say what might be better said in a few. Another capital objection is, that subjects of importance, instead of being treated *de suite* for illustration or comparison, are given by scraps as received, without order, and without connection; a mode which lessens the effect of writing, and destroys much of its utility.

In favour of composing essays on the principal objects that have been observed, that is, giving the result of travels and not the travels themselves, there is this obvious and great advantage, that the subjects thus treated are in as complete a state of combination and illustration as the abilities of the author can make them; the matter comes with full force and effect. Another admirable circumstance is brevity; for by the rejection of all useless details, the reader has nothing before him but what tends to the full explanation of the subject: of the disadvantages, I need not speak; they are sufficiently noted by shewing the benefits of the diary form; for proportionably to the benefits of the one will clearly be the disadvantages of the other.

After weighing the *pour* and the *contre*, I think that it is not impracticable in my peculiar case to retain the benefits of both these plans.

With one leading and predominant object in view, namely agriculture, I have conceived that I might throw each subject of it into distinct chapters, retaining all the advantages which arise from composing the result only of my travels.

At the same time, that the reader may have whatever satisfaction flows from the diary form, the observations which I made upon the face of the countries through which I passed; and upon the manners, customs, amusements, towns, roads, seats, &c., may, without injury, be given in a journal, and thus satisfy the reader in all those points, with which he ought in candour to be made acquainted, for the reasons above intimated.

It is upon this idea that I have reviewed my notes, and executed the work I now offer to the public.

But travelling upon paper, as well as moving amongst rocks and rivers, hath its difficulties. When I had traced my plan, and begun to work upon it, I rejected without mercy a variety of little circumstances relating to myself only, and of conversations with various persons which I had thrown upon paper for the amusement of my family and intimate friends. For this I was remonstrated with by a person, of whose judgment I think highly, as having absolutely spoiled my diary, by expunging the very passages that would best please the mass of common readers; in a word, that I must give up the journal plan entirely or let it go as it was written.—To treat the public like a friend, let them see all, and trust to their candour for forgiving trifles. He reasoned thus: *Depend on it, Young, that those notes you wrote at the moment, are more likely to please than what you will now produce coolly, with the idea of reputation in your head: whatever you strike out will be what is most interesting, for you will be guided by the importance of the subject; and believe me, it is not this consideration that pleases so much as a careless and easy mode of thinking and writing, which every man exercises most when he does not compose for the press. That I am right in this opinion you yourself afford a proof. Your tour of Ireland* (he was pleased to say) *is one of the best accounts of a country I have read, yet it had no great success. Why? Because the chief part of it is a farming diary, which, however valuable it may be to consult, nobody will read. If, therefore, you print your journal at all, print it so as to be read; or reject the method entirely, and confine yourself to set dissertations. Remember the travels of Dr.* —— *and Mrs.* ——, *from which it would be difficult to gather one single important idea, yet they were received with applause; nay, the bagatelles of Baretti, amongst the Spanish muleteers were read with avidity.*

The high opinion I have of the judgment of my friend, induced me to follow his advice; in consequence of which, I venture to offer my itinerary to the public, just as it was written on the spot: requesting my reader, if much should be found of a trifling nature, to pardon it, from a reflection, that the chief object of my travels is to be found in another part of the work, to which he may at once have recourse, if he wish to attend only to subjects of a more important character.

JOURNAL.

May 15, 1787.

THE streight that separates England, so fortunately for her, from all the rest of the world, must be crossed many times before a traveller ceases to be surprised at the sudden and universal change that surrounds him on landing at Calais. The scene, the people, the language, every object is new; and in those circumstances in which there is most resemblance, a discriminating eye finds little difficulty in discovering marks of distinctions.

The noble improvement of a salt marsh, worked by Mons. Mouron of this town, occasioned my acquaintance some time ago with that gentleman; and I had found him too well informed, upon various important objects, not to renew it with pleasure. I spent an agreeable and instructive evening at his house.—165 miles.

The 17th. Nine hours rolling at anchor had so fatigued my mare, that I thought it necessary for her to rest one day; but this morning I left Calais. For a few miles the country resembles parts of Norfolk and Suffolk; gentle hills, with some inclosures around the houses in the vales, and a distant range of wood. The country is the same to Boulogne. Towards that town, I was pleased to find many seats belonging to people who reside there. How often are false ideas conceived from reading and report! I imagined that nobody but farmers and labourers in France lived in the country; and the first ride I take in that kingdom shews me a score of country seats. The road excellent.

Boulogne is not an ugly town; and from the ramparts

of the upper part the view is beautiful, though low water in the river would not let me see it to advantage. It is well known that this place has long been the resort of great numbers of persons from England, whose misfortunes in trade, or extravagance in life, have made a residence abroad more agreeable than at home. It is easy to suppose that they here find a *level* of society that tempts them to herd in the same place. Certainly it is not cheapness, for it is rather dear. The mixture of French and English women makes an odd appearance in the streets; the latter are dressed in their own fashion; but the French heads are all without hats, with close caps, and the body covered with a long cloak that reaches to the feet. The town has the appearance of being flourishing: the buildings good, and in repair, with some modern ones; perhaps as sure a test of prosperity as any other. They are raising also a new church, on a large and expensive scale. The place on the whole is chearful, and the environs pleasing; and the sea-shore is a flat strand of firm sand as far the tide reaches. The high land adjoining is worth viewing by those who have not already seen the petrification of clay; it is found in the stoney and argilaceous state, just as what I described at Harwich. ("Annals of Agriculture," vol. vi. p. 218.)—24 miles.

The 18th. The view of Boulogne from the other side, at the distance of a mile is a pleasing landscape; the river meanders in the vale, and spreads in a fine reach under the town, just before it falls into the sea, which opens between two high lands, one of which backs the town.— The view wants only wood; for if the hills had more, fancy could scarcely paint a more agreeable scene. The country improves, more inclosed, and some parts strongly resembling England. Some fine meadows about Bonbrie,[1] and several chateaus. I am not professedly in this diary on husbandry, but must just observe, that it is to the full as bad as the country is good; corn miserable and yellow with weeds, yet all summer fallowed with lost attention, On the hills, which are at no great distance from the sea, the trees turn their heads from it, shorn of their foliage: it is not therefore to the S.W. alone that we should attri-

[1] Pont de Brique (Pas de Calais).

bute this effect.—If the French have not husbandry to shew us, they have roads; nothing can be more beautiful, or kept in more garden order, if I may use the expression, than that which passes through a fine wood of Mons. Neuvillier's; and indeed for the whole way from Samer[1] it is wonderfully formed: a vast causeway, with hills cut to level vales; which would fill me with admiration, if I had known nothing of the abominable *corveès*,[2] that make me commiserate the oppressed farmers, from whose extorted labour, this magnificence has been wrung. Women gathering grass and weeds by hand in the woods for their cows is a trait of poverty.

Pass *turbarries*,[3] near Montreuil,[4] like those at Newbury. The walk round the ramparts of that town is pretty: the little gardens in the bastions below are singular. The place has many English; for what purpose not easy to conceive, for it is unenlivened by those circumstances that render towns pleasant. In a short conversation with an English family returning home, the lady, who is young, and I conjecture agreeable, assured me I should find the court of Versailles amazingly splendid. Oh! how she loved France!—and should regret going to England if she did not expect soon to return. As she had crossed the kingdom of France, I asked her what part of it pleased her best; the answer was, such as a pair of pretty lips would be sure to utter, "Oh! Paris and Versailles." Her husband, who is not so young, said "Touraine." It is probable, that a farmer is much more likely to agree with the sentiments of the husband than of the lady, notwithstanding her charms.—24 miles.

The 19th. Dined, or rather starved, at Bernay,[5] where

[1] (Pas de Calais).
[2] "Un malheureux corvoyeur, qui pays quarante sous de capitation, et qui n'a pour vivre que ce qu'il peut gagner dans la journée, sera tenu d'entretenir environ six toises (measure of six feet) de chemin, entretien évalué à neuf livres (the livre varied in value from twenty to twenty-five sous) chaque année. De plus on la transportait d'une route sur une autre, loin de chez lui."—*Petition of the Parliament of Rennes.* H. Martin, Histoire de France, vol. xvi., p. 237. When Arthur Young wrote, the *corvée* had in certain regions been commuted into a fixed money payment, paid by the Commune. [3] Turbary; Fr. Tourbière (peat-bed).
[4] Montreuil-sur-mer (Pas de Calais). [5] (Pas de Calais).

for the first time I met with that wine of whose ill fame I had heard so much in England, that of being worse than small beer. No scattered farm-houses in this part of Picardy, all being collected in villages which is as unfortunate for the beauty of a country, as it is inconvenient to its cultivation. To Abbeville,[1] unpleasant, nearly flat; and though there are many and great woods, yet they are uninteresting. Pass the new chalk chateau of Mons. St. Maritan, who, had he been in England, would not have built a good house in that situation, nor have projected his walls like those of an alms-house.

Abbeville is said to contain 22,000 souls; it is old, and disagreeably built; many of the houses of wood, with a greater air of antiquity than I remember to have seen; their brethren in England have been long ago demolished. Viewed the manufacture of Van Robais,[2] which was established by Lewis XIV. and of which Voltaire and others have spoken so much. I had many enquiries concerning wool and woollens to make here; and, in conversation with the manufacturers, found them great politicians, condemning with violence the new commercial treaty[3] with England. —30 miles.

The 21st. It is the same flat and unpleasing country to Flixcourt.[4]—15 miles.

The 22d. Poverty and poor crops to Amiens; women are now ploughing with a pair of horses to sow barley. The difference of the customs of the two nations is in nothing more striking than in the labours of the sex; in England, it is very little that they will do in the fields except to glean and make hay; the first is a party of pilfering, and the second of pleasure: in France, they plough and

[1] (Pas de Calais.)
[2] The Van Robais, Dutch cloth manufacturers invited to France by Colbert.
[3] This treaty, so liberal in spirit, was signed at Versailles in Sept. 1786, and ratified the following year. The trade between the two countries had been up to that time comparatively small; imports and exports were doubled within twelve months after the treaty had come into force. Among the clauses was one providing entire religious liberty for subjects of both countries, and the right of sepulture "in convenient places to be appointed for that purpose." These friendly and profitable commercial relations were soon interrupted by war. Knight's Hist. Eng., vol. vi., p. 797.   [4] (Somme.)

fill the dung-cart. Lombardy poplars seem to have been introduced here about the same time as in England.

Picquigny[1] has been the scene of a remarkable transaction, that does great honour to the tolerating spirit of the French nation. Mons. Colmar, a Jew, bought the seignory and estate, including the viscounty of Amiens, of the Duke of Chaulnes, by virtue of which he appoints the canons of the cathedral of Amiens. The bishop resisted his nomination, and it was carried by appeal to the parliament of Paris, whose decree was in favour of Mons. Colmar. The immediate seignory of Picquigny, but without its dependences, is resold to the Count d'Artois.

At Amiens, view the cathedral, said to be built by the English; it is very large and beautifully light and decorated. They are fitting it up in black drapery, and a great canopy, with illuminations for the burial of the prince de Tingry, colonel of the regiment of cavalry, whose station is here. To view this was an object among the people, and crouds were at each door. I was refused entrance, but some officers being admitted, gave orders that an English gentleman without should be let in, and I was called back from some distance and desired very politely to enter, as they did not know at first that I was an Englishman. These are but trifles, but they show liberality, and it is fair to report them. If an Englishman receives attention in France, *because he is an Englishman*, what return ought to be made to a Frenchman in England is sufficiently obvious. The château d'eau or machine for supplying Amiens with water is worth viewing; but plates only could give an idea of it. The town abounds with woollen manufactures. I conversed with several masters who united entirely with those of Abbeville in condemning the treaty of commerce.—15 miles.

The 23rd. To Breteuil[2] the country is diversified, woods everywhere in sight the whole journey.—21 miles.

The 24th. A flat and uninteresting chalky country continues about to Clermont,[3] where it improves; is hilly and has wood. The view of the town as soon as the dale is seen, with the Duke of Fitzjames' plantation is pretty.—24 miles.

[1] (Somme.)   [2] (Oise.)   [3] (Oise.)

The 25th. The environs of Clermont are picturesque. The hills about Liancourt are pretty and spread with a sort of cultivation I had never seen before, a mixture of vineyards (for here the vines first appear), gardens and corn. A piece of wheat, a scrap of lucerne, a patch of clover or vetches, a bit of vine with cherry and other fruit trees scattered among all, and the whole cultivated with the spade; it makes a pretty appearance, but must form a poor system of trifling.

Chantilly—magnificence is its reigning character, it is never lost. There is not taste or beauty enough to soften it into milder features; all but the château [1] is great, and there is something imposing in that; except the gallery of the great Condé's battles and the cabinet of natural history, which is rich in very fine specimens, most advantageously arranged; it contains nothing that demands particular notice; nor is there one room which in England would be called large. The stable is truly great and exceeds very much indeed anything of the kind I had ever seen. It is 580 feet long and 40 broad, and is sometimes filled with 240 English horses. I had been so accustomed to the imitation in water of the waving and irregular lines of nature that I came to Chantilly [2] prepossessed against the idea of a canal, but the view of one here is striking and had the effect which magnificent scenes impress. It arises from extent and from the right lines of the water uniting with the regularity of the objects in view. It is Lord Kames,[3] I think, who says the part of the garden contiguous to the house should partake of the regularity of the building; with much magnificence about a place this is unavoidable. The effect here, however, is lessened by the parterre before the castle, in which the division and the diminutive jets d'eau are not of a size to correspond with the magnificence of the canal. The menagerie is very pretty, and exhibits a prodigious variety of domestic poultry, from all parts of the world; one of the best objects

---

[1] The château here spoken of was razed as a fortress in 1792, and replaced in 1880 by the elegant construction of the Duc d'Aumale, presented to the Institut in 1886.
[2] (Oise.)
[3] Home, Henry, Lord Kames, Scotch judge and author, died 1782.

to which a menagerie can be applied; these, and the Corsican stag had all my attention. The *hameau* contains an imitation of an English garden; the taste is but just introduced into France, so that it will not stand a critical examination.[1] The most English idea I saw is the lawn in front of the stables; it is large, of a good verdure, and well kept; proving clearly that they may have as fine lawns in the north of France as in England. The labyrinth is the only complete one I have seen, and I have no inclination to see another: it is in gardening what a rebus is in poetry. In the Sylvae are many very fine and scarce plants. I wish those persons who view Chantilly, and are fond of fine trees would not forget to ask for the great beech; this is the finest I ever saw; strait as an arrow, and, as I guess, not less than 80 or 90 feet high; 40 feet to the first branch, and 12 feet diameter at five from the ground. It is in all respects one of the finest trees that can anywhere be met with. Two others are near it, but not equal to this superb one. The forest around Chantilly, belonging to the Prince of Condé,[1] is immense, spreading far and wide; the Paris road crosses it for ten miles, which is its least extent. They say the capitainerie, or paramountship, is above 100 miles in circumference. That is to say, all the inhabitants for that extent are pestered with game, without permission to destroy it, in order to give one man diversion. Ought not these capitaineries to be extirpated?

At Luzarch,[2] I found that my mare, from illness, would travel no further; French stables, which are covered dunghills, and the carelessness of *garcons d'ecuries*, an execrable set of vermin, had given her cold. I therefore left her to send for from Paris, and went thither post; by which experiment I found that posting in France is much worse,

---

[1] This prince headed the emigration, a movement that sealed the fate of Louis XVI. The vast Bourbon-Condé estate became the property of the Duke d'Aumale on the mysterious death of the last duke (son of the above-mentioned) in 1830. The old man was found at the château of St. Leu, hanging by his cravat from the sill of a window, and foul play was suspected. He was father of the Duke d'Enghien, foully murdered by the first Napoleon.

[2] Luzarches (connected with Paris by a railway branching from the Boulogne and Calais line) (Seine et Oise).

and even, upon the whole, dearer than in England. Being in a post-chaise I travelled to Paris, as other travellers in post-chaises do, knowing little or nothing. The last ten miles I was eagerly on the watch for that throng of carriages which near London impede the traveller. I watched in vain; for the road, quite to the gates, is, on comparison, a perfect desert. So many great roads join here, that I suppose this must be accidental. The entrance has nothing magnificent; ill built and dirty. To get to the Rue de Varenne Faubourg St. Germain, I had the whole city to cross, and passed it by narrow, ugly, and crouded streets.

At the hotel de la Rochefoucauld I found the Duke of Liancourt[1] and his sons, the Count de la Rochefoucauld, and the Count Alexander, with my excellent friend Monsieur de Lazowski,[2] all of whom I had the pleasure of knowing in Suffolk. They introduced me to the Duchess d'Estissac, mother of the Duke of Liancourt, and to the Duchess of Liancourt. The agreeable reception and friendly attentions I met with from all this liberal family were well calculated to give me the most favourable impression * * * *.—42 miles.

The 26th. So short a time had I passed before in France, that the scene is totally new to me. Till we have been accustomed to travelling we have a propensity to stare at and admire everything—and to be on the search for novelty, even in circumstances in which it is ridiculous to

---

[1] It was the Duke de Liancourt who summoned courage to break to Louis XVI. the fall of the Bastille. "It is a revolt!" said the King. "No, sire," replied the Duke, "it is a revolution!" His leanings were to constitutional monarchy, and he made every effort to reconcile the court and the assembly. Finding the cause of the Revolution, from his point of view, hopeless, he quitted France, and after years of exile quietly ended his days at Liancourt among the country people by whom he was so deservedly beloved. Died 1827, in the Rue St. Honoré, No. 29.

[2] Madame Roland gives a painful portrait of this Polish *protégé* of the Duke. The National Assembly having suppressed his office as inspector of manufactures, he threw himself into *sans-culottism*, took part in the terrible events of September, 1792, and died soon after. His funeral oration was pronounced by Robespierre. See "Mémoires de Madame Roland." Paris, 1885. See also for Lazowski's services to French agriculture, "L'agriculture in 1785-1787," par MM. Pigeonneau and De Foville. Paris, 1882.

look for it. I have been upon the full silly gape to find out things that I had not found before, as if a street in Paris could be composed of anything but houses, or houses formed of anything but brick or stone—or that the people in them, not being English, would be walking on their heads. I shall shake off this folly as fast as I can, and bend my attention to mark the character and disposition of the nation. Such views naturally lead us to catch the little circumstances which sometimes express them; not an easy task, but subject to many errors.

I have only one day to pass at Paris, and that is taken up with buying necessaries. At Calais, my abundant care produced the inconvenience it was meant to avoid; I was afraid of losing my trunk, by leaving it at Dessein's for the diligence; so I sent it to M. Mouron's.—The consequence is, that it is not to be found at Paris, and its contents are to be bought again before I can leave this city on our journey to the Pyrenees. I believe it may be received as a maxim, that a traveller should always trust his baggage to the common voitures of the country, without any extraordinary precautions.

After a rapid excursion, with my friend Lazowski, to see many things; but too hastily to form any correct idea, spend the evening at his brother's, where I had the pleasure of meeting Mons. de Broussonet,[1] secretary of the Royal Society of Agriculture,[2] and Mons. Desmarets, both of the Academy of Sciences. As Mons. Lazowski is well informed in the manufactures of France, in the police of which he enjoys a post of consideration, and as the other gentlemen have paid much attention to agriculture, the conversation was in no slight degree instructive, and I regretted that a very early departure from Paris would not let me promise myself a further enjoyment so congenial with my feelings, as the company of men, whose conversation shewed a marked attention to objects of national

---

[1] Broussonet, Pierre Auguste, a distinguished naturalist, and no insignificant politician, whose life was a long series of adventures. Proscribed as a Girondin, he crossed to Africa. In 1805 he became member of the corps Législatif. Died 1807.

[2] Founded 1761. An account of the labours of M. Desmarets and his colleagues is given in the work named in note 2, preceding page.

importance. On the breaking up of the party, went with count Alexander de la Rochefoucauld post to Versailles, to be present at the fête of the day following; (whitsunday) slept at the duke de Liancourt's hotel.

The 27th. Breakfasted with him at his apartments in the palace, which are annexed to his office of grand master of the wardrobe, one of the principal in the court of France.—Here I found the duke surrounded by a circle of noblemen, among whom was the duke de la Rochefoucauld,[1] well known for his attention to natural history; I was introduced to him, as he is going to Bagnere de Luchon in the Pyrenees, where I am to have the honour of being in his party.

The ceremony of the day was, the King's investing the Duke of Berri, son of the count D'Artois, with the cordon blue. The Queen's band was in the chapel where the ceremony was performed, but the musical effect was thin and weak. During the service the King was seated between his two brothers, and seemed by his carriage and inattention to wish himself a hunting. He would certainly have been as well employed, as in hearing afterwards from his throne a feudal oath of chivalry, I suppose, or some such nonsense, administered to a boy of ten years old. Seeing much pompous folly I imagined it was the dauphin, and asked a lady of fashion near me; at which she laughed in my face, as if I had been guilty of the most egregious idiotism: nothing could be done in a worse manner; for the stifling of her expression only marked it the more. I applied to Mons. de la Rochefoucauld to learn what gross absurdity I had been guilty of so unwittingly; when, forsooth, it was because the dauphin, *as all the world knows in* France, has the cordon blue put around him as soon as he is born. So unpardonable was it for a foreigner to be ignorant of such an important part of French history, as that of giving a babe a blue slobbering bib instead of a white one!

---

[1] Like his kinsman the Duc de Liancourt, one of the public-spirited noblemen who welcomed the Revolution. "La constitution sera faite ou nous ne serons plus" were his words two years later. Of liberal mind and sterling worth the Duke de la Rochefoucauld deserved a better fate. Killed at Gisors, 1794.

After this ceremony was finished, the King and the knights walked in a sort of procession to a small apartment in which he dined, saluting the Queen as they passed. There appeared to be more ease and familiarity than form in this part of the ceremony; her majesty, who, by the way, is the most beautiful woman I saw to-day, received them with a variety of expression. On some she smiled; to others she talked; a few seemed to have the honour of being more in her intimacy. Her return to some was formal, and to others distant. To the gallant Suffrein [1] it was respectful and benign. The ceremony of the King's dining in public is more odd than splendid. The Queen sat by him with a cover before her, but ate nothing; conversing with the duke of Orleans, and the duke of Liancourt, who stood behind her chair. To me it would have been a most uncomfortable meal, and were I a sovereign, I would sweep away three-fourths of these stupid forms; if Kings do not dine like other people, they lose much of the pleasure of life; their station is very well calculated to deprive them of much, and they submit to nonsensical customs, the sole tendency of which is to lessen the remainder. The only comfortable or amusing dinner is a table of ten or twelve covers for the people whom they like; travellers tell us that this was the mode of the late King of Prussia, who knew the value of life too well to sacrifice it to empty forms on the one hand, or to a monastic reserve on the other.

The palace of Versailles, one of the objects of which report had given me the greatest expectation, is not in the least striking: I view it without emotion: the impression it makes is nothing. What can compensate the want of unity? From whatever point viewed, it appears an assemblage of buildings; a splendid quarter of a town, but not a fine edifice; an objection from which the garden front is not free, though by far the most beautiful.—The great gallery is the finest room I have seen; the other apart-

---

[1] This brave admiral had commanded the French fleets in the East (1773, 1783), coming to sharp encounters with our own off the coasts of Madras and Ceylon. His most brilliant exploit was the capture of Trincomalee, but these successes were not seconded by the weak government at home, and the Treaty of Versailles cut short his career. Died 1788.

ments are nothing; but the pictures and statues are well known to be a capital collection. The whole palace, except the chapel, seems to be open to all the world; we pushed through an amazing croud of all sorts of people to see the procession, many of them not very well dressed, whence it appears, that no questions are asked. But the officers at the door of the apartment in which the King dined, made a distinction, and would not permit all to enter promiscuously.

Travellers speak much, even very late ones, of the remarkable interest the French take in all that personally concerns their King, shewing by the eagerness of their attention not curiosity only, but love. Where, how, and in whom those gentlemen discovered this I know not.—It is either misrepresentation, or the people are changed in a few years more than is credible. Dine at Paris, and in the evening the duchess of Liancourt, who seems to be one of the best of women, carried me to the opera at St. Cloud,[1] where also we viewed the palace which the Queen is building; it is large, but there is much in the front that does not please me.—20 miles.

The 28th. Finding my mare sufficiently recovered for a journey, a point of importance to a traveller so weak in cavalry as myself, I left Paris, accompanying the count de la Rochefoucauld and my friend Lazowski, and commencing a journey that is to cross the whole kingdom to the Pyrenees. The road to Orleans is one of the greatest that leads from Paris, I expected, therefore, to have my former impression of the little traffic near that city removed; but on the contrary, it was confirmed; it is a desert compared with those around London. In ten miles we met not one stage or diligence; only two messageries, and very few chaises; not a tenth of what would have been met had we been leaving London at the same hour. Knowing how great, rich, and important a city Paris is, this circumstance perplexes me much. Should it afterwards be confirmed, conclusions in abundance are to be drawn.

For a few miles, the scene is everywhere scattered with

---

[1] This château, famous as the scene of Napoleon's Coup d'état of the 18 Brumaire, from which also emanated the ordonnances of Charles X., was destroyed by the Prussian fire in 1870.

the shafts of quarries, the stone drawn up by lanthorn wheels of a great diameter. The country diversified; and its greatest want to please the eye is a river; woods generally in view; the proportion of the French territory covered by this production for want of coals, must be prodigious, for it has been the same all the way from Calais. At Arpajon,[1] the maréchal duke de Mouchy[2] has a small house, which has nothing to recommend it.—20 miles.

The 29th. To Estamps[3] is partly through a flat country, the beginning of the famous Pays de Beauce. To Toury,[4] flat and disagreeable, only two or three gentlemen's seats in sight.—31 miles.

The 30th. One universal flat, uninclosed, uninteresting, and even tedious, though small towns and villages are every where in sight; the features that might compound a landscape are not brought together. This Pays de Beauce contains, by reputation, the cream of French husbandry; the soil excellent; but the management all fallow. Pass through part of the forest of Orleans belonging to the duke of that name: it is one of the largest in France.

From the steeple of the cathedral at Orleans, the prospect is very fine. The town large, and its suburbs, of single streets, extend near a league. The vast range of country, that spreads on every side, is an unbounded plain, through which the magnificent Loire bends his stately way, in sight for 14 leagues; the whole scattered with rich meadows, vineyard, gardens, and forests. The population must be very great; for, beside the city, which contains near 40,000 people, the number of smaller towns and villages strewed thickly over the plain is such as to render the whole scene animated. The cathedral, from which we had this noble prospect is a fine building, the

---

[1] (Seine et Oise.)
[2] Philippe Comte de Noailles, Duc de Mouchy, with his wife, guillotined during the Terror. He was son of Adrian Maurice, Maréchal de France and Duc de Noailles, and father of that public-spirited viscount who took the lead in renouncing feudal privileges on the assemblage of the States General.
[3] Étampes (Seine et Oise).
[4] Station on the Orleans railway (Loiret).

choir raised by Henry IV. The new church is a pleasing edifice; the bridge a noble structure of stone, and the first experiment of the flat arch made in France, where it is now so fashionable. It contains nine, and is 410 yards long, and 45 feet wide. To hear some Englishmen talk, one would suppose there was not a fine bridge in all France; not the first, nor the last error I hope that travelling will remove. There are many barges and boats at the quay, built upon the river in the Bourbonnois, &c. loaded with wood, brandy, wine, and other goods; on arriving at Nantes, the vessels are broken up and sold with the cargo. Great numbers built with spruce fir. A boat goes from hence to that city, when demanded by six passengers, each paying a louis-d'or:[1] they lie on shore every night, and reach Nantes in four days and a half. The principal street leading to the bridge is a fine one, all busy and alive, for trade is brisk here. Admire the fine acacias scattered about the town.—20 miles.

The 31st. On leaving it, enter soon the miserable province of Sologne, which the French writers call the *triste* Sologne.[2] Through all this country they have had severe spring frosts, for the leaves of the walnuts are black and cut off. I should not have expected this unequivocal mark of a bad climate after passing the Loire. To La Ferté Lowendahl,[3] a dead flat of hungry sandy gravel, with much heath. The poor people, who cultivate the soil here, are *métayers*,[4] that is, men who hire the land without ability to stock it; the proprietor is forced to provide cattle and seed, and he and his tenant divide the produce; a miserable system, that perpetuates poverty and excludes instruction. Meet a man employed on the roads who was

[1] Coin thus called in the reign of Louis XIII.; value in 1787 twenty-four francs.

[2] Plantations, irrigation, canalization and improved methods of agriculture are gradually transforming this region. La Sologne forms part of the two departments of Loiret and Loir and Cher.

[3] La Ferté-Saint-Aubin (Loiret).

[4] Métayage, Lat. Medietarius, is the system of farming on half profits, so successful in various parts of France. The owner of the land supplies the soil rent-free, the farmer gives the necessary labour, the fruits being equally shared. Complex as such an arrangement may appear at first sight, métayage must be counted as a factor of great importance in the agricultural prosperity of France.

prisoner at Falmouth four years; he does not seem to have any rancour against the English; nor yet was he very well pleased with his treatment. At La Ferté[1] is a handsome chateau of the marquis de Croix, with several canals, and a great command of water. To Nonant-le-Fuzelier,[2] a strange mixture of sand and water. Much inclosed, and the houses and cottages of wood filled between the studs with clay or bricks, and covered not with slate but tile, with some barns boarded like those in Suffolk—rows of pollards in some of the hedges; an excellent road of sand; the general features of a woodland country; all combined to give a strong resemblance to many parts of England; but the husbandry is so little like that of England, that the least attention to it destroyed every notion of similarity.—27 miles.

JUNE 1. The same wretched country continues to La Loge;[3] the fields are scenes of pitiable management, as the houses are of misery. Yet all this country highly improveable, if they knew what to do with it: the property, perhaps, of some of those glittering beings, who figured in the procession the other day at Versailles. Heaven grant me patience while I see a country thus neglected—and forgive me the oaths I swear at the absence and ignorance of the possessors.—Enter the generality[4] of Bourges, and soon after a forest of oak belonging to the count d'Artois; the trees are dying at top, before they attain any size. There the miserable Sologne ends; the first view of Verson[5] and its vicinity is fine. A noble vale spreads at your feet, through which the river Cher[6] leads, seen in several places to the distance of some leagues, a bright sun burnished the water, like a string of lakes amidst the shade of a vast woodland. See Bourges to the left.—18 miles.

The 2d. Pass the rivers Cher and Lave; the bridges well built; the stream fine, and with the wood, buildings, boats, and adjoining hills, form an animated scene. Several

[1] The Château de Lowendal (Loiret).
[2] Nouant-le-Fuzelier (Loir and Cher). This little town is an active centre of bee-farming.
[3] (Loir and Cher.)
[4] Généralité, ancient fiscal division.
[5] Vierzon (Cher).
[6] (Cher.)

new houses, and buildings of good stone in Verson; the place appears thriving, and doubtless owes much to the navigation. We are now in Berri, a province governed by a provincial assembly, consequently the roads good, and made without *corvées*. Vatan [1] is a little town that subsists chiefly by spinning. We drank there excellent Sancere [2] wine, of a deep colour, rich flavour, and good body, 20*f*.[3] the bottle; but in the country 10. An extensive prospect before we arrived at Chateauroux [4] where we viewed the manufactures.—40 miles.

The 3d. Within about three of Argenton [5] come upon a fine scene, beautiful, yet with bold features; a narrow vale bounded on every side with hills covered with wood, all of which are immediately under the eye, without a level acre, except the bottom of the vale, through which a river flows, by an old castle picturesquely situated to the right; and to the left, a tower rising out of a wood.

At Argenton, walk up a rock that hangs almost over the town. It is a delicious scene. A natural ledge of perpendicular rock pushes forward abruptly over the vale, which is half a mile broad, and two or three long: at one end closed by hills, and at the other filled by the town with vineyards rising above it; the surrounding scene that hems in the vale is high enough for relief; vineyards, rocks or hills covered with wood. The vale cut into inclosures of a lovely verdure, and a fine river winds through it, with an outline that leaves nothing to wish. The venerable fragments of a castle's ruins, near the point of view, are well adapted to awaken reflections on the triumph of the arts of peace over the barbarous ravages of the feudal ages, when every class of society was involved in commotion, and the lower ranks were worse slaves than at present.

The general face of the country, from Verson to Argenton, is an uninteresting flat with many heaths of ling.

---

[1] Vatan (Indre).   [2] Sancerre (Cher), famous for its wines.

[3] Sol. sou.

[4] Châteauroux (Indre). From time immemorial this town has been celebrated for its cloth manufactures.

[5] (Indre), within easy reach of the valley of La Creuse, immortalized by George Sand.

No appearance of population, and even towns are thin. The husbandry poor and the people miserable. By the circumstances to which I could give attention I conceive them to be honest and industrious; they seem clean; are civil, and have good countenances. They appear to me as if they would improve their country, if they formed the part of a system, the principles of which tended to national prosperity.—18 miles.

The 4th. Pass an inclosed country, which would have a better appearance if the oaks had not lost their foliage by insects, whose webs hang over the buds. They are but now coming into leaf again. Cross a stream which separates Berri from La Marche;[1] chesnuts appear at the same time; they are spread over all the fields, and yield the food of the poor. A variety of hill and dale, with fine woods, but little signs of population. Lizards for the first time also. There seems a connection relative to climate between the chesnuts and these harmless animals. They are very numerous, and some of them near a foot long. Sleep at La Ville au Brun.[2]—24 miles.

The 5th. The country improves in beauty greatly; pass a vale, where a causeway stops the water of a small rivulet and swells it into a lake, that forms one feature of a delicious scene. The indented outlines and the swells margined with wood are beautiful; the hills on every side in unison; one now covered with ling the prophetic eye of taste may imagine lawn. Nothing is wanted to render the scene a garden, but to clear away rubbish.

The general face of the country, for 16 miles, by far the most beautiful I have seen in France; it is thickly inclosed, and full of wood; the umbrageous foliage of the chesnuts gives the same beautiful verdure to the hills, as watered meadows (seen for the first time to day) to the vales. Distant mountainous ridges form the back ground, and make the whole interesting. The declivity of country, as we go down to Bassies,[3] offers a beautiful view; and

---

[1] The tract of uncultivated land serving as a frontier between two states or seignorial domains. Thus we find la Marche between le Berri, and le Limousin, les Marches in Savoy, &c. From the first-named was formed the department of la Corrèze.

[2] (Indre.)   [3] Bassines (Hte. Vienne).

the approach to the town, presents a landscape fancifully grouped of rock, and wood, and water. To Limoge, pass another artificial lake between cultivated hills; beyond are wilder heights, but mixed with pleasant vales; still another lake more beautiful than the former, with a fine accompanyment of wood; across a mountain of chesnut copse, which commands a scene of a character different from any I have viewed either in France or England, a great range of hill and dale all covered with forest, and bounded by distant mountains. Not a vestige of any human residence; no village: no house or hut, no smoke to raise the idea of a peopled country; an American scene; wild enough for the tomohawk of the savage. Stop at an execrable auberge, called Maison Rouge, where we intended to sleep; but, on examination, found every appearance so forbidding, and so beggarly an account of a larder, that we passed on to Limoge. The roads through all this country, are truly noble, far beyond any thing I have seen in France or elsewhere.—44 miles.

The 6th. View Limoge, and examine its manufactures. It was certainly a Roman station, and some traces of its antiquity are still remaining. It is ill built, with narrow and crooked streets, the houses high and disagreeable. They are raised of granite, or wood with lath and plaister, which saves lime, an expensive article here, being brought from a distance of twelve leagues; the roofs are of pantiles, with projecting eaves, and almost flat; a sure proof we have quitted the region of heavy snows. The best of their public works is noble fountain, the water conducted three quarters of a league by an arched aqueduct brought under the bed of a rock 60 feet deep to the highest spot in the town, where it falls into a bason 15 feet diameter, cut out of one piece of granite; thence the water is let into reservoirs, closed by sluices, which are opened for watering the streets, or in cases of fires.

The cathedral is ancient, and the roof of stone; there are some arabesque ornaments cut in stone, as light, airy, and elegant as any modern house can boast, whose decorations are in the same taste.

The present bishop has erected a large and handsome palace, and his garden is the finest object to be seen at

Limoge, for it commands a landscape hardly to be equalled for beauty: it would be idle to give any other description than just enough to induce travellers to view it. A river winds through a vale, surrounded by hills that present the gayest and most animated assemblage of villas, farms, vines, hanging meadows, and chesnuts blended so fortunately as to compose a scene truly smiling. This bishop is a friend of the count de la Rochefoucauld's family; he invited us to dine, and gave us a very handsome entertainment. Lord Macartney,[1] when a prisoner in France, after the Grenades were taken, spent some time with him; there was an instance of French politeness shewn to his lordship, that marks the urbanity of this people. The order came from court to sing Te Deum on the very day that Lord Macartney was to arrive. Conceiving that the public demonstrations of joy for a victory that brought his noble guest a prisoner, might be personally unpleasant to him, the bishop proposed to the intendant to postpone the ceremony for a few days, in order that he might not meet it so abruptly; this was instantly acceded to, and conducted in such a manner afterwards as to mark as much attention to Lord Macartney's feelings as to their own. The bishop told me, that Lord Macartney spoke better French than he could have conceived possible for a foreigner, had he not heard him; better than many well educated Frenchmen.

The post of intendant here was rendered celebrated by being filled by that friend of mankind, Turgot, whose well earned reputation in this province placed him at the head of the French finances, as may be very agreeably learned, in that production of equal truth and elegance, his life by the marquis of Condorcet. The character which Turgot left here is considerable. The noble roads we have passed, so much exceeding any other I have seen in France, were amongst his *good* works; an epithet due to them because not made by *corvées*. There is here a society of

[1] Lord Macartney was appointed envoy extraordinary to the Empress of Russia in 1764, and later governor of Tobago. On the capture of that island he was sent to France. In 1780 he became governor of Madras, and afterwards Governor-General of Bengal. St. Lucia, St. Vincent, Grenada, and Tobago (the Windward Islands) now belong to England.

agriculture, which owes it origin to the same distinguished patriot: but in that most unlucky path of French exertion he was able to do nothing: evils too radically fixed were in the way of the attempt. This society does like other societies,—they meet, converse, offer premiums, and publish nonsense. This is not of much consequence, for the people, instead of reading their memoirs, are not able to read at all. They can however *see;* and if a farm was established in that good cultivation which they ought to copy, something would be presented from which they *might* learn. I asked particularly if the members of this society had land in their own hands, from which it might be judged if they knew anything of the matter themselves: I was assured that they had; but the conversation presently explained it: they had *métayers* around their country-seats, and this was considered as farming their own lands, so that they assume something of a merit from the identical circumstance, which is the curse and ruin of the whole country. In the agricultural conversations we have had on the journey from Orleans, I have not found one person who seemed sensible of the mischief of this system.

The 7th. No chesnuts for a league before we reach Piere Bussiere,[1] they say because the basis of the country is a hard granite; and they assert also at Limoge, that in this granite there grow neither vines, wheat, nor chesnuts, but that on the softer granites these plants thrive well: it is true, that chesnuts and this granite appeared together when we entered Limosin. The road has been incomparably fine, and much more like the well kept alleys of a garden than a common high way. See for the first time old towers, that appear in this country.—33 miles.

The 8th. Pass an extraordinary spectacle for English eyes, of many houses too good to be called cottages, without any glass windows. Some miles to the right is Pompadour,[2] where the King has a stud; there are all kinds of horses, but chiefly Arabian, Turkish and English. Three years ago four Arabians were imported, which had

[1] Pierrebussière (Hte. Vienne).
[2] (Dordogne.) This village was created a marquisate by Louis XV. for his mistress. Château and haras remain.

been procured at the expence of 72,000 livres (3149l.)[1] the price of covering a mare is only three livres to the groom; the owners are permitted to sell their colts as they please, but if these came up to the standard height, the King's officers have the preference, provided they give the price offered by others. These horses are not saddled till six years old. They pasture all day, but at night are confined on account of wolves, which are so common as to be a great plague to the people. A horse of six years old, a little more than four feet six inches high, is sold for 70l.; and 15l. has been offered for a colt of one year old. Pass Uzarch;[2] dine at Donzenac;[3] between which place and Brive meet the first maize, or Indian corn.

The beauty of the country, through the 34 miles from St. George[4] to Brive,[5] is so various, and in every respect so striking and interesting, that I shall attempt no particular description, but observe in general, that I am much in doubt, whether there be anything comparable to it either in England or Ireland. It is not that a fine view breaks now and then upon the eye to compensate the traveller for the dulness of a much longer district; but a quick succession of landscapes, many of which would be rendered famous in England, by the resort of travellers to view them. The country is all hill or valley; the hills are very high, and would be called with us mountains, if waste and covered with heated; but being cultivated to the very tops, their magnitude is lessened to the eye. Their forms are various: they swell in beautiful semi-globes; they project in abrupt masses, which inclose deep glens: they expand into amphitheatres of cultivation that rise in gradation to the eye: in some places tossed into a thousand inequalities of surface; in others the eye reposes on scenes of the softest verdure. Add to this, the rich robe with which nature's bounteous hand has dressed the slopes, with hanging woods of chesnut. And whether the vales open their verdant bosoms, and admit the sun to illumine the rivers in their comparative repose; or whether they be closed in deep glens, that afford a passage with difficulty

---

[1] The livre differed in value from twenty to twenty-five sous.
[2] Uzerche (Corrèze). [3] (Corrèze.)
[4] St. Germain-les-Belles (Hte. Vienne). [5] (*Ibid.*)

to the water rolling over their rocky beds, and dazzling the eye with the lustre of cascades; in every case the features are interesting and characteristic of the scenery. Some views of singular beauty rivetted us to the spot; that of the town of Uzarch, covering a conical hill, rising in the hollow of an amphitheatre of wood, and surrounded at its feet by a noble river, is unique. Derry in Ireland has something of its form, but wants some of its richest features. The water-scenes from the town itself, and immediately after passing it, are delicious. The immense view from the descent to Donzenac is equally magnificent. To all this is added the finest road in the world, every where formed in the most perfect manner, and kept in the highest preservation, like the well ordered alley of a garden, without dust, sand, stones, or inequality, firm and level, of pounded granite, and traced with such a perpetual command of prospect, that had the engineer no other object in view, he could not have executed it with a more finished taste.

The view of Brive, from the hill is so fine, that it gives the expectation of a beautiful little town, and the gaiety of the environs encourages the idea; but on entering, such a contrast is found as disgusts completely. Close, ill built, crooked, dirty, stinking streets, exclude the sun, and almost the air from every habitation, except a few tolerable ones on the promenade.—34 miles.

The 9th. Enter a different country with the new province of Quercy,[1] which is a part of Guienne; not near so beautiful as Limosin, but, to make amends, it is far better cultivated. Thanks to maize, which does wonders! Pass Noailles, on the summit of a high hill, the chateau[2] of the Marshal Duke of that name.—Enter a calcareous country, and lose chesnuts at the same time.

In going down to Souillac,[3] there is a prospect that must universally please: it is a bird's eye view of a delicious little valley, sunk deep amongst some very bold hills that

---

[1] Formerly le pays de Cadurques, now the department of the Lot.

[2] The château still remains. The Duc de Noailles here mentioned was brother of the unfortunate Duc de Mouchy. He was created Marshall of France by Louis XV. without having rendered any services deserving the honour. Died 1793. (H. Martin.)

[3] Souillac (Lot).

inclose it; a margin of wild mountain contrasts the extreme beauty of the level surface below, a scene of cultivation scattered with fine walnut trees; nothing can apparently exceed the exuberant fertility of this spot.

Souillac is a little town in a thriving state, having some rich merchants. They receive staves from the mountains of Auvergne by their river Dordonne, which is navigable eight months in the year; these they export to Bordeaux and Libourn; also wine, corn, and cattle, and import salt in great quantities. It is not in the power of an English imagination to figure the animals that waited upon us here, at the Chapeau Rouge. Some things that called themselves by the courtesy of Souillac women, but in reality walking dung-hills.—But a neatly dressed clean waiting girl at an inn, will be looked for in vain in France. —34 miles.

The 10th. Cross the Dordonne by a ferry; the boat well contrived for driving in at one end, and out at the other, without the abominable operation, common in England, of beating horses till they leap into them; the price is as great a contrast as the excellence; we paid for an English whisky,[1] a French cabriolet, one saddle-horse and six persons, no more than 50s. (2s. 1d.) I have paid half-a-crown a wheel in England for execrable ferries, passed over at the hazard of the horses limbs.—This river runs in a very deep valley between two ridges of high hills: extensive views, all scattered with villages and single houses; an appearance of great population. Chesnuts on a calcareous soil, contrary to the Limosin maxim.

Pass Payrac,[2] and meet many beggars, which we had not done before. All the country, girls and women, are without shoes or stockings; and the ploughmen at their work have neither sabots nor feet to their stockings. This is a poverty, that strikes at the root of national prosperity; a large consumption among the poor being of more consequence than among the rich: the wealth of a nation lies in its circulation and consumption; and the case of poor people abstaining from the use of manufactures of leather and wool ought to be considered as an evil of the first magnitude. It reminded me of the misery of Ireland.

[1] A light carriage, also called *tim-whiskey*.   [2] (Lot).

Pass Pont-de-Rodez,[1] and come to high land, whence we enjoyed an immense and singular prospect of ridges, hills, vales, and gentle slopes, rising one beyond another in every direction, with few masses of wood, but many scattered trees. At least forty miles are tolerably distinct to the eye, and without a level acre; the sun, on the point of being set, illumined part of it, and displayed a vast number of villages and scattered farms. The mountains of Auvergne, at the distance of 100 miles, added to the view. Pass by several cottages, exceedingly well built, of stone and slate or tiles, yet without any glass to the windows; can a country be likely to thrive where the great object is to spare manufactures? Women picking weeds into their aprons for their cows, another sign of poverty I observed, during the whole way from Calais.—30 miles.

The 11th. See for the first time the Pyrenees, at the distance of 150 miles.—To me, who had never seen an object farther than 60 or 70, I mean the Wicklow mountains, as I was going out of Holyhead, this was interesting. Wherever the eye wandered in search of new objects it was sure to rest there. Their magnitude, their snowy height, the line of separation between two great kingdoms, and the end of our travels altogether account for this effect. Towards Cahors[2] the country changes, and has something of a savage aspect; yet houses are seen every where, and one-third of it under vines.

That town is bad; the streets neither wide nor strait, but the new road is an improvement. The chief object of its trade and resource are vines and brandies. The true Vin de Cahors, which has a great reputation, is the produce of a range of vineyards, very rocky, on a ridge of hills full to the south, and is called Vin de Grave, because growing on a gravelly soil. In plentiful years, the price of good wine here does not exceed that of the cask; last year it was sold at 10s. 6d. a barique, or 8d. a dozen. We drank it at the Trois Rois from three to ten years old, the latter at 30*s*. (1s. 3d.) the bottle; both excellent, full bodied, great spirit, without being fiery, and to my palate much better than our ports. I liked it so well, that I established

---

[1] Pont de Rode (Lot).   [2] (Lot).

a correspondence with Mons. Andoury, the innkeeper.[1] The heat of this country is equal to the production of strong wine. This was the most burning day we had experienced.

On leaving Cahors, the mountain of rock rises so immediately, that it seems as if it would tumble into the town. The leaves of walnuts are now black with frosts that happened within a fortnight. On enquiry, I found they are subject to these frosts all through the spring months; and though rye is sometimes killed by them, the mildew in wheat is hardly known;—a fact sufficiently destructive of the theory of frosts being the cause of that distemper. It is very rare that any snow falls here. Sleep at Ventillac.[2] —22 miles.

The 12th. The shape and colour of the peasants houses here add a beauty to the country; they are square, white, and with rather flat roofs, but few windows. The peasants are for the most part land-proprietors. Immense view of the Pyrenees before us, of an extent and height truly sublime: near Perges,[3] the view of a rich vale, that seems to reach uninterruptedly to those mountains is a glorious scenery; one vast sheet of cultivation: every where chequered with these well built white houses;—the eye losing itself in the vapour, which ends only with that stupendous ridge, whose snow-capped heads are broken into the boldest outline. The road to Caussade[4] leads through a very fine avenue of six rows of trees, two of them mulberries, which are the first we have seen. Thus we have travelled almost to the Pyrenees before we met with an article of culture which some want to introduce into England. The vale here is all on a dead level; the roads finely made, and mended with gravel. Montauban[5] is old, but not ill built. There are many good houses, without forming handsome streets. It is said to be very populous, and the eye confirms the intelligence. The cathedral is modern, and pretty well built, but too heavy. The public college, the seminary,

---

[1] I since had a barrique of him; but whether he sent bad wine, which I am not willing to believe, or that it came through bad hands, I know not. It is, however, so bad, as to be item for folly.—*Author's note.*

[2] Ventaillac (Lot).   [3] (Tarn et Garonne).
[4] (Tarn et Garonne.)   [5] Montauban (*ibid.*).

the bishop's palace, and the house of the first president of the court of aids are good buildings: the last large, with a most shewy entrance. The promenade is finely situated; built on the highest part of the rampart, and commanding that noble vale, or rather plain, one of the richest in Europe, which extends on one side to the sea, and in front to the Pyrenees; whose towering masses, heaped one upon another, in a stupendous manner, and covered with snow, offer a variety of lights and shades from indented forms, and the immensity of their projections. This prospect, which contains a semi-circle of an hundred miles diameter, has an oceanic vastness, in which the eye loses itself; an almost boundless scene of cultivation; an animated, but confused mass of infinitely varied parts—melting gradually into the distant obscure, from which emerges the amazing frame of the Pyrenees, rearing their silvered heads far above the clouds. At Montauban, I met Capt. Plampin, of the royal navy; he was with Major Crew, who has a house and family here, to which he politely carried us; it is sweetly situated on the skirts of the town, commanding a fine view; they were so obliging as to resolve my enquiries upon some points, of which a residence made them complete judges. Living is reckoned cheap here; a family was named to us, whose income was supposed to be about 1500 louis a-year, and who lived as handsomely as in England on 5000l. The comparative dearness and cheapness of different countries, is a subject of considerable importance, but difficult to analize. As I conceive the English to have made far greater advances in the useful arts, and in manufactures, than the French have done, England ought to be the cheaper country. What we meet with in France, is a cheap *mode of living*, which is quite another consideration.—30 miles.

The 13th. Pass Grisolles,[1] where are well built cottages without glass, and some with no other light than the door. Dine at Pompinion,[2] at the Grand Soleil, an uncommonly good inn, where Capt. Plampin, who accompanied us thus far, took his leave. Here we had a violent storm of thunder and lightning, with rain much heavier I thought than I had known in England; but, when we set out for Tou-

[1] (Tarn et Garonne.)   [2] Pompignon (Tarn et Garonne).

louze, I was immediately convinced that such a violent shower had never fallen in that kingdom; for the destruction it had poured on the noble scene of cultivation, which but a moment before was smiling with exuberance, was terrible to behold. All now one scene of distress: the finest crops of wheat beaten so flat to the ground, that I question whether they can ever rise again; other fields so inundated, that we were actually in doubt whether we were looking on what was lately land or always water. The ditches had been filled rapidly with mud, had overflowed the road, and swept dirt and gravel over the crops.

Cross one of the finest plains of wheat that is any where to be seen; the storm, therefore, was fortunately partial. Pass St. Jorry;[1] a noble road, but not better than in Limosin. It is a desert to the very gates; meet not more persons than if it were 100 miles from any town. —31 miles.

The 14th. View the city,[2] which is very ancient and very large, but not peopled in proportion to its size: the buildings are a mixture of brick and wood, and have consequently a melancholy appearance. This place has always prided itself on its taste for literature and the fine arts. It has had a university since 1215; and it pretends that its famous academy of Jeux Floraux[3] is as old as 1323. It has also a royal academy of sciences, another of painting, sculpture, and architecture. The church of the Cordelliers[4] has vaults, into which we descended, that have the property of preserving dead bodies from corruption; we saw many that they assert to be 500 years old. If I had a vault well lighted, that would preserve the countenance and physiognomy as well as the flesh and bones, I should like to have it peopled with all my ancestors; and this desire would, I suppose, be proportioned to their merit and celebrity; but to one like this, that preserves cada-

---

[1] St. Jory (Hte. Garonne).   [2] Toulouse.
[3] The *jeux floraux* or poetic tourneys celebrated the visit of Charles Le Bel to Toulouse in 1323 or 1324. A golden violet was given to the author of the best poem, also the title of *docteur du gai saber*. But the days of Provençal poetry were over, and the king did not even attend the crowning of the successful candidate.
[4] Now desecrated, and used for the storage of hay.

verous deformity, and gives perpetuity to death, the voracity of a common grave is preferable. But Toulouze is not without objects more interesting than churches and academies; these are the new quay, the corn mills, and the canal de Brien. The quay is of a great length, and in all respects a noble work: the houses intended to be built will be regular like those already erected, in a stile aukward and inelegant. The canal de Brien,[1] so called from the archbishop of Toulouze,[2] afterwards prime minister and cardinal, was planned and executed in order to join the Garonne at Toulouze with the canal of Languedoc, which is united at two miles from the town with the same river. The necessity of such a junction arises from the navigation of the river in the town being absolutely impeded by the wear which is made across it in favour of the corn mills. It passes arched under the quay to the river, and one sluice levels the water with that of Languedoc canal. It is broad enough for several barges to pass abreast. These undertakings have been well planned, and their execution is truly magnificent: there is however more magnificence than trade; for while the Languedoc canal is alive with commerce, that of Brien is a desert.

Among other things we viewed at Toulouze, was the house[3] of Mons. du Barrè,[4] brother of the husband of the celebrated countess. By some transactions, favourable to anecdote, which enabled him to draw her from obscurity, and afterwards to marry her to his brother, he contrived to make a pretty considerable fortune. On the first floor

---

[1] The canal de Brienne, joining the canals de Languedoc and du Midi.

[2] The anti-Protestant Loménie de Brienne, in power at the time this was written, dismissed the following year.

[3] The Hotel Dubarry, now No. 13, Place St. Raymond, is occupied by nuns of the Benedictine Order. What became of the portrait here mentioned is not known, no mention of it occurring in the list of objects confiscated in 1794.

[4] Madame du Barry, the favourite of Louis XV. She had fled from Paris on the outbreak of the Revolution, but ventured to the Bernardine Convent at Couilly (Seine and Marne), now destroyed, in order to get her diamonds there hidden. She was seized and guillotined during the Terror. Helen Maria Williams gives a fearful picture of her execution. See Memoir De Goncourts.

is one principal and complete apartment, containing seven or eight rooms, fitted up and furnished with such profusion of expence, that if a fond lover, at the head of a kingdom's finances, were decorating for his mistress, he could hardly give in large any thing that is not here to be seen on a moderate scale. To those who are fond of gilding here is enough to satiate; so much that to an English eye it has too gaudy an appearance. But the glasses are large and numerous. The drawing-room very elegant (gilding always excepted).—Here I remarked a contrivance which has a pleasing effect; that of a looking-glass before the chimnies, instead of those various screens used in England: it slides backwards and forwards into the wall of the room. There is a portrait of Madame du Barrè, which is said to be very like; if it really is, one would pardon a King some follies committed at the shrine of so much beauty—As to the garden, it is beneath all contempt, except as an object to make a man stare at the efforts to which folly can arrive: in the space of an acre, there are hills of genuine earth, mountains of pasteboard, rocks of canvass: abbés, cows, sheep, and shepherdesses in lead; monkeys and peasants, asses and altars, in stone. Fine ladies and blacksmiths, parrots and lovers, in wood. Windmills and cottages, shops and villages, nothing excluded except nature.

The 15th. Meet Highlanders, who put me in mind of those of Scotland; saw them first at Montauban; they have round flat caps, and loose breeches: "Pipers, blue bonnets, and oat-meal, are found," says Sir James Stuart, "in Catalonia, Auvergne and Swabia, as well as in Lochabar." Many of the women here are without stockings. Meet them coming from the market, with their shoes in their baskets. The Pyrenees, at sixty miles distance, appear now so distinct, that one would guess it not more than fifteen; the lights and shades of the snow are seen clearly.—30 miles.

The 16th. A ridge of hills on the other side of the Garonne, which began at Toulouze, became more and more regular yesterday; and is undoubtedly the most distant ramification of the Pyrenees, reaching into this vast vale quite to Toulouze, but no farther. Approach the mountains; the lower ones are all cultivated, but the higher seem covered with wood: the road now is bad all the way. Meet many waggons, each loaded with two casks of wine, quite backward in the carriage and as the hind wheels are much higher than the lower ones, it shews that these mountaineers have more sense than John Bull. The wheels of these waggons are all shod with wood instead of iron. Here, for the first time, see rows of maples, with vines, trained in festoons, from tree to tree; they are conducted by a rope of bramble, vine cutting, or willow. They give many grapes, but bad wine. Pass St. Martino,[1] and then a large village of well built houses, without a single glass window.—30 miles.

The 17th. St. Gaudens[2] is an improving town, with many new houses, something more than comfortable. An uncommon view of St. Bertrand;[3] you break at once upon a vale sunk deep enough beneath the point of view to command every hedge and tree, with that town clustered round its large cathedral, on a rising ground; if it had been built purposely to add a feature to a singular prospect, it could not have been better placed. The mountains rise proudly around, and give their rough frame to this exquisite little picture.

Cross the Garonne, by a new bridge of one fine arch, built of hard blue limestone. Medlars, plumbs, cherries, maples in every hedge, with vines trained.—Stop at Lauresse;[4] after which the mountains almost close, and leave only a narrow vale, the Garonne and the road occupying some portion of it. Immense quantities of poultry in all this country; most of it the people salt and keep in grease. We tasted a soup made of the leg of a goose thus kept, and it was not nearly so bad as I expected.

Every crop here is backward, and betrays a want of sun; no wonder, for we have been long travelling on the banks of a rapid river, and must now be very high, though still apparently in vales. The mountains, in passing on, grow more interesting. Their beauty, to northern eyes, is very singular; the black and dreary prospects which our

---

[1] St. Martory (Hte. Garonne).
[2] (Hte. Garonne.)
[3] St. Bertrand de Comminges (Hte. Garonne)
[4] Loures (Hte. Pyrenees).

mountains offer are known to every one; but here the climate cloaths them with verdure, and the highest summits in sight are covered with wood; there is snow on still higher ridges.

Quit the Garonne some leagues before Sirpe,[1] where the river Neste[2] falls into it. The road to Bagnere is along this river, in a very narrow valley, at one end of which is built the town of Luchon,[3] the termination of our journey; which to me has been one of the most agreeable I ever undertook; the good humour and good sense of my companions are well calculated for travelling; one renders a journey pleasing, and the other instructive.—Having now crossed the kingdom, and been in many French inns, I shall in general observe, that they are on an average better in two respects, and worse in all the rest, than those in England. We have lived better in point of eating and drinking beyond a question, than we should have done in going from London to the Highlands of Scotland, at double the expence. But if in England the best of every thing is ordered, without any attention to the expence, we should for double the money have lived better than we have done in France; the common cookery of the French gives great advantage. It is true, they roast every thing to a chip, if they are not cautioned: but they give such a number and variety of dishes, that if you do not like some, there are others to please your palate. The desert at a French inn has no rival at an English one; nor are the liqueurs to be despised.—We sometimes have met with bad wine, but upon the whole, far better than such port as English inns give. Beds are better in France; in England they are good only at good inns; and we have none of that torment, which is so perplexing in England, to have the sheets aired; for we never trouble our heads about them, doubtless on account of the climate. After these two points, all is a blank. You have no parlour to eat in; only a room with two, three, or four beds. Apartments badly fitted up; the walls white-washed; or paper of dif-

[1] Cierp (Hte. Garonne).
[2] This word Neste, meaning a torrent stream, is frequently found in the Pyrenees.
[3] Bagnères de Luchon (Hte. Garonne).

ferent sorts in the same room ; or tapestry so old, as to be a fit nidus for moths and spiders; and the furniture such, that an English innkeeper would light his fire with it. For a table, you have every where a board laid on cross bars, which are so conveniently contrived, as to leave room for your legs only at the end.—Oak chairs with rush bottoms, and the back universally a direct perpendicular, that defies all idea of rest after fatigue. Doors give music as well as entrance ; the wind whistles through their chinks; and hinges grate discord. Windows admit rain as well as light ; when shut they are not so easy to open ; and when open not easy to shut. Mops, brooms, and scrubbing-brushes are not in the catalogue of the necessaries of a French inn. Bells there are none ; the *fille* must always be bawled for; and when she appears, is neither neat well dressed, nor handsome. The kitchen is black with smoke ; the master commonly the cook, and the less you see of the cooking, the more likely you are to have a stomach to your dinner ; but this is not peculiar to France. Copper utensils always in great plenty, but not always well tinned. The mistress rarely classes civility or attention to her guests among the requisites of her trade.—30 miles.

The 28th. Having being now ten days fixed in our lodgings, which the Count de la Rochefoucauld's friends had provided for us ; it is time to minute a few particulars of our life here. Mons. Lazowski and myself have two good rooms on a ground floor, with beds in them, and a servant's room, for 4 liv. (3s. 6d.) a-day. We are so unaccustomed in England to live in our bed-chambers, that it is at first aukward in France to find that people live no where else: At all the inns I have been in, it has been always in bed-rooms ; and here I find, that every body, let his rank be what it may, lives in his bed-chamber. This is novel; our English custom is far more convenient, as well as more pleasing. But this habit I class with the œconomy of the French, The day after we came, I was introduced to the La Rochefoucauld party, with whom we have lived; it consists of the duke and dutchess de la Rochefoucauld, daughter of the duke de Chabot ; her brother, the prince de Laon and his princess, the daughter of the duke de Montmorenci ; the count de Chabot, another brother of the dutchess de la Rochefoucauld; the marquis D'Aubourval, who, with my two fellow-travellers and myself, made a party of nine at dinner and supper. A traiteur serves our table at 4 liv. a head for the two meals, two courses and a good desert for dinner; for supper one, and a desert; the whole very well served, with every thing in season: the wine separate, at 6*f*. (3d.) a bottle. With difficulty the Count's groom found a stable. Hay is little short of 5l. English per ton; oats much the same price as in England, but not so good: straw dear, and so scarce, that very often there is no litter at all.

The States of Languedoc are building a large and handsome bathing house, to contain various separate cells, with baths, and a large common room, with two arcades to walk in, free from sun and rain. The present baths are horrible holes; the patients lie up to their chins in hot sulphureous water, which, with the beastly dens they are placed in, one would think sufficient to cause as many distempers as they cure. They are resorted to for cutaneous eruptions. The life led here has very little variety. Those who bathe or drink the waters, do it at half after five or six in the morning; but my friend and myself are early in the mountains, which are here stupendous; we wander among them to admire the wild and beautiful scenes which are to be met with in almost every direction. The whole region of the Pyrenees is of a nature and aspect so totally different from every thing that I had been accustomed to, that these excursions were productive of much amusement. Cultivation is here carried to a considerable perfection in several articles, especially in the irrigation of meadows: we seek out the most intelligent peasants, and have many and long conversations with those who understand French, which however is not the case with all, for the language of the country is a mixture of Catalan, Provencal, and French.— This, with examining the minerals (an article for which the duke de la Rochefoucauld likes to accompany us, as he possesses a considerable knowledge in that branch of natural history), and with noting the plants with which we are acquainted, serves well to keep our time employed sufficiently to our taste. The ramble of the morning finished, we return in time to dress for dinner, at half after twelve or one: then adjourn to the drawing-room of madam de la Rochefoucauld, or the countess of Grandval alternately, the only ladies who have apartments large enough to contain the whole company. None are excluded; as the first thing done, by every person who arrives, is to pay a morning visit to each party already in the place; the visit is returned, and then every body is of course acquainted at these assemblies, which last till the evening is cool enough for walking. There is nothing in them but cards, tricktrack, chess, and sometimes music; but the great feature is cards: I need not add, that I absented myself often from these parties, which are ever mortally insipid to me in England, and not less so in France. In the evening, the company splits into different parties, for their promenade, which lasts till half an hour after eight; supper is served at nine: there is, after it, an hour's conversation in the chamber of one of our ladies; and this is the best part of the day,—for the chat is free, lively, and unaffected; and uninterrupted, unless on a post-day, when the duke has such packets of papers and pamphlets, that they turn us all into politicians. All the world are in bed by eleven. In this arrangement of the day, no circumstance is so objectionable as that of dining at noon, the consequence of eating no breakfast; for as the ceremony of dressing is kept up, you must be at home from any morning's excursion by twelve o'clock. This single circumstance, if adhered to, would be sufficient to destroy any pursuits, except the most frivolous. Dividing the day exactly in halves, destroys it for any expedition, enquiry, or business that demands seven or eight hours attention, uninterrupted by any calls to the table or the toilette: calls which, after fatigue or exertion, are obeyed with refreshment and with pleasure. We dress for dinner in England with propriety, as the rest of the day is dedicated to ease, to converse, and relaxation; but by doing it at noon, too much time is lost. What is a man good for after his silk breeches and stockings are on, his hat under his arm, and his head *bien poudrè?*—Can he botanize in a watered meadow?—Can he clamber the rocks to mineralize?—Can he farm with the peasant and the ploughman?—He is in order for the conversation of the ladies, which to be sure is in every country, but particularly in France, where the women are highly cultivated, an excellent employment; but it is an employment that never relishes better than after a day spent in active toil or animated pursuit; in something that has enlarged the sphere of our conceptions, or added to the stores of our knowledge.—I am induced to make this observation, because the noon dinners are customary all over France, except by persons of considerable fashion at Paris. They cannot be treated with too much ridicule or severity, for they are absolutely hostile to every view of science, to every spirited exertion, and to every useful pursuit in life.

Living in this way, however, with several persons of the first fashion in the kingdom, is an object to a foreigner solicitous to remark the manners and character of the nation. I have every reason to be pleased with the experiment, as it affords me a constant opportunity to enjoy the advantages of an unaffected and polished society, in which an invariable sweetness of disposition, mildness of character, and what in English we emphatically call *good temper*, eminently prevails:—seeming to arise—at least I conjecture it, from a thousand little nameless and peculiar circumstances; not resulting entirely from the personal character of the individuals, but apparently holding of the national one.—Beside the persons I have named, there are among others at our assemblies, the marquis and marchioness de Hautfort; the duke and dutchess de Ville (this dutchess is among the good order of beings); the chevalier de Peyrac; Mons. l'Abbé Bastard; baron de Serres; viscountess Duhamel; the bishops of Croire[1] and Montauban; Mons. de la Marche; the baron de Montagu, a chess player; the chevalier de Cheyron; and Mons. de Bellecomb, who commanded in Pondicherry, and was taken by the English. There are also about half a dozen young officers, and three or four abbes.

If I may hazard a remark on the conversation of French assemblies, from what I have known here, I should praise them for equanimity but condemn them for insipidity. All vigour of thought seems so excluded from expression, that characters of ability and of inanity meet nearly on a par: tame and elegant, uninteresting and polite, the

---

[1] Cahors or Aire (Landes) is evidently meant.

mingled mass of communicated aside has powers neither to offend nor instruct; where there is much polish of character there is little argument; and if you neither argue nor discuss, what is conversation?—Good temper, and habitual ease, are the first ingredients in private society; but wit, knowledge, or originality, must break their even surface into some inequality of feeling, or conversation is like a journey on an endless flat.

Of the rural beauties we have to contemplate, the valley of Larbousse,[1] in a nook of which the town of Luchon is situated, is the principal, with its surrounding accompanyment of mountain. The range that bounds it to the north, is bare of wood but covered with cultivation; and a large village, about three parts of its height, is perched on a steep, that almost makes the unaccustomed eye tremble with apprehension, that the village, church, and people will come tumbling into the valley. Villages thus perched, like eagles nests on rocks, are a general circumstance in the Pyrenees, which appear to be wonderfully peopled. The mountain, that forms the western wall of the valley, is of a prodigious magnitude. Watered meadow and cultivation rise more than one-third the height. A forest of oak and beech forms a noble belt above it; higher still is a region of ling; and above all snow. From whatever point viewed, this mountain is commanding from its magnitude, and beautiful from its luxuriant foliage. The range which closes in the valley to the east is of a character different from the others; it has more variety, more cultivation, villages, forests, glens, and cascades. That of Gouzat, which turns a mill as soon as it falls from the mountain, is romantic, with every accompanyment necessary to give a high degree of picturesque beauty. There are features in that of Montauban, which Claude Loraine would not have failed transfusing on his canvass; and the view of the vale from the chesnut rock is gay and animated. The termination of our valley to the south is striking; the river Neste pours in incessant cascades over the rocks that seem an eternal resistance. The eminence in the centre of a small vale, on which is an old tower, is a wild and romantic spot the roar of the waters beneath unites in effect with the

[1] Larboust, or de l'Arboust, east of Bagnères-de-Luchon.

mountains, whose towering forests, finishing in snow, give an awful grandeur, a gloomy greatness to the scene; and seem to raise a barrier of separation between the kingdoms, too formidable even for armies to pass. But what are rocks, and mountains, and snow, when opposed to human ambition?—In the recesses of the pendent woods, the bears find their habitation on the rocks, and above, the eagles have their nests. All around is great; the sublime of nature, with imposing majesty, impresses awe upon the mind; attention is rivetted to the spot; and imagination, with all its excursive powers, seeks not to wander beyond the scene.

> Deepens the murmurs of the falling floods,
> And breathes a browner horror o'er the woods.[1]

To view these scenes tolerably, is a business of some days; and such is the climate here, or at least has been since I was at Bagnere de Luchon, that not more than one day in three is to be depended on for fine weather. The heights of the mountains is such, that the clouds, perpetually broken, pour down quantities of rain. From June 26th to July 2d, we had one heavy shower, which lasted without intermission for sixty hours. The mountains, though so near, were hidden to their bases in the clouds. They do not only arrest the fleeting ones, which are passing in the atmosphere, but seem to have a generative power; for you see small ones at first, like thin vapour rising out of glens, forming on the sides of the hills, and increasing by degrees, till they become clouds heavy enough to rest on the tops, or else rise into the atmosphere, and pass away with others.

Among the original tenants of this immense range of mountains, the first in point of dignity, from the importance of the mischief they do, are the bears. There are both sorts, carnivorous and vegetable-eaters; the latter are more mischievous than their more terrible brethren, coming down in the night and eating the corn, particularly buckwheat and maize; and they are so nice in choosing the sweetest ears of the latter, that they trample and spoil infinitely more than they eat. The carnivorous bears wage

[1] Pope, Eloisa to Abelard, lines 169, 170.

war against the cattle and sheep, so that no stock can be left in the fields at night. Flocks must be watched by shepherds, who have fire-arms, and the assistance of many stout and fierce dogs; and cattle are shut up in stables every night in the year. Sometimes, by accident, they wander from their keepers, and if left abroad, they run a considerable risque of being devoured.—The bears attack these animals by leaping on their back, force the head to the ground, thrust their paws into the body in the violence of a dreadful hug. There are many hunting days every year for destroying them; several parishes joining for that purpose. Great numbers of men and boys form a cordon, and drive the wood where the bears are known or suspected to be. They are the fattest in winter, when a good one is worth three louis. A bear never ventures to attack a wolf; but several wolves together, when hungry, will attack a bear, and kill and eat him. Wolves are here only in winter. In summer, they are in the very remotest parts of the Pyrenees—the most distant from human habitations: they are here, as every where else in France, dreadful to sheep.

A part of our original plan of travelling to the Pyrenees, was an excursion into Spain. Our landlord at Luchon had before procured mules and guides for persons travelling on business to Saragossa and Barcelona, and at our request wrote to Vielle,[1] the first Spanish town across the mountains, for three mules and a conductor, who speaks French; and being arrived according to appointment, we set out on our expedition. *For the register of this Tour into Spain, I must refer the reader to the Annals of Agriculture*, vol. viii. p. 193.

JULY 21. Return.—Leave Jonquieres,[2] where the countenances and manners of the people would make one believe all the inhabitants were smugglers. Come to a most noble road, which the King of Spain is making; it begins at the pillars that mark the boundaries of the two monarchies, joining with the French road: it is admirably executed. Here take leave of Spain and re-enter France: the contrast is striking. When one crosses the sea from

---

[1] Viella (Catalonia).   [2] Jonquiera (Catalonia).

Dover to Calais, the preparation and circumstance of a naval passage, leave the mind by some gradation to a change: but here, without going through a town, a barrier, or even a wall, you enter a new world. From the natural and miserable roads of Catalonia, you tread at once on a noble causeway, made with all the solidity and magnificence that distinguishes the highways of France. Instead of beds of torrents you have well built bridges; and from a country wild, desert, and poor, we found ourselves in the midst of cultivation and improvement. Every other circumstance spoke the same language, and told us by signs not to be mistaken, and some great and operating cause worked an effect too clear to be misunderstood. The more one sees, the more I belive we shall be led to think, that there is but one all-powerful cause that instigates mankind, and that is GOVERNMENT!—Others form exceptions, and give shades of difference and distinction, but this acts with permanent and universal force. The present instance is remarkable; for Roussillon[1] is in fact a part of Spain; the inhabitants are Spaniards in language and in customs; but they are under a French government.

Great range of the Pyrenees at a distance. Meet shepherds that speak the Catalan. The cabriolets we meet are Spanish. The farmers thresh their corn like the Spaniards. The inns and the houses are the same. Reach Perpignan;[2] there I parted with Mons. Lazowski. He returned to Bagnere de Luchon, but I had planned a tour in Languedoc, to fill up the time to spare—15 miles.

The 22d. The Duke de la Rochefoucauld had given me a letter to Mons. Barri de Lasseuses, major of a regiment at Perpignan, and who, he said, understood agriculture, and would be glad to converse with me on the subject. I sallied out in the morning to find him, but being Sunday, he was at his country-seat at Pia, about a league from the town. I had a roasting walk thither, over a dry stony country under vines. Mons. Madame, and Mademoiselle de Lasseuses, received me with great politeness. I ex-

---

[1] Le Roussillon, now forming the department of Les Pyrenées-Orientales, was added to the French crown in 1659 by the treaty of the Pyrenees.
[2] (Pyrenées-Orientales.)

plained the motives of my coming to France, which were not to run idly through the kingdom with the common herd of travellers, but to make myself a master of their agriculture; that if I found any thing good and applicable to England, I might copy it. He commended the design greatly; said it was travelling with a truly laudable motive; but expressed much astonishment, as it was so uncommon; and was very sure there was not a single Frenchman in all England on such an errand. He desired I would spend the day with him. I found the vineyard the chief part of his husbandry, but he had some arable land, managed in the singular manner of that province. He pointed to a village which he said was Rivesalta,[1] which produced some of the most famous wine in France; at dinner I found that it merited its reputation. In the evening returned to Perpignan, after a day fertile in useful information.—8 miles.

The 23d. Take the road to Narbonne. Pass Rivesalta. Under the mountain there is the largest spring I ever saw. Otters-Pool and Holly-well are bubbles to it. It rises at the foot of the rock, and is able to turn immediately many mills; being at once rather a river than a spring. Pass an uninterrupted flat waste, without a single tree, house, or village for a considerable distance: by much the ugliest country I have seen in France. Great quantities of corn every where treading out with mules, as in Spain. Dine at Sejean,[2] at the Soleil, a good new inn, where I accidentally met with the marquis de Tressan. He told me, that I must be a singular person to travel so far with no other object than agriculture: he never knew nor heard of the like; but approved much of the plan, and wished he could do the same.

The roads here are stupendous works. I passed a hill, cut through to ease a descent, that was all in the solid rock, and cost 90,000 liv. (3,937l.) yet it extends but a few hundred yards. Three leagues and an half from Sejean to Narbonne cost 1,800,000 liv. (78,750l.) These ways are superb even to a folly. Enormous sums have been spent to level even gentle slopes. The causeways are raised and

---

[1] Rivesaltes, station and seat of the wine trade (Pyrenées-Orientales).
[2] Sigean, on the lagoon of that name (Aude).

walled on each side, forming one solid mass of artificial road, carried across the vallies to the height of six, seven, or eight feet, and never less than 50 wide. There is a bridge of a single arch, and a causeway to it, truly magnificent; we have not an idea of what such a road is in England. The traffic of the way, however, demands no such exertions; one-third of the breadth is beaten, one-third rough, and one-third covered with weeds. In 36 miles, I have met one cabriolet, half a dozen carts, and some old women with asses. For what all this waste of treasure?—In Languedoc, it is true, these works are not done by corvées; but there is an injustice in levying the amount not far short of them. The money is raised by tailles, and, in making the assessment, lands held by a noble tenure are so much eased, and others by a base one so burthened, that 120 arpents in this neighbourhood held by the former, pay 90 liv. and 400 possessed by a plebeian right, which ought proportionally to pay 300 liv. is, instead of that, assessed at 1400 liv. At Narbonne, the canal[1] which joins that of Languedoc, deserves attention; it is a very fine work, and will, they say, be finished next month. —36 miles.

The 24th. Women without stockings, and many without shoes; but if their feet are poorly clad they have a *superb* consolation in walking upon magnificent causeways: the new road is 50 feet wide, and 50 more digged away or destroyed to make it.

The vintage itself can hardly be such a scene of activity and animation as this universal one of treading out the corn, with which all the towns and villages in Languedoc are now alive. The corn is all roughly stacked around a dry firm spot, where great numbers of mules and horses are driven on a trot round a centre, a woman holding the reins, and another, or a girl or two, with whips drive; the men supply and clear the floor; other parties are dressing, by throwing the corn into the air for the wind to blow away the chaff. Every soul is employed, and with such an air of cheerfulness, that the people seem as well pleased with their labour, as the farmer himself with his great

---

[1] La Robine.

heaps of wheat. The scene is uncommonly animated and joyous. I stopped and alighted often to see their method; I was always very civilly treated, and my wishes for a good price for the farmer, and not too good a one for the poor, well received. This method, which entirely saves barns, depends absolutely on climate: from my leaving Bagnere de Luchon to this moment, all through Catalonia, Roussillon, and this part of Languedoc, there has been nothing like rain; but one unvarying clear bright sky and burning sun, yet not at all suffocating, or to me even unpleasant. I asked whether they were not sometimes caught in the rain? they said, very rarely indeed; but if rain did come, it is seldom more than a heavy shower, which a hot sun quickly succeeds and dries every thing speedily.

The canal of Languedoc[1] is the capital feature of all this country. The mountain through which it pierces is insulated, in the midst of an extended valley, and only half a mile from the road. It is a noble and stupendous work, goes through the hill about the breadth of three toises, and was digged without shafts.

Leave the road, and crossing the canal, follow it to Beziers;[2] nine sluice-gates let the water down the hill to join the river at the town.—A noble work! The port is broad enough for four large vessels to lie abreast; the greatest of them carries from 90 to 100 tons. Many of them were at the quay, some in motion, and every sign of an animated business. This is the best sight I have seen in France. Here Lewis XIV. thou art truly great!—Here, with a generous and benignant hand, thou dispensest ease and wealth to thy people!—*Si sic omnia*, thy name would indeed have been revered. To effect this noble work, of uniting the two seas, less money was expended than to besiege Turin, or to seize Strasbourg like a robber. Such an employment of the revenues of a great kingdom is the only laudable way of a monarch's acquiring immortality; all other means make their names survive with those only of the incendiaries, robbers, and violators of mankind.

[1] The canal de Languedoc or du Midi, called also Le canal des deux Mers, which unites the Mediterranean with the Atlantic, was created under Louis XIV. by Riquet.

[2] Béziers (Hérault).

The canal passes through the river for about half a league, separated from it by walls which are covered in floods; and then turns off for Cette. Dine at Beziers. Knowing that Mons. l'Abbé Rozier,[1] the celebrated editor of the Journal Physique, and who is now publishing a dictionary of husbandry, which in France has much reputation, lived and farmed near Beziers, I enquired at the inn the way to his house. They told me that he had left Beziers two years, but that the house was to be seen from the street, and accordingly shewed it me from something of a square open on one side to the country; adding, that it belonged now to a Mons. de Rieuse, who had purchased the estate of the Abbé. To view the farm of a man celebrated for his writings, was an object, as it would, at least, enable me, in reading his book, to understand better the allusions he might make to the soil, situation, and other circumstances. I was sorry to hear, at the table d'hôte, much ridicule thrown on the Abbé Rozier's husbandry, that it had *beaucoup de fantasie mais rien solide*; in particular, they treated his paving his vineyards as a ridiculous circumstance. Such an experiment seemed remarkable, and I was glad to hear it, that I might desire to see these paved vineyards. The Abbé here, as a farmer, has just that character which every man will be sure to have who departs from the methods of his neighbours; for it is not in the nature of countrymen, that any body should come among them who can presume with impunity to think for themselves. I asked why he left the country? and they gave me a curious anecdote of the bishop of Beziers cutting a road through the Abbé's farm, at the expence of the province, to lead to the house of his (the bishop's) mistress, which occasioned such a quarrel that Mons. Rozier could stay no longer in the country. This is a pretty feature of a government: that a man is to be forced to sell his estate, and driven out of a country, because bishops make love.—I suppose to their neighbours wives, as no other love is fashionable in France. Which of my neighbours' wives will tempt the bishop of Norwich to make a road through my farm, and drive me to sell Bradfield?—

[1] Rozier (François), an ecclesiastic and agricultural writer, born 1754, killed at the siege of Lyons, 1793.

I give my authority for this anecdote, the chat of a table d'hôte; it is as likely to be false as true; but Languedocian bishops are certainly not English ones.—Mons. de Rieuse received me politely, and satisfied as many of my enquiries as he could; for he knew little more of the Abbe's husbandry than common report, and what the farm itself told him, As to paved vineyards, there was no such thing; the report must have taken rise from a vineyard of Burgundy grapes, which the Abbé planted in a new manner; he set them in a curved form, in a foss, covering them only with flints instead of earth; this succeeded well. I walked over the farm, which is beautifully situated, on the slope and top of a hill, which commands Beziers, its rich vale, its navigation, and a fine accompanyment of mountains.

Beziers has a fine promenade; and is becoming, they say, a favourite residence for the English, preferring the air to that of Montpellier. Take the road to Pezenas.[1] It leads up a hill, which commands, for some time, a view of the Mediterranean. Through all this country, but particularly in the olive grounds, the cricket (*cicala*) makes a constant, sharp, monotonous noise; a more odious companion on the road can hardly be imagined. Pezenas opens on a very fine country, a vale of six or eight leagues extent all cultivated; a beautiful mixture of vines, mulberries, olives, towns, and scattered houses, with a great deal of fine lucerne; the whole bounded by gentle hills, cultivated to their tops.—At supper, at the table d'hôte, we were waited on by a female without shoes or stockings, exquisitely ugly, and diffusing odours not of roses: there were, however, a croix de St. Louis,[2] and two or three mercantile-looking people that prated with her very familiarly: at an ordinary of farmers, at the poorest and remotest market village in England, such an animal would not be allowed by the landlord to enter his house; or by the guests their room.—32 miles.

The 25th. The road, in crossing a valley to and from a

---

[1] Pézenas (Hérault).

[2] An order created by Louis XIV., and conferred only on officers, naval and military. Suppressed by the Convention, 1792, re-established under the Restoration, this order was finally abolished in July, 1830.

bridge, is a magnificent walled causeway, more than a mile long, ten yards wide, and from eight to twelve feet high; with stone posts on each side at every six yards—a prodigious work.—I know nothing more striking to a traveller than the roads of Languedoc: we have not in England a conception of such exertions; they are splendid and superb; and if I could free my mind of the recollection of the unjust taxation which pays them, I should travel with admiration at the magnificence displayed by the states of this province. The police of these roads is however execrable—for I scarcely meet a cart but the driver is asleep in it.

Taking the road to Montpellier, pass through a pleasing country; and by another immense walled causeway, twelve yards broad and three high, leading close to the sea. To Pijan,[1] and near Frontignan[2] and Montbasin,[3] famous for their muscat wines.—Approach Montpellier; the environs, for near a league, are delicious, and more highly ornamented than any thing I have seen in France.—Villas well built, clean, and comfortable, with every appearance of wealthy owners, are spread thickly through the country. They are, in general, pretty square buildings; some very large. Montpellier, with the air rather of a great capital than of a provincial town, covers a hill that swells proudly to the view.—But on entering it, you experience a disappointment from narrow, ill-built, crooked streets, but full of people, and apparently alive with business; yet there is no considerable manufacture in the place; the principal are verdigrease, silk handkerchiefs, blankets, perfumes and *liqueurs*. The great object for a stranger to view is the promenade or square, for it partakes of both, called the Perou.[4]—There is a magnificent aqueduct on three tires of arches for supplying the city with water, from a hill at a considerable distance; a very noble work; a *chateau d'eau* receives the water in a circular bason, from which it falls into an external reservoir, to supply the city, and the *jets d'eau* that cool the air of a garden below, the whole in a fine square considerably elevated above the surrounding ground, walled in with a ballustrade, and other mural decorations, and in the centre a good equestrian statue of

---

[1] Pignan (Hérault).
[2] (Hérault.)
[3] Montbazin (Hérault).
[4] Place du Peyrou.

Louis XIV. There is an air of real grandeur and magnificence in this useful work, that struck me more than any thing at Versailles. The view is also singularly beautiful. To the south, the eye wanders with delight over a rich vale, spread with villas, and terminated by the sea. To the north, a series of cultivated hills. On one side, the vast range of the Pyrenees trend away till lost in remoteness. On the other, the eternal snows of the Alps pierce the clouds. The whole view one of the most stupendous to be seen, when a clear sky approximates these distant objects.—32 miles.

The 26th. The fair of Beaucaire[1] fills the whole country with business and motion; meet many carts loaded; and nine diligences going or coming. Yesterday and to day the hottest I ever experienced; we had none like them in Spain—the flies much worse than the heat.—30 miles.

The 27th. The amphitheatre of Nismes is a prodigious work, which shews how well the Romans had adapted these edifices to the abominable uses to which they were erected. The convenience of a theatre that could hold 17000 spectators without confusion; the magnitude; the massive and substantial manner in which it is built without mortar, that has withstood the attacks of the weather, and the worse depredations of the barbarians in the various revolutions of sixteen centuries, all strike the attention forcibly.

I viewed the Maison Quarré last night; again this morning, and twice more in the day; it is beyond all comparison the most light, elegant, and pleasing building I ever beheld. Without any magnitude to render it imposing; without any extraordinary magnificence to surprize, it rivets attention. There is a magic harmony in the proportions that charms the eye. One can fix on no particular part of pre-eminent beauty; it is one perfect whole of symmetry and grace. What an infatuation in modern architects, that can overlook the chaste and elegant simplicity of taste, manifest in such a work; and yet rear such piles of laboured foppery and heaviness as are to be met

---

[1] (Gard.) The celebrated fairs formerly held here have much decreased in importance.

with in France. The temple of Diana, as it is called, and the ancient baths, with their modern restoration, and the promenade, form parts of the same scene, and are magnificent decorations of the city. I was, in relation to the baths, in ill luck, for the water was all drawn off, in order to clean them and the canals.—The Roman pavements are singularly beautiful, and in high preservation. My quarters at Nismes were at the Louvre, a large, commodious, and excellent inn, the house was almost as much a fair from morning to night as Beaucaire itself could be. I dined and supped at the table d'hôte; the cheapness of these tables suits my finances, and one sees something of the manners of the people; we sat down from twenty to forty at every meal, most motley companies of French, Italians, Spaniards, and Germans, with a Greek and Armenian; and I was informed, that there is hardly a nation in Europe or Asia; that have not merchants at this great fair, chiefly for raw silk, of which many millions in value are sold in four days: all the other commodities of the world are to be found there.

One circumstance I must remark on this numerous table d'hôte, because it has struck me repeatedly, which is the taciturnity of the French. I came to the kingdom expecting to have my ears constantly fatigued with the infinite volubility and spirits of the people, of which so many persons have written, sitting, I suppose, by their English fire-sides. At Montpellier, though 15 persons and some of them ladies were present, I found it impossible to make them break their inflexible silence with more than a monosyllable, and the whole company sat more like an assembly of tongue-tied quakers, than the mixed company of a people famous for loquacity. Here also, at Nismes, with a different party at every meal it is the same; not a Frenchman will open his lips. To day at dinner, hopeless of that nation, and fearing to lose the use of an organ they had so little inclination to employ, I fixed myself by a Spaniard, and having been so lately in his country, I found him ready to converse, and tolerably communicative; but we had more conversation than thirty other persons maintained among themselves.

The 28th. Early in the morning to the Pont du Gard,

through a plain covered with vast plantations of olives to the left, but much waste rocky land. At the first view of that celebrated aqueduct, I was rather disappointed, having expected something of greater magnitude; but soon found the error: I was, on examining it more nearly, convinced that it possessed every quality that ought to make a strong impression. It is a stupendous work; the magnitude, and the massive solidity of the architecture, which may probably endure two or three thousand years more, united with the undoubted utility of the undertaking, to give us a high idea of the spirit of exertion which executed it for the supply of a provincial town: the surprize, however, may cease, when we consider the nations enslaved that were the workmen.—Returning to Nismes, meet many merchants returning from the fair; each with a child's drum tied to their cloakbag: my own little girl was too much in my head not to love them for this mark of attention to their children;—but why a drum?—Have they not had enough of the military in a kingdom, where they are excluded from all the honours, respect, and emolument, that can flow from the sword?—I like Nismes much; and if the inhabitants are at all on a par with the appearance of their city, I should prefer it for a residence to most, if not all the towns I have seen in France. The theatre, however, is a capital point, in that Montpellier is said to exceed it.—24 miles.

The 29th. Pass six leagues of a disagreeable country to Sauve.[1] Vines and olives. The chateau of Mons. Sabbatier[2] strikes in this wild country; he has inclosed much with dry walls, planted many mulberries and olives, which are young, thriving, and well inclosed, yet the soil is so stony, that no earth is visible; some of his walls are four feet thick, and one of them twelve thick and five high, whence it seems, he thinks moving the stones a necessary improvement, which I much question. He has built three or four new farm-houses; I suppose he resides on this estate for improving it. I hope he does not *serve;* that no moon-shine pursuit may divert him from a conduct honour-

---

[1] (Gard.)
[2] The château Sabatier is seen to the right on the railway from Nîmes to Le Vigan.

able to himself, and beneficial to his country.—Leaving Sauve, I was much struck with a large tract of land, seemingly nothing but huge rocks; yet most of it inclosed and planted with the most industrious attention. Every man has an olive, a mulberry, an almond, or a peach-tree, and vines scattered among them; so that the whole ground is covered with the oddest mixture of these plants, and bulging rocks that can be conceived. The inhabitants of this village deserve encouragement for their industry; and if I was a French minister, they should have it. They would soon turn all the deserts around them into gardens. Such a knot of active husbandmen, who turn their rocks into scenes of fertility, because I suppose THEIR OWN, would do the same by the wastes, if animated by the same omnipotent principle. Dine at St. Hyppolite,[1] with eight protestant merchants returning home to Rouverge,[2] from the fair of Beaucaire; as we parted at the same time, we travelled together; and from their conversation, I learned some circumstances of which I wanted to be informed; they told me also, that mulberries extend beyond Vigan,[3] but then, and especially about Milhaud,[4] almonds take their place, and are in very great quantities.

My Rouverge friends pressed me to pass with them to Milhaud and Rodez, assured me, that the cheapness of their province was so great, that it would tempt me to live some time amongst them. That I might have a house at Milhaud, of four tolerable rooms on a floor furnished, for 12 louis a-year; and live in the utmost plenty with all my family, if I would bring them over, for 100 louis a-year: that there were many families of noblesse, who subsisted on 50, and even on 25 a-year. Such anecdotes of cheapness are only curious when considered in a political light, as contributing on one hand to the welfare of individuals; and on the other, as contributing to the prosperity, wealth, and power of the kingdom; if I should meet with many such instances, and also with others directly contrary, it will be necessary to consider them more at large.—30 miles.

[1] St. Hippolyte du Fort (Gard).
[2] The Rouergue (Aveyron).
[3] Le Vigan (Gard).   [4] Millau (Aveyron).

The 30th. Going out of Gange,[1] I was surprised to find by far the greatest exertion in irrigation which I had yet seen in France; and then pass by some steep mountains, highly cultivated in terraces. Much watering at St. Laurence.[2] The scenery very interesting to a farmer. From Gange, to the mountain of rough ground which I crossed, the ride has been the most interesting which I have taken in France; the efforts of industry the most vigorous; the animation the most lively. An activity has been here, that has swept away all difficulties before it, and has cloathed the very rocks with verdure. It would be a disgrace to common sense to ask the cause: the enjoyment of property *must* have done it. Give a man the secure possession of a bleak rock, and he will turn it into a garden; give him a nine years lease of a garden, and he will convert it into a desert. To Montadier,[3] over a rough mountain covered with box and lavender; it is a beggarly village, with an auberge that made me almost shrink. Some cut throat figures were eating black bread, whose visages had so much of the gallies that I thought I heard their chains rattle. I looked at their legs, and could not but imagine they had no business to be free. There is a species of countenance here so horridly bad, that it is impossible to be mistaken in one's reading. I was quite alone, and absolutely without arms. Till this moment, I had not dreamt of carrying pistols: I should now have been better satisfied, if I had had them. The master of the auberge, who seemed first cousin to his guests, procured for me some wretched bread with difficulty, but it was not black. —No meat, no eggs, no legumes, and execrable wine: no corn for my mule; no hay; no straw; no grass: the loaf fortunately was large; I took a piece, and sliced the rest for my four-footed Spanish friend, who ate it thankfully, but the aubergiste growled.—Descend by a winding and excellent road to Maudieres,[4] where a vast arch is thrown across the torrent. Pass St. Maurice,[5] and cross a ruined forest amongst fragments of trees. Descend three hours, by a most noble road hewn out of the mountain side to

---

[1] Ganges (Hérault). [2] St. Laurence le Minier (Hérault).
[3] Mondardier (Hérault). [4] Madières (Hérault).
[5] (Hérault.)

Lodeve,[1] a dirty, ugly, ill built town, with crooked close streets, but populous, and very industrious.—Here I drank excellent light and pleasing white wine at 5*f.* a bottle.—36 miles.

The 31st. Cross a mountain by a miserable road, and reach Beg de Rieux,[2] which shares with Carcassonne, the fabric of Londrins,[3] for the Levant trade.—Cross much waste to Beziers.—I met to-day with an instance of ignorance in a well dressed French merchant, that surprised me. He had plagued me with abundance of tiresome foolish questions, and then asked for the third or fourth time what country I was of. I told him I was a Chinese. How far off is that country?—I replied, 200 leagues. *Deux cents lieus! Diable! c'est un grand chemin!* The other day a Frenchman asked me, after telling him I was an Englishman, if we had trees in England?—I replied, that we had a few. Had we any rivers?—Oh, none at all. *Ah ma foi c'est bien trieste!* This incredible ignorance, when compared with the knowledge so universally disseminated in England, is to be attributed, like every thing else, to government.—40 miles.

August 1. Leave Beziers, in order to go to Capestan[4] by the pierced mountain. Cross the canal of Languedoc several times; and over many wastes to Pleraville.[5] The Pyrenees now full to the left, and their roots but a few leagues off. At Carcassonne they carried me to a fountain of muddy water, and to a gate of the barracks; but I was better pleased to see several large good houses of manufacturers, that shew wealth.—40 miles.

The 2d. Pass a considerable convent, with a long line of front, and rise to Fanjour.[6]—16 miles.

The 3d. At Mirepoix[7] they are building a most magnificent bridge of seven flat arches, each of 64 feet span,

---

[1] Lodève (Hérault).
[2] Bédarieux (Hérault).
[3] Londrins, cloth, imitating that of London, hence the name, manufactured in Languedoc, Provence, and Dauphiné.
[4] Capestang, Caput Stagnum, see for a most interesting account of the Lagoons of Languedoc, M. Lenthéric's "Les Villes Mortes du Golfe du Lyon."
[5] Prouille (Hérault). [6] Faujeaux (Hérault).
[7] (Ariège.)

which will cost 1,800,000 liv. (78,750l.); it has been 12 years erecting, and will be finished in two more. The weather for several days has been as fine as possible, but very hot; to-day the heat was so disagreeable, that I rested from 12 to 3 at Mirepoix; and found it so burning, that it was an effort to go half a quarter of a mile to view the bridge. The myriads of flies were ready to devour me, and I could hardly support any light in the room. Riding fatigued me, and I enquired for a carriage of some sort to carry me, while these great heats should continue; I had done the same at Carcassonne; but nothing like a cabriolet of any sort was to be had. When it is recollected that that place is one of the most considerable manufacturing towns in France, containing 15,000 people, and that Mirepoix is far from being a mean place, and yet not a voiture of any kind to be had, how will an Englishman bless himself for the universal conveniences that are spread through his own country, in which I believe there is not a town of 1500 people in the kingdom where post chaises and able horses are not to be had at a moment's warning? What a contrast! This confirms the fact deducible from the little traffic on the roads even around Paris itself. Circulation is stagnant in France.—The heat was so great that I left Mirepoix disordered with it: This was by far the hottest day that I ever felt. The hemisphere seemed almost in a flame with burning rays that rendered it impossible to turn ones eyes within many degrees of the radiant orb that now blazed in the heavens. —Cross another fine new bridge of three arches; and come to a woodland, the first I have seen for a great distance. Many vines about Pamiers,[1] which is situated in a beautiful vale, upon a fine river. The place itself is ugly, stinking, and ill built; with an inn! Adieu, Mons. Gascit; if fate sends me to such another house as thine— be it an expiation for my sins!—28 miles.

The 4th. Leaving Amous,[2] there is the extraordinary spectacle of a river issuing out of a cavern in a mountain of rock; on crossing the hill you see where it enters by another cavern.—It pierces the mountain. Most countries,

---

[1] (Ariège.)
[2] Amous. Aulus is evidently here meant (Ariège).

however, have instances of rivers passing under ground. At St. Geronds[1] go to the Croix Blanche, the most execrable receptacle of filth, vermin, impudence, and imposition that ever exercised the patience, or wounded the feelings of a traveller. A withered hag, the dæmon of beastliness, presides there. I laid, not rested, in a chamber over a stable, whose effluviæ through the broken floor were the least offensive of the perfumes afforded by this hideous place. —It could give me nothing but two stale eggs, for which I paid, exclusive of all other charges, 20/. Spain brought nothing to my eyes that equalled this sink, from which an English hog would turn with disgust. But the inns all the way from Nismes are wretched, except at Lodeve, Gange, Carcassonne, and Mirepoix. St. Geronds must have, from its appearance, four or five thousand people. Pamiers near twice that number. What can be the circulating connection between such masses of people and other towns and countries, that can be held together and supported by such inns? There have been writers who look upon such observations as rising merely from the petulance of travellers, but it shews their extreme ignorance. Such circumstances are political data. We cannot demand all the books of France to be opened in order to explain the amount of circulation in that kingdom: a politician must therefore collect it from such circumstances as he can ascertain; and among these, traffic on the great roads, and the convenience of the houses prepared for the reception of travellers, tell us both the number and the condition of those travellers; by which term I chiefly allude to the natives, who move on business or pleasure from place to place; for if they are not considerable enough to cause good inns, those who come from a distance will not, which is evident from the bad accommodations even in the high road from London to Rome. On the contrary, go in England to towns that contain 1500, 2000, or 3000 people, in situations absolutely cut off from all dependence, or almost the expectation of what are properly called travellers, yet you will meet with neat inns, well dressed and clean people keeping them, good furniture, and a refreshing

---

[1] St. Girons (Basses-Pyrenées).

civility; your senses may not be gratified, but they will not be offended; and if you demand a post chaise and a pair of horses, the cost of which is not less than 80l. in spite of a heavy tax, it will be ready to carry you whither you please. Are no political conclusions to be drawn from this amazing contrast? It proves that such a population in England have connections with other places to the amount of supporting such houses. The friendly clubs of the inhabitants, the visits of friends and relations, the parties of pleasure, the resort of farmers, the intercourse with the capital and with other towns, form the support of good inns; and in a country where they are not to be found, it is a proof that there is not the same quantity of motion; or that it moves by means of less wealth, less consumption, and less enjoyment. In this journey through Languedoc, I have passed an incredible number of splendid bridges, and many superb causeways. But this only proves the absurdity and oppression of government. Bridges that cost 70 or 80,000l. and immense causeways to connect towns, that have no better inns than such as I have described, appear to be gross absurdities. They cannot be made for the mere use of the inhabitants, because one-fourth of the expense would answer the purpose of real utility. They are therefore objects of public magnificence, and consequently for the eye of travellers. But what traveller, with his person surrounded by the beggarly filth of an inn, and with all his senses offended, will not condemn such inconsistencies as folly, and will not wish for more comfort and less appearance of splendour.—30 miles.

The 5th. To St. Martory[1] is an almost uninterrupted range of well inclosed and well cultivated country.—For an hundred miles past, the women generally without shoes, even in the towns; and in the country many men also.— The heat yesterday and to-day as intense as it was before: there is no bearing any light in the rooms: all must be shut close, or none are tolerably cool: in going out of a light room into a dark one, tho' both to the north, there is a very sensible coolness; and out of a dark one into a

---

[1] (Hte. Garonne.)

roofed balcony, is like going into an oven. I have been advised every day not to stir till four o'clock. From ten in the morning till five in the afternoon, the heat makes all exercise most uncomfortable ; and the flies are a curse of Egypt. Give me the cold and fogs of England, rather than such a heat, should it be lasting. The natives, however, assert, that this intensity has now continued as long as it commonly does, namely, four or five days; and that the greatest part even of the hottest months is much cooler than the weather is at present.—In 250 miles distant, I have met on the road two cabriolets only, and three miserable things like old English one-horse chaises ; not one gentleman ; though many merchants, as they call themselves, each with two or three cloak-bags behind him: —a paucity of travellers that is amazing.—28 miles.

The 6th. To Bagnere de Luchon, rejoining my friends, and not displeased to have a little rest in the cool mountains, after so burning a ride.—28 miles.

The 10th. Finding our party not yet ready to set out on their return to Paris, I determined to make use of the time there was yet to spare, ten or eleven days, in a tour to Bagnere de Bigorre to Bayonne,[1] and to meet them on the way to Bourdeaux, at Auch. This being settled, I mounted my English mare, and took my last leave of Luchon.—28 miles.

The 11th. Pass a convent[2] of Bernardine monks, who have a revenue of 30,000 liv. It is situated in a vale, watered by a charming chrystal stream, and some hills, covered with oak, shelter it behind.—Arrive at Bagnere, which contains little worthy of notice, but it is much frequented by company on account of its waters. To the valley of Campan,[3] of which I had heard great things, and which yet much surpassed my expectation. It is quite different from all the other vales I have seen in the Pyrenees or in Catalonia. The features and the arrangement novel. In general the richly cultivated slopes of those mountains are thickly inclosed ; this, on the contrary, is open. The vale itself is a flat range of cultivation and

---

[1] (Hte. Pyrénées.)   [2] No longer in existence.
[3] (Hte. Pyrénées.) " Celebrated perhaps beyond its deserts from the time of Arthur Young to the present."—*Murray's Guide.*

watered meadow, spread thickly with villages and scattered houses. The eastern boundary is a rough, steep, and rocky mountain, and affords pasturage to goats and sheep; a contrast to the western, which forms the singular feature of the scene. It is one noble sheet of corn and grass uninclosed, and intersected only by lines that mark the division of properties, or the channels that conduct water from the higher regions for irrigating the lower ones; the whole hanging is one matchless slope of the richest and most luxuriant vegetation. Here and there are scattered some small masses of wood, which chance has grouped with wonderful happiness for giving variety to the scene. The season of the year, by mixing the rich yellow of ripe corn, with the green of the watered meadows, added greatly to the colouring of the landscape, which is upon the whole the most exquisite for *form* and *colour* that my eye has ever been regaled with.—Take the road to Lourde,[1] where is a castle on a rock, garrisoned for the mere purpose of keeping state prisoners, sent hither by *lettres de cachet*. Seven or eight are *known* to be here at present; thirty have been here at a time; and many for life—torn by the relentless hand of jealous tyranny from the bosom of domestic comfort; from wives, children, friends, and hurried for crimes unknown to themselves—more probably for virtues—to languish in this detested abode of misery—and die of despair. Oh, liberty! liberty!—and yet this is the mildest government of any considerable country in Europe, our own excepted. The dispensations of providence seem to have permitted the human race to exist only as the prey of tyrants, as it has made pigeons for the prey of hawks—35 miles.

The 12th. Pau[2] is a considerable town, that has a parliament and a linen manufacture; but it is more famous for being the birth-place of Henry IV. I viewed the castle, and was shewn, as all travellers are, the room in which that amiable prince was born, and the cradle, the shell of a tortoise, in which he was nursed. What an effect on

---

[1] Lourdes (Hte. Pyrénées), celebrated in these days for its so-called miraculous fountain and pilgrimages. The castle is now used as a barrack.

[2] (Basses-Pyrénées.)

posterity have great and distinguished talents! This is a considerable town, but I question whether any thing would ever carry a stranger to it but its possessing the cradle of a favourite character.

Take the road to Moneng,[1] and come presently to a scene which was so new to me in France, that I could hardly believe my own eyes. A succession of many well built, tight, and COMFORTABLE farming cottages, built of stone, and covered with tiles; each having its little garden, inclosed by clipt thorn hedges, with plenty of peach and other fruit-trees, some fine oaks scattered in the hedges, and young trees nursed up with so much care, that nothing but the fostering attention of the owner could effect any thing like it. To every house belongs a farm, perfectly well inclosed, with grass borders mown and neatly kept around the corn fields, with gates to pass from one inclosure to another. The men are all dressed with red caps, like the highlanders of Scotland. There are some parts of England (where small yeomen still remain) that resemble this country of Bearne; but we have very little that is equal to what I have seen in this ride of twelve miles from Pau [2] to Moneng. It is all in the hands of little proprietors, without the farms being so small as to occasion a vicious and miserable population. An air of neatness, warmth, and comfort breathes over the whole. It is visible in their new built houses and stables; in their little gardens; in their hedges; in the courts before their doors; even in the coops for their poultry, and the sties for their hogs. A peasant does not think of rendering his pig comfortable, if his own happiness hangs by the thread of a nine years lease. We are now in Bearne, within a few miles of the cradle of Henry IV. Do they inherit these blessings from that good prince? The benignant genius of that good monarch, seems to reign still over the country; each peasant has *the fowl in the pot.* —34 miles.

The 13th. The agreeable scene of yesterday continues; many small properties; and every appearance of rural

[1] Monein (Basses-Pyrenées).
[2] "Dans nos campagnes, tout le monde est propriétaire."—*Remonstrance of the Parliament of Pau,* 1788. See H. Martin's "Histoire de France," vol. xvi., p. 668.

happiness. Navareen[1] is a small walled and fortified town, consisting of three principal streets, which cross at right angles, with a small square. From the ramparts there is the view of a fine country. The linen fabric spreads through it. To St. Palais[2] the country is mostly inclosed, and much of it with thorn-hedges, admirably trained, and kept neatly clipped.—25 miles.

The 14th. Left St. Palais, and took a guide to conduct me four leagues to Anspan.[3] Fair day, and the place crouded with farmers; I saw the soup prepared for what we should call the farmer's ordinary. There was a mountain of sliced bread, the colour of which was not inviting; ample provision of cabbage, grease, and water, and about as much meat for some scores of people, as half a dozen English farmers would have eaten, and grumbled at their host for short commons.—26 miles.

The 15th. Bayonne is by much the prettiest town I have seen in France; the houses are not only well built of stone, but the streets are wide and there are many openings which, though not regular squares, have a good effect. The river is broad, and many of the houses being fronted to it, the view of them from the bridge is fine. The promenade is charming; it has many rows of trees, whose heads join and form a shade delicious in this hot climate. In the evening, it was thronged with well dressed people of both sexes: and the women, through all the country, are the handsomest I have seen in France. In coming hither from Pau, I saw what is very rare in that kingdom, clean and pretty country girls; in most of the provinces, hard labour destroys both person and complexion. The bloom of health on the cheeks of a well dressed country girl is not the worst feature in any landscape. I hired a chaloup for viewing the embankment at the mouth of the river. By the water spreading itself too much, the harbour was injured; and government, to contract it, has built a wall on the north bank a mile long, and another on the south shore of half the length. It is from ten to 20 feet wide, and

[1] Navarrenx (Basses Pyrénées).
[2] St. Palais (Basses Pyrénées).
[3] Hasparren (Basses Pyrénées), an important Basque town, still celebrated for its fairs.

about twelve high, from the top of the base of rough stone, which extends twelve or fifteen feet more. Towards the mouth of the harbour, it is twenty feet wide, and the stones on both sides crampt together with irons. They are now driving piles of pine 16 feet deep, for the foundation. It is, on the whole, a work of great expence, magnificence and utility.

The 16th. To Dax is not the best way to Auch, but I had a mind to see the famous waste called *Les Landes de Bourdeaux*,[1] of which I had long heard and read so much. I was informed, that by this route, I should pass through more than twelve leagues of them. They reach almost to the gates of Bayonne; but broken by cultivated spots for a league or two. These *landes* are sandy tracts covered with pine trees, cut regularly for resin. Historians report, that when the moors were expelled from Spain, they applied to the court of France for leave to settle on and cultivate these *landes*; and that the court was much condemned for refusing them. It seems to have been taken for granted, that they could not be peopled with French; and therefore ought rather to be given to Moors, than to be left waste.—At Dax, there is a remarkably hot spring in the middle of the town. It is a very fine one, bubbling powerfully out of the ground in a large bason, walled in; it is boiling hot; it tastes like common water, and I was told that it was not impregnated with any mineral. The only use to which it is applied is for washing linen. It is at all seasons of the same heat, and in the same quantity. —27 miles.

The 17th. Pass district of sand as white as snow, and so loose as to blow; yet has oaks two feet in diameter, by reason of a bottom of white adhesive earth like marl. Pass three rivers, the waters of which might be applied in irrigation, yet no use made of them. The duke de

---

[1] Some notion of the transformation effected in this region since Arthur Young's time may be gathered from the following facts: 290,000 hectares have been rendered fertile by canals, which in 1877 reached a total of 2,200 kilomètres. 90,000 hectares, lying between the mouth of the Garonne and of the Adour, are now covered with pine forests, the creation of this century. A very small portion of the Landes remains in the condition our author found it just a hundred years ago. See E. Réclus, "Géographie de la France."

Bouillon[1] has vast possessions in these lands. A Grand Seigneur will at any time, and in any country, explain the reason of improveable land being left waste.—29 miles.

The 18th. As dearness is, in my opinion, the general feature of all money exchanges in France, it is but candid to note instances to the contrary. At Airé,[2] they gave me, at the Croix d'Or, soup, eels, sweet bread, and green-peas, a pigeon, a chicken, and veal-cutlets, with a dessert of biscuits, peaches, nectarines, plumbs, and glass of *liqueur*, with a bottle of good wine, all for 40*f.* (20d.) oats for my mare 20*f.* and hay 10*f.* At the same price at St. Severe,[3] I had a supper last night not inferior to it. Every thing at Airé seemed good and clean; and what is very uncommon, I had a parlour to eat my dinner in, and was attended by a neat well dressed girl. The last two hours to Airé it rained so violently, that my silk surtout was an insufficient defence; and the old landlady was in no haste to give me fire enough to be dried. As to supper, I had the idea of my dinner.—35 miles.

The 19th. Pass Beek,[4] which seems a flourishing little place, if we may judge by the building of new houses. The Clef d'Or is a large, new, and good inn.

In the 270 miles, from Bagnere de Luchon to Auch,[5] a general observation I may make is, that the whole, with very few exceptions, is inclosed; and that the farm-houses are every where scattered, instead of being, as in so many parts of France collected in towns. I have seen scarcely any gentlemen's country seats that seem at all modern; and, in general, they are thin to a surprising degree. I have not met with one country equipage, nor any thing like a gentleman riding to see a neighbour. Scarcely a gentleman at all. At Auch, met by appointment my friends, on their return to Paris. The town is almost without manufactures or commerce, and is supported chiefly by the rents of the country. But they have many

---

[1] The duchy of Bouillon was incorporated with French territory in 1793, but annexed to Luxemburg in 1815, and now forms part of Belgian Luxembourg. See Lalanne's "Dictionnaire historique de la France."
[2] Aire (Landes). [3] St. Sever (Landes).
[4] Beek. Vic-Bigorre (Landes).
[5] Auch (Gers). This name is **Basque**.

of the noblesse in the province, too poor to live here; some indeed so poor, that they plough their own fields; and these may possibly be much more estimable members of society, than the fools and knaves that laugh at them.—31 miles.

The 20th. Pass Fleuran,[1] which contains many good houses, and go through a populous country to La Tour,[2] a bishoprick, the diocesan of which we left at Bagnere de Luchon. The situation is beautiful on the point of a ridge of hills.—20 miles.

The 22d. By Leyrac,[3] through a fine country, to the Garonne, which we cross by a ferry. This river is here a quarter of a mile broad, with every appearance of commerce. A large barge passed loaded with cages of poultry; of such consequence throughout the extent of this navigation is the consumption of the great city of Bourdeaux. The rich vale continues to Agen,[4] and is very highly cultivated; but has not the beauty of the environs of Leitour. If new buildings are a criterion of the flourishing state of a place, Agen prospers. The bishop has raised a magnificent palace, the centre of which is in good taste; but the junction with the wings not equally happy.—23 miles.

The 23d. Pass a rich and highly cultivated vale to Aguillon;[5] much hemp, and every woman in the country employed on it. Many neat well built farm-houses on small properties, and all the country very populous. View the chateau of the Duc d'Aguillon,[6] which, being in the town, is badly situated, according to all rural ideas; but a town is ever an accompanyment of a chateau in France, as it was formerly in most parts of Europe; it seems to have

[1] Fleurance (Gers), one of the numerous towns in this department having a foreign name. We find Barcelone, Cologne, Pis (Pisa), Valence, originally seigneurial fortresses.
[2] Lectoure (Gers), no longer an episcopate.
[3] Leyrac (Lot and Garonne).
[4] (Lot and Garonne).
[5] Aigullon (Lot and Garonne).
[6] That cruel and lawless governor of Brittany whose conduct was the subject of a petition to Louis XV. from the Parliament of Rennes. He was disgraced by Louis XVI. His son rehabilitated family honour with the Vicomte de Noailles and others, surrendering feudal privileges on the outbreak of the Revolution. The chateau here spoken of was never completed, and the title is now extinct.

resulted from a feudal arrangement, that the Grand Seigneur might keep his slaves the nearer to his call, as a man builds his stables near his house. This edifice is a considerable one, built by the present Duke; begun about twenty years ago, when he was exiled here during eight years. And, thanks to that banishment, the building went on nobly; the body of the house done, and the detached wings almost finished. But as soon as the sentence was reversed, the duke went to Paris, and has not been here since, consequently all now stands still. It is thus that banishment alone will force the French nobility to execute what the English do for pleasure—reside upon and adorn their estates. There is one magnificent circumstance, namely, an elegant and spacious theatre; it fills one of the wings. The orchestra is for twenty-four musicians, the number kept, fed, and paid, by the duke when here. This elegant and agreeable luxury, which falls within the compass of a very large fortune is known in every country in Europe except England: the possessors of great estates here preferring horses and dogs very much before any entertainment a theatre can yield. To Tonnance.[1]—25 miles.

The 24th. Many new and good country seats, of gentlemen, well built, and set off with gardens, plantations, &c. These are the effects of the wealth of Bourdeaux. These people, like other Frenchmen, eat little meat; in the town of Levrac five oxen only are killed in a year; whereas an English town with the same population would consume two or three oxen a week. A noble view towards Bourdeaux for many leagues, the river appearing in four or five places. Reach Langon,[2] and drink of its excellent white wine—32 miles.

The 25th.—Pass through Barsac,[3] famous also for its wines. They are now ploughing with oxen between the rows of the vines, the operation which gave Tull[4] the idea of horse-hoeing corn. Great population and country seats all the way. At Castres[5] the country changes to an un-

---

[1] Tonneins (Lot and Garonne).   [2] (Gironde.)
[3] (Gironde.)
[4] Tull, Jethro, agricultural writer who made the tour of Europe, died 1740.
[5] (Tarn.)

interesting flat. Arrive at Bourdeaux,[1] through a continued village.—30 miles.

26th. Much as I had read and heard of the commerce, wealth, and magnificence of this city, they greatly surpassed my expectations. Paris did not answer at all, for it is not to be compared to London; but we must not name Liverpool in competition with Bourdeaux. The grand feature here, of which I had heard most, answers the least; I mean the quay, which is respectable only for length, and its quantity of business, neither of which, to the eye of a stranger, is of much consequence, if devoid of beauty. The row of houses is regular, but without either magnificence or beauty. It is a dirty, sloping, muddy shore; parts without pavement, incumbered with filth and stones; barges lie here for loading and unloading the ships, which cannot approach to what should be a quay. Here is all the dirt and disagreeable circumstances of trade, without the order, arrangement, and magnificence of a quay. Barcelona is unique in this respect. When I presumed to find fault with the buildings on the river, it must not be supposed that I include the whole; the crescent which is in the same line is better. The *place royale*, with the statute of Lewis XV. in the middle, is a fine opening, and the buildings which form it regular and handsome. But the quarter of the *chapeau rouge* is truly magnificent, consisting of noble houses, built, like the rest of the city, of white hewn stone. It joins the *chateau trompette*, which occupies near half a mile of the shore. This fort is bought of the king, by a company of speculators, who are now pulling it down with an intention of building a fine square and many new streets, to the amount of 1800 houses. I have seen a design of the square and the streets, and it would, if executed, be one of the most splendid additions to a city that is to be seen in Europe. This great work stands still at present through a fear of resumptions. The theatre, built about ten or twelve years ago, is by far the most magnificent in France. I have seen nothing that approaches it. The building is insulated; and fills up a space of 306 feet by 165, one end being the principal front,

[1] I leave the spelling of Bordeaux as Arthur Young wrote. Bourdeaux is a little town in the Drôme.

containing a portico the whole length of it, of twelve very large Corinthian columns. The entrance from this portico is by a noble vestibule, which leads not only to the different parts of the theatre, but also to an elegant oval concert-room and saloons for walking and refreshments. The theatre itself is of a vast size; in shape the segment of an oval. The establishment of actors, actresses, singers, dancers, orchestra, &c. speak the wealth and luxury of the place. I have been assured, that from thirty to fifty louis a night have been paid to a favourite actress from Paris. Larrive,[1] the first tragic actor of that capital, is now here, at 500 liv. (211. 12s. 6d.) a night, with two benefits. Dauberval, the dancer and his wife (the Mademoiselle Theodore of London) are retained as principal ballet-master and first female dancer, at a salary of 28,000 liv. (1225l.) Pieces are performed every night, Sundays not excepted, as every where in France. The mode of living that takes place here among merchants is highly luxurious. Their houses and establishments are on expensive scales. Great entertainments, and many served on plate: high play is a much worse thing;—and the scandalous chronicle speaks of merchants keeping the dancing and singing girls of the theatre at salaries which ought to import no good to their credit. This theatre, which does so much honour to the pleasures of Bourdeaux, was raised at the expence of the town, and cost 270,000l. The new tide corn-mill, erected by a company, is very well worth viewing. A large canal is dug and formed in masonry of hewn stone, the walls four feet thick, leading under the building for the tide coming in, to turn the water wheels. It is then conducted in other equally well formed canals to a reservoir; and when the tide returns it gives motion to the wheels again. Three of these canals pass under the building for containing 24 pairs of stones. Every part of the work is on a scale of solidity and duration, admirably executed. The estimate of the expence is 8,000,000 liv. (350,000l.); but I know not how to credit such a sum. How far the erection of steam engines to do the same business would have been found a cheaper method, I shall

---

[1] Larrive, Henri, 1733-1802, celebrated actor and vocalist.

not enquire; but I should apprehend that the common water mills, on the Garonne, which start without such enormous expences for their power, must in the common course of common events ruin this company. The new houses that are building in all quarters of the town, mark, too clearly to be misunderstood, the prosperity of the place. The skirts are every where composed of new streets; with still newer ones marked out, and partly built. These houses are in general small, or on a middling scale, for inferior tradesmen. They are all of white stone, and add, as they are finished, much to the beauty of the city. I enquired into the date of these new streets, and found that four or five years were in general the period: that is to say, since the peace; and from the colour of the stone of those streets next in age, it is plain that the spirit of building was at a stop during the war. Since the peace they had gone on with great activity. What a satire on the government of the two kingdoms, to permit in one the prejudices of manufacturers and merchants, and in the other the insidious policy of an ambitious court, to hurry the two nations for ever into wars that check all beneficial works, and spread ruin where private exertion was busied in deeds of prosperity. The rent of houses and lodgings rises every day, as it has done since the peace considerably, at the same time that so many new houses have been and are erecting, unites with the advance in the prices of every thing: they complain that the expences of living have risen in ten years full 30 per cent.—There can hardly be a clearer proof of an advance in prosperity.

The commercial treaty with England being a subject too interesting not to have demanded attention, we made the necessary enquiries.—Here it is considered in a very different light from Abbeville and Rouen: at Bourdeaux they think it a wise measure, that tends equally to the benefit of both countries. This is not the place for being more particular on the trade of this town.

We went twice to see Larrive do his two capital parts of the Black Prince in Mons. du Belloy's [1] Piere le Cruel, and Philoctete, which gave me a very high idea of the French

---

[1] De Belloy, a dramatic writer famous in his day, now forgotten.

theatre. The inns at this city are excellent; the hotel d'Angletere and the Prince of Asturias; at the latter we found every accommodation to be wished, but with an inconsistence that cannot be too much condemned: we had very elegant apartments, and were served on plate, yet the necessary-house the same temple of abomination that is to be met in a dirty village.

The 28th. Leave Bourdeaux;—cross the river by a ferry, which employs twenty-nine men and fifteen boats, and lets at 18,000 liv. (787l.) a year. The view of the Garonne is very fine, appearing to the eye twice as broad as the Thames at London; and the number of large ships lying in it, makes it, I suppose, the *richest* water view that France has to boast. From hence to the Dordonne, a noble river, though much inferior to the Garonne, which we cross by another ferry that lets at 6000 liv. Reach Cavignac.[1]—20 miles.

The 29th. To Barbesieux,[2] situated in a beautiful country, finely diversified and wooded; the marquisate of which, with the chateau, belongs to the duke de la Rochefoucauld, whom we met here; he inherits this estate from the famous Louvois, the minister of Louis XIV. In this thirty-seven miles of country, lying between the great rivers Garonne, Dordonne, and Charente, and consequently in one of the best parts of France for markets, the quantity of waste land is surprising: it is the predominant feature the whole way. Much of these wastes belonged to the prince de Soubise,[3] who would not sell any part of them. Thus it is whenever you stumble on a Grand Seigneur, even one that was worth millions, you are sure to find his property desert. The duke of Bouillon's and this prince's are two of the greatest properties in France;

---

[1] (Gironde.)   [2] Barbézieux (Charente).
[3] The so-called "roi de la Maraude," who commanded the French forces during the régime of the " Reine Pompadour." His men gave him the above sobriquet because of the unlimited license allowed them to pillage and plunder. With an army demoralized by debauchery and want, the officers being followed by a train of courtezans, pedlars, and hangers-on, the soldiers dependent entirely on black mail, he set out for the defeat of Rosbach. For a victory gained by another later, Madame de Pompadour gave Soubise a marshal's bâton. See H. Martin, vol xv. pp. 517-21.

and all the signs I have yet seen of their greatness, are wastes, *landes*, deserts, fern, ling.—Go to their residence, wherever it may be, and you would probably find them in the midst of a forest, very well peopled with deer, wild boars, and wolves. Oh! if I was the legislator of France for a day, I would make such great lords skip again.[1] We supped with the duke de la Rochefoucauld; the provincial assembly of Saintonge is soon to meet, and this nobleman, being the president, is waiting for their assembling.

The 30th. Through a chalk country, well wooded, though without inclosures to Angoulême; the approach to that town is fine; the country around being beautiful with the fine river Charente,[2] here navigable, flowing through it, the effect striking.—25 miles.

The 31st. Quitting Angoulême, pass through a country almost covered with vines, and across a noble wood belonging to the duchess d'Anville, mother of the duke de la Rochefoucauld, to Verteul,[3] a chateau of the same lady, built in 1459, where we found every thing that travellers could wish in a hospitable mansion. The Emperor Charles V. was entertained here by Anne de Polignac, widow of Francis II. count de la Rochefoucauld, and that prince, said aloud, *n'avoir jamais été en maison qui sentit mieux sa grande vertu honnêteté & seigneurie que celle la*.—It is excellently kept; in thorough repair, fully furnished, and all in order, which merits praise, considering that the family rarely are here for more than a few days in a year, having many other and more considerable seats in different parts of the kingdom. If this just attention to the interests of posterity was more general, we should not see the melancholy spectacle of ruined chateaus in so many parts of France. In the gallery is a range of portraits from the tenth century; by one of which it appears, that this estate

---

[1] I can assure the reader that these sentiments were those of the moment; the events that have taken place almost induced me to strike many such passages out, but it is fairer to all parties to leave them.—*Author's note.*

[2] "The fairest river in my kingdom," said Henri IV.

[3] Verteuil, in the valley of the Charente. The château has been in part reconstructed by M. de la Rochefoucauld, and is not to be confounded with the magnificent château de la Rochefoucauld, near Angoulême.

came by a Mademoiselle la Rochefoucauld, in 1470. The park, woods, and river Charente here are fine: the last abounds greatly in carp, tench, and perch. It is at any time easy to get from 50 to 100 brace of fish that weigh from three to 10lb. each: we had a brace of carp for supper, the sweetest, without exception, I ever tasted. If I pitched my tent in France, I should choose it to be by a river that gave such fish. Nothing provokes one so in a country residence as a lake, a river, or the sea within view of the windows, and a dinner every day without fish, which is so common in England.—27 miles.

SEPTEMBER 1st. Pass Caudec,[1] Ruffec,[2] Maisons-Blanches,[3] and Chaunay.[4] At the first of these places, view a very fine flour-mill built by the late count de Broglio,[5] brother of the marechal de Broglio, one of the ablest and most active officers in the French service. In his private capacity, his undertakings were of a national kind; this mill, an iron forge, and the project of a navigation, proved, that he had a disposition for every exertion that could, according to the prevalent ideas of the times, benefit his country; that is to say, in every way except the one in which it would have been effective—practical agriculture. This day's journey has been, with some exceptions, through a poor, dull, and disagreeable country.—35 miles.

The 2d. Poitou,[6] from what I see of it, is an unimproved, poor, and ugly country. It seems to want communication, demand, and activity of all kinds; nor does it, on an average, yield the half of what it might. The lower part of the province is much richer and better.

[1] (Charente.)   [2] *Ibid.*   [3] *Ibid.*   [4] *Ibid.*

[5] Father of the unfortunate Prince Claude Victor, who accepted command under the Convention, but refusing to acknowledge the Déchéance, was guillotined 1794.

[6] No part of France has more rapidly improved in our own time than Poitou, now forming the three departments of Vendée, Deux Sèvres, and la Vienne. I revisited La Vendée in 1885, after an interval of ten years, to find extraordinary progress: agriculture has made great strides, works of public utility have been erected, railways now intersect the country, and, owing to the indefatigable labours of peasant owners, hundreds of thousands of acres of waste land have been put under cultivation. The "unimproved, poor, and ugly country" of Arthur Young is now one vast garden. La Vendée is the region of large farms and stock raising. Mule breeding is carried on largely around Niort.—ED.

Arrive at Poitiers, which is one of the worst built towns I have seen in France; very large and irregular, but containing scarcely any thing worthy of notice, except the cathedral, which is well built, and very well kept.—The finest thing by far in the town is the promenade, which is the most extensive I have seen; it occupies a considerable space of ground, with gravelled walks, &c. excellently kept.—12 miles.

The 3d. A white chalky country to Chateaurault,[1] open, and thinly peopled, though not without country-seats. That town has some animation, owing to its navigable river, which falls into the Loire. There is a considerable cutlery manufacture: we were no sooner arrived, than our apartment was full of the wives and daughters of manufacturers, each with her box of knives, scissars, toys, &c. and with so much civil solicitude to have something bought, that had we wanted nothing it would have been impossible to let so much urgency prove vain. It is remarkable, as the fabrics made here are cheap, that there is scarcely any division of labour in this manufacture; it is in the hands of distinct and unconnected workmen, who go through every branch on their own account, and without assistance, except from their families.—25 miles.

The 4th. Pass a better country, with many chateaus, to Les Ormes,[2] where we stopped to see the seat built by the late count de Voyer d'Argenson. This chateau is a large handsome edifice of stone, with two very considerable wings for offices and strangers' apartments: the entrance is into a neat vestibule, at the end of which is the saloon, a circular marble room, extremely elegant and well furnished; in the drawing-room are paintings of the four French victories of the war of 1744: in every apartment there is a strong disposition to English furniture and modes. This pleasing residence belongs at present to the count d'Argenson. The late count who built it formed with the present duke of Grafton, in England, the scheme of a very agreeable party. The duke was to go over with his horses and pack of fox-hounds, and live here for some

---

[1] Châtellerault (Vienne).
[2] This château, with its fine gardens, still remains, and is in the possession of the Argenson family.

months, with a number of friends. It originated in the proposal to hunt French wolves with English fox-dogs. Nothing could be better planned than the scheme, for Les Ormes is large enough to have contained a numerous party; but the count's death destroyed the plan. This is a sort of intercourse between the nobility of two kingdoms, which I am surprised does not take place sometimes; it would vary the common scenes of life very agreeably, and be productive of some of the advantages of travelling in the most eligible way.—23 miles.

The 5th. Through a dead flat and unpleasant country, but on the finest road I have seen in France—nor does it seem possible that any should be finer; not arising from great exertions, as in Languedoc, but from being laid flat with admirable materials. Chateaus are scattered every where in this part of Touraine; but farm houses and cottages thin, till you come in sight of the Loire, the banks of which seem one continued village. The vale, through which that river flows, may be three miles over; a dead level of burnt russet meadow.

The entrance of Tours[1] is truly magnificent, by a new street of large houses, built of hewn white stone, with regular fronts. This fine street, which is wide, and with foot pavements on each side, is cut in a strait line through the whole city to the new bridge, of fifteen flat arches, each of seventy-five feet span. It is altogether a noble exertion for the decoration of a provincial town. Some houses remain yet to be built, the fronts of which are done; some reverend fathers are satisfied with their old habitations, and do not choose the expence of filling up the elegant design of the Tours projectors; they ought, however, to be unroosted if they will not comply, for fronts without houses behind them have a ridiculous appearance. From the tower of the cathedral there is an extensive view of the adjacent country; but the Loire, for so considerable a river, and for being boasted as the most beautiful in Europe, exhibits such a breadth of shoals and sands as to be almost subversive of beauty. In the chapel of the old palace of Louis XI. Les Plessis les Tours,[2] are three

---

[1] (Indre and Loire.)   [2] Plessis-lès-Tours.

pictures which deserve the travellers notice; a holy family, St. Catharine, and the daughter of Herod; they seem to be of the best age of Italian art. There is a very fine promenade here; long and admirably shaded by four rows of noble and lofty elms, which for shelter against a burning sun can have no superior; parallel with it is another on the rampart of the old walls, which looks down on the adjacent gardens; but these walks, of which the inhabitants have long boasted, are at present objects of melancholy; the corporation has offered the trees to sale, and I was assured they would be cut down the ensuing winter.—One would not wonder at an English corporation sacrificing the ladies' walk for plenty of turtle, venison, and madeira; but that a French one should have so little gallantry, is inexcusable.

The 9th. The count de la Rochefoucauld having a feverish complaint when he arrived here, which prevented our proceeding on the journey, it became the second day a confirmed fever; the best physician of the place was called in, whose conduct I liked much, for he had recourse to very little physick, but much attention to keep his apartment cool and airy; and seemed to have great confidence in leaving nature to throw off the malady that oppressed her. Who is it that says there is a great difference between a good physician and a bad one; yet very little between a good one and none at all?

Among other excursions, I took a ride on the banks of the Loire towards Saumur, and found the country the same as near Tours; but the chateaus not so numerous or good. Where the chalk hills advance perpendicularly towards the river, they present a most singular spectacle of uncommon habitations;[1] for a great number of houses are cut out of the white rock, fronted with masonry, and holes cut above for chimnies, so that you sometimes know not where the house is from which you see the smoke issuing. These cavern-houses are in some places in tires one above another. Some with little scraps of gardens have a pretty effect. In general, the proprietors occupy them; but many are let at 10, 12, and 15 liv. a year. The people I talked

[1] These strange dwellings are being superseded in Maine and Loire by neatly-built cottages, homes of peasant owners.

with seemed well satisfied with their habitations, as good and comfortable: a proof of the dryness of the climate. In England the rheumatism would be the chief inhabitant. Walked to the Benedictine convent of Marmoutier,[1] of which the cardinal de Rohan, at present here, is abbot.

The 10th. Nature, or the Tours doctor, having recovered the count, we set forward on our journey. The road to Chanteloup is made on an embankment, that secures a large level tract from floods. The country more uninteresting than I could have thought it possible for the vicinity of a great river to be.—View Chanteloup, the magnificent seat of the late duke de Choiseul.[2] It is situated on a rising ground, at some distance from the Loire, which in winter, or after great floods, is a fine object, but at present is scarcely seen. The ground-floor in front consists of seven rooms: the dining-room of about thirty by twenty, and the drawing-room thirty by thirty-three: the library is seventy-two by twenty, but now fitted up by the present possessor, the duke de Penthievre, with very beautiful tapestry from the Gobelins.—In the pleasure-ground, on a hill commanding a very extensive prospect; is a Chinese pagoda, 120 feet high, built by the duke, in commemoration of the persons who visited him in his exile. On the walls of the first room in it their names are engraved on marble tablets. The number and rank of the persons do honour to the duke and to themselves. The idea was a happy one. The forest you look down on from this building is very extensive; they say eleven leagues across: ridings are cut pointing to the pagoda; and when the duke was alive, these glades had the mischievous animation of a vast hunt, supported so liberally as to ruin the master of it, and transferred the property of this noble estate and residence from his family to the last hands I

---

[1] Now a ruin.

[2] The able and patriotic minister of Louis XV. who restored the French navy, effected the annexation of Lorraine and Corsica to the crown, expelled the Jesuits, and protected Poland. He was banished because he would not acknowledge the authority of the infamous Dubarry. " Tout ce qui restait de l'honneur Française à Versailles en sortit avec Choiseul." H. Martin, vol. xv. The château was destroyed in 1830.

should wish to see it in—a prince of the blood. Great lords love too much an environ of forest, boars, and huntsmen, instead of marking their residence by the accompanyment of neat and well cultivated farms, clean cottages, and happy peasants. In such a method of shewing their magnificence, rearing forests, gilding domes, or bidding aspiring columns rise, might be wanting; but they would have, instead of them, erections of comfort, establishments of ease, and plantations of felicity: and their harvest, instead of the flesh of boars, would be in the voice of chearful gratitude—they would see public prosperity flourish on its best basis of private happiness.—As a farmer, there is one feature which shews the duke had some merit; he built a noble cow-house; a platform leads along the middle, between two rows of mangers, with stalls for seventy-two, and another apartment, not so large, for others, and for calves. He imported 120 very fine Swiss cows, and visited them with his company every day, as they were kept constantly tied up. To this I may add the best built sheephouse I have seen in France: and I thought I saw from the pagoda part of the farm better laid out and ploughed than common in the country, so that he probably imported some ploughmen.—This has merit in it; but it was all the merit of banishment. Chanteloup would neither have been built nor decorated, nor furnished, if the duke had not been exiled. It was the same with the duke d'Aguillon. These ministers would have sent the country to the devil before they would have reared such edifices, or formed such establishments, if they had not both been sent from Versailles. View the manufacture of steel at Amboise,[1] established by the duke de Choiseul. Vineyards the chief feature of agriculture.—37 miles.

The 11th. To Blois,[2] an old town, prettily situated on the Loire, with a good stone bridge of eleven arches. We viewed the castle, for the historical monument it affords that has rendered it so famous. They shew the room where the council assembled, and the chimney in it before which the duke of Guise was standing when the king's page came to demand his presence in the royal closet: the door he was

---

[1] (Indre and Loire.)   [2] (Loir and Cher.)

entering when stabbed: the tapestry he was in the act of turning aside: the tower where his brother the cardinal suffered; with a hole in the floor into the dungeon of Louis XI. of which the guide tells many horrible stories, in the same tone, from having told them so often, in which the fellow in Westminster Abbey gives his monotonous history of the tombs. The best circumstance attending the view of the spots, or the walls within which great, daring, or important actions have been performed, is the impression they make on the mind, or rather on the heart of the spectator, for it is an emotion of feeling, rather than an effort of reflection. The murders, or political executions perpetrated in this castle, though not uninteresting, were inflicted on, and by men that command neither our love, nor our veneration. The character of the period, and of the men that figured in it, were alike disgusting. Bigotry and ambition, equally dark, insidious, and bloody, allow no feelings of regret. The parties could hardly be better employed than in cutting each others throats. Quit the Loire, and pass to Chambord. The quantity of vines is very great; they have them very flourishing on a flat poor blowing sand. How well satisfied would my friend Le Blanc be if his poorest sands at Cavenham gave him 100 dozen of good wine per acre per annum! See at one *coup d'œil* 2000 acres of them. View the royal chateau of Chambord,[1] built by that magnificent prince Francis I. and inhabited by the late marechal de Saxe. I had heard much of this castle, and it more than answered my expectation. It gives a great idea of the splendor of that prince. Comparing the centuries, and the revenues of Louis XIV. and Francis I. I prefer Chambord infinitely to Versailles. The apartments are large, numerous, and well contrived. I admired particularly the stone stair-case in the centre of the house, which, being in a double spiral line, contains two distinct stair-cases, one above another, by which means people are going up and down at the same time, without seeing each other. The four apartments in the attic, with arched stone roofs, were in no mean taste. One of these count Saxe turned into a neat well contrived theatre. We

[1] (Loir and Cher.)

were shewn the apartment which that great soldier occupied, and the room in which he died. Whether in his bed or not is yet a problem for anecdote hunters to solve. A report not uncommon in France was, that he was ran through the heart in a duel with the Prince of Conti, who came to Chambord for that purpose; and great care was taken to conceal it from the king (Louis XV.), who had such a friendship for the marechal, that he would certainly have driven the prince out of the kingdom. There are several apartments modernized, either for the marechal or for the governors that have resided here since. In one there is a fine picture of Louis XIV. on horseback. Near the castle are the barracks for the regiment of 1500 horse, formed by marechal de Saxe, and which Louis XV. gave him, by appointing them to garrison Chambord while their colonel made at his residence. He lived here in great splendour, and highly respected by his sovereign, and the whole kingdom.—The situation of the castle is bad; it is low, and without the least prospect that is interesting; indeed the whole country is so flat that a high ground is hardly to be found in it. From the battlements we saw the environs, of which the park or forest forms three-fourths; it contains within a wall about 20,000 arpents, and abounds with all sorts of game to a degree of profusion. Great tracts of this park are waste or under heath, &c. or at least a very imperfect cultivation: I could not help thinking, that if the king of France ever formed the idea of establishing one compleat and perfect farm under the turnip culture of England, here is the place for it. Let him assign the chateau for the residence of the director and all his attendants; and the barracks, which are now applied to no use whatever, for stalls for cattle, and the profits of the wood would be sufficient to stock and support the whole undertaking.[1] What comparison between the utility of such an establishment, and that of a much greater expence applied here at present for supporting a wretched haras (stud), which has not a tendency but to mischief! I may,

[1] Numerous schools of agriculture, to which are attached model farms, now exist in France, supported by the State. State-paid professors of agriculture who lecture gratuitously in the country are now appointed to many chef-lieux.

however, recommend such agricultural establishments; but they never were made in any country, and never will be, till mankind are governed on principles absolutely contrary to those which prevail at present—until something more is thought requisite for a national husbandry than academies and memoirs.—35 miles.

The 12th. In two miles from the park wall regain the high road on the Loire. In discourse with a vigneron, we were informed that it froze this morning hard enough to damage the vines; and I may observe, that for four or five days past the weather has been constantly clear, with a bright sun, and so cold a north-east wind as to resemble much our cold clear weather in England in April; we have all our great coats on the day through. Dine at Clarey,[1] and view the monument of that able but bloody tyrant Louis XI. in white marble; he is represented in a kneeling posture, praying forgiveness, I suppose, which doubtless was promised him by his priests for his basenesses and his murders. Reach Orleans.—30 miles.

The 13th. Here my companions, wanting to return as soon as possible to Paris, took the direct road thither; but, having travelled it before, I preferred that by Petivier[2] in the way to Fountainbleau. One motive for my taking this road was its passing by Denainvilliers, the seat of the late celebrated Mons. du Hamel,[3] and where he made those experiments in agriculture which he has recited in many of his works. At Petivier I was just by, and walked thither for the pleasure of viewing grounds I had read of so often, considering them with a sort of classic reverence. His *homme d'affaire*, who conducted the farm, being dead, I could not get many particulars to be depended upon. Mons. Fougeroux, the present possessor, was not at home, or I should doubtless have had all the information I wished. I examined the soil, a principal point in all ex-

---

[1] Notre Dame de Cléry (Loiret).
[2] Pithivier (Loiret).
[3] The works of this celebrated writer on rural economy and vegetable physiology have been translated into English. "A Practical Treatise on Husbandry," London, 1750; "The Elements of Agriculture," translated by Philip Miller, London, 1764. Duhamel died 1782. The château still exists.

periments, when conclusions are to be drawn from them; and I also took notes of the common husbandry. Learning from the labourer who attended me that the drill-ploughs, &c., were yet in being, on a loft in one of the offices, I viewed them with pleasure, and found them as well as I can remember, very accurately represented in the plates which their ingenious author has given. I was glad to find them laid up in a place out of common traffic, where they may remain safe till some other farming traveller, as enthusiastic as myself, may view the venerable remains of a useful genius. Here is a stove and bath for drying wheat, which he also has described. In an inclosure behind the house is a plantation of various curious exotic trees, finely grown, also several rows of ash, elm, and poplar along the roads, near the chateau, all planted by Mons. du Hamel. It gave me still greater pleasure to find that Denainvilliers is not an inconsiderable estate. The lands extensive; the chateau respectable; with offices, gardens, &c. that prove it the residence of a man of fortune; from which it appears, that this indefatigable author, however he might have failed in some of his pursuits, met with that reward from his court which did it credit to bestow; and that he was not like others, left in obscurity to the simple rewards which ingenuity can confer on itself. Four miles before Malsherbs [1] a fine plantation of a row of trees on each side the road begins, formed by Mons. de Malsherbs, and is a striking instance of attention to decorating an open country. More than two miles of them are mulberries. They join his other noble plantations at Malsherbs, which contain a great variety of the most curious trees that have been introduced in France.—36 miles.

The 14th. After passing three miles through the forest of Fountainbleau, arrive at that town, and view the royal palace, which has been so repeatedly added to by several kings, that the share of Francis I. its original founder, is not easily ascertained. He does not appear to such advantage as at Chambord. This has been a favourite with the Bourbons, from there having been so many Nimrods of that family. Of the apartments which are shewn here,

[1] (Loiret.) The château of Malesherbes still belongs to the descendants of the noble defender of Louis XVI. here mentioned.

the king's, the queen's, monsieur's, and madame's, are the chief. Gilding seems the prevalent decoration: but in the queen's cabinet it is well and elegantly employed. The painting of that delicious little room is exquisite; and nothing can exceed the extremity of ornament that is here with taste bestowed. The tapestries of Beauvais and the Gobelins, are seen in this palace to great advantage. I liked to see the gallery of Francis I. preserved to its ancient state, even to the andirons in the chimney, which are those that served that monarch. The gardens are nothing; and the grand canal, as it is called, not to be compared with that at Chantilly. In the pond that joins the palace, are carp as large and as tame as the Prince of Condè's. The landlord of the inn at Fountainbleau thinks that royal palaces should not be seen for nothing; he made me pay 10 liv. for a dinner, which would have cost me not more than half the money at the star and garter at Richmond. Reach Meulan.[1]—34 miles.

The 15th. Cross, for a considerable distance, the royal oak forest of Senár.[2]—About Montgeron,[3] all open fields, which produce corn and partridges to eat it, for the number is enormous. There is on an average a covey of birds on every two acres, besides favourite spots, where they abound much more. At St. George[4] the Seine is a much more beautiful river than the Loire. Enter Paris once more, with the same observation I made before, that there is not one-tenth of the motion on the roads around it that there is around London. To the hotel de la Rochefoucauld.—20 miles.

The 16th. Accompanied the count de la Rochefoucauld to Liancourt.—38 miles.

I went thither on a visit for three or four days; but the whole family contributed so generally to render the place in every respect agreeable, that I staid more than three weeks. At about half a mile from the chateau is a range of hill that was chiefly a neglected waste: the duke of Liancourt has lately converted this into a plantation, with winding walks, benches, and covered seats, in the English

---

[1] Melun (Seine and Marne).   [2] Sénart (Seine and Marne).
[3] Montgeron (Seine and Oise).
[4] Villeneuve St. Georges (Seine and Oise).

style of gardening. The situation is very fortunate. These ornamented paths follow the edge of the declivity to the extent of three or four miles. The views they command are every where pleasing, and in some places great. Nearer to the chateau the dutchess of Liancourt has built a menagerie and dairy in a pleasing taste. The cabinet and anti-room are very pretty; the saloon elegant, and the diary entirely constructed of marble. At a village near Liancourt, the duke has established a manufacture of linen and stuffs mixed with thread and cotton, which promises to be of considerable utility; there are 25 looms employed, and preparations making for more. As the spinning for these looms is also established, it gives employment to great numbers of hands who were idle, for they have no sort of manufacture in the country though it is populous. Such efforts merit great praise. Connected with this is the execution of an excellent plan of the duke's for establishing habits of industry in the rising generation. The daughters of the poor people are received into an institution to be educated to useful industry: they are instructed in their religion, taught to write and read, and to spin cotton: are kept till marriageable, and then a regulated proportion of their earnings given them as a marriage portion. There is another establishment of which I am not so good a judge; it is for training the orphans of soldiers to be soldiers themselves. The duke of Liancourt has raised some considerable buildings for their accommodation well adapted to the purpose. The whole is under the superintendance of a worthy and intelligent officer, Mons. le Roux, captain of dragoons, and croix de St. Louis, who sees to every thing himself. There are at present 120 boys, all dressed in uniform.—My ideas have all taken a turn which I am too old to change: I should have been better pleased to see 120 lads educated to the plough, in habits of culture superior to the present; but certainly the establishment is humane, and the conduct of it excellent.[1]

[1] A French traveller, Vaysse de Villiers, visiting Liancourt in 1816, gives a delightful picture of the progress effected by this true humanitarian; numerous industries established, and agriculture furthered by the introduction of hemp, flax, colza, the hop, the vine, besides many vegetables hitherto unknown in these regions.

The ideas I had formed, before I came to France, of a country residence in that kingdom, I found at Liancourt to be far from correct. I expected to find it a mere transfer of Paris to the country, and that all the burthensome forms of a city were preserved, without its pleasures; but I was deceived; the mode of living, and the pursuits, approach much nearer to the habits of a great nobleman's house in England, than would commonly be conceived. A breakfast of tea for those that chose to repair to it; riding, sporting, planting, gardening, till dinner, and that not till half after two o'clock, instead of their old fashioned hour of twelve; music, chess, and the other common amusements of a rendezvouz-room, with an excellent library of seven or eight thousand volumes, were well calculated to make the time pass agreeably; and to prove that there is a great approximation in the modes of living at present in the different countries of Europe. Amusements, in truth, ought to be numerous within doors; for, in such a climate, none are to be depended on without: the rain that has fallen here is hardly credible. I have, for five-and-twenty years past, remarked in England, that I never was prevented by rain from taking a walk every day without going out while it actually rains; it may fall heavily for many hours; but a person who watches an opportunity gets a walk or a ride. Since I have been at Liancourt, we have had three days in succession of such incessantly heavy rain, that I could not go an hundred yards from the house to the duke's pavilion, without danger of being quite wet. For ten days more rain fell here, I am confident, had there been a guage to measure it, than ever fell in England in thirty. The present fashion in France, of passing some time in the country is new; at this time of the year, and for many weeks past, Paris is, comparatively speaking, empty. Every body that have country-seats are at them; and those who have none visit others who have. This remarkable revolution in the French manners is certainly one of the best customs they have taken from England; and its introduction was effected the easier, being assisted by the magic of Rousseau's writings. Mankind are much indebted to that splendid genius, who, when living, was hunted from country to country, to seek an asylum, with as much venom as if he had been a mad dog; thanks to the vile spirit of bigotry, which has not yet received its death's wound. Women of the first fashion in France are now ashamed of not nursing their own children; and stays are universally proscribed from the bodies of the poor infants, which were for so many ages tortured in them, as they are still in Spain. The country residence may not have effects equally obvious; but they will be no less sure in the end, and in all respects beneficial to every class in the state.

The duke of Liancourt being president of the provincial assembly of the election of Clermont,[1] and passing several days there in business, asked me to dine with the assembly, as he said there were to be some considerable farmers present. These assemblies, which had been proposed many years past by the French patriots, and especially by the marquis de Mirabeau,[2] the celebrated *l'ami des hommes*; which had been treated by M. Necker, and which were viewed with eyes of jealousy by certain persons who wished for no better government than one whose abuses were the chief foundation of their fortunes; these assemblies were to me interesting to see. I accepted the invitation with pleasure. Three considerable farmers, renters, not proprietors of land, were members, and present. I watched their carriage narrowly, to see their behaviour in the presence of a great lord of the first rank, considerable property, and high in royal favour; and it was with pleasure that I found them behaving with becoming ease and freedom, and though modest, and without anything like flippancy, yet without any obsequiousness offensive to English ideas. They started their opinions freely, and adhered to them with becoming confidence. A more singular spectacle, was to see two ladies present at a dinner of this sort, with five or six and twenty gentlemen; such a thing could not happen in England. To say that the French manners

---

[1] Clermont de l'Oise (Oise).
[2] Father and persecutor of the great tribune. His famous pamphlet " L'Ami des Hommes," was followed by the " Théorie de l'Impôt," which consigned its author to the Bastille. " L'Ami des hommes et le tyran de sa famille," is the historic verdict passed on the father of Mirabeau.—H. Martin, vol. xvi., p. 180.

in this respect, are better than our own, is the assertion of an obvious truth. If the ladies are not present at meetings where the conversation has the greatest probability of turning on subjects of more importance than the frivolous topics of common discourse, the sex must either remain on one hand in ignorance, or, on the other, filled with the foppery of over education, learned, affected, and forbidding. The conversation of men, not engaged in trifling pursuits, is the best school for the education of a woman.

The political conversation of every company I have seen has turned much more on the affairs of Holland than on those of France. The preparations going on for a war with England, are in the mouths of all the world; but the finances of France are in such a state of derangement, that the people best informed assert a war to be impossible; the marquis of Verac, the late French ambassador at the Hague, who was sent thither, as the English politicians assert, expressly to bring about a revolution in the government, has been at Liancourt three days. It may easily be supposed, that he is cautious in what he says in such a mixed company; but it is plain enough, that he is well persuaded that that revolution, change, or lessening the Stadtholder's power; that plan, in a word, whatever it was, for which he negotiated in Holland, had for some time been matured and ready for execution, almost without a possibility of failure, had the count de Vergennes consented, and not spun out the business by refinement on refinement, to make himself the more necessary to the French cabinet; and it unites with the idea of some sensible Dutchmen, with whom I have conversed on the subject.

During my stay at Liancourt, my friend Lazowski accompanied me on a little excursion of two days to Ermenonville, the celebrated seat of the marquis de Girardon. We passed by Chantilly to Morefountain,[1] the country-seat of Mons. de Morefountain, *prevost des merchands* of Paris; the place has been mentioned as decorated in the English style. It consists of two scenes; one a garden of winding walks, and ornamented with a profusion of temples, benches, grottos, columns, ruins, and I know not what: i

---

[1] Mortefontaine (Oise).

hope the French who have not been in England do not consider this as the English taste. It is in fact as remote from it as the most regular stile of the last age. The water view is fine. There is a gaiety and chearfulness in it that contrast well with the brown and unpleasing hills that surround it, and which partake of the waste character of the worst part of the surrounding country. Much has been done here; and it wants but few additions to be as perfect as the ground admits.

Reach Ermenonville,[1] through another part of the prince of Condè's forest, which joins the ornamented grounds of the marquis Girardon.[2] This place, after the residence and death of the persecuted but immortal Rousseau, whose tomb every one knows is here, became so famous as to be resorted to very generally. It has been described, and plates published of the chief views; to enter into a particular description would therefore be tiresome, I shall only make one or two observations, which I do not recollect having been touched on by others. It consists of three distinct water scenes; or of two lakes and a river. We were first shewn that which is so famous for the small isle of poplars, in which reposes all that was mortal of that extraordinary and inimitable writer. This scene is as well imagined, and as well executed as could be wished. The water is between forty and fifty acres; hills rise from it on both sides, and it is sufficiently closed in by tall wood at both ends, to render it sequestered. The remains of departed genius stamp a melancholy idea, from which decoration would depart too much, and accordingly there is little. We viewed the scene in a still evening. The declining sun threw a lengthened shade on the lake, and silence seemed to repose on its unruffled bosom; as some poet says, I forget who. The worthies to whom the temple of philosophers is dedicated, and whose names are marked on the columns, are NEWTON, *Lucem.*—DESCARTES. *Nil in rebus inane.*—VOLTAIRE, *Ridiculum.*—ROUSSEAU, *Naturam.*—And on another unfinished column, *Quis hoc perficiet?* The other

---

[1] Ermenonville (Oise), on the Soissons railway. Rousseau was interred here in the Ile de Peupliers, but his remains were removed to the Panthéon in 1794.

[2] Marquis de Girardin, the friend of Rousseau, died 1808.

lake is larger; it nearly fills the bottom of the vale, around which are some rough, rocky, wild, and barren sand hills; either broken or spread with heath; in some places wooded, and in others scattered thinly with junipers. The character of the scene is that of wild and undecorated nature, in which the hand of art was meant to be concealed as much as was consistent with ease of access. The last scene is that of a river, which is made to wind through a lawn, receding from the house, and broken by wood: the ground is not fortunate; it is too dead a flat, and no where viewed to much advantage.

From Ermenonville we went, the morning after, to Brasseuse,[1] the seat of Madame du Pont, sister to the dutchess of Liancourt. What was my surprize at finding this viscountess a great farmer! A French lady, young enough to enjoy all the pleasures of Paris, living in the country and minding her farm, was an unlooked for spectacle. She has probably more lucerne than any other person in Europe—250 arpents. She gave me, in a most unaffected and agreeable manner, both lucerne and dairy intelligence; but of that more elsewhere. Returned to Liancourt by Pont,[2] where there is a handsome bridge, of three arches, the construction uncommon, each pier consisting of four pillars, with a towing-path under one of the arches for the barge-horses, the river being navigable.

Amongst the morning amusements I partook at Liancourt was *la chasse*. In deer shooting, the sportsmen place themselves at distances around a wood, then beat it, and seldom more than one in a company gets a shot; it is more tedious than is easily conceived: like angling, incessant expectation, and perpetual disappointment. Partridge and hare shooting are almost as different from that of England. We took this diversion in the fine vale of Catnoir,[3] five or six miles from Liancourt; arranging ourselves in a file at about thirty yards from person to person, and each with a servant and a loaded gun, ready to present when his master fires: thus we marched across and cross the vale, treading up the game. Four or five brace of hares, and twenty

---

[1] (Oise).   [2] Pont St. Maixence (Oise).   [3] Catenoy (Oise).

brace of partridges were the spoils of the day. I like this mode of shooting but little better than waiting for deer. The best circumstance to me of exercise in company (it was not so once) is the festivity of the dinner at the close of the day. To enjoy this, it must not be pushed to great fatigue. Good spirits, after violent exercise, are always the affectation of silly young folks (I remember being that sort of fool myself, when I was young), but with something more than moderate, the exhilaration of body is in unison with the flow of temper, and agreeable company is then delicious On such days as these we were too late for the regular dinner, and had one by ourselves, with no other dressing than the refreshment of clean linen; and these were not the repasts when the dutchess's champaigne had the worst flavour. A man is not worth hanging that does not drink a little too much on such occasions: *mais prenez-y-garde*: repeat it often; and make it a mere drinking party, the lustre of the pleasure fades, and you become what *was* an English fox-hunter. One day while we were thus dining *à l'Anglais*, and drinking the plough, the chace, and I know not what, the dutchess of Liancourt and some of her ladies came in sport to see us. It was a moment for them to have betrayed ill-nature in the contempt of manners not French, which they might have endeavoured to conceal under a laugh:—but nothing of this; it was a good humoured curiosity; a natural inclination to see others pleased and in spirits. *Ils ont été de grands chasseurs aujourd'hui*, said one. *Oh! ils s'applaudissent de leurs exploites.* Do they drink the gun? said another. *Leurs maitresses certainement*, added a third. *J'aime a les voir en gaieté; il y a quelque chose d'aimable dans tout ceci.* To note such trifles may seem superfluous to many: but what is life when trifles are withdrawn? and they mark the temper of a nation better than objects of importance. In the moments of council, victory, flight, or death, mankind, I suppose, are nearly the same. Trifles discriminate better, and the number is infinite that gives me an opinion of the good temper of the French. I am fond neither of a man nor a recital that can appear only on stilts and dressed in holiday geers. It is every-day feelings that decide the colour of our lives; and he who values them the most plays the best for the stake of happiness. But it is time to quit Liancourt, which I do with regret. Take leave of the good old dutchess, whose hospitality and kindness ought long to be remembered.—51 miles.

The 9th, 10th, and 11th. Return by Beauvais[1] and Pontoise,[2] and enter Paris for the fourth time, confirmed in the idea that the roads immediately leading to that capital are deserts, comparatively speaking, with those of London. By what means can the connnection be carried on with the country? The French must be the most stationary people upon earth, when in a place they must rest without a thought of going to another. Or the English must be the most restless; and find more pleasure in moving from one place to another, than in resting to enjoy life in either. If the French nobility went to their country seats only when exiled there by the court, the roads could not be more solitary.—25 miles.

The 12th. My intention was to take lodgings; but on arriving at the hotel de la Rochefoucauld, I found that my hospitable dutchess was the same person at the capital as in the country; she had ordered an apartment to be ready for me. It grows so late in the season, that I shall make no other stay in this capital than what will be necessary for viewing public buildings. This will unite well enough with delivering some letters I brought to a few men of science; and it will leave me the evenings for the theatres, of which there are many in Paris. In throwing on paper a rapid *coup d'œil*, of what I see of a city, so well known in England, I shall be apt to delineate my own ideas and feelings, perhaps more than the objects themselves; and be it remembered, that I profess to dedicate this careless itinerary to trifles, much more than to objects that are of real consequence. From the tower of the cathedral, the view of Paris is complete. It is a vast city, even to the eye that has seen London from St. Paul's; being circular, gives an advantage to Paris; but a much greater is the atmosphere. It is now so clear, that one would suppose it the height of summer: the clouds of coal-smoke that envelope London, always prevent a distinct view of

---

[1] (Oise.)   [2] (Seine and Oise.)

that capital, but I take it to be one-third at least larger than Paris. The buildings of the parliament-house [1] are disfigured by a gilt and taudry gate, and a French roof. The hotel des Monoies is a fine building; and the facade of the Louvre one of the most elegant in the world, because they have (to the eye) no roofs; in proportion as a roof is seen a building suffers. I do not recollect one edifice of distinguished beauty (unless with domes) in which the roof is not so flat as to be hidden, or nearly so. What eyes then must the French architects have had, to have loaded so many buildings with coverings of a height destructive of all beauty? Put such a roof as we see on the parliament-house or on the Thuilleries, upon the facade of the Louvre, and where would its beauty be?—At night to the opera,[2] which I thought a good theatre, till they told me it was built in six weeks; and then it became good for nothing in my eyes, for I suppose it will be tumbling down in six years. Durability is one of the essentials of building; what pleasure would a beautiful front of painted pasteboard give? The Alceste of Gluck was performed; that part by Mademoiselle St. Huberti, their first singer, an excellent actress. As to scenes, dresses, decorations, dancing, &c. this theatre beats the Haymarket to nothing.

The 13th. Across Paris to the rue des blancs Manteaux, to Mons. Broussonet, secretary of the Society of Agriculture; he is in Burgundy. Called on Mr. Cook from London, who is at Paris with his drill-plough,[3] waiting for weather to shew its performance to the duke of Orleans;

---

[1] The Palais de Justice, made over to the Parliament of Paris by Charles VII. Very little remains of the original building, which was almost as ancient as the Palais de Thermes. See Lalanne's "Dictionnaire historique de la France."

[2] The opera-house having been burnt in 1781, the Théâtre de la Porte St. Martin for a time used in its stead, was planned and built in seventy-five days. It was completely destroyed by fire during the Commune (1871), and has been since rebuilt.—Lalanne.

[3] At this time the improvement of the plough occupied the attention of all interested in agriculture. In spite of many improvements, the old system remained in vogue throughout the greater part of England, the plough being very heavy, two-wheeled and requiring four horses, a ploughman and a driver! The single-wheeled drill-plough was an immense advance.

this is a French idea, improving France by drilling. A man should learn to walk before he learns to dance. There is agility in cutting capers, and it may be done with grace; but where is the necessity to cut them at all. There has been much rain to day; and it is almost incredible to a person used to London, how dirty the streets of Paris are, and how horribly inconvenient and dangerous walking is without a foot-pavement. We had a large party at dinner, with politicians among them, and some interesting conversation on the present state of France. The feeling of every body seems to be that the archbishop[1] will not be able to do any thing towards exonerating the state from the burthen of its present situation; some think that he has not the inclination; others that he has not the courage; others that he has not the ability. By some he is thought to be attentive only to his own interest; and by others, that the finances are too much deranged to be within the power of any system to recover, short of the states-general of the kingdom; and that it is impossible for such an assembly to meet without a revolution in the government ensuing. All seem to think that something extraordinary will happen; and a bankruptcy is an idea not at all uncommon. But who is there that will have the courage to make it?

The 14th. To the benedictine abbey of St. Germain, to see pillars of African marble, &c. It is the richest abbey in France: the abbot has 300,000 liv. a year (13,125*l*.) I lose my patience at such revenues being thus bestowed; consistent with the spirit of the tenth century, but not with that of the eighteenth. What a noble farm would the fourth of this income establish! what turnips, what cabbages, what potatoes, what clover, what sheep, what wool! —Are not these things better than a fat ecclesiastic? If an active English farmer was mounted behind this abbot, I think he would do more good to France with half the income than half the abbots of the kingdom with the whole of theirs. Pass the bastile; another pleasant object to make agreeable emotions vibrate in a man's bosom. I search for good farmers, and run my head at every turn

---

[1] Loménie de Brienne, minister. See p. 97.

against monks and state prisoners.—To the arsenal, to wait on Mons. Lavoisier,[1] the celebrated chemist, whose theory of the non-existence of phlogiston, has made as much noise in the chemical world as that of Stahl, which established its existence. Dr. Priestly had given me a letter of introduction. I mentioned in the course of conversation his laboratory, and he appointed Tuesday. By the Boulevards, to the *Place Louis XV*,[2] which is not properly a square, but a very noble entrance to a great city. The facades of the two buildings erected are highly finished. The union of the *Place Louis XV*. with the champs Elisées, the gardens of the Thuilleries and the Seine is open, airy, elegant, and superb; and is the most agreeable and best built part of Paris; here one can be clean and breathe freely. But by far the finest thing I have yet seen at Paris is the *Halle aux bleds*, or corn market: it is a vast rotunda; the roof entirely of wood, upon a new principle of carpentry, to describe which would demand plates and long explanations; the gallery is 150 yards round, consequently the diameter is as many feet: it is as light as if suspended by the fairies. In the ground area, wheat, pease, beans, lentils, are stored and sold. In the surrounding divisions, flour on wooden stands. You pass by stair-cases doubly winding within each other to spacious apartments for rye, barley, oats, &c. The whole is so well planned, and so admirably executed, that I know of no public building that exceeds it in either France or England. And if an appropriation of the parts to the conveniences wanted, and an adaptation of every circumstance to the end required, in union with that elegance which is consistent with use, and that magnificence which results from stability and duration are the criteria of public edifices, I know nothing that equals it:—it has but one fault, and that is situation; it should have been upon the banks of the river, for the convenience of unloading barges without land carriage. In

---

[1] Lavoisier. guillotined in 1794, fell a victim to the proscription of the "fermiers-généraux," or collectors of the revenue, to which hated body he had belonged in 1769. His wife, daughter of a "fermier-général," escaped the fate of her husband, and married Count Romford in 1805, from whom she was shortly afterwards separated. She aided Lavoisier in his experiments and published his "Mémoires de Chimie." See for his efforts on behalf of French agriculture the work of MM. Pigeonneau and de Foville before named. [2] The Place de la Concorde.

the evening, to the *Comedie Italienne*,[1] the edifice fine; and the whole quarter regular and new built, a private speculation of the duke de Choiseul, whose family has a box entailed for ever.—L'Aimant jaloux. Here is a young singer, Mademoiselle Rénard, with so sweet a voice, that if she sung Italian, and had been taught in Italy, would have made a delicious performer.

To the tomb of Cardinal de Richlieu,[2] which is a noble production of genius: by far the finest statue I have seen. Nothing can be wished more easy and graceful than the attitude of the cardinal, nor more expressive nature than the figure of weeping science. Dine with my friend at the Palais Royale, at a coffee-house; well dressed people; every thing clean, good, and well served: but here, as every where else, you pay a good price for good things; we ought never to forget that a low price for bad things is not cheapness. In the evening to *l'Ecole des Peres*, at the *Comedie Francaise*, a crying *larmoyant* thing. This theatre, the principal one at Paris, is a fine building, with a magnificent portico. After the circular theatres of France, how can any one relish our ill contrived oblong holes of London?

The 16th. To Mons. Lavoisier, by appointment. Madame Lavoisier, a lively, sensible, scientific lady, had prepared a *dejeuné Anglois* of tea and coffee, but her conversation on Mr. Kirwan's Essay on Phlogiston,[3] which she is translating from the English, and on other subjects, which a woman of understanding, that works with her husband in his laboratory, knows how to adorn, was the best repast. That apartment, the operations of which

---

[1] The privilege of holding an opéra comique in Paris was first accorded in 1647, and this opera was afterwards amalgamated with the Comédie Italienne, under which title Louis XVI. granted state patronage to the company. When Arthur Young wrote, representations were given in a building occupying the site of the Opéra Comique, recently destroyed by fire. The Comédie Française mentioned above, was installed in the building erected in 1782, and burnt down in 1799, afterwards reconstructed, and now known as the Odéon. By the Théâtre Français alluded to further on, is evidently meant the above company.—Lalanne.

[2] This masterpiece of Girardon, hidden during the Revolution, is replaced in the church of the Sorbonne. The *pleureuses*, or weeping figures are portraits of the cardinal's nieces

[3] Richard Kirwan, 1734-1812, author of many scientific and philosophical works.

have been rendered so interesting to the philosophical world, I had pleasure in viewing. In the apparatus for aërial experiments, nothing makes so great a figure as the machine for burning inflammable and vital air, to make, or deposit water; it is a splendid machine. Three vessels are held in suspension with indexes for marking the immediate variations of their weights; two that are as large as half hogsheads, contain the one inflammable, the other the vital air, and a tube of communication passes to the third, where the two airs unite and burn; by contrivances, too complex to describe without plates, the loss of weight of the two airs, as indicated by their respective balances, equal at every moment to the gain in the third vessel from the formation or deposition of the water, it not being yet ascertained whether the water be actually made or deposited. If accurate (of which I must confess I have little conception), it is a noble machine. Mons. Lavoisier, when the structure of it was commended, said, *Mais oüi monsieur, & même par un artiste Francois!* with an accent of voice that admitted their general inferiority to ours. It is well known that we have a considerable exportation of mathematical and other curious instruments to every part of Europe, and to France amongst the rest. Nor is this new, for the apparatus with which the French academicians measured a degree in the polar circle was made by Mr. George Graham.[1] Another engine Mons. Lavoisier shewed us was an electrical apparatus inclosed in a balloon, for trying electrical experiments in any sort of air. His pond of quicksilver is considerable, containing 250lb. and his water apparatus very great, but his furnaces did not seem so well calculated for the higher degrees of heat as some others I have seen. I was glad to find this gentleman splendidly lodged, and with every appearance of a man of considerable fortune. This ever gives one pleasure: the employments of a State can never be in better hands than of men who thus apply the superfluity of their wealth. From the use that is generally made of money, one would think it the assistance of all others of the least consequence in affecting any business truly useful to mankind, many of

[1] Whitehurst's "Formation of the Earth," 2nd edit. p. 6.—Author's note.

the great discoveries that have enlarged the horizon of science having been in this respect the result of means seemingly inadequate to the end: the energic exertions of ardent minds, bursting from obscurity, and breaking the bands inflicted by poverty, perhaps by distress. To the *hotel des invalids*, the major of which establishment had the goodness to shew the whole of it. In the evening to Mons. Lomond,[1] a very ingenious and inventive mechanic, who has made an improvement of the jenny for spinning cotton. Common machines are said to make too hard a thread for certain fabrics, but this forms it loose and spongy. In electricity he has made a remarkable discovery: you write two or three words on a paper; he takes it with him into a room, and turns a machine inclosed in a cylindrical case, at the top of which is an electrometer, a small fine pith ball; a wire connects with a similar cylinder and electrometer in a distant apartment; and his wife, by remarking the corresponding motions of the ball, writes down the words they indicate: from which it appears that he has formed an alphabet of motions. As the length of the wire makes no difference in the effect, a correspondence might be carried on at any distance: within and without a besieged town, for instance; or for a purpose much more worthy, and a thousand times more harmless, between two lovers prohibited or prevented from any better connection. Whatever the use may be, the invention is beautiful. Mons. Lomond has many other curious machines, all the entire work of his own hands: mechanical invention seems to be in him a natural propensity. In the evening to the *Comedie Francaise*. Mola did the *Bourru Bienfaisant*, and it is not easy for acting to be carried to greater perfection.

The 17th. To Mons. l'Abbé Messier,[2] astronomer royal, and of the Academy of Sciences. View the exhibition, at the Louvre, of the Academy's paintings. For one history piece in our exhibitions at London here are ten; abundantly more than to balance the difference between an annual and

---

[1] No mention of this inventor of a mechanical system of telegraph occurs in Lalanne's biographical dictionary, but aerial telegraphy invented by Chappe was put into use by the Convention in 1794. See Lalanne. [2] Messier, Charles, 1770-1817.

biennial exhibition. Dined to-day with a party, whose conversation was entirely political. Mons. de Calonne's [1] *Requête au Roi* is come over, and all the world are reading and disputing on it. It seems, however, generally agreed that, without exonerating himself from the charge of the agiotage, he has thrown no inconsiderable load on the shoulders of the archbishop of Toulouze, the present premier, who will be puzzled to get rid of the attack. But both these ministers were condemned on all hands in the lump; as being absolutely unequal to the difficulties of so arduous a period. One opinion pervaded the whole company, that they are on the eve of some great revolution in the government: that every thing points to it: the confusion in the finances great; with a *deficit* impossible to provide for without the states-general of the kingdom, yet no ideas formed of what would be the consequence of their meeting: no minister existing, or to be looked to in or out of power, with such decisive talents as to promise any other remedy than palliative ones: a prince on the throne, with excellent dispositions, but without the resources of a mind that could govern in such a moment without ministers: a court buried in pleasure and dissipation; and adding to the distress, instead of endeavouring to be placed in a more independent situation: a great ferment amongst all ranks of men, who are eager for some change, without knowing what to look to, or to hope for: and a strong leaven of liberty, increasing every hour since the American revolution; altogether form a combination of circumstances that promise e'er long to ferment into motion, if

---

[1] It was the fate of Louis XVI. to have the worst ministers as well as the best; after Turgot and Malesherbes, Calonne and Loménie de Brienne, Archbishop of Toulouse. Called to a task for which Sully or Richelieu must have proved inadequate, Calonne played with the fortunes of France as a desperate gamester, doubling the stakes in the face of ruin During the space of a few years the loans had reached the figure of 1,250 millions, and the annual deficit of the budget, 115 millions. This revelation resulted in his fall. In 1789 he became the agent of the emigrant nobles at Turin. His successor Loménie de Brienne, Archbishop of Toulouse, afterwards of Sens, had, in the words of Mignet, only hopeless courses before him, and could decide upon none. The queen's favour followed him into exile, and he received a cardinal's hat, but went over to the popular side when revolution seemed the winning game. He committed suicide in 1794.—Mignet. vol. i., H. Martin, vol. xvi.

some master hand, of very superior talents, and inflexible courage, is not found at the helm to guide events, instead of being driven by them. It is very remarkable, that such conversation never occurs, but a bankruptcy is a topic: the curious question on which is, *would a bankruptcy occasion a civil war, and a total overthrow of the government?* The answers that I have received to this question, appear to be just: such a measure, conducted by a man of abilities, vigour, and firmness, would certainly not occasion either one or the other. But the same measure, attempted by a man of a different character, might possibly do both. All agree, that the states of the kingdom cannot assemble without more liberty being the consequence; but I meet with so few men that have any just ideas of freedom, that I question much the species of this new liberty that is to arise. They know not how to value the privileges of THE PEOPLE: as to the nobility and the clergy, if a revolution added any thing to their scale, I think it would do more mischief than good.[1]

The 18th. To the Gobelins, which is undoubtedly the first manufacture of tapestry in the world, and such an one as could be supported only by a crowned head. In the evening to that incomparable comedy *La Metromanie*, of Pyron, and well acted. The more I see of it the more I like the French theatre; and have no doubt in preferring it far to our own. Writers, actors, buildings, scenes, decorations, music, dancing, take the whole in a mass, and it is unrivalled by London. We have certainly a few brilliants of the first water; but throw all in the scales, and that of England kicks the beam. I write this passage with a lighter heart than I should do were it giving the palm to the French plough.

The 19th. To Charenton, near Paris, to see *l'Ecole Veterinaire*,[2] and the farm of the Royal Society of Agricul-

---

[1] In transcribing these papers for the press, I smile at some remarks and circumstances which events have since placed in a singular position; but I alter none of these passages; they explain what were the opinions in France, before the revolution, on topics of importance; and the events which have since taken place render them the more interesting. June, 1790.—*Author's note.*

[2] This veterinary school still exists.

ture. Mons. Chabert,[1] the directeur-general, received us with the most attentive politeness. Mons. Flandrein, his assistant, and son-in-law, I had had the pleasure of knowing in Suffolk. They shewed the whole veterinary establishment, and it does honour to the government of France. It was formed in 1766 : in 1783 a farm was annexed to it, and four other professorships established ; two for rural œconomy, one for anatomy, and another for chemistry.— I was informed that Mons. d'Aubenton, who is at the head of this farm with a salary of 6000 liv. a year, reads lectures of rural œconomy, particularly on sheep, and that a flock was for that purpose kept in exhibition. There is a spacious and convenient apartment for dissecting horses and other animals ; a large cabinet, where the most interesting parts of all domestic animals are preserved in spirits ; and also of such parts of their bodies that mark the visible effect of distempers. This is very rich. This, with a similar one near Lyons, is kept up (exclusive of the addition of 1783), at the moderate expence, as appears by the writings of M. Necker, of about 60,000 liv. (2600l.) Whence, as in many other instances, it appears that the most useful things cost the least. There are at present about one hundred elèves from different parts of the kingdom, as well as from every country in Europe, *except England*; a strange exception, considering how grossly ignorant our farriers are ; and that the whole expence of supporting a young man here does not exceed forty louis a-year; nor more than four years necessary for his complete instruction. As to the farm, it is under the conduct of a great naturalist, high in royal academies of science, and whose name is celebrated through Europe for merit in superior branches of knowledge. It would argue in me a want of judgment in human nature, to expect good practice from such men. They would probably think it beneath their pursuits and situation in life to be good ploughmen, turnip-hoers, and shepherds ; I should therefore betray my own ignorance of life, if I was to express any surprize at finding this farm in a situation that—I had rather forget than describe. In the evening, to a field much more successfully cultivated, Mademoiselle St. Huberti, in the Penelope of Picini.

[1] Philibert Chabert, 1734-1814.

The 20th. To the *Ecole Militaire*,[1] established by Louis XV. for the education of 140 youths, the sons of the nobility; such establishments are equally ridiculous and unjust. To educate the son of a man who cannot afford the education himself, is a gross injustice, if you do not secure a situation in life answerable to that education. If you do secure such a situation, you destroy the result of the education, because nothing but merit ought to give that security. You educate the children of men, who are well able to give the education themselves, you tax the people who cannot afford to educate their children, in order to ease those who can well afford the burthen; and in such institutions, this is sure to be the case. At night to *l'Ambigu Comique*,[2] a pretty little theatre, with plenty of rubbish on it. Coffee-houses on the boulevards, music, noise, and *filles* without end; every thing but scavengers and lamps. The mud is a foot deep; and there are parts of the boulevards without a single light.

The 21st. Mons. de Broussonet being returned from Burgundy, I had the pleasure of passing a couple of hours at his lodgings very agreeably. He is a man of uncommon activity, and possessed of a great variety of useful knowledge in every branch of natural history; and he speaks English perfectly well. It is very rare that a gentleman is seen better qualified for a post than Mons. de Broussonet for that which he occupies, of secretary to a Royal Society.

The 22d. To the bridge of Neuilié,[3] said to be the finest in France. It is by far the most beautiful one I have any where seen. It consists of five vast arches; flat, from the Florentine model; and all of equal span; a mode of building incomparably more elegant, and more striking than our system of different sized arches. To the machine at Marly; which ceases to make the least impression. Madame du Barré's residence, Lusienne,[4] is on the hill just above this machine; she has built a pavilion on the brow of the de-

---

[1] The Ecole Militaire was suppressed by the Revolution, and from that time the building has been used as cavalry barracks.
[2] Like most of the theatres mentioned here, since burnt and rebuilt.
[3] Neuilly, this famous bridge was built by Perronet.
[4] Lucienne, the pavilion of Madame Dubarry, still stands.

clivity, for commanding the prospect, fitted up and decorated with much elegance. There is a table formed of Seve[1] porcelain, exquisitely done. I forget how many thousand louis d'ors it cost. The French, to whom I spoke of Lusienne, exclaimed against mistresses and extravagance, with more violence than reason in my opinion. Who, in common sense, would deny a king the amusement of a mistress, provided he did not make a business of his plaything? *Mais Frederic le Grand avoit-il une maitresse, lui fasoit-il batir des pavillons, et les meubloit-il de tables de porcelaine?* No: but he had that which was fifty times worse: a king had better make love to a handsome woman than to one of his neighbour's provinces. The king of Prussia's mistress cost an hundred millions sterling, and the lives of 500,000 men; and before the reign of that mistress is over, may yet cost as much more. The greatest genius and talents are lighter than a feather, weighed philosophically, if rapine, war, and conquest, are the effects of them.

To St. Germain's, the terrace of which is very fine. Mons. de Broussonet met me here, and we dined with Mons. Breton, at the maréchal duc de Noailles, who has a good collection of curious plants. Here is the finest *sophora japonica*[2] I have seen.—10 miles.

The 23d. To Trianon, to view the Queen's *Jardin Anglois*. I had a letter to Mons. Richard, which procured admittance. It contains about 100 acres, disposed in the taste of what we read of in books of Chinese gardening, whence it is supposed the English style was taken. There is more of Sir William Chambers[3] here than of Mr. Brown[4] —more effort than nature—and more expence than taste. It is not easy to conceive any thing that art can introduce in a garden that is not here; woods, rocks, lawns, lakes, rivers, islands, cascades, grottos, walks, temples, and even

---

[1] Sèvres (Seine and Oise). The famous porcelain manufactory was established by Louis XV. in 1756.

[2] Japanese Japonica.

[3] Sir W. Chambers (1726-1796), an architect of distinction, laid out the royal gardens at Kew, wrote *inter alia*, " Dissertation on Chinese Gardening."

[4] Mr. Brown seems to be Robert Brown of Mickle, contributor to the " Edinburgh Farmers' Magazine," 1757-1831.

villages. There are parts of the design very pretty, and well executed. The only fault is too much crouding; which has led to another, that of cutting the lawn by too many gravel walks, an error to be seen in almost every garden I have met with in France. But the glory of *La Petite Trianon* is the exotic trees and shrubs. The world has been successfully rifled to decorate it. Here are curious and beautiful ones to please the eye of ignorance; and to exercise the memory of science. Of the buildings, the temple of love is truly elegant.

Again to Versailles. In viewing the king's apartment, which he had not left a quarter of an hour, with those slight traits of disorder that shewed he *lived* in it, it was amusing to see the blackguard figures that were walking unconfrouled about the palace, and even in his bed-chamber; men whose rags betrayed them to be in the last stage of poverty, and I was the only person that stared and wondered how the devil they got there. It is impossible not to like this careless indifference and freedom from suspicion. One loves the master of the house, who would not be hurt or offended at seeing his apartment thus occupied, if he returned suddenly; for if there was danger of this, the intrusion would be prevented. This is certainly a feature of that *good temper* which appears to me so visible every where in France. I desired to see the Queen's apartments, but I could not. Is her majesty in it? No. Why then not see it as well as the king's? *Ma foi, Mons. c'est un autre chose.* Ramble through the gardens, and by the grand canal, with absolute astonishment at the exaggerations of writers and travellers. There is magnificence in the quarter of the orangerie, but no beauty any where; there are some statues good enough to wish them under cover. The extent and breadth of the canal are nothing to the eye; and it is not in such good repair as a farmer's horse-pond. The menagerie is well enough, but nothing great. Let those who desire that the buildings and establishments of Louis XIV. should continue the impression made by the writings of Voltaire, go to the canal of Languedoc, and by no means to Versailles.—Return to Paris. —14 miles.

The 24th. With Mons. de Broussonet to the King's

cabinet of natural history and the botanical garden, which is in beautiful order. Its riches are well known, and the politeness of Mons. Thouin, which is that of a most amiable disposition, renders this garden the scene of other rational pleasures besides those of botany. Dine at the Invalides, with Mons. Parmentier,[1] the celebrated author of many œconomical works, particularly on the *boulangerie* of France. This gentleman, to a considerable mass of useful knowledge, adds a great deal of that fire and vivacity for which his nation has been distinguished, but which I have not recognized so often as I expected.

The 25th. This great city appears to be in many respects the most ineligible and inconvenient for the residence of a person of small fortune of any that I have seen; and vastly inferior to London. The streets are very narrow, and many of them crouded, nine tenths dirty, and all without foot-pavements. Walking, which in London is so pleasant and so clean, that ladies do it every day, is here a toil and a fatigue to a man, and an impossibility to a well dressed woman. The coaches are numerous, and, what are much worse, there are an infinity of one-horse cabriolets, which are driven by young men of fashion and their imitators, alike fools, with such rapidity as to be real nuisances, and render the streets exceedingly dangerous, without an incessant caution. I saw a poor child run over and probably killed, and have been myself many times blackened with the mud of the kennels. This beggarly practice, of driving a one-horse booby hutch about the streets of a great capital, flows either from poverty or wretched and despicable œconomy; nor is it possible to speak of it with too much severity. If young noblemen at London were to drive their chaises in streets without foot-ways, as their brethren do at Paris, they would speedily and justly get

---

[1] Parmentier was the apostle of the potato in France. Turgot had indeed introduced it as an article of human food into the Limousin and the south. Parmentier was mainly instrumental in extending its use throughout the entire country. The poor king aided him, and wore as a "button-hole," a potato blossom. This worthy follower of Olivier de Serres devoted his whole life to the solution of two problems, the arrest of periodic famines, and the increase of food supplies. He also greatly furthered the cultivation of maize and improved bread baking; died 1813.—See H. Martin, vol. xvi. p. 523.

very well threshed, or rolled in the kennel. This circumstance renders Paris an ineligible residence for persons, particularly families that cannot afford to keep a coach; a convenience which is as dear as at London. The *fiacres*, hackney-coaches, are much worse than at that city; and chairs there are none, for they would be driven down in the streets. To this circumstance also it is owing, that all persons of small or moderate fortune, are forced to dress in black, with black stockings; the dusky hue of this in company is not so disagreeable a circumstance as being too great a distinction; too clear a line drawn in company between a man that has a good fortune, and another that has not. With the pride, arrogance, and ill temper of English wealth this could not be borne; but the prevailing good humour of the French eases all such untoward circumstances. Lodgings are not half so good as at London, yet considerably dearer. If you do not hire a whole suite of rooms at an hotel, you must probably mount three, four, or five pair of stairs, and in general have nothing but a bedchamber. After the horrid fatigue of the streets, such an elevation is a delectable circumstance. You must search with trouble before you will be lodged in a private family, as gentlemen usually are at London, and pay a higher price. Servants wages are about the same as at that city. It is to be regretted that Paris should have these disadvantages, for in other respects I take it to be a most eligible residence for such as prefer a great city. The society for a man of letters, or who has any scientific pursuit, cannot be exceeded. The intercourse between such men and the great, which, if it is not upon an equal footing, ought never to exist at all, is respectable. Persons of the highest rank pay an attention to science and literature, and emulate the character they confer. I should pity the man who expected, without other advantages of a very different nature, to be well received in a brilliant circle at London, because he was a fellow of the Royal Society. But this would not be the case with a member of the Academy of Sciences at Paris; he is sure of a good reception every where. Perhaps this contrast depends in a great measure on the difference of the governments of the two countries. Politics are too much attended to in England to allow a due respect to be paid to any thing else; and should the French establish a freer government, academicians will not be held in such estimation, when rivalled in the public esteem by the orators who hold forth liberty and property in a free parliament.

The 28th. Quit Paris, and take the road to Flanders. Mons. de Broussonet was so obliging as to accompany me to Dugny, to view the farm of Mons. Creté de Palieul, a very intelligent cultivator. Take the road to Senlis:[1] at Dammertin,[2] I met by accident a French gentleman, a Mons. du Pré du St. Cotin. Hearing me conversing with a farmer on agriculture, he introduced himself as an amateur, gave me an account of several experiments he had made on his estate in Champagne, and promised a more particular detail; in which he was as good as his word.—22 miles.

The 29th. Pass Nanteul,[3] where the Prince of Condé has a chateau, to Villes-Coterets,[4] in the midst of immense forests belonging to the duke of Orleans. The crop of this country, therefore, is princes of the blood; that is to say, hares, pheasants, deer, boars!—26 miles.

The 30th. Soissons[5] seems a poor town, without manufactures, and chiefly supported by a corn-trade, which goes hence by water to Paris and Rouen.—25 miles.

The 31st. Coucy[6] is beautifully situated on a hill, with a fine vale winding beside it. At St. Gobin,[7] which is in the midst of great woods, I viewed the fabric of plate-glass the greatest in the world. I was in high luck, arriving about half an hour before they begun to run glasses for the day. Pass La Fere.[8] Reach St. Quintin,[9] where are considerable manufactures that employed me all the afternoon. From St. Gobin, are the most beautiful slate roofs I have any where seen.—30 miles.

NOVEMBER 1. Near Belle Angloise[10] I turned aside half a league to view the canal of Picardy, of which I had heard

[1] (Oise.)   [2] Dammartin (Seine and Marne).
[3] Nanteuil-le-Hardouin (Oise).   [4] Villers-Cotterets (Aisne).
[5] Soissons (*Ibid.*).   [6] Coucy (*Ibid.*).
[7] St. Gobain (*Ibid.*).   [8] La Fère (*Ibid.*).
[9] St. Quintin (*Ibid.*).   [10] Bellenglise (*Ibid.*).

much. In passing from St. Quintin to Cambray the country rises so much, that it was necessary to carry it in a tunnel under ground for a considerable depth, even under many vales as well as hills. In one of these vallies there is an opening for visiting it by an arched stair-case, on which I descended 134 steps to the canal, and, as this valley is much below the adjacent and other hills, the great depth at which it is dug, may be conceived. Over the door of the descent, is the following inscription:— *L'ann. 1781.—Mons. le Comte d'Agay etant intendant de cette province, Mons. Laurent de Lionni etant directeur de l'ancien & nouveau canal de Picardie, & Mons. de Champrosé inspecteur, Joseph II. Empereur Roi des Romaines, a parcourru en batteau le canal sous terrain depuis cet endroit jusques au puit, No. 20, le 28, & a temoigné sa satisfaction d'avoir vu cet ouvrage en ces termes:* "*Je suis fier d'etre homme, quand je vois qu'un de mes semblables a ose imaginer & executer un ouvrage aussi vaste et aussi hardie. Cette idea me leve l'ame.*"—These three Messieurs lead the dance here in a very French style. The great Joseph follows humbly in their train; and as to poor Louis XVI. at whose expence the whole was done, these gentlemen certainly thought that no name less than that of an emperor ought to be annexed to theirs. When inscriptions are fixed to public works, no names ought to be permitted but those of the king, whose merit patronizes, and the engineer or artist whose genius executes the work. As to a mob of intendants, directors, and inspectors, let them go to the devil! The canal at this place is ten French feet wide and twelve high, hewn entirely out of the chalk rock, imbedded, in which are many flints—no masonry. There is only a small part finished of ten toises long for a pattern, twenty feet broad and twenty high. Five thousand toises are already done in the manner of that part which I viewed; and the whole distance under ground, when the tunnel will be complete, is 7020 toises (each six feet) or about nine miles. It has already cost 1,200,000 liv. (52,500l.) and there wants 2,500,000 liv. (109,375l.) to complete it; so that the total estimate is near four millions. It is executed by shafts. At present there is not above five or six inches of water in it. This great work has stood still entirely since the administration of the archbishop of

Toulouze.¹ When we see such works stand still for want of money, we shall reasonably be inclined to ask, What are the services that continue supplied? and to conclude, that amongst kings, and ministers, and nations, œconomy is the first virtue:—without it, genius is a meteor; victory a sound; and all courtly splendour a public robbery.

At Cambray,² view the manufacture. These frontier towns of Flanders are built in the old style, but the streets broad, handsome, well paved, and lighted. I need not observe, that all are fortified, and that every step in this country has been rendered famous or infamous according to the feelings of the spectator, by many of the bloodiest wars that have disgraced and exhausted christendom. At the hotel de Bourbon I was well lodged, fed, and attended: an excellent inn.—22 miles.

The 2d. Pass Bouchaine³ to Valenciennes,⁴ another old town, which, like the rest of the Flemish ones, manifests more the wealth of former than of present times.—18 miles.

The 3d. To Orchees;⁵ and the 4th to Lisle,⁶ which is surrounded by more windmills for expressing the oil of coleseed, than are to be seen any where else I suppose in the world. Pass fewer drawbridges and works of fortification here than at Calais; the great strength of this place is in its mines and other *souteraines*. In the evening to the play.

The cry here for a war with England amazed me. Every one I talked with said, it was beyond a doubt the English had called the Prussian army into Holland; and that the motives in France for a war were numerous and manifest. It is easy enough to discover, that the origin of all this violence is the commercial treaty, which is execrated here, as the most fatal stroke to their manufactures they ever experienced. These people have the

---

[1] This canal was completed by Napoleon I. in 1810. A communication was thereby opened between the river Scheldt and the extreme eastern departments of France and the Atlantic through the rivers Somme, Seine and Loire.

[2] (Nord.) Famous for its *batiste* or cambric, so called after Baptiste, the inventor, whose statue adorns the Esplanade.

[3] Bouchain (Nord).   [4] (Nord).

[5] Orchies (*Ibid.*).   [6] Lille (*Ibid.*).

true monopolizing ideas; they would involve four-and-twenty millions of people in the certain miseries of a war, rather than see the interest of those who consume fabrics, preferred to the interest of those who make them. The advantages reaped by four-and-twenty millions of consumers are lighter than a feather compared with the inconveniences sustained by half a million of manufacturers. Meet many small carts in the town, drawn each by a dog: I was told by the owner of one, what appears to me incredible, that his dog would draw 700lb. half a league. The wheels of these carts are very high, relative to the height of the dog, so that his chest is a good deal below the axle.

The 6th. In leaving Lisle, the reparation of a bridge made me take a road on the banks of the canal, close under the works of the citadel. They appear to be very numerous, and the situation exceedingly advantageous, on a gently rising ground, surrounded by low watry meadows, which may with ease be drowned. Pass Darmentiers,[1] a large paved town. Sleep at Mont. Cassel.[2]—30 miles.

The 7th. Cassel is on the summit of the only hill in Flanders. They are now repairing the bason at Dunkirk,[3] so famous in history for an imperiousness in England, which she must have paid dearly for. Dunkirk, Gibraltar, and the statue of Louis XIV. in the *Place de Victoire*, I place in the same political class of national arrogance. Many men are now at work on this bason, and, when finished, it will not contain more than twenty or twenty-five frigates; and appears to an unlearned eye, a ridiculous object for the jealousy of a great nation, unless it professes to be jealous of privateers.—I made enquiries concerning the import of wool from England, and was assured that it was a very trifling object. I may here observe, that when I left the town, my little cloak-bag was examined as scrupulously as if I had just left England, with a cargo of prohibited goods, and again at a fort two miles of Dunkirk being a free port, the custom-house is at the gates.

---

[1] D'armentières or Armentières (Nord).
[2] Cassel on the Mont Cassel (Nord).
[3] (Nord.)

What are we to think of our woollen manufacturers in England, when suing for their wool-bill, of infamous memory, bringing one Thomas Wilkinson from Dunkirk quay, to the bar of the English House of Lords to *swear* that wool passes from Dunkirk without entry, duty, or any thing being required, at double custom-houses, for a check on each other, where they examine even a cloak-bag. On such evidence, did our legislature, in the true shop-keeping spirit, pass an act of fines, pains, and penalties against all the wool-growers of England. Walk to Rossendal[1] near the town, where Mons. le Brun has an inprovement on the Dunes, which he very obligingly shewed me. Between the town and that place are a great number of neat little houses, built with each its garden, and one or two fields inclosed of most wretched blowing *dune* sand, naturally as white as snow, but improved by industry. The magic of PROPERTY turns sand to gold.—18 miles.

The 8th. Leave Dunkirk, where the *Concierge*, a good inn, as indeed I have found all in Flanders. Pass Gravelline,[2] which, to my unlearned eyes, seems the strongest place I have yet seen, at least the works above ground are more numerous than at any other. Ditches, ramparts, and drawbridges without end. This is a part of the art military I like: it implies defence, and leaving rascality to neighbours. If Gengischan or Tamerlane had met with such places as Gravelline or Lisle in their way, where would their conquests and extirpations of the human race have been?—Reach Calais. And here ends a journey which has given me a great deal of pleasure, and more information than I should have expected in a kingdom not so well cultivated as our own. It has been the first of my foreign travels; and has with me confirmed the idea, that to know our own country well, we must see something of others. Nations figure by comparison; and those ought to be esteemed the benefactors of the human race, who have most established public prosperity on the basis of private happiness. To ascertain how far this has been the case with the French, has been one material object of my tour. It is an enquiry of great range, and no trifling complexity; but a

---

[1] Le Rosendael.   [2] (Nord.)

single excursion is too little to trust to. I must come again and again before I venture conclusions.—25 miles.

Wait at Desseins three days for a wind (the duke and dutchess of Gloucester are in the same inn and situation) and for a pacquet. A captain behaved shabbilly: deceived me, and was hired by a family that would admit nobody but themselves:—I did not ask what nation this family was of.—Dover—London—Bradfield;—and have more pleasure in giving my little girl a French doll, than in viewing Versailles.

1788.

THE long journey I had last year taken in France, suggested a variety of reflections on the agriculture, and on the sources and progress of national prosperity in that kingdom; in spite of myself, these ideas fermented in my mind; and while I was drawing conclusions relative to the political state of that great country, in every circumstance connected with its husbandry. I found, at each moment of my reflection, the importance of making as regular a survey of the whole as was possible for a traveller to effect. Thus instigated, I determined to attempt finishing what I had fortunately enough begun.

JULY 30. Left Bradfield; and arrived at Calais.—161 miles.

AUGUST 5. The next day I took the road to St. Omers.[1] Pass the bridge *Sans Pareil*, which serves a double purpose, passing two streams at once; but it has been praised beyond its merit, and cost more than it was worth. St. Omers contains little deserving notice; and if I could direct the legislatures of England and Ireland, should contain still less:—why are catholics to emigrate in order to be ill educated abroad, instead of being allowed institutions that would educate them well at home? The country is seen to advantage from St. Bertin's steeple.—25 miles.

The 7th. The canal of St. Omers is carried up a hill by a series of sluices. To Aire,[2] and Lilliers,[3] and Bethune,[4] towns well known in military story.—25 miles.

The 8th. The country now a champaign, one changes; from Bethune to Arras[5] an admirable gravel road. At the last town there is nothing but the great and rich abbey of Var,[6] which they would not shew me—it was not the right day—or some frivolous excuse. The cathedral is nothing. —17½ miles.

[1] (Pas de Calais.)
[2] Aire-sur-la-Lys (Pas de Calais).
[3] Lillers (Pas de Calais).
[4] Béthune (Pas de Calais).
[5] Arras (Pas de Calais).
[6] Ancient Benedictine abbey of St. Vaast, now appropriated to the bishop's palace, seminary, museum, and public library.

The 9th. Market-day; coming out of the town I met at least an hundred asses, some loaded with a bag, others a sack, but all apparently with a trifling burthen, and swarms of men and women. This is called a market, being plentifully supplied; but a great proportion of all the labour of a country is idle in the midst of harvest, to supply a town which in England would be fed by $\frac{1}{40}$ of the people: whenever this swarm of triflers buz in a market, I take a minute and vicious division of the soil for granted. Here my only companion *de voyage*, the English mare that carries me, discloses by her eye a secret not the most agreeable, that she is going rapidly blind. She is moon-eyed; but our fool of a Bury farrier assured me I was safe for above a twelvemonth. It must be confessed this is one of those agreeable situations which not many will believe a man would put himself into. *Ma foy*! this is a piece of my good luck;—the journey at best is but a drudgery, that others are paid for performing on a good horse, and I pay myself for doing it on a blind one;—I shall feel this inconvenience perhaps at the expence of my neck.—20 miles.

The 10th. To Amiens.[1] Mr. Fox slept here last night, and it was amusing to hear the conversation at the table d'hôte; they wondered that so great a man should not travel in a greater style:—I asked what was his style? Monsieur and *Madame* were in an English post-chaise, and the fille and valet de chambre in a cabriolet, with a French courier to have horses ready. What would they have? but a style both of comfort and amusement? A plague on a blind mare!—But I have worked through life; and he TALKS.

The 11th. By Poix[2] to Aumale;[3] enter Normandy.—25 miles.

The 12th. From thence to Newchatel,[4] by far the finest country since Calais. Pass many villas of Rouen merchants.—40 miles.

---

[1] (Somme.)

[2] Passed on the railway from Rouen to Amiens (Seine Inférieure).

[3] Aumale, the ancient Albemarle (Seine Inférieure).

[4] Neufchâtel, anciently a fortress (Seine Inférieure).

The 13th. They are right to have country villas—to get out of this great ugly, stinking, close, and ill built town, which is full of nothing but dirt and industry. What a picture of new buildings does a flourishing manufacturing town in England exhibit! The choir of the cathedral is surrounded by a most magnificent railing of solid brass. They shew the monument of Rollo, the first duke of Normandy, and of his son; of William Longsword; also those of Richard Cœur de Lion; his brother Henry; the Duke of Bedford, regent of France; of their own King Henry V.; of the Cardinal d'Amboise, minister of Louis XII. The altar-piece is an adoration of the shepherds, by Philip of Champagne. Rouen [1] is dearer than Paris, and therefore it is necessary for the pockets of the people that their bellies should be wholesomely pinched. At the table d'hôte, at the hotel *pomme du pin* we sat down, sixteen, to the following dinner, a soup, about 3lb. of bouilli, one fowl, one duck, a small fricassee of chicken, rote of veal, of about 2lb. and two other small plates with a sallad: the price 45*f.* and 20*f.* more for a pint of wine; at an ordinary of 20d. a head in England there would be a piece of meat which would, literally speaking, outweigh this whole dinner! The ducks were swept clean so quickly, that I moved from table without half a dinner. Such table d'hôtes are among the cheap things of France! Of all *sombre* and *triste* meetings a French table d'hôte is foremost; for eight minutes a dead silence, and as to the politeness of addressing a conversation to a foreigner, he will look for it in vain. Not a single word has any where been said to me unless to answer some question: Rouen not singular in this. The parliament-house here is shut up, and its members exiled a month past to their country seats, because they would not register the edict for a new land-tax. I enquired much into the common sentiments of the people, and found that the King personally from having been here, is more popular than the parliament, to whom they attribute the general dearness of every thing. Called on Mons.

---

[1] (Seine Inférieure.) A very different impression is now made on the traveller by the French Manchester, one of the handsomest provincial towns in France. It is odd that so many-sided an observer should have halted at Rouen without a souvenir of Jeanne d'Arc.

d'Ambournay, the author of a treatise on using madder green instead of dried, and had the pleasure of a long conversation with him on various farming topics, interesting to my enquiries.

The 14th. To Barentin,[1] through abundance of apples and pears, and a country better than the husbandry: to Yvelt[2] richer, but miserable management.—21 miles.

The 15th. Country the same to Bolbec;[3] their inclosures remind me of Ireland, the fence is a high broad parapet bank, very well planted with hedges and oak and beech trees. All the way from Rouen there is a scattering of country seats, which I am glad to see; farm-houses and cottages every where, and the cotton manufacture in all. Continues the same to Harfleur.[4] To Havre de Grace,[5] the approach strongly marks a very flourishing place: the hills are almost covered with little new built villas, and many more are building; some are so close as to form almost streets, and considerable additions are also making to the town.—30 miles.

The 16th. Enquiries are not necessary to find out the prosperity of this town; it is nothing equivocal: fuller of motion, life, and activity, than any place I have been at in France. A house here, which in 1779 let without any fine on a lease of six years for 240 liv. per annum, was lately let for three years at 600 liv. which twelve years past was to be had at 24 liv. The harbour's[6] mouth is narrow and formed by a mole, but it enlarges into two oblong basons of greater breadth; these are full of ships, to the number of some hundreds, and the quays around are thronged with business, all hurry, bustle, and animation. They say a fifty gun ship can enter, but I suppose without her guns. What is better, they have merchant-men of five and six hundred tons: the state of the harbour has however given them much alarm and perplexity; if nothing had been done to improve it, the mouth would have been filled up with

[1] On the railway from Rouen to Havre (Seine Inférieure).
[2] Yvetot (Seine Inférieure).
[3] Bolbec-Nointat, station, omnibus to Bolbec. There is a river of the same name.
[4] Le Hâvre (Seine Inférieure). [5] (Seine Inférieure).
[6] The harbour consists now of the Avant-Port, or tidal harbour and eight floating docks.

sand, an increasing evil; to remedy which, many engineers have been consulted. The want of a back water to wash it out is so great, that they are now, at the King's expence, forming a most noble and magnificent work, a vast bason, walled off from the ocean, or rather an inclosure of it by solid masonry, 700 yards long, five yards broad, and 10 or 12 feet above the surface of the sea at high water; and for 400 yards more it consists of two exterior walls, each three yards broad, and filled up seven yards wide between them with earth; by means of this new and enormous bason, they will have an artificial back-water capable, they calculate, of sweeping out the harbour's mouth clean from all obstructions. It is a work that does honour to the kingdom. The view of the Seine from this mole is striking; it is five miles broad, with high lands for its opposite shore; and the chalk cliffs and promontories, that recede to make way for rolling its vast tribute to the ocean, bold and noble.

Wait on Mons. l'Abbé Dicquemarre,[1] the celebrated naturalist, where I had also the pleasure of meeting Mademoiselle le Masson Golft, author of some agreeable performances; among others, *Entretien sur le Havre*, 1781, when the number of souls was estimated at 25,000. The next day Mons. le Reiseicourt, captain of the *corps royale du Génie*, to whom also I had letters, introduced me to Messrs. Hombergs, who rank amongst the most considerable merchants of France. I dined with them at one of their country houses, meeting a numerous company and splendid entertainment. These gentlemen have wives and daughters, cousins and friends, cheerful, pleasing, and well informed. I did not like the idea of quitting them so soon, for they seemed to have a society that would have made a longer residence agreeable enough. It is no bad prejudice surely to like people that like England; most of them have been there.—*Nous avons assurément en France de belles, d'agreables et de bonnes choses, mais on trouve une telle enérgie dans votre nation—*

The 18th. By the passage-packet, a decked vessel, to Honfleur, seven and a half miles, which we made with a strong north wind in an hour, the river being rougher than

[1] Dicquemare (Jacques François), 1733-1789, a distinguished naturalist and astronomer.

I thought a river could be. Honfleur is a small town, full of industry, and a bason full of ships, with some Guineamen[1] as large as at Havre. At Pont au de Mer,[2] wait on Mons. Martin, director of the *manufacture royale* of leather. I saw eight or ten Englishmen that are employed here (there are 40 in all), and conversed with one from Yorkshire, who told me he had been deceived into coming; for though they are well paid, yet they find things very dear, instead of very cheap, as they had been given to understand.—20 miles.

The 19th. To Pont l'Eveque,[3] towards which town the country is richer, that is, has more pasturage; the whole has singular features, composed of orchard inclosures, with hedges so thick and excellent, though composed of willow, with but a sprinkling of thorns, that one can scarcely see through them; chateaus are scattered, and some good, yet the road is villainous. Pont l'Eveque is situated in the Pay d'Auge,[4] celebrated for the great fertility of its pastures. To Lisieux,[5] through the same rich district, fences admirably planted, and the country thickly inclosed and wooded.—At the hotel d'Angleterre, an excellent inn, new, clean, and well furnished; and was well served and well fed.—26 miles.

The 20th. To Caen;[6] the road passes on the brow of a hill, that commands the rich valley of Corbon, still in the Pays d'Auge, the most fertile of the whole, all is under fine Poictou bullocks, and would figure in Leicester or Northampton.—28 miles.

The 21st. The marquis de Guerchy, who I had had the pleasure of seeing in Suffolk, being colonel of the regiment of Artois, quartered here, I waited on him; he introduced me to his lady, and remarked, that as it was the fair of Guibray,[7] and himself going, I could not do better than

---

[1] Probably slavers. See for particulars of this horrible traffic, E. Souvestre's " En Bretagne," p. 166. The Convention in 1794 abolished slavery throughout the French dominions, prohibited slave-dealing, and granted full civil rights to negroes. Napoleon I. (1802) re-established slavery and slave-dealing, and it remained for the second republic to undo his work in 1848.—See Lalanne's " Dict. Hist. de la France."

[2] Pont Audemer.   [3] Pont l'Evêque (Calvados).
[4] La vallée d'Auge, celebrated for its pastures (Calvados).
[5] (Calvados.)   [6] (Calvados.)
[7] A suburb of Falaise (Calvados).

accompany him, since it was the second fair in France. I readily agreed: in our way, we called at Bon, and dined with the marquis of Turgot, elder brother of the justly celebrated comptroller-general: this gentleman is author of some memoirs on planting, published in the Trimestres of the Royal Society of Paris: he shewed and explained to us all his plantations, but chiefly prides himself on the exotics; and I was sorry to find in proportion not to their promised utility, but merely to their rarity. I have not found this uncommon in France; and it is far from being so in England. I wished every moment, of a long walk to change the conversation from trees to husbandry, and made many efforts, but all in vain. In the evening to the fair playhouse—*Richard Cœur de Lion;* and I could not but remark an uncommon number of pretty women. Is there no antiquarian that deduces English beauty from the mixture of Norman blood? or who thinks, with Major Jardine, that nothing improves so much as crossing; to read his agreeable book of travels, one would think none wanting, and yet to look at his daughters, and hear their music, it would be impossible to doubt his system. Supped at the marquis d'Ecougal's, at his chateau *a la Frenaye.* If these French marquisses cannot shew me good crops of corn and turnips, here is a noble one of something else—of beautiful and elegant daughters, the charming copies of an agreeable mother: the whole family I pronounced at the first blush amiable: they are chearful, pleasing, interesting: I want to know them better, but it is the fate of a traveller to meet opportunities of pleasure, and merely see to quit them. After supper, while the company were at cards, the marquis conversed on topics interesting to my enquiries.— $22\frac{1}{2}$ miles.

The 22d. At this fair of Guilbray, merchandize is sold, they say, to the amount of six millions (262,500l.) but at that of Beaucaire to ten: I found the quantity of English goods considerable, hard and queen's ware; cloths and cottons. A dozen of common plain plates, 3 liv. and 4 liv. for a French imitation, but much worse; I asked the man (a Frenchman) if the treaty of commerce would not be very injurious with such a difference—*C'est précisement le contraire Mons.—quelque mauvaise que soit cette imitation, on n'a encore rien fait d'aussi bien en France ; l'année prochaine ou fera mieux—nous perfectionnerons—et en fin nous l'emporterans sur vous.*—I believe he is a very good politician, and that without competition, it is not possible to perfect any fabric. A dozen with blue or green edges, English, 5 liv. 5s. Return to Caen; dine with the marquis of Guerchy, lieutenant-colonel, major, &c. of the regiment, and their wives present a large and agreeable company. View the Abbey of Benedictines,[1] founded by W. the Conqueror. It is a splendid building, substantial, massy, and magnificent, with very large apartments, and stone stair-cases worthy of a palace. Sup with Mons. du Mesni, captain of the *corps de Genie*, to whom I had letters; he had introduced me to the engineer employed on the new port, which will bring ships of three or four hundred tons to Caen, a noble work, and among those which do honour to France.

The 23d. Mons. de Guerchy and the Abbée de——, accompanied me to view Harcourt,[2] the seat of the duke d'Harcourt, governor of Normandy, and of the Dauphin; I had heard it called the finest English garden in France, but Ermenonville will not allow that claim, though not near its equal as a residence. Found at last a horse to try in order to prosecute my journey a little less like Don Quixotte, but it would by no means do, an uneasy stumbling beast, at a price that would have bought a good one, so my blind friend and I must jog on still further.—30 miles.

The 24th. To Bayeux;[3] the cathedral has three towers, one of which is very light, elegant, and highly ornamented.

The 25th. In the road to Carentan,[4] pass an arm of the sea at Issigny,[5] which is fordable. At Carentan I found myself so ill, from accumulated colds I suppose, that I was seriously afraid of being laid up—not a bone without its aches; and a horrid dead leaden weight all over me.

---

[1] The church of St. Etienne, or the Abbaye aux Hommes.
[2] The château de Fontaine-Henri, a few miles from Caen, built in the early part of sixteenth century, interior not shown to strangers.
[3] (Calvados).
[4] Here is entered the peninsula of the Cotentin (Manche).
[5] Isigny (Manche).

I went early to bed, washed down a dose of antimonial powders, which proved sudorific enough to let me prosecute my journey.—23 miles.

The 26th. To Volognes;[1] thence to Cherbourg, a thick woodland, much like Sussex. The marquis de Guerchy had desired me to call on Mons. Doumerc, a great improver at Pierbutte near Cherbourg, which I did; but he was absent at Paris: however his bailiff, Mons. Baillio, with great civility shewed me the lands, and explained every thing.—30 miles.

The 27th. Cherbourg. I had letters to the duke de Beuvron, who commands here; to the count de Chavagnac, and M. de Meusnier, of the Academy of Sciences, and translator of Cook's Voyages; the count is in the country. So much had I heard of the famous works erecting to form a harbour here, that I was eager to view them without the loss of a moment: the duke favoured me with an order for that purpose, I therefore took a boat, and rowed across the artificial harbour formed by the celebrated cones. As it is possible that this itinerary may be read by persons that have not either time or inclination to seek other books for an account of these works, I will in a few words sketch the intention and execution. The French possess no port for ships of war from Dunkirk to Brest, and the former capable of receiving only frigates. This deficiency has been fatal to them more than once in their wars with England, whose more favourable coast affords not only the Thames, but the noble harbour of Portsmouth. To remedy the want, they planned a mole across the open bay of Cherbourg; but to inclose a space sufficient to protect a fleet of the line, would demand so extended a wall, and so exposed to heavy seas, that the expence would be far too great to be thought of; and at the same time the success too dubious to be ventured. The idea of a regular mole was therefore given up, and a partial one, on a new plan adopted; this was to erect in the sea, a line where a mole is wanted, insulated columns of timber and masonry, of so vast a size, as to resist the violence of the ocean, and to break its waves sufficiently to permit a bank being formed between column and

---

[1] Valognes (Manche).

column. These have been called cones from their form. They are 140 feet diameter at the base; 60 diameter at the top, and 60 feet vertical height, being, when sunk in the sea, 30 to 34 feet, immersed at the low water of high tides. These enormous broad-bottomed tubs being constructed of oak, with every attention to strength and solidity, when finished for launching, were loaded with stone just sufficient for sinking, and in that state each cone weighed 1000 tons (of 2000 lb.) To float them, sixty empty casks, each of ten pipes, were attached around by cords, and in this state of buoyancy the enormous machine was floated to its destined spot, towed by numberless vessels, and before innumerable spectators. At a signal the cords are cut in a moment, and the pile sinks: it is then filled instantly with stone from vessels ready attending, and capped with masonry. The contents of each filled only to within four feet of the surface, 2500 cubical toises of stone.[1] A vast number of vessels are then employed to form a bank of stone from cone to cone, visible at low water in neap tides. Eighteen cones, by one account, but 33 by another, would complete the work, leaving only two entrances, commanded by two very fine new-built forts, *Royale* and *d'Artois*, thoroughly well provided, it is said, for they do not shew them, with an apparatus for heating cannon balls. The number of cones will depend on the distances at which they are placed. I found eight finished, and the skeleton frames of two more in the dock-yard; but all is stopped by the archbishop of Toulouze, in favour of the œconomical plans at present in speculation. Four of them, the last sunk, being most exposed, are now repairing, having been found too weak to resist the fury of the storms, and the heavy westerly seas. The last cone is much the most damaged, and, in proportion as they advance, they will be still more and more exposed, which gives rise to the opinion of many skilful engineers, that the whole scheme will prove fruitless, unless such an expence is bestowed on the remaining cones as would be sufficient to exhaust the revenues of a kingdom. The eight already erected have for some years given a new appearance to Cherbourg; new houses, and even streets,

---

[1] The toise, measure of six feet.

and such a face of activity and animation, that the stop to the works was received with blank countenances. They say, that, quarry-men included, 3000 were employed. The effect of the eight cones already erected, and the bank of stone formed between them has been to give perfect security to a considerable portion of the intended harbour. Two 40 gun ships have lain at anchor within them these eighteen months past, by way of experiment, and though such storms have happened in that time as have put all to severe trials, and, as I mentioned before, considerably damaged three of the cones, yet these ships have not received the smallest agitation; hence it is a harbour for a small fleet without doing more. Should they ever proceed with the rest of the cones, they must be built much stronger, perhaps larger, and far greater precautions taken in giving them firmness and solidity: it is also a question, whether they must not be sunk much nearer to each other; at all events, the proportional expence will be nearly doubled, but for wars with England, the importance of having a secure harbour, so critically situated, they consider as equal almost to any expence; at least this importance has its full weight in the eyes of the people of Cherbourg. I remarked, in rowing across the harbour, that while the sea without the artificial bar was so rough, that it would have been unpleasant for a boat, within it was quite smooth. I mounted two of the cones, one of which has this inscription:— *Louis* XVI.—*Sur ce premiere cône echoue le 6 Juin* 1784, *a vu l'immersion de celui de l'est, le 23 Juin* 1786.—On the whole, the undertaking is a prodigious one, and does no trifling credit to the spirit of enterprize of the present age in France.[1] The service of the marine is a favourite; whether justly or not, is another question; and this harbour shews, that when this great people undertake any capital works, that are really favourites, they find inventive genius to plan, and engineers of capital talents to execute whatever is devised, in a manner that does honour to their kingdom. The duke de Beuvron had asked me to dinner,

---

[1] The famous breakwater or digue of Cherbourg was not completed till our own time at a cost of two and a half millions sterling, fifty years' labour and four million cubic feet of stone. The area enclosed by the digue amounts to 1,000 hectares.

but I found that if I accepted his invitation, it would then take me the next day to view the glass manufacture; I preferred therefore business to pleasure, and taking with me a letter from that nobleman to secure a sight of it, I rode thither in the afternoon; it is about three miles from Cherbourg. Mons. de Puye, the director, explained every thing to me in the most obliging manner. Cherbourg is not a place for a residence longer than necessary; I was here fleeced more infamously than at any other town in France; the two best inns were full; I was obliged to go to the *barque*, a vile hole, little better than a hog-sty; where, for a miserable dirty wretched chamber, two suppers composed chiefly of a plate of apples and some butter and cheese, with some trifle besides too bad to eat, and one miserable dinner, they brought me in a bill of 31 liv. (1l. 7s. 1d.) they not only charged the room 3 liv. a night, but even the very stable for my horse, after enormous items for oats, hay, and straw. This is a species of profligacy which debases the national character. Calling, as I returned, on Mons. Baillio, I shewed him the bill, at which he exclaimed for imposition, and said the man and woman were going to leave off their trade; and no wonder, if they had made a practice of fleecing others in that manner. Let no one go to Cherbourg without making a bargain for everything he has, even to the straw and stable; pepper, salt, and table-cloth.—10 miles.

The 28th, return to Carentan; and the 29th, pass through a rich and thickly inclosed country, to Coutances, capital of the district called the Cotentin. They build in this country the best mud houses and barns I ever saw, excellent habitations, even of three stories, and all of mud, with considerable barns and other offices. The earth (the best for the purpose is a rich brown loam) is well kneaded with straw; and being spread about four inches thick on the ground, is cut in squares of nine inches, and these are taken with a shovel and tossed to the man on the wall who builds it; and the wall built, as in Ireland, in layers, each three feet high, that it may dry before they advance. The thickness about two feet. They make them project about an inch, which they cut off layer by layer perfectly smooth. If they had the English way of white washing, they would look as well as our lath and plaister, and are much more durable. In good houses the doors and windows are in stone work.—20 miles.

The 30th. A fine sea view of the Isles of Chausée,[1] at five leagues distant; and afterwards Jersey, clear at about forty miles, with that of the town of Grandval[2] on a high peninsula: entering the town, every idea of beauty is lost; a close, nasty, ugly, ill built hole: market day, and myriads of triflers, common at a French market. The bay of Caucalle, all along to the right, and St. Michael's rock rising out of the sea, conically, with a castle on the top, a most singular and picturesque object.—30 miles.

The 31st. At Pont Orsin,[3] enter Bretagne; there seems here a more minute division of farms than before. There is a long street in the episcopal town of Doll,[4] without a glass window; a horrid appearance. My entry into Bretagne gives me an idea of its being a miserable province.—22 miles.

SEPTEMBER 1st. To Combourg,[5] the country has a savage aspect; husbandry not much further advanced, at least in skill, than among the Hurons, which appears incredible amidst inclosures; the people almost as wild as their country, and their town of Combourg one of the most brutal filthy places that can be seen; mud houses, no windows, and a pavement so broken, as to impede all passengers, but ease none—yet here is a chateau, and inhabited; who is this Mons. de Chateaubriant,[6] the owner, that has nerves strung for a residence amidst such filth and poverty? Below this hideous heap of wretchedness is a fine lake, surrounded by well wooded inclosures. Coming out of Hedé,[7] there is a beautiful lake belonging to Mons. de Blassac,[8] intendant of Poictiers, with a fine accompanyment of wood. A very little cleaning would make here a delicious scenery. There is a chateau, with four rows of

---

[1] Archipelago of Chausey. [2] Granville (Manche).
[3] Pontorson, on the branch railway from Vitré (Manche).
[4] Dol (Ille and Vilaine). [5] (Ille and Vilaine.)
[6] Chateaubriand, the writer, spent part of his childhood here. In his "Mémoires d'outre Tombe," he often recurs to the scenes amid which his youth was past.
[7] Hédé (Ille and Vilaine).
[8] The Count de Blossac, after whom the promenade of Poitiers is called.

trees, and nothing else to be seen from the windows in the true French stile. Forbid it, taste, that this should be the house of the owner of that beautiful water; and yet this Mons. de Blassac has made at Poictiers the finest promenade in France! But that taste which draws a strait line, and that which traces a waving one, are founded on feelings and ideas as separate and distinct as painting and music—as poetry or sculpture. The lake abounds with fish, pike to 36lb. carp to 24lb. perch 4lb. and tench 5lb. To Rennes the same strange wild mixture of desert and cultivation, half savage, half human.—31 miles.

The 2d. Rennes[1] is well built, and it has two good squares; that particularly of Louis XV. where is his statue. The parliament being in exile, the house is not to be seen. The Benedictines garden, called the *Tabour*,[2] is worth viewing. But the object at Rennes most remarkable at present is a camp, with a marshal of France (de Stainville), and four regiments of infantry, and two of dragoons, close to the gates. The discontents of the people have been double, first on account of the high price of bread, and secondly for the banishment of the parliament. The former cause is natural enough, but why the people should love their parliament was what I could not understand, since the members, as well as of the states, are all noble, and the distinction between the *noblesse* and *roturiers* no where stronger, more offensive, or more abominable than in Bretagne. They assured me, however, that the populace have been blown up to violence by every art of deception, and even by money distributed for that purpose. The commotions rose to such a height before the camp was established, that the troops here were utterly unable to keep the peace. Mons. Argentaise, to whom I had brought letters, had the goodness, during the four days I was here, to shew and explain every thing to be seen. I find Rennes very cheap; and it appears the more so to me just come from Normandy, where every thing is extravagantly dear. The table d'hôte, at the *grand maison*, is well served; they give two courses, containing plenty of good things, and a very ample regular dessert: the supper one good course, with a large

---

[1] (Ille and Vilaine.) [2] Le Thabor.

joint of mutton, and another good dessert; each meal, with the common wine, 40*f.* and for 20 more you have very good wine, instead of the ordinary sort: 30*f.* for the horse: thus, with good wine, it is no more than 6 liv. 10*f.* a day, or 5s. 10d. Yet a camp which they complain has raised prices enormously.

The 5th. To Montauban.[1] The poor people seem poor indeed; the children terribly ragged, if possible worse clad than if with no cloaths at all; as to shoes and stockings they are luxuries. A beautiful girl of six or seven years playing with a stick, and smiling under such a bundle of rags as made my heart ache to see her: they did not beg, and when I gave them any thing seemed more surprized than obliged. One third of what I have seen of this province seems uncultivated, and nearly all of it in misery. What have kings, and ministers, and parliaments, and states, to answer for their prejudices, seeing millions of hands that would be industrious, idle and starving, through the execrable maxims of despotism, or the equally detestable prejudices of a feudal nobility.[2] Sleep at the *lion d'or*, at Montauban, an abominable hole.—20 miles.

The 6th. The same inclosed country to Brooms;[3] but near that town improves to the eye, from being more hilly. At the little town of Lamballe,[4] there are above fifty families of noblesse that live in winter, who reside on their estates in the summer. There is probably as much foppery and nonsense in their circles, and for what I know as much happiness, as in those of Paris. Both would be better employed in cultivating their lands, and rendering the poor industrious.—30 miles.

The 7th. Leaving Lamballe, the country immediately changes. The marquis d'Urvoy, who I met at Rennes, and has a good estate at St. Brieux,[5] gave me a letter for his agent, who answered my questions.—12½ miles.

The 8th. To Guingamp,[6] a *sombre* inclosed country.

---

[1] Montauban-de-Bretagne (Ille and Vilaine).

[2] See, for an account of the extraordinary progress in Brittany, the contributions of M. H. Baudrillart, of the Institut, to the " Revue des deux Mondes," Oct. 15, Nov. 15, 1884.

[3] Broons (Côtes du Nord).   [4] (Côtes du Nord.)

[5] (Côtes du Nord.)   [6] (Côtes du Nord.)

Pass Chateaulandrin,[1] and enter Bas Bretagne. One recognizes at once another people, meeting numbers who have not more French than *Je ne sai pas ce que vous dites*, or *Je n'entend rien*. Enter Guingamp by gateways, towers, and battlements, apparently of the oldest military architecture; every part denoting antiquity, and in the best preservation. The poor people's habitations are not so good; they are miserable heaps of dirt; no glass, and scarcely any light; but they have earth chimnies. I was in my first sleep at Belleisle,[2] when the aubergiste came to my bedside, undrew a curtain, that I expected to cover me with spiders, to tell me that I had *une jument Anglois superbe*, and that a signeur wished to buy it of me: I gave him half a dozen flowers of French eloquence for his impertinence, when he thought proper to leave me and his spiders at peace. There was a great *chasse* assembled. These Bas Bretagne signeurs are capital hunters, it seems, that fix on a blind mare for an object of admiration. *A-propos* to the breeds of horses in France; this mare cost me twenty-three guineas when horses were dear in England, and had been sold for sixteen when they were rather cheaper; her figure may therefore be guessed; yet she was much admired, and often in this journey; and as to Bretagne, she rarely met a rival. That province, and it is the same in parts of Normandy, is infested in every stable with a pack of garran poney stallions, sufficient to perpetuate the miserable breed that is every where seen. This villainous hole, that calls itself the *grand maison*, is the best inn at a post town on the great road to Brest, at which marshals of France, dukes, peers, countesses, and so forth, must now and then, by the accidents to which long journies are subject to, have found themselves. What are we to think of a country that has made, in the eighteenth century, no better provision for its travellers!—30 miles.

The 9th. Morlaix[3] is the most singular port I have seen. It has but one feature, a vale just wide enough for a fine canal with two quays, and two rows of houses; behind them the mountain rises steep, and woody on one side; on the other gardens, rocks, and wood; the effect

---

[1] Chateaulandrin (Côtes du Nord).
[2] Belle-Isle-Bégard (Côtes du Nord).   [3] (Finistère.)

romantic and beautiful. Trade now very dull, but flourished much in the war.—20 miles.

The 10th. Fair day at Landervisier,[1] which gave me an opportunity of seeing numbers of Bas Bretons collected, as well as their cattle. The men dress in great trowsers like breeches, many with naked legs, and most with wooden shoes, strong marked features like the Welch, with countenances a mixture of half energy half laziness; their persons stout, broad, and square. The women furrowed without age by labour, to the utter extinction of all softness of sex. The eye discovers them at first glance to be a people absolutely distinct from the French. Wonderful that they should be found so, with distinct language, manners, dress, &c. after having been settled here 1300 years.—35 miles.

The 11th. I had respectable letters, and to respectable people at Brest, in order to see the dock-yard, but they were vain; Mons. le Chevalier de Tredairne particularly applied for me earnestly to the commandant, but the order, contrary to its being shewn either to Frenchmen or foreigners, was too strict to be relaxed without an express direction from the minister of the marine, given very rarely, and to which, when it does come, they give but an unwilling obedience. Mons. Tredairne, however, informed me, that lord Pembroke saw it not long since by means of such an order: and he remarked himself, knowing that I could not fail doing the same, that it was strange to shew the port to an English general and governor of Portsmouth, yet deny it to a farmer. He however assured me, that the duke of Chartres went away but the other day without being permitted to see it. Gretry's music at the theatre, which, though not large, is neat and even elegant, was not calculated to put me in good humour; it was *Panurge*.— Brest is a well built town, with many regular and handsome streets, and the quay where many men of war are laid up, and other shipping has much of that life and motion which animates a sea-port.

The 12th. Return to Landernau,[2] where, at the *duc de Chartre*, which is the best and cleanest inn in the bishopric,

---

[1] Landivisiau (Finistère).   [2] Landerneau (Finistère).

as I was going to dinner, the landlord told me, there was a *Monsieur un homme comme il faut*, and the dinner would be better if we united; *de tout mon cœur*. He proved a Bas Breton noble, with his sword and a little miserable but nimble nag. This seigneur was ignorant that the duke de Chartres, the other day at Brest, was not the duke that was in Mons. d'Orvillier's fleet. Take the road to Nantes. —25 miles.

The 13th. The country to Chateaulin[1] more mountainous; one-third waste. All this region far inferior to Leon[2] and Traguer;[3] no exertions, nor any marks of intelligence, yet all near to the great navigation and market of Brest water, and the soil good. Quimper,[4] though a bishopric, has nothing worth seeing but its promenades which are among the finest in France.—25 miles.

The 14th. Leaving Quimper, the seem to be more cultivated features; but this only for a moment;—wastes—wastes—wastes. Reach Quimperly.[4]—27 miles.

The 15th. The same *sombre* country to l'Orient,[5] but with a mixture of cultivation and much wood.—I found l'Orient so full of fools, gaping to see a man of war launched, that I could get no bed for myself, nor stable for my horse at the *epeè royale*. At the *cheval blanc*, a poor hole, I got my horse crammed among twenty others, like herrings in a barrel, but could have no bed. The duke de Brissac, with a suite of officers, had no better success. If the governor of Paris could not, without trouble, get a bed at l'Orient, no wonder Arthur Young found obstacles. I went directly to deliver my letters, found Mons. Besné, a merchant, at home; he received me with a frank civility better than a million of compliments; and the moment he understood my situation, offered me a bed in his house, which I accepted. The Tourville, of 84 guns, was to be launched at three o'clock, but put off till the next day,

---

[1] (Finistère.)
[2] The Léonnais of which St. Pol de Léon was formerly capital (Finistère).
[3] Tréguier (Côtes du Nord).
[4] Quimper and Quimperle (Finistère) are beautifully situated and possess beautiful churches.
[5] Lorient (Morbihan).

much to the joy of the aubergistes, &c. who were well pleased to see such a swarm of strangers kept another day. I wished the ship in their throats, for I thought only of my poor mare being squeezed a night amongst the Bretagne garrans; sixpence, however to the garcon, had effects marvelously to her ease. The town is modern, and regularly built, the streets diverge in rays from the gate, and are crossed by others at right angles, broad, handsomely built, and well paved; with many houses that make a good figure. But what makes l'Orient more known is being the appropriated port for the commerce of India, containing all the shipping and magazines of the company. The latter are truly great, and speak the royal munificence from which they arose. They are of several stories, and all vaulted in stone, in a splendid style, and of vast extent. But they want, at least at present, like so many other magnificent establishments in France, the vigour and vivacity of an active commerce. The business transacting here seems trifling. Three 84 gun ships, the Tourville, l'Eole, and Jean Bart, with a 32 gun frigate, are upon the stocks. They assured me, that the Tourville has been only nine months building: the scene is alive, and fifteen large men of war being laid up here in ordinary, with some Indiamen, and a few traders, render the port a pleasing spectacle. There is a beautiful round tower, 100 feet high, of white stone, with a railed gallery at top; the proportions light and agreeable; it is for looking out and making signals. My hospitable merchant, I find a plain unaffected character, with some whimsical originalities, that make him more interesting; he has an agreeable daughter, who entertains me with singing to her harp. The next morning the Tourville quitted her stocks, to the music of the regiments, and the shouts of thousands collected to see it. Leave l'Orient. Arrive at Hennebon.[1]—7½ miles.

The 17th. To Auray,[2] the eighteen poorest miles I have yet seen in Bretagne. Good houses of stone and slate, without glass. Auray has a little port, and some sloops, which always give an air of life to a town. To Vannes,[3] the country various, but *landes* the more permanent feature.

---

[1] Hennebont (Morbihan).   [2] (Morbihan.)
[3] (Morbihan.)

Vannes is not an inconsiderable town, but its greatest beauty is its port and promenade.

The 18th. To Musiliac.¹ Belleisle² with the smaller ones, d'Hedic³ and d'Honat, are in sight. Musiliac, if it can boast of nothing else, may at least vaunt its cheapness. I had for dinner two good flat fish, a dish of oysters, soup, a fine duck roasted; with an ample dessert of grapes, pears, walnuts, biscuits, liqueur, and a pint of good Bourdeaux wine: my mare, besides hay, had three-fourths of a peck of corn, and the whole 56*f*. 2*f*. to the fille and two to the garcon, in all 2s. 6d. Pass *landes—landes—landes—*to la Roche Bernard. The view of the river Villaine, is beautiful from the boldness of the shores, there are no insipid flats; the river is two-thirds of the width of the Thames at Westminster, and would be equal to any thing in the world if the shores were woody, but they are the savage wastes of this country.—33 miles.

The 19th. Turned aside to Auvergnac,⁴ the seat of the count de la Bourdonaye,⁵ to whom I had a letter from the dutchess d'Anville, as a person able to give me every species of intelligence relative to Bretagne, having for five-and-twenty years been first syndic of the noblesse. A fortuitous jumble of rocks and steeps could scarcely form a worse road than these five miles: could I put as much faith in two bits of wood laid over each other, as the good folks of the country do, I should have crossed myself, but my blind friend, with the most incredible sure-footedness, carried me safe over such places, that if I had not been in the every day habit of the saddle, I should have shuddered at, though guided by eyes keen as Eclipse's; for I suppose a fine racer, on whose velocity so many fools have been ready to lose their money, must have good eyes, as well as good legs. Such a road, leading to several villages, and one of the first noblemen of the province, shews what the state of

---

¹ Muzillac (Morbihan).
² Belle-île-en-Mer (Morbihan), the most important island of the department, and well cultivated.
³ The isles of Hœdic and Honat (Le Canard and Le Canelot).
⁴ Lauvergnac (Loire Inférieure), now the seat of M. de Mondoret; it is passed on the way from Guérande to St. Nazaire.
⁴ Afterwards General of Division of the Republican armies in Belgium and La Vendée, died 1793.

society must be;—no communication—no neighbourhood —no temptation to the expences which flow from society; a mere seclusion to save money in order to spend it in towns. The count received me with great politeness; I explained to him my plan and motives for travelling in France, which he was pleased very warmly to approve, expressing his surprise that I should attempt so large an undertaking, as such a survey of France, unsupported by my government; I told him he knew very little of our government, if he supposed they would give a shilling to any agricultural project or projector; that whether the minister was whig or tory made no difference, the party of THE PLOUGH never yet had one on its side; and that England has had many Colberts but not one Sully. This led to much interesting conversation on the balance of agriculture, manufactures, and commerce, and on the means of encouraging them; and, in reply to his enquiries, I made him understand their relations in England, and how our husbandry flourished, in spite of the teeth of our ministers, merely by the protection which civil liberty gives to property: and consequently that it was in a poor situation, comparatively with what it would have been in had it received the same attention as manufactures and commerce. I told M. de la Bourdonaye that his province of Bretagne seemed to me to have nothing in it but privileges and poverty, he smiled, and gave me some explanations that are important; but no nobleman can ever probe this evil as it ought to be done, resulting as it does from the privileges going to themselves, and the poverty to the people. He shewed me his plantations, which are very fine and well thriven, and shelter him thoroughly on every side, even from the S.W. so near to the sea; from his walks we see Belleisle and its neighbours, and a little isle or rock belonging to him, which he says the King of England took from him after Sir Edward Hawke's victory, but that his majesty was kind enough to leave him his island after one night's possession.—20 miles.

The 20th. Take my leave of Monsieur and Madame de la Bourdonaye, to whose politeness as well as friendly attentions I am much obliged. Towards Nazaire[1] there is a fine view of the mouth of the Loire, from the rising grounds,

[1] St. Nazaire (Loire Inférieure).

but the headlands that form the embouchure are low, which takes off from that greatness of the effect which highlands give to the mouth of the Shannon. The swelling bosom of the Atlantic boundless to the right. Savanal[1] poverty itself.—33 miles.

The 21st. Come to an improvement in the midst of these deserts, four good houses of stone and slate, and a few acres run to wretched grass, which have been tilled, but all savage, and become almost as rough as the rest. I was afterwards informed that this improvement, as it is called, was wrought by Englishmen, at the expence of a gentleman they ruined as well as themselves.—I demanded how it had been done? Pare and burn, and sow wheat, then rye, and then oats. Thus it is for ever and ever! the same follies, the same blundering, the same ignorance; and then all the fools in the country said, as they do now, that these wastes are good for nothing. To my amazement find the incredible circumstance, that they reach within three miles of the great commercial city of Nantes! This is a problem and a lesson to work at, but not at present. Arrive—go to the theatre, new built of fine white stone, and has a magnificent portico front of eight elegant Corinthian pillars, and four others within, to part the portico from a grand vestibule. Within all is gold and painting, and *a coup d'œil* at entering, that struck me forcibly. It is, I believe, twice as large as Drury-Lane, and five times as magnificent. It was Sunday, and therefore full. *Mon Dieu!* cried I to myself, do all the wastes, the deserts, the heath, ling, furz, broom, and bog, that I have passed for 300 miles lead to this spectacle? What a miracle, that all this splendour and wealth of the cities in France should be so unconnected with the country! There are no gentle transitions from ease to comfort, from comfort to wealth: you pass at once from beggary to profusion,—from misery in mud cabins to Mademoiselle St. Huberti, in splendid spectacles at 500 liv. a night, (21l. 17s. 6d.) The country deserted, or if a gentleman in it, you find him in some wretched hole, to save that money which is lavished with profusion in the luxuries of a capital.—20 miles.

[1] Savenay (Loire Inférieure), here took place the final dispersion of the Vendean army.

The 22d. Deliver my letters. As much as agriculture is the chief object of my journey, it is necessary to acquire such intelligence of the state of commerce, as can be best done from merchants, for abundance of useful information is to be gained, without putting any questions that a man would be cautious of answering, and even without putting any questions at all. Mons. Riédy was very polite, and satisfied many of my enquiries; I dined once with him, and was pleased to find the conversation take an important turn on the relative situations of France and England in trade, particularly in the West Indies. I had a letter also to Mons. Epivent, *consilier* in the parliament of Rennes, whose brother, Mons. Epivent de la Villesboisnet, is a very considerable merchant here. It was not possible for any person to be more obliging than these two gentlemen; their attentions to me were marked and friendly, and rendered a few days residence here equally instructive and agreeable. The town has that sign of prosperity of new buildings, which never deceives. The quarter of the *comedie* is magnificent, all the streets at right angles and of white stone. I am in doubt whether the *hotel de Henri* IV. is not the finest inn in Europe: Dessein's at Calais is larger, but neither built, fitted up, nor furnished like this, which is new. It cost 400,000 liv. (17,500l.) furnished, and is let at 14,000 liv. per ann. (612l. 10s.) with no rent for the first year. It contains 60 beds for masters, and 25 stalls for horses. Some of the apartments of two rooms, very neat, are 6 liv. a day; one good 3 liv. but for merchants 5 liv. per diem for dinner, supper, wine, and chamber, and 35*f.* for his horse. It is, without comparison, the first inn I have seen in France, and very cheap. It is in a small square close to the theatre, as convenient for pleasure or trade as the votaries of either can wish. The theatre cost 450,000 liv. and lets to the comedians at 17,000 liv. a year; it holds, when full, 120 louis d'or. The land the inn stands on was bought at 9 liv. a foot: in some parts of the city it sells as high as 15 liv. This value of the ground induces them to build so high as to be destructive of beauty. The quay has nothing remarkable; the river is choaked with islands, but at the furthest part next to the sea is a large range of houses regularly fronted. An institution common in the great commercial towns of France, but particularly flourishing in Nantes, is a *chambre de lecture*, or what we should call a book-club, that does not divide its books, but forms a library. There are three rooms, one for reading, another for conversation, and the third is the library; good fires in winter are provided, and wax candles. Messrs. Epivent had the goodness to attend me in a water expedition, to view the establishment of Mr. Wilkinson, for boring cannon, in an island in the Loire below Nantes.[1] Until that well known English manufacturer arrived, the French knew nothing of the art of casting cannon solid, and then boring them. Mr. Wilkinson's machinery, for boring four cannons, is now at work, moved by tide wheels; but they have erected a steam engine, with a new apparatus for boring seven more; M. de la Motte, who has the direction of the whole, shewed us also a model of this engine, about six feet long, five high, and four or five broad; which he worked for us, by making a small fire under the boiler that is not bigger than a large tea-kettle; one of the best machines for a traveling philosopher that I have seen. Nantes is as *enflammé* in the cause of liberty, as any town in France can be; the conversations I witnessed here, prove how great a change is effected in the minds of the French, nor do I believe it will be possible for the present government to last half a century longer, unless the clearest and most decided talents are at the helm. The American revolution has laid the foundation of another in France, if government does not take care of itself.[2] The 23d one of the twelve prisoners[3] from the Bastile arrived here—he was the most violent of them all—and his imprisonment has been far enough from silencing him.

[1] The island of Indret is evidently meant, the great State factory of arms at the present day.

[2] It wanted no great spirit of prophecy to foretell this; but latter events have shewn that I was very wide of the mark when I talked of fifty years.—*Author's Note*.

[3] Twelve Breton gentlemen deputed to Versailles with a denunciation of the ministers for their suspension of provincial parliaments. They were at once sent to the Bastille. It was this war of the king and the parliaments that brought about the assembly of the States-General, the step being decided on by the assembly of Grenoble, July 21, 1788. See H. Martin, vol. xvi., p 608, *et seq.*

The 25th. It was not without regret that I quitted a society both intelligent and agreeable, nor should I feel comfortably if I did not hope to see Messrs. Epivents again; I have little chance of being at Nantes, but if they come a second time to England, I have a promise of seeing them at Bradfield. The younger of these gentlemen spent a fortnight with Lord Shelburne at Bowood, which he remembers with much pleasure; Colonel Barré and Dr. Priestley were there at the same time. To Aucenis[1] is all inclosed: for seven miles many seats.—22½ miles.

The 26th. To the scene of the vintage. I had not before been witness to so much advantage as here; last autumn the heavy rains made it a melancholy business. At present, all is life and activity. The country all thickly and well inclosed. Glorious view of the Loire from a village, the last of Bretagne, where is a great barrier across the road and custom-houses, to search every thing coming from thence. The Loire takes the appearance of a lake large enough to be interesting. There is on both sides an accompanyment of wood, which is not universal on this river. The addition of towns, steeples, windmills, and a great range of lovely country, covered with vines; the character gay as well as noble. Enter Anjou, with a great range of meadows. Pass St. George,[2] and take the road to Angers. For ten miles quit the Loire and meet it again at Angers. Letters from Mons. de Broussonet; but he is unable to inform me in what part of Anjou was the residence of the marquis de Tourbilly; to find out that nobleman's farm, where he made those admirable improvements, which he describes in the *Memoire sur les defrichemens*, was such an object to me, that I was determined to go to the place, let the distance out of my way be what it might.—30 miles.

The 27th. Among my letters, one to Mons. de la Livoniere, perpetual secretary of the Society of Agriculture here. I found he was at his country-seat, two leagues off at Mignianne.[3] On my arrival at his seat, he was sitting down to dinner with his family; not being past twelve, I

---

[1] Ancenis (Loire Inférieure).
[2] St. Georges-sur-Loire (Maine and Loire).
[3] La Meignanne.

thought to have escaped this awkwardness; but both himself and Madame prevented all embarrassment by very unaffectedly desiring me to partake with them, and making not the least derangement either in table or looks, placed me at once at my ease, to an indifferent dinner, garnished with so much ease and chearfulness that I found it a repast more to my taste than the most splendid tables could afford. An English family in the country, similar in situation, taken unawares in the same way, would receive you with an unquiet hospitality, and an anxious politeness; and after waiting for a hurry-scurry derangement of cloth, table, plates, sideboard, pot and spit, would give you perhaps so good a dinner, that none of the family, between anxiety and fatigue, could supply one word of conversation, and you would depart under cordial wishes that you might never return.—This folly, so common in England, is never met with in France: the French are quiet in their houses, and do things without effort.—Mons. Livoniere conversed with me much on the plan of my travels, which he commended greatly, but thought it very extraordinary that neither government, nor the Academy of Sciences, nor the Academy of Agriculture, should at least be at the expence of my journey. This idea is purely French; they have no notion of private people going out of their way for the public good, without being paid by the public; nor could he well comprehend me, when I told him that every thing is well done in England, except what is done with public money. I was greatly concerned to find that he could give me no intelligence concerning the residence of the late marquis of Tourbilly, as it would be a provoking circumstance to pass all through the province without finding his house, and afterwards hear perhaps that I had been ignorantly within a few miles of it. In the evening returned to Angers.—20 miles.

The 28th. To La Flêche. The chateau of Duretal,[1] belonging to the dutchess d'Estissac, is boldly situated above the little town of that name, and on the banks of a beautiful river, the slopes to which that hang to the south are covered with vines. The country chearful, dry, and plea-

---

[1] Durtal (Maine and Loire). This château still exists, partly restored. It belonged to the two Marshals Schomberg.

sant for residence. I enquired here of several gentlemen for the residence of the marquis of Tourbilly, but all in vain. The 30 miles to La Flêche the road is a noble one; of gravel, smooth, and kept in admirable order. La Flêche is a neat, clean, little town, not ill built, on the river that flows to Duretal, which is navigable; but the trade is inconsiderable. My first business here, as every where else in Anjou, was to enquire for the residence of the marquis de Tourbilly. I repeated my enquiries till I found that there was a place not far from La Flêche, called Tourbilly, but not what I wanted, as there was no Mons. de Tourbilly there, but a marquis de Galway, who inherited Tourbilly from his father. This perplexed me more and more; and I renewed my enquiries with so much eagerness, that several people, I believe, thought me half mad. At last I met with an ancient lady who solved my difficulty; she informed me, that Tourbilly, about twelve miles from La Flêche, was the place I was in search of: that it belonged to the marquis of that name, who had written some books she believed; that he died twenty years ago insolvent; that the father of the present marquis de Galway bought the estate. This was sufficient for my purpose; I determined to take a guide the next morning, and, as I could not visit the marquis, at least see the remains of his improvements. The news, however, that he died insolvent, hurt me very much; it was a bad commentary on his book, and foresaw, that whoever I should find at Tourbilly, would be full of ridicule, on a husbandry that proved the loss of the estate on which it was practised.—30 miles.

The 29th. This morning I executed my project; my guide was a countryman with a good pair of legs, who conducted me across a range of such ling wastes as the marquis speaks of in his memoir. They appear boundless here; and I was told that I could travel many--many days, and see nothing else: what fields of improvement to make, not to lose estates! At last we arrived at Tourbilly,[1] a poor village, of a few scattered houses, in a vale between two rising grounds, which are yet heath and waste; the chateau in the midst, with plantations of fine poplars lead-

[1] Turbilly (Maine and Loire). This château, XVIIth. Cent., still exists, and is in possession of the De Broc family.

ing to it. I cannot easily express the anxious inquisitive curiosity I felt to examine every scrap of the estate; no hedge or tree, no bush but what was interesting to me; I had read the translation of the marquis's history of his improvements in Mr. Mills' husbandry,[1] and thought it the most interesting morsel I had met with, long before I procured the original *Memoire sur les defrichemens;* and determined that if ever I should go to France to view improvements the recital of which had given me such pleasure. I had neither letter nor introduction to the present owner, the marquis de Galway. I therefore stated to him the plain fact, that I had read Mons. de Tourbilly's book with so much pleasure, that I wished much to view the improvements described in it; he answered me directly in good English, received me with such cordiality of politeness, and such expressions of regard for the purport of my travels, that he put me perfectly in humour with myself, and consequently with all around me. He ordered breakfast *a l'Angloise;* gave orders for a man to attend us in our walk, who I desired might be the oldest labourer to be found of the late marquis de Tourbilly's. I was pleased to hear that one was alive who had worked with him from the beginning of his improvement. At breakfast Mons. de Galway introduced me to his brother, who also spoke English, and regretted that he could not do the same to Madame de Galway, who was in the straw: he then gave me an account of his father's acquiring the estate and chateau of Tourbilly. His great-grand-father came to Bretagne with King James II. when he fled from the English throne; some of the same family are still living in the county of Cork, particularly at Lotta. His father was famous in that province for his skill in agriculture; and, as a reward for an improvement he had wrought on the *landes*, the states of the province gave him a waste tract in the island of Belleisle, which at present belongs to his son. Hearing that the marquis de Tourbilly was totally ruined, and his estates in Anjou to be sold by the creditors,

---

[1] This writer would appear to be the translator of Count Gyllenborg's "Elements of Husbandry," 1770, and spoken of in no polite terms as "Agriculture Mills" in a letter from John Gray to Smollett, 1771. Mills also translated Virgil's "Georgics," 1780.

he viewed them, and finding the land very improveable, made the purchase, giving about 15,000 louis d'ors for Tourbilly, a price which made the acquisition highly advantageous, notwithstanding his having bought some law-suits with the estate. It is about 3000 arpents, nearly contiguous, the seigneury of two parishes, with the *haute justice*, &c. a handsome, large, and convenient chateau, offices very compleat, and many plantations, the work of the celebrated man concerning whom my enquiries were directed. I was almost breathless on the question of so great an improver being ruined! " You are unhappy that a man should be ruined by an art you love so much." Precisely so. But he eased me in a moment, by adding, that if the marquis had done nothing but farm and improve, he had never been ruined. One day, as he was boring to find marl, his ill stars discovered a vein of earth, perfectly white, which on trial did not effervesce with acids.[1] It struck him as an acquisition for porcelain—he shewed it to a manufacturer ——it was pronounced excellent: the marquis's imagination took fire, and he thought of converting the poor village of Tourbilly into a town, by a fabric of china—— he went to work on his own account——raised buildings ——and got together all that was necessary, except skill and capital.——In fine, he made good porcelain, was cheated by his agents, and people, and at last ruined. A soap manufactory, which he established also, as well as some law-suits relative to other estates, had their share in causing his misfortunes: his creditors seized the estate, but permitted him to administer it till his death, when it was sold. The only part of the tale that lessened my regret was, that, though married, he left no family; so that his ashes will sleep in peace, without his memory being reviled by an indigent posterity. His ancestors acquired the estate by marriage in the fourteenth century. His agricultural improvements, Mons. Galway observed, certainly did not hurt him; they were not well done, nor well supported by himself, but they rendered the estate more valuable; and he never heard that they had brought him into any difficulties. I cannot but observe here, that there

[1] Kaolin was discovered in France in 1760. The magnificent beds near Limoges were discovered by the wife of a country doctor in 1768.

seems a fatality to attend country gentlemen whenever they attempt trade or manufacture. In England I never knew a man of landed property, with the education and habits of landed property, attempt either, but they were infallibly ruined; or if not ruined, considerably hurt by them. Whether it is that the ideas and principles of trade have something in them repugnant to the sentiments which *ought* to flow from education — or whether the habitual inattention of country gentlemen to small gains and savings, which are the soul of trade, renders their success impossible; to whatever it may be owing, the fact is such, not one in a million succeeds. Agriculture, in the improvement of their estates, is the only proper and legitimate sphere of their industry; and though ignorance renders this sometimes dangerous, yet they can with safety attempt no other. The old labourer, whose name is Piron (as propitious I hope to farming as to wit), being arrived, we sallied forth to tread what to me was a sort of classic ground. I shall dwell but little on the particulars: they make a much better figure in the *Memoire sur les defrichemens* than at Tourbilly; the meadows, even near the chateau, are yet very rough; the general features are rough: but the alleys of poplars, of which he speaks in the memoirs, are nobly grown indeed, and do credit to his memory; they are 60 or 70 feet high, and girt a foot: the willows are equal. Why were they not oak? to have transmitted to the farming travellers of another century the pleasure I feel in viewing the more perishable poplars of the present time; the causeways near the castle must have been arduous works. The mulberries are in a state of neglect; Mons. Galway's father not being fond of that culture, destroyed many, but some hundreds remain, and I was told that the poor people had made as far as 25 lbs. of silk, but none attempted at present. The meadows had been drained and improved near the chateau to the amount of 50 or 60 arpents, they are now rushy, but valuable in such a country. Near them is a wood of Bourdeaux pines, sown 35 years ago, and are now worth five or six liv. each. I walked into the boggy bit that produced the great cabbages he mentioned, it joins a large and most improveable bottom. Piron informed me that the marquis pared and burnt about 100 arpents in all, and he folded 250 sheep. On our return to the chateau, Mons. de Galway, finding what an enthusiast I was in agriculture, searched among his papers to find a manuscript of the marquis de Tourbilly's, written with his own hand, which he had the goodness to make me a present of, and which I shall keep amongst my curiosities in agriculture. The polite reception I had met from Mons. Galway, and the friendly attention he had given to my views, entering into the spirit of my pursuits, and wishing to promote it, would have induced me very cheerfully to have accepted his invitation of remaining some days with him; had I not been apprehensive that the moment of madame Galway's being in bed, would render such an unlooked for visit inconvenient. I took my leave therefore in the evening, and returned to La Flèche by a different road.—25 miles.

The 30th. A quantity of moors to Le Mans,[1] they assured me at Guerces,[2] that they are here 60 leagues in circumference, with no great interruptions. At Le Mans I was unlucky in Mons. Tournai, secretary to the Society of Agriculture, being absent.—28 miles.

October 1. Towards Alençon,[3] the country a contrast to what I passed yesterday; good land, well inclosed, well built, and tolerably cultivated, with marling. A noble road of dark coloured stone, apparently ferruginous, that binds well. Near Beaumont[4] vineyards in sight on the hills, and these are the last in thus travelling northwards; the whole country finely watered by rivers and streams, yet no irrigation.—30 miles.

The 2d. Four miles to Nouant,[5] of rich herbage, under bullocks.—28 miles.

The 3d. From Gacé[6] towards Bernay.[7] Pass the marishal duc de Broglio's chateau at Broglio,[8] which is surrounded by such a multiplicity of clipt hedges, double, treble, and quadruple, that he must half maintain the poor of the little town in clipping.—25 miles.

The 4th. Leave Bernay; where, and at other places in this country, are many mud walls, made of rich red loam,

---

[1] (Sarthe.)   [2] La Guierche (Sarthe).
[3] (Orne.)   [4] Beaumont-sur-Sarthe (Sarthe).
[5] Nouans (Sarthe).   [6] (Orne.)
[7] (Eure.)   [8] Broglie (Eure). This château still exists.

thatched at top, and well planted with fruit-trees: a hint very well worth taking for copying in England, where brick and stone are dear. Come to one of the richest countries in France, or indeed in Europe. There are few finer views than the first of Elbeuf,[1] from the eminence above it, which is high; the town at your feet in the bottom; on one side the Seine presents a noble reach, broken by wooded islands, and an immense amphitheatre of hill, covered with a prodigious wood, surrounding the whole.

The 5th. To Rouen, where I found the *hotel royal*, a contrast to that dirty, impertinent, cheating hole the *pomme de pin*. In the evening to the theatre, which is not so large, I think, as that of Nantes, but not comparable in elegance or decoration; it is *sombre* and dirty. Gretty's *Caravanne de Caire*, the music of which, though too much chorus and noise, has some tender and pleasing passages. I like it better than any other piece I have heard of that celebrated composer. The next morning waited on Mons. Scanegatty, *professeur de physique dans la Société Royale d'Agriculture;* he received me with politeness. He has a considerable room furnished with mathematical and philosophical instruments and models. He explained some of the latter to me that are of his own invention, particularly one of a furnace for calcining gypsum, which is brought here in large quantities from Montmartre.[2] Waited on Messrs. Midy, Rossec and Co., the most considerable wool merchants in France, who were so kind as to shew me a great variety of wools, from most of the European countries, and permitted me to take specimens. The next morning I went to Darnetal,[3] where Mons. Curmer shewed me his manufacture. Return to Rouen, and dined with Mons. Portier, *directeur general des fermes*, to whom I had brought a letter from the duc de la Rochefoucauld. The conversation turned, among other subjects, on the want of new streets at Rouen, on comparison with Havre, Nantes, and Bourdeaux; at the latter places it was remarked, that a merchant makes a fortune in ten or fifteen years, and builds away; but at Rouen, it is a commerce of œconomy, in which a man is long doing it, and therefore unable with

---

[1] (Seine Inférieure.) [2] (Seine Inférieure.)
[3] Three miles from Rouen on the Amiens railway (*ibid.*).

prudence to make the same exertions. Every person at table agreed in another point which was discussed, that the wine provinces are the poorest in all France: I urged the produce being greater per arpent by far than of other lands; they adhered to the fact as one generally known and admitted. In the evening at the theatre, Madame du Fresne entertained me greatly; she is an excellent actress, never overdoes her parts, and make one feel by feeling herself. The more I see of the French theatre, the more I am forced to acknowledge the superiority to our own, in the number of good performers, and in the paucity of bad ones; and in the quantity of dancers, singers, and persons on whom the business of the theatre depends, all established on a great scale. I remark, in the sentiments that are applauded, the same generous feelings in the audience in France, that have many times in England put me in good humour with my countrymen. We are too apt to hate the French, for myself I see many reasons to be pleased with them; attributing faults very much to their government; perhaps in our own, our roughness and want of good temper are to be traced to the same origin.

The 8th. My plan had for some time been to go directly to England, on leaving Rouen, for the post-offices had been cruelly uncertain. I had received no letters for some time from my family, though I had written repeatedly to urge it; they passed to a person at Paris who was to forward them; but some carelessness, or other cause, impeded all, at a time that others directed to the towns I passed, came regularly; I had fears that some of my family were ill, and that they would not write bad news to me in a situation where knowing the worst could have no influence in changing it for better. But the desire I had to accept the invitation to La Roche Guyon, of the dutchess d'Anville's and the duc de la Rochefoucauld, prolonged my journey, and I set forward on this further excursion. A truly noble view from the road above Rouen; the city at one end of the vale, with the river flowing to it perfectly checkered with isles of wood. The other divides into two great channels, between which the vale is all spread with islands, some arable, some meadow, and much wood on all. Pass Pont l'Arch[1] to Louviers.[2] I had letters for the celebrated manufacturer Mons. Decretot, who received me with a kindness that ought to have some better epithet than polite; he shewed me his fabric, unquestionably the first woollen one in the world, if success, beauty of fabric, and an inexhaustible invention to supply with taste all the cravings of fancy, can give the merit of such superiority. Perfection goes no further than the Vigonia cloths of Mons. Decretot, at 110 liv. (4l. 16s. 3d.) the aulne. He shewed me also his cotton-mills, under the direction of two Englishmen. Near Louviers is a manufacture of copper plates for the bottoms of the King's ships; a colony of Englishmen. I supped with Mons. Decretot, passing a very pleasant evening in the company of some agreeable ladies.—17 miles.

The 9th. By Guillon[3] to Vernon;[4] the vale flat rich arable. Among the notes, I had long ago taken of objects to see in France, was the plantation of mulberries, and the silk establishment of the marechal de Belleisle, at Bissy,[5] near Vernon; the attempts repeatedly made by the society for the encouragement of arts, at London, to introduce silk into England, had made the similar undertakings in the north of France more interesting. I accordingly made all the enquiries that were necessary for discovering the success of this meritorious attempt. Bissy is a fine place, purchased on the death of the duc de Belleisle by the duc de Penthievre, who has but one amusement, which is that of varying his residence at the numerous seats he possesses in many parts of the kingdom. There is something rational in this taste; I should like myself to have a score of farms from the vale of Valencia to the Highlands of Scotland, and to visit and direct their cultivation by turns. From Vernon, cross the Seine, and mount the chalk hills again; after which mount again, and to La Roche Guyon,[6] the

---

[1] Pont de l'Arche, Junction Station.
[2] One of the principal cloth manufacturing towns of France (Seine Inférieure).
[3] (Eure.)   [4] (Seine Inférieure.)
[5] The old château de Bizy was replaced in 1866 by a new building in the style of Louis XIV.
[6] This château has been reconstructed, parts of the ancient building remaining. It still belongs to the family of La Rochefoucauld-Liancourt.

most singular place I have seen. Madame d'Anville and the duc de la Rochefoucauld received me in a manner that would have made me pleased with the place had it been in the midst of a bog. It gave me pleasure to find also the dutchess de la Rochefoucauld here, with whom I had passed so much agreeable time at Bagnere de Luchon, a thoroughly good woman, with that simplicity of character which is banished by pride of family or foppery of rank. The Abbé Rochon,[1] the celebrated astronomer, of the academy of sciences, with some other company which, with the domestics and trappings of a grand seigneur, gave La Roche Guyon exactly the resemblance of the residence of a great lord in England. Europe is now so much assimilated, that if one goes to a house where the fortune is 15 or 20,000*l*. a-year, we shall find in the mode of living much more resemblance than a young traveller will ever be prepared to look for.—23 miles.

The 10th. This is one of the most singular places I have been at. The chalk rock has been cut perpendicularly, to make room for the chateau. The kitchen, which is a large one, vast vaults, and extensive cellars (magnificently filled by the way) with various other offices, are all cut out of the rock, with merely fronts of brick; the house is large, containing thirty-eight apartments. The present dutchess has added a handsome saloon of forty-eight feet long, and well proportioned, with four fine tablets of the Gobelin tapestry, also a library well filled. Here I was shewn the ink-stand that belonged to the famous Louvois, the minister of Louis XIV. known to be the identical one from which he signed the revocation of the edict of Nantes, and I suppose also the order to Turenne to burn the Palatinate. This marquis de Louvois was grandfather to the two dutchesses d'Anville and d'Estissac, who inherited all his fortune, as well as their own family one of the house of La Rochefoucauld, from which family I conceive, and not from Louvois, they inherited their dispositions. From the principal apartment, there is a balcony that leads to the walks which serpentine up the mountain. Like all French seats, there is a town, and a great *potager* to remove before it would be

[1] Author of "Voyage à Madagascar et aux Indes Orientales," died 1817.

consonant with English ideas. Bissy, the duc de Penthievre's, is just the same; before the chateau there is a gently falling vale with a little stream through it, that might be made any thing of for *lawning and watering*; exactly there, in full front of the house, they have placed a great kitchen-garden, with walls enough for a fortress. The houses of the poor people here, as on the Loire in Touraine, are burrowed into the chalk rock, and have a singular appearance: here are two streets of them, one above another; they are asserted to be wholesome, warm in winter, and cool in summer, but others thought differently; and that they were bad for the health of the inhabitants. The duc de la Rochefoucauld had the kindness to order the steward to give me all the information I wanted relative to the agriculture of the country, and to speak to such persons as was necessary on points that he was in doubt about. At an English nobleman's, there would have been three or four farmers asked to meet me, who would have dined with the family amongst the ladies of the first rank. I do not exaggerate, when I say, that I have had this at least an hundred times in the first houses of our islands. It is however, a thing that in the present state of manners in France, would not be met with from Calais to Bayonne, except by chance in the house of some great lord that had been much in England,[1] and then not unless it was asked for. The nobility in France have no more idea of practising agriculture, and making it an object of conversation, except on the mere theory, as they would speak of a loom or a bowsprit, than of any other object the most remote from their habits and pursuits. I do not so much blame them for this neglect, as I do that herd of visionary and absurd writers on agriculture, who, from their chambers in cities, have, with an impertinence almost incredible, deluged France with nonsense and theory, enough to disgust and ruin the whole nobility of the kingdom.

The 12th. Part with regret from a society I had every reason to be pleased with.—35 miles.

The 13th. The 20 miles to Rouen, the same features.

---

[1] I once knew it at the duc de Liancourt's.—*Author's Note.*

First view of Rouen sudden and striking; but the road doubling, in order to turn more gently down the hill, presents from an elbow the finest view of a town I have ever seen; the whole city, with all its churches and convents, and its cathedral proudly rising in the midst, fills the vale. The river presents one reach, crossed by the bridge, and then dividing into two fine channels, forms a large island covered with wood; the rest of the vale of verdure and cultivation, of gardens and habitations, finish the scene, in perfect unison with the great city that forms the capital feature. Wait on Mons. d'Ambournay, secretary of the society of agriculture, who was absent when I was here before; we had an interesting conversation on agriculture, and on the means of encouraging it. I found, from this very ingenious gentleman, that his plan of using madder green, which many years ago made so much noise in the agricultural world, is not practised at present any where; but he continues to think it perfectly practicable. In the evening to the play, where Madame Cretal, from Paris, acted *Nina*; and it proved the richest treat I have received from the French theatre. She performed it with an inimitable expression, with a tenderness, a *naiveté*, and an elegance withal, that mastered every feeling of the heart, against which the piece was written: her expression is as delicious, as her countenance is beautiful; in her acting, nothing overcharged, but all kept within the simplicity of nature. The house was crouded, garlands of flowers and laurel were thrown on the stage, and she was crowned by the other actors, but modestly removed them from her head, as often as they were placed there.—20 miles.

The 14th. Take the road to Dieppe. Meadows in the vale well watered, and hay now making. Sleep at Tote.[1]—17¼ miles.

The 15th. To Dieppe. I was lucky enough to find the passage-boat ready to sail; go on board with my faithful sure-footed blind friend. I shall probably never ride her again, but all my feelings prevent my selling her in France. —Without eyes she has carried me in safety above 1,500 miles; and for the rest of her life she shall have no other

---

[1] Tôtes (Seine Inférieure).

master than myself; could I afford it, this should be her last labour: some ploughing, however, on my farm, she will perform for me, I dare say, chearfully.

Landing at the neat, new-built town of Brighthelmstone, offers a much greater contrast to Dieppe, which is old and dirty, than Dover does to Calais; and in the castle inn I seemed for a while to be in fairy land; but I paid for the enchantment. The next day to lord Sheffield's, a house I never go to, but to receive equal pleasure and instruction. I longed to make one for a few days in the evening library circle, but I took it strangely into my head, from one or two expressions, merely accidental, in the conversation, coming after my want of letters to France, that I had certainly lost a child in my absence; and I hurried to London next morning, where I had the pleasure of finding my alarm a false one; letters enough had been written, but all failed. To Bradfield.—202 miles.

1789.

MY two preceding journies had crossed the whole western half of France, in various directions; and the information I had received in making them, had made me as much a master of the general husbandry, the soil, management and productions, as could be expected, without penetrating in every corner; and residing long in various stations, a method of surveying such a kingdom as France, that would demand several lives instead of years. The eastern part of the kingdom remained. The great mass of country, formed by the triangle, whose three points are Paris, Strasbourg and Moulins, and the mountainous region S.E. of the last town, presented in the map an ample space, which it would be necessary to pass before I could have such an idea of the kingdom as I had planned the acquisition; I determined to make this third effort, in order to accomplish a design which appeared more and more important, the more I reflected on it; and less likely to be executed by those whose powers are better adapted to the undertaking than mine. The meeting of the States General of France also, who were now assembled, made it the more necessary to lose no time; for in all human probability, that assembly will be the epoch of a new constitution, which will have new effects, and, for what I know, attended with a new agriculture; and to have the regal sun in such a kingdom, both rise and set without the territory being known, must of necessity be regretted by every man solicitous for real political knowledge. The events of a century and half, including the brilliant reign of Louis XIV. will for ever render the sources of the French power interesting to mankind, and particularly that its state may be known previous to the establishment of an improved government, as the comparison of the effects of the old and new system will be not a little curious in future.

JUNE 2. To London. At night, *Il Generosité d' Alessandro*, by Tarchi, in which Signor Marchesi exerted his powers, and sung a duet, that made me for some moments forget all the sheep and pigs of Bradfield. I was, however, much better entertained after it, by supping at my friend Dr. Burney's, and meeting Miss Burney; how seldom it is that we can meet two characters at once in whom great celebrity deducts nothing from private amiableness; how many dazzling ones that we have no desire to live with! give me such as to great talents, add the qualities that make us wish to *shut up doors* with them.

The 3d. Nothing buzzing in my ears but the fête given last night by the Spanish ambassador. The best fête of the present period is that which ten millions of people are giving to themselves,

The feast of reason and the flow of soul.

The animated feelings of bosoms beating with gratitude for the escape of one common calamity, and the thrilling hope of the continuance of common blessings. Meet the count de Berchtold [1] at Mr. Songa's; a reach [2] of good sense and important views:—Why does not the Emperor call him to his own country, and make him his prime minister? The world will never be well governed till princes know their subjects.

The 4th. To Dover in the machine, with two merchants from Stockholm, a German and a Swede; we shall be companions to Paris. I am more likely to learn something useful from the conversation of a Swede and a German, than from the chance medley Englishmen of a stage-coach. —72 miles.

The 5th. Passage to Calais; 14 hours for reflection in a vehicle that does not allow one power to reflect.—21 miles.

The 6th. A Frenchman and his wife, and a French

---

[1] Berchtold, Count Leopold de, a distinguished German philanthropist, born 1738, died 1809. He travelled for fifteen years over Europe, Asia, and Africa, for the purpose of disseminating philanthropic tracts, and was one of the most active members of the Royal Humane Society. He fell a victim to his devotion in attending the sick and wounded Austrian soldiers after the battle of Wagram.

[2] Reach, used in a sense now obsolete—extent of capacity.

"Be sure yourself and your own reach to know."—POPE.

teacher from Ireland, full of foppery and affectation, which her own nation did not give her, were our company, with a young good-natured raw countryman of hers, at whom she played off many airs and graces. The man and his wife contrived to produce a pack of cards, to banish, they said, *l'enuye* of the journey; but they contrived also to fleece the young fellow of five louis. This is the first French diligence I have been in, and shall be the last; they are detestable. Sleep at Abbeville.—78 miles.

These men and women, girls and boys, think themselves (except the Swede) very cheerful because very noisy; they have stunned me with singing; my ears have been so tormented with French airs, that I would almost as soon have rode the journey blindfold on an ass. This is what the French call good spirits; no truly chearful emotion in their bosoms; silent or singing; but for conversation they had none. I lose all patience in such company. Heaven send me a blind mare rather than another diligence! We were all this night, as well as all the day, on the road, and reached Paris at nine in the morning.—102 miles.

The 8th. To my friend Lazowski, to know where were the lodgings I had written him to hire me, but my good dutchess d'Estissac would not allow him to execute my commission. I found an apartment in her hotel prepared for me. Paris is at present in such a ferment about the States General,[1] now holding at Versailles, that conversation is absolutely absorbed by them. Not a word of any thing else talked of. Every thing is considered, and justly so, as important in such a crisis of the fate of four-and-twenty millions of people. It is now a serious contention whether the representatives are to be called the *Commons* or *Tiers Etat*; they call themselves steadily the former, while the court and the great lords reject the term with a species of apprehension, as if it involved a meaning not easily to be fathomed. But this point is of little consequence, compared with another, that has kept the states for sometime in inactivity, the verification of their power separately or in common. The nobility and the clergy de-

---

[1] The States-General had assembled 5th May of this year, composed of 308 representatives of the clergy, 285 of the nobles, 621 of the Tiers état, or Commons (Lalanne).

mand the former, but the Commons steadily refuse it; the reason why a circumstance, apparently of no great consequence, is thus tenaciously regarded, is that it may decide their sitting for the future in separate houses or in one.[1] Those who are warm for the interest of the people declare that it will be impossible to reform some of the grossest abuses in the state, if the nobility, by sitting in a separate chamber, shall have a negative on the wishes of the people: and that to give such a *veto* to the clergy would be still more preposterous; if therefore, by the verification of their powers in one chamber, they shall once come together, the popular party hope that there will remain, no power afterwards to separate. The nobility and clergy foresee the same result, and will not therefore agree to it. In this dilemma it is curious to remark the *feelings* of the moment. It is not my business to write memoirs of what passes, but I am intent to catch, as well as I can, the opinions of the day most prevalent. While I remain at Paris, I shall see people of all descriptions, from the coffee-house politicians to the leaders in the states; and the chief object of such rapid notes as I throw on paper, will be to catch the ideas of the moment; to compare them afterwards with the actual events that shall happen, will afford amusement at least. The most prominent feature that appears at present is, that an idea of common interest and common danger does not seem to unite those, who, if not united, may find themselves too weak to oppose the common danger that must arise from the people being sensible of a strength the result of *their* weakness. The king, court, nobility, clergy, army, and parliament, are nearly in the same situation. All these consider, with equal dread, the ideas of liberty, now afloat; except the first, who, for reasons obvious to those who know his character, troubles himself little, even with circumstances that concern his power the most intimately. Among the rest, the feeling of danger is common, and they would unite, were there a head to render it easy, in order to do without the states at all. That the commons themselves look for some such hostile union as more than probable, appears from an idea

[1] "Tout l'avenir de la France était dans la séparation ou dans la réunion des ordres" (Mignet).

which gains ground, that they will find it necessary should the other two orders continue to unite with them in one chamber, to declare themselves boldly the representatives of the kingdom at large, calling on the nobility and clergy to take their places—and to enter upon deliberations of business without them, should they refuse it. All conversation at present is on this topic, but opinions are more divided than I should have expected. There seem to be many who hate the clergy so cordially, that rather than permit them to form a distinct chamber would venture on a new system, dangerous as it might prove.

The 9th. The business going forward at present in the pamphlet shops of Paris is incredible. I went to the Palais Royal to see what new things were published, and to procure a catalogue of all. Every hour produces something new. Thirteen came out to-day, sixteen yesterday, and ninety-two last week. We think sometimes that Debrett's or Stockdale's shops at London are crouded, but they are mere deserts, compared to Desein's, and some others here, in which one can scarcely squeeze from the door to the counter. The price of printing two years ago was from 27 liv. to 30 liv. per sheet, but now it is from 60 liv. to 80 liv. This spirit of reading political tracts, they say, spreads into the provinces, so that all the presses of France are equally employed. Nineteen-twentieths of these productions are in favour of liberty, and commonly violent against the clergy and nobility; I have to-day bespoke many of this description, that have reputation; but enquiring for such as had appeared on the other side of the question, to my astonishment I find there are but two or three that have merit enough to be known. Is it not wonderful, that while the press teems with the most levelling and even seditious principles, that if put in execution would overturn the monarchy, nothing in reply appears, and not the least step is taken by the court to restrain this extreme licentiousness of publication. It is easy to conceive the spirit that must thus be raised among the people. But the coffee-houses in the Palais Royal present yet more singular and astonishing spectacles; they are not only crouded within, but other expectant crouds are at the doors and windows, listening *a gorge deployé* to certain orators, who from chairs or tables harangue each his little audience: the eagerness with which they are heard, and the thunder of applause they receive for every sentiment of more than common hardiness or violence against the present government, cannot easily be imagined. I am all amazement at the ministry permitting such nests and hotbeds of sedition and revolt, which disseminate amongst the people, every hour, principles that by and by must be opposed with vigour, and therefore it seems little short of madness to allow the propagation at present.

The 10th. Every thing conspires to render the present period in France critical: the want of bread is terrible: accounts arrive every moment from the provinces of riots and disturbances, and calling in the military, to preserve the peace of the markets. The prices reported are the same as I found at Abbeville and Amiens 5f. (2$\frac{1}{2}$.) a pound for white bread, and 3$\frac{1}{2}f$. to 4f. for the common sort, eaten by the poor: these rates are beyond their faculties, and occasion great misery. At Meudon, the police, that is to say the intendant, ordered that no wheat should be sold on the market without the person taking at the same time an equal quantity of barley. What a stupid and ridiculous regulation, to lay obstacles on the supply, in order to be better supplied; and to shew the people the fears and apprehensions of government, creating thereby an alarm, and raising the price at the very moment they wish to sink it. I have had some conversation on this topic with well informed persons, who have assured me that the price is, as usual, much higher than the proportion of the crop demanded, and there would have been no real scarcity if Mr. Necker would have let the corn-trade alone; but his edicts of restriction, which have been mere comments on his book on the legislation of corn, have operated more to raise the price than all other causes together. It appears plain to me, that the violent friends of the commons are not displeased at the high price of corn, which seconds their views greatly, and makes any appeal to the common feeling of the people more easy, and much more to their purpose than if the price was low. Three days past, the chamber of the clergy contrived a cunning proposition; it was to send a deputation to the commons, proposing to name a commission from the three orders to take into consideration the misery of the people, and to deliberate on the means of lowering the price of bread. This would have led to the deliberation by order, and not by heads, consequently must be rejected, but unpopularly so from the situation of the people: the commons were equally dextrous; in their reply, they prayed and conjured the clergy to join them in the common hall of the states to deliberate, which was no sooner reported at Paris than the clergy became doubly an object of hatred; and it became a question with the politicians of the *Caffé de Foy*,[1] whether it was not lawful for the commons to decree the application of their estates towards easing the distress of the people?

The 11th. I have been in much company all day, and cannot but remark, that there seem to be no settled ideas of the best means of forming a new constitution. Yesterday the Abbé Syeyes[2] made a motion in the house of commons, to declare boldly to the privileged orders, that if they will not join the commons, the latter will proceed in the national business without them; and the house decreed it, with a small amendment. This causes much conversation on what will be the consequence of such a proceeding; and on the contrary, on what may flow from the nobility and clergy continuing steadily to refuse to join the commons, and should they so proceed, to protest against all they decree, and appeal to the King to dissolve the states, and recal them in such a form as may be practicable for business. In these most interesting discussions, I find a general ignorance of the principles of government; a strange and unaccountable appeal, on one side, to ideal and visionary rights of nature; and, on the other, no settled plan that shall give security to the people for being in

[1] The Café Foy (J. Bignon), Boulevard des Italiens, No. 38, corner of the Chaussée d'Antin.

[2] The author of the most famous pamphlet ever written, began his political career as a pioneer of democracy, and ended it as an apostle of despotism. He voted the death of the king, but knew how to take care of his own head. His maxim was " Vivre." Effacing himself completely during the Terror, he appeared again on the scene under the Directory, and was the main abettor of Napoleon to the Coup d'Etat of the 18th Brumaire. Died 1836.

future in a much better situation than hitherto; a security absolutely necessary. But the nobility, with the principles of great lords that I converse with, are most disgustingly tenacious of all old rights, however hard they may bear on the people; they will not hear of giving way in the least to the spirit of liberty, beyond the point of paying equal land-taxes, which they hold to be all that can with reason be demanded. The popular party, on the other hand, seem to consider all liberty as depending on the privileged classes being lost, and outvoted in the order of the commons, at least for making the new constitution; and when I urge the great probability, that should they once unite, there will remain no power of ever separating them; and that in such case, they will have a very questionable constitution, perhaps a very bad one; I am always told, that the first object must be for the people to get the power of doing good; and that it is no argument against such a conduct to urge that an ill use may be made of it. But among such men, the common idea is, that any thing tending towards a separate order, like our house of lords, is absolutely inconsistent with liberty; all which seems perfectly wild and unfounded.

The 12th. To the royal society of agriculture, which meets at the *hotel de ville*, and of which being an *associé*, I voted, and received a *jetton*, which is a small medal given to the members, every time they attend, in order to induce them to mind the business of their institution; it is the same at all royal academies, &c., and amounts, in a year, to a considerable and ill-judged expence; for what good is to be expected from men who would go only to receive their *jetton?* Whatever the motive may be, it seems well attended: near thirty were present; among them Parmentier, vice-president, Cadet de Vaux, Fourcroy, Tillet, Desmarets, Broussonet, secretary, and Creté de Palieul, at whose farm I was two years ago, and who is the only practical farmer in the society. The secretary reads the titles of the papers presented, and gives some little account of them; but they are not read unless particularly interesting, then memoirs are read by the members, or reports of references; and when they discuss or debate, there is no order, but all speak together as in a warm private conversation. The Abbé Reynal[1] has given them 1200 liv. (52l. 10s.) for a premium on some important subject; and my opinion was asked what it should be given for. Give it, I replied, in some way for the introduction of turnips.[2] But that they conceive to be an object of impossible attainment; they have done so much, and the government so much more, and all in vain, that they consider it as a hopeless object. I did not tell them that all hitherto done has been absolute folly; and that the right way to begin, was to undo every thing done. I am never present at any societies of agriculture, either in France or England, but I am much in doubt with myself whether, when best conducted, they do most good or mischief; that is, whether the benefits a national agriculture may by great chance owe to them, are not more than counterbalanced by the harm they effect; by turning the public attention to frivilous objects, instead of important ones, or dressing important ones in such a garb as to make them trifles? The only society that could be really useful would be that which, in the culture of a large farm, should exhibit a perfect example of good husbandry, for the use of such as would resort to it; consequently one that should consist solely of practical men; and then query whether many good cooks would not spoil a good dish. The ideas of the public on the great business going on at Versailles change daily and even hourly. It now seems the opinion, that the commons, in their late violent vote, have gone too far; and that the union of the nobility, clergy, army, parliament, and King, will be by far too many for them; such an union is said to be in agitation; and that the count d'Artois, the Queen, and the party usually known by her name, are taking steps to effect it, against the moment when the proceedings of the commons shall make it necessary to act with unity and vigour. The abolition of the

[1] The brilliant, but somewhat unscrupulous Jesuit, expelled his order for free theological views. Although latterly obnoxious to the Revolutions, Raynal escaped the Terror, and died poor in 1796. Charlotte Corday delighted in his writings.

[2] Arthur Young's enthusiasm on the subject of turnips may be understood when we remember that this invaluable esculent was not cultivated as food for cattle till the latter part of the last century.

parliaments is common conversation among the popular leaders, as a step essentially necessary; because, while they exist, they are tribunals to which the court can have resort, should they be inclined to take any step against the existence of the states: those bodies are alarmed, and see with deep regret, that their refusal to register the royal edicts, has created a power in the nation not only hostile, but dangerous to their own existence. It is now very well known and understood on all hands, that should the King get rid of the states, and govern on any tolerable principles, all the edicts would be enregistered by all the parliaments. In the dilemma and apprehension of the moment, the people look very much to the duc d'Orleans,[1] as to a head; but with palpable and general ideas of distrust and want of confidence; they regret his character, and lament that they cannot depend on him in any severe and difficult trial: they conceive him to be without steadiness, and that his greatest apprehension is to be exiled from the pleasures of Paris, and tell of many littlenesses he practised before, to be recalled from banishment. They are, however, so totally without a head, that they are contented to look to him as one; and are highly pleased with what is every moment reported, that he is determined to go at the head of a party of the nobility, and verify their powers in common with the commons. All agree, that had he firmness, in addition to his vast revenue of seven millions (306,250l.) and four more (175,000l.) in reversion, after the death of his father-in-law, the duc de Penthievre,[2] he might, at the head of the popular cause do any thing.

The 13th. In the morning to the King's library,[3] which

[1] Here is a portrait of Philippe Egalité by a contemporary. "Le duc, sans talents, décrié par une vie crapuleuse, par une avidité d'argent, répréhensible dans un particulier, honteuse, avillissante dans un prince, avait tous les vices qui font haïr les crimes, et n'avait pas une des qualités brillantes qui l'illustrent en quelque sorte aux yeux de la posterité. Il fallait animer ce cadavre moral, lui donner une apparente volonté; on lui montre le pouvoir suprême sous le nom de lieutenant général du royaume, tout l'argent du trésor public à sa disposition, et dans un avenir qu'il ne tiendrait qu'à lui de rapprocher. la couronne pour ses enfans."—*Mémoires du Marquis de Ferrières*, p. 9, Paris, 1880.

[2] The Duc de Penthièvre was grandson of Louis XIV. and Mdme. de Montespan, and son of the Count of Toulouse.

[3] The Bibliothèque Nationale, Rue de Richelieu.

I had not seen when before at Paris; it is a vast apartment, and, as all the world knows, nobly filled. Every thing is provided to accommodate those who wish to read or transcribe—of whom there were sixty or seventy present. Along the middle of the rooms are glass cases, containing models of the instruments of many trades preserved for the benefit of posterity, being made on the most exact scale of proportion; among others the potter, founder, brickmaker, chymist, &c., &c., and lately added a very large one of the English garden, most miserably imagined; but with all this not a plough, or an iota of agriculture; yet a farm might be much easier represented than the garden they have attempted, and with infinitely more use. I have no doubt but there may arise many cases, in which the preservation of instruments unaltered, may be of considerable utility; I think I see clearly, that such a use would result in agriculture, and if so, why not in other arts? These cases of models, however, have so much the air of childrens' play-houses, that I would not answer for my little girl, if I had her here, not crying for them. At the dutchess of d'Anville's, where meet the archbishop of Aix,[1] bishop of Blois,[2] Prince de Laon, and duc and dutchess de la Rochefoucauld, the three last of my old Bagnere de Luchon acquaintance, lord[3] and lady Camelford, lord Eyre,[4] &c., &c.

All this day I hear nothing but anxiety of expectation for what the crisis in the states will produce. The embarrassment of the moment is extreme. Every one agrees that there is no ministry: the Queen is closely connecting herself with the party of the princes, with the count d'Artois at their head; who are all so adverse to Mons. Necker that every thing is in confusion: but the King,

[1] The Archbishop of Aix was a staunch upholder of the supremacy the Church, and headed the refractory clergy after the decrees of June and July, 1790.
[2] The Bishop of Blois was replaced by an "évêque constitutionel" in 1790.
[3] Thomas Pitt, nephew of the first Earl of Chatham, author of "Tracts on the American War."
[4] Sir James Eyre, afterwards Baron of the Exchequer. In 1793 one of the commissioners of the Great Seal, afterwards Chief Justice of the Common Pleas.

who is personally the honestest man in the world, has but one wish, which is to do right; yet, being without those decisive parts that enable a man to foresee difficulties and to avoid them, finds himself in a moment of such extreme perplexity, that he knows not what council to take refuge in: it is said that Mons. Necker is alarmed for his power, and anecdote reports things to his disadvantage, which probably are not true:—of his trimming—and attempting to connect himself to the Abbé de Vermont,[1] reader to the Queen, and who has great influence in all affairs in which he chuses to interfere; this is hardly credible, as that party are known to be exceedingly adverse to Mons. Necker; and it is even said, that, as the count d'Artois, Madame de Polignac,[2] and a few others were, but two days ago, walking in the private garden of Versailles they met Madame Necker, and descended even to hissing: if half this is true, it is plain enough that this minister must speedily retire. All who adhere to the antient constitution, or rather government, consider him as their mortal enemy; they assert, and truly, that he came in under circumstances that would have enabled him to do every thing he pleased— he had king and kingdom at command—but that the errors he was guilty of, for want of some settled plan, have been the cause of all dilemmas experienced since. They accuse him heavily of assembling the notables, as a false step that did nothing but mischief: and assert that his letting the king go to the states-general, before their powers were verified, and the necessary steps taken to keep the orders separate, after giving double the representation to the *tiers* to that of the other two orders, was madness. That he ought to have appointed commissaries to have received the verification before admittance: they accuse him further of

---

[1] "Ancien précepteur et conseiller intime de Marie Antoinette, précepteur qui ne lui avait rien appris, conseiller qui ne lui donnait—jamais que de pernicieux avis, vrai Maurepas de Marie Antoinette, aussi égoïste et moins sagace que le fatal ministre de Louis XVI. H. Martin, vol. xvi. p. 556. The Abbé de Vermont very prudently quitted France after the fall of the Bastille.

[2] The Duke and Duchess de Polignac, after having received countless honours, privileges, and substantial favours from Louis XVI. and the queen, were the first to desert them. Like the Abbé de Vermont, they fled after the 14th July, 1789.

having done all this through an excessive and insufferable vanity, which gave him the idea of guiding the deliberation of the states by his knowledge and reputation. The character of a man, drawn by his enemies, must necessarily be charged; but these are his features here, of which all parties recognize some truth, however rejoiced they may be that error was a part of his constitution. It is expressly asserted by M. Necker's [1] most intimate friends, that he has acted with good faith, and that he has been in principle a friend to the regal power, as well as to an amelioration of the condition of the people. The worst thing I know of him is his speech to the states on their assembling,—a great opportunity, but lost,—no great leading or masterly views,—no decision on circumstances in which the people ought to be relieved, and new principles of government adopted;—it is the speech you would expect from a banker's clerk of some ability. Concerning it there is an anecdote worth inserting; he knew his voice would not enable him to go through the whole of it, in so large a room, and to so numerous an assembly; and therefore he had spoken to Mons. de Broussonet, of the academy of sciences, and secretary to the royal society of agriculture, to be in readiness to read it for him. He had been present at an annual general meeting of that society, when Mons. Broussonet had read a discourse with a powerful piercing voice, that was heard distinctly to the greatest distance. This gentleman attended him several times to take his instructions, and be sure of understanding the interlineations that were made, even after the speech was finished. M. Broussonet was with him the evening before the assembly of the states, at nine o'clock: and next day, when he came to read it in public, he found still more corrections and alterations, which Mons. Necker had made after quitting him; they were chiefly in stile, and shew how very solicitous he was in regard to the form and decoration of his matter: the ideas in my opinion wanted this attention more than the stile. Mons. Broussonet himself told me this little anecdote. This morning in the states

---

[1] See Mémoires de Montlosier for many interesting notes on Necker and his fall, chs. 3, 4, 5.

three curées of Poitou have joined themselves to the commons, for the verification of their powers, and were received with a kind of madness of applause; and this evening at Paris nothing else is talked of. The nobles have been all day in debate, without coming to any conclusion, and have adjourned to Monday.

The 14th. To the king's garden, where Mons. Thouin had the goodness to shew me some small experiments he has made on plants that promise greatly for the farmer, particularly the *lathyrus biennis*,[1] and the *melilotus syberica*,[1] which now make an immense figure for forage; both are biennial; but will last three or four years if not seeded; the *Achillæa syberica* promises well, and an *astragalus*; he has promised me seeds. The Chinese hemp has perfected its seeds, which it had not done before in France.[2] The more I see of Mons. Thouin the better I like him, he is one of the most amiable men I know.

To the repository of the royal machines, which Mons. Vandermond shewed and explained to me with great readiness and politeness. What struck me most was Mons. Vaucusson's machine for making a chain, which I was told Mr. Watt of Birmingham admired very much, at which my attendants seemed not displeased. Another for making the cogs indented in iron wheels. There is a chaff cutter, from an English original; and a model of the nonsensical plough to go without horses, these are the only ones in agriculture. Many of very ingenious contrivance for winding silk, &c. In the evening to the theatre *Francoise*, the

[1] I have since cultivated these plants in small quantities, and believe them to be a very important object.—*Author's Note.*

[2] An eminent botanist has kindly elucidated this passage:—" A very full list of the plants in cultivation at Paris was published by Desfontaines, first edition, 1804. Ours (Royal Herbarium, Kew) is the third edition, and is called 'Catalogus Plantarum Horti Regii Parisiensis,' 1829. Hortus regii evidently means the Jardin des Plantes. I find no mention of any Lathyrus biennis, and should guess that it means Lathyrus sativus (Chickling Vetch). There is also named a Melilotus Siberiei, afterwards called Medicago Siberiei by De Candolle, but it is unknown to the last author of a Russian flora. Achillæa Siberiei is a near ally of our common English Achillæa Ptarmica (Sneezewort). Astragalus may well have been some specimen of that very large genus. Chinese hemp is evidently one of the many varieties of Cannabis sativa."

Siege of Calais, by Mons. de Belloy, not a good, but a popular performance.

It is now decided by the popular leaders, that they will move to-morrow to declare all taxes illegal not raised by authority of the states general, but to grant them immediately for a term; either for two years, or for the duration of the present session of the states. This plan is highly approved at Paris by all the friends of liberty; and it is certainly a rational mode of proceeding, founded on just principles, and will involve the court in a great dilemma.

The 15th. This has been a rich day, and such an one as ten years ago none could believe would ever arrive in France; a very important debate being expected on what, in our house of commons, would be termed the state of the nation. My friend Mons. Lazowski and myself were at Versailles by eight in the morning. We went immediately to the hall of the states to secure good seats in the gallery; we found some deputies already there, and a pretty numerous audience collected. The room is too large; none but stentorian lungs, or the finest clearest voices can be heard; however the very size of the apartment, which admits 2000 people, gave a dignity to the scene. It was indeed an interesting one. The spectacle of the representatives of twenty-five millions of people, just emerging from the evils of 200 years of arbitrary power, and rising to the blessings of a freer constitution, assembled with open doors under the eye of the public, was framed to call into animated feelings every latent spark, every emotion of a liberal bosom. To banish whatever ideas might intrude of their being a people too often hostile to my own country,—and to dwell with pleasure on the glorious idea of happiness to a great nation—of felicity to millions yet unborn. Mons. l'Abbé Syeyes opened the debate. He is one of the most zealous sticklers for the popular cause; carries his ideas not to a regulation of the present government, which he thinks too bad to be regulated at all, but wishes to see it absolutely overturned; being in fact a violent republican: this is the character he commonly bears, and in his pamphlets he seems pretty much to justify such an idea. He speaks ungracefully, and uneloquently, but logically, or rather reads so, for he read his speech, which was prepared. His motion, or rather string of motions, was to declare themselves the representatives known and verified of the French nation, admitting the right of all absent deputies (the nobility and clergy) to be received among them on the verification of their powers. Mons. de Mirabeau spoke without notes, for near an hour, with a warmth, animation, and eloquence, that entitles him to the reputation of an undoubted orator. He opposed the words *known* and *verified*, in the proposition of Abbé Syeyes, with great force of reasoning; and proposed, in lieu, that they should declare themselves simply *Representatives du peuple Francoise*: that no *veto* should exist against their resolves in any other assembly: that all taxes are illegal, but should be granted during the present session of the states, and no longer: that the debt of the king should become the debt of the nation, and be secured on funds accordingly. Mons. de Mirabeau was well heard, and his proposition much applauded. Mons. de Mounier,[1] a deputy from Dauphine, of great reputation, and who has also published some pamphlets, very well approved by the public, moved a different resolution to declare themselves the legitimate representatives of the majority of the nation: that they should vote by head and not by order: and that they should never acknowledge any right in the representatives of the clergy or nobility to deliberate separately. Mons. Rabaud St. Etienne,[2] a protestant from Languedoc, also an author,

---

[1] Mounier (Jean Joseph), député of the Dauphiné, and friend of Necker, is a leading figure in the early period of the Revolution. On his proposition, the members of the Tiers Etat took the celebrated oath of the Jeu de Paume. He was in favour of a constitutional monarchy on the English model, but retired from the assembly when all hopes of an understanding between the court and the nation were at an end.

[2] Rabaud St. Etienne was one of the first Protestant ministers in France to exercise his newly acquired civil rights. Imbued with the revolutionary spirit, yet an eloquent pleader for law, order, and mercy, he fell a victim to his generous defence of royalty. In the letters of Helen Maria Williams (1795) she thus describes him:—"A few weeks after our release from prison Rabaud St. Etienne was put to death. He was one of the most enlightened and virtuous men whom the revolution had called forth, and had acquired general esteem by his conduct as a legislator, and considerable reputation by his talents as a writer. I saw him on that memorable day (the expulsion of the Girondins from the

who has written in the present affairs, and a man of considerable talents, spoke also, and made his proposition, which was to declare themselves the representatives of the people of France; to declare all taxes null; to regrant them during the sitting of the states; to verify and consolidate the debt; and to vote a loan. All which were well approved except the loan, which was not at all to the feeling of the assembly. This gentleman speaks clearly and with precision, and only passages of his speech from notes. Mons. Bernarve,[1] a very young man, from Grenoble, spoke without notes with great warmth and animation. Some of his periods were so well rounded, and so eloquently delivered, that he met with much applause, several members crying—*bravo!*

In regard to their general method of proceeding, there are two circumstances in which they are very deficient: the spectators in the galleries are allowed to interfere in the debates by clapping their hands, and other noisy expressions of approbation: this is grossly indecent; it is also dangerous; for, if they are permitted to express approbation, they are, by parity of reason, allowed expressions of dissent; and they may hiss as well as clap; which it is said, they have sometimes done:—this would be, to overrule the debate and influence the deliberations. Another circumstance, is the want of order among themselves; more than once to-day there were an hundred members on their legs at a time, and Mons. Bailly[2] absolutely without

---

convention) filled with despair, not so much from the loss of his own life, which he considered inevitable, as for that of the liberty of his country, now falling under the vilest despotism." Betrayed by a friend, he was guillotined 1793.

[1] Barnave, 1761-1793. Ardent revolutionary, and chivalrous gentleman, deputed by the assembly to meet the captured royal family at Epernay and escort them to Paris. Barnave's sympathies were evoked by the sufferings of the prisoners, and in trying to save their lives he lost his own. What irony is lent to Burke's famous peroration by the careers of such men as Barnave and Rabaud St. Etienne! If, indeed, a thousand swords did not leap from their scabbards to avenge so much as a look that threatened Marie Antoinette with insult, many brave, ambitious, and generous patriots were cut off in the flower of their youth for having interceded on behalf of royalty. Barnave was a Protestant.

[2] Bailly, Jean Sylvain, more familiar to us as President of the National Assembly, and first Mayor of Paris, than a brilliant astronomer,

power to keep order. This arises very much from complex motions being admitted; to move a declaration relative to their title, to their powers, to taxes, to a loan, &c. &c. all in one proposition, appears to English ears preposterous, and certainly is so. Specific motions, founded on single and simple propositions, can alone produce order in debate; for it is endless to have five hundred members declaring their reasons of assent to one part of a complex proposition, and their dissent to another part. A debating assembly should not proceed to any business whatever till they have settled the rules and orders of their proceedings, which can only be done by taking those of other experienced assemblies, confirming them as they find useful, and altering such as require to be adapted to different circumstances. The rules and orders of debate in the house of commons of England, as I afterwards took the liberty of mentioning to Mons. Rabaud St. Etienne, might have been taken at once in Mr. Hatsel's[1] book, and would have saved them at least a fourth of their time. They adjourned for dinner. Dined ourselves with the duc de Liancourt, at his apartments in the palace, meeting twenty deputies.—I sat by M. Rabaud St. Etienne, and had much conversation with him; they all speak with equal confidence on the fall of despotism. The foresee, that attempts very adverse to the spirit of liberty will be made, but the spirit of the people is too much excited at present to be crushed any more. Finding that the question of to-day's debate cannot be decided to-day, and that in all probability it will be unfinished even to-morrow, as the number that will speak on it is very great. Return in the evening to Paris.

The 16th. To Dugny, ten miles from Paris, again with Mons. de Broussonet, to wait on Mons. Creté de Palieul, the only practical farmer in the society of agriculture. Mons. Broussonet, than whom no man can be more eager for the honour and improvement of agriculture, was desi-

---

was born 1736. Guillotined 1793. This single-minded patriot forfeited his popularity for having allowed the National Guard to fire on the people in 1791 when riotously demanding "la déchéance." Bailly's great " History of Astronomy " was published in Paris, 1775-87.

[1] Hatsell's " Precedents of the House of Commons."

rous that I should witness the practice and improvements of a gentleman who stands so high in the list of good French farmers. Called first on the brother of Mons. Creté who at present has the *poste*, and consequently 140 horses; walked over his farm, and the crops he shewed me of wheat and oats were on the whole very fine, and some of them superior; but I must confess I should have been better pleased with them if he had not had his stables so well filled with a view different from that of the farm. And to look for a course of crops in France is vain; he sows white corn twice, thrice, and even four times in succession. At dinner, &c. had much conversation with the two brothers, and with some other neighbouring cultivators present on this point, in which I recommended either turnips or cabbages, according to the soil, for breaking their rotations of white corn. But every one of them, except Mons. de Broussonet, was against me; they demanded, *Can* we sow wheat after turnips and cabbages? On a small portion you may with great success; but the time of consuming the greater part of the crop renders it impossible. *That is sufficient, if we cannot sow wheat after them, they cannot be good in France.* This idea is everywhere nearly the same in that kingdom. I then said, that they might have half their land under wheat and yet be good farmers; thus;—1. Beans;—2. Wheat;—3. Tares; 4. Wheat;—5. Clover;—6. Wheat;—this they approved better of, but thought their own courses more profitable. But the most interesting circumstance of their farms is the chicory (*chicorium intybus*).[1] I had the satisfaction to find, that Mons. Creté de Palieul had as great an opinion of it as ever; that his brother had adopted it; that it was very flourishing on both their farms; and on those of their neighbours also: I never see this plant but I congratulate myself on having travelled for something more than to write in my closet: and that the introduction of it in England would alone, if no other result had flowed from one man's existence, have been enough to shew that he did not live in vain. Of this excellent plant, and Mons. Creté's experiments on it, more elsewhere.

---

[1] Wild chicory, succory.

The 17th. All conversation on the motion of l'Abbé Syeyes being accepted, yet that of the Count de Mirabeau better relished. But his character is a dead weight upon him; there is a suspicion that he has received 100,000 liv. from the Queen; a blind, improbable report;[1] for his conduct would in every probability be very different had any such transaction taken place: but when a man's life has not passed free from gross errors, to use the mildest language, suspicions are ever ready to fix on him, even when he is as free from what ought at the moment to give the imputation as any the most immaculate of their patriots. This report brings out others from their lurking holes; that he published, at her instigation, the anecdotes of the court of Berlin; and that the king of Prussia, knowing the causes of that publication, circulated the memoirs of Madame de la Motte[2] all over Germany. Such are the eternal tales, suspicions, and improbabilities for which Paris has always been so famous. One clearly, however, gathers from the complexion of conversation, even on the most ridiculous topics, provided of a public nature, how far, and for what reason, confidence is lodged in certain men. In every company, of every rank, you hear of the count de Mirabeau's talents; that he is one of the first pens of France, and the first orator; and yet that he could not carry from confidence six votes on any question in the states. His writings, however, spread in Paris and the provinces: he published a journal of the states, written for a few days with such force, and such severity, that it was silenced by an express edict of government. This is attributed to Mons. Necker, who was treated in it with so little ceremony, that his vanity was wounded to the quick. The number of subscribers to the journal was such, that I have heard the profit, to Mons. Mirabeau, calculated at 80,000 liv. (3,500l.) a year. Since its suppression, he publishes once or twice a week a small pamphlet, to answer

---

[1] Reports verified later. "In the beginning of the year 1790 Mirabeau entered into relations with the court, and pledged himself to its interests in consideration of a large bribe."—Lalanne. See for much light on this subject the Mémoires de Ferrières, and Mémoires de Montlosier The first interview between Mirabeau and the king and queen took place in a cellar of the Tuilleries.

[2] See Carlyle on "The Diamond Necklace," "Misc. Essays."

the same purpose of giving an account of the debates, or rather observations on them, entitled 1, 2, 3, &c. *Lettre des Comte de Mirabeau a ses Commettans*, which, though violent, sarcastic, and severe, the court has not thought proper to stop, respecting, I suppose, its title. It is a weak and miserable conduct, to single out any particular publication for prohibition, while the press groans with innumerable productions, whose tendency is absolutely to overturn the present government; to permit such pamphlets to be circulated all over the kingdom, even by the posts and diligences in the hands of government, is a blindness and folly, from which there are no effects that may not be expected. In the evening to the comic opera; Italian music, Italian words, and Italian performers; and the applause so incessant and rapturous, that the ears of the French must be changing apace. What could Jean Jacques have said, could he have been a witness to such a spectacle at Paris!

The 18th. Yesterday the commons decreed themselves, in consequence of the Abbé Syeyes's amended motion, the title of *Assembleé Nationale*; and also, considering themselves then in activity, the illegality of all taxes; but granted them during the session, declaring that they would, without delay, deliberate on the consolidating of the debt; and on the relief of the misery of the people. These steps give great spirits to the violent partizans of a new constitution, but amongst more sober minds, I see evidently an apprehension that it will prove a precipitate measure. It is a violent step, which may be taken hold of by the court, and converted very much to the people's disadvantage. The reasoning of Mons. de Mirabeau against it was forcible and just—*Si je voulois employer contre les autres motions les armes dont on se sert pour attaquer la mienne, ne pourrois-je pas dire a montour: de quelque maniere que vous-vous qualifiez que vous soyez les representans connus & verifies de la nation, les représentans de 25 millions d'hommes, les representans de la majorité du peuple, dussiez-vous même vous appeller l'Assembleé Nationalé, les etats généraux, empecherez-vous les classes privilegieés de continuer des assembleés que sa majesté a reconnues? Les empecherez-vous de prendre des deliberationes? Les empecherez-vous de pretendre au veto? Empecherez-vous le Roi de les recevoir? Des les reconnoitre, de leur continuer les mêmes titres qu'il leur adonnès jusqu'a present? Enfin, empecherez-vous la nation d'appeller le clergé, le clergé, la noblesse, la noblesse?*

To the royal society of agriculture, where I gave my vote with the rest, who were unanimous for electing general Washington an honorary member; this was a proposal of Mons. Broussonet, in consequence of my having assured him, that the general was an excellent farmer, and had corresponded with me on the subject. Abbé Commerel[1] was present; he gave a pamphlet of his on a new project, the *choux a fauché*, and a paper of the seed.

The 19th. Accompanied Mons. de Broussonet to dine with Mons. de Parmentier, at the *hotel des invalids*. A president of the parliament, a Mons. Mailly, brother-in-law to the chancellor, was there; Abbé Commerel, &c. &c. I remarked two years ago that Mons. Parmentier is one of the best of men, and beyond all question understands every circumstance of the *boulangerie* better than any other writer, as his productions clearly manifest. After dinner, to the plains of Sablon,[2] to see the society's potatoes and preparation for turnips, of which I shall only say that I wish my brethren to stick to their *scientific* farming, and leave the practical to those who understand it. What a sad thing for philosophical husbandmen that God Almighty created such a thing as couch (*triticum repens*).

The 20th. News!—News!—Every one stares at what every one might have expected.[3] A message from the King to the presidents of the three orders, that he should meet them on Monday; and, under pretence of preparing the hall for the *seance royale*, the French guards were placed with bayonets to prevent any of the deputies entering the room. The circumstances of doing this ill-judged act of violence have been as ill-advised as the act itself. Mons. Bailly received no other notice of it than by a letter from the marquis de Brézé, and the deputies met at the door of the hall, without knowing that it was shut. Thus the seeds of disgust were sown wantonly in the manner of

---

[1] The Abbé Commerell introduced mangel wurzel into France.

[2] Sablonville, between Neuilly and St. Denis.

[3] "Ce jour-là fut perdue l'autorité royale. L'initiative des lois et la puissance morale passèrent du monarque à l'assemblée" (Mignet).

doing a thing, which in itself was equally impalatable and unconstitutional. The resolution taken on the spot was a noble and firm one; it was to assemble instantly at the *Jeu de paume*,[1] and there the whole assembly took a solemn oath never to be dissolved but by their own consent, and consider themselves, and act as the national assembly, let them be wherever violence or fortune might drive them, and their expectations were so little favourable, that expresses were sent off to Nantes, intimating that the national assembly might possibly find it necessary to take refuge in some distant city. This message, and placing guards at the hall of the states, are the result of long and repeated councils, held in the king's presence at Marly, where he has been shut up for some days, seeing nobody; and no person admitted, even to the officers of the court, without jealousy and circumspection. The king's brothers have no seat in the council, but the count d'Artois incessantly attends the resolutions, conveys them to the Queen, and has long conferences with her. When this news arrived at Paris, the Palais Royal was in a flame, the coffee-houses, pamphlet-shops, corridores, and gardens were crouded,—alarm and apprehension sat in every eye,—the reports that were circulated eagerly, tending to shew the violent intentions of the court, as if it was bent on the utter extirpation of the French nation, except the party of the Queen, are perfectly incredible for their gross absurdity; but nothing was so glaringly ridiculous but the mob swallowed it with undiscriminating faith. It was, however, curious to remark, among people of another description (for I was in several parties after the news arrived), that the balance of opinions was clearly that the national assembly, as it called itself, had gone too far—had been too precipitate—and too violent—had taken steps that the mass of the people would not support. From which we may conclude, that if the court, having seen the tendency of their late proceedings, shall pursue a firm and politic plan, the popular cause will have little to boast.

The 21st. It is impossible to have any other employment at so critical a moment, than going from house to

[1] This historic tennis-court is still to be seen in the Rue St. François, Versailles.

house demanding news; and remarking the opinions and ideas most current. The present moment is, of all others, perhaps that which is most pregnant with the future destiny of France. The step the commons have taken of declaring themselves the national assembly, independent of the other orders, and of the king himself, precluding a dissolution, is in fact an assumption of all the authority in the kingdom. They have at one stroke converted themselves into the long parliament of Charles I. It needs not the assistance of much penetration to see that if such a pretension and declaration are not done away, king, lords, and clergy are deprived of their shares in the legislature of France. So bold, and apparently desperate a step, full in the teeth of every other interest in the realm, equally destructive to the royal authority, by parliaments and the army, can never be allowed. If it is not opposed, all other powers will lie in ruins around that of the common. With what anxious expectation must one therefore wait to see if the crown will exert itself firmly on the occasion, with such an attention to an improved system of liberty, as is absolutely necessary to the moment! All things considered, that is, the characters of those who are in possession of power, no well digested system and steady execution are to be looked for. In the evening to the play: Madame Rocquere did the queen in Hamlet; it may easily be supposed how that play of Shakespeare is cut in pieces. It has however effect by her admirable acting.

The 22nd. To Versailles at six in the morning, to be ready for the *seance royale*. Breakfasting with the duc de Liancourt, we found that the king had put off going to the states, till to-morrow morning. A committee of council was held last night, which sat till midnight, at which were present Mons. and the count d'Artois for the first time: an event considered as extraordinary, and attributed to the influence of the Queen. The count d'Artois, the determined enemy of Mons. Necker's plans, opposed his system, and prevailed to have the *seance* put off to give time for a council in the king's presence to-day. From the chateau we went to find out the deputies; reports were various where they were assembling. To the *Recolets*, where they had been, but finding it incommodious they went to the church of St. Louis,[1] whither we followed them, and were in time to see M. Bailly take the chair, and read the king's letter, putting off the *seance* till to-morrow. The spectacle of this meeting, was singular—the crowd that attended in and around the church was great,—and the anxiety and suspense in every eye, with the variety of expression that flowed from different views and different characters, gave to the countenances of all the world an impression I had never witnessed before. The only business of importance transacted, but which lasted till three o'clock, was receiving the oaths and the signatures of some deputies, who had not taken them at the *Jeu de paume*; and the union of three bishops and 150 of the deputies of the clergy, who came to verify their powers, and were received by such applause, with such clapping and shouting, from all present, that the church resounded. Apparently the inhabitants of Versailles, which having a population of 60,000 people can afford a pretty numerous mob, are to the last person in the interest of the commons; remarkable, as this town is absolutely fed by the palace, and if the cause of the court is not popular here, it is easy to suppose what it must be in all the rest of the kingdom. Dine with the duc de Liancourt, in the palace, a large party of nobility and deputies of the commons, the duc d'Orleans, amongst them; the bishop of Rodez, Abbé Syeyes, and Mons. Rabaud St. Etienne. This was one of the most striking instances of the impression made on men of different ranks by great events. In the streets, and in the church of St. Louis, such anxiety was in every face, that the importance of the moment was written in the physiognomy; and all the common forms and salutations of habitual civility lost in attention: but amongst a class so much higher as those I dined with, I was struck with the difference. There were not, in thirty persons, five in whose countenances you could guess that any extraordinary event was going forward: more of the conversation was indifferent than I should have expected. Had it all been so, there would have been no room for wonder; but observations were made of the greatest freedom, and so received as to mark that there was not the least impropriety in

[1] The cathedral church of St. Louis, built 1743.

making them. In such a case, would not one have expected more energy of feeling and expression, and more attention in conversation to the crisis that must in its nature fill every bosom? Yet they eat, and drank, and sat, and walked, loitered and smirked and smiled, and chatted with that easy indifference, that made me stare at their insipidity. Perhaps there is a certain nonchalance that is natural to people of fashion from long habit, and which marks them from the vulgar, who have a thousand asperities in the expression of their feelings, that cannot be found on the polished surface of those whose manners are smoothed by society, not worn by attrition. Such an observation would therefore in all common cases be unjust; but I confess the present moment, which is beyond all question the most critical that France has seen from the foundation of the monarchy, since the council was assembled that must finally determine the king's conduct, was such as might have accounted for a behaviour totally different. The duc d'Orleans presence might do a little, but not much; his manner might do more; for it was not without some disgust, that I observed him several times playing off that small sort of wit, and flippant readiness to titter, which, I suppose, is a part of his character, or it would not have appeared to-day. From his manner, he seemed not at all displeased. The Abbé Syeyes has a remarkable physiognomy, a quick rolling eye; penetrating the ideas of other people, but so cautiously reserved as to guard his own. There is as much character in his air and manner as there is vacuity of it in the countenance of Mons. Rabaud St. Etienne, whose physiognomy, however, is far from doing him justice, for he has undoubted talents. It seems agreed, that if, in the council the count d'Artois, carries his point, Mons. Necker, the count de Montmorin,[1] and Mons. de St. Priest[2] will resign; in which case Mons. Necker's return to power, and in triumph, will inevitably

---

[1] Armand, Marc, 1745-1792, Ambassador in Spain, afterwards Minister of Foreign Affairs, and in the confidence of Louis XVI. and Marie Antoinette. A victim of the September massacres.

[2] François, Emmanuel, 1735-1821, Ambassador in Spain, Turkey, and Holland, afterwards Minister of the Interior. He quitted France in Dec., 1790, and was afterwards Private Secretary of Louis XVIII.

happen. Such a turn, however, must depend on events.—
Evening.—The count d'Artois plan accepted; the king will
declare it in his speech to-morrow. Mons. Necker demanded to resign, but it was refused by the king. All is
now anxiety to know what the plan is.

The 23rd. The important day is over: in the morning
Versailles seemed filled with troops: the streets, about ten
o'clock, were lined with the French guards, and some Swiss
regiments, &c.: the hall of the states was surrounded, and
centinels fixed in all the passages, and at the doors; and
none but deputies admitted. This military preparation
was ill-judged, for it seemed admitting the impropriety
and unpopularity of the intended measure, and the expectation, perhaps fear of popular commotions. They pronounced, before the king left the chateau, that his plan
was adverse to the people, from the military parade with
which it was ushered in. The contrary, however, proved
to be the fact; the propositions are known to all the
world: the plan was a good one; much was granted to the
people in great and essential points; and as it was granted
before they had provided for these public necessities of
finance, which occasioned the states being called together;
and consequently left them at full power in future to procure for the people all that opportunity might present, they
apparently ought to accept them, provided some security is
given for the future meetings of the states, without which
all the rest would be insecure; but as a little negociation
may easily secure this, I apprehend the deputies will accept them conditionally: the use of soldiers, and some im-
prudencies in the manner of forcing the king's system, relative to the interior constitution, and assembling of the
deputies, as well as the ill-blood which had had time to
brood for three days past in their minds, prevented the
commons from receiving the king with any expressions of
applause; the clergy, and some of the nobility, cried *vive
le Roi!* but treble the number of mouths being silent, took
off all effect. It seems they had previously determined to
submit to no violence: when the king was gone, and the
clergy and nobility retired, the marquis de Brézé waiting a
moment to see if they meant to obey the king's express
orders, to retire also to another chamber prepared for

them, and perceiving that no one moved, addressed them,
—*Messieurs, vous connoissez les intentions du Roi.* A dead
silence ensued; and then it was that superior talents bore
the sway, that overpowers in critical moments all other
considerations. The eyes of the whole assembly were
turned on the count de Mirabeau, who instantly replied to
the marquis de Brézé—*Oui, Monsieur, nous avons entendu
les intentions qu'on a suggéreés au Roi, & vous qui ne sauriez
être son organe auprès des etats généraux, vous qui n'ávez ici
ni place, ni voix, ni droit de parler, vous n'êtes pas fait pour
nous rapeller son discours. Cependant pour eviter toute
equivoque, & tout delai, je vous declare que si l'on vous a
chargé de nous faire sortir d'ici, vous devez demander des
ordres pour employer la force, car nous ne quitterons nos
places que par la puissance de la baionette.*—On which there
was a general cry of—*Tel est le vœu del l'Assembleé.* They
then immediately passed a confirmation of their preceding
arrets; and, on the motion of the count de Mirabeau, a
declaration that their persons, individually and collectively,
were sacred; and that all who made any attempts against
them should be deemed infamous traitors to their country.

The 24th. The ferment at Paris is beyond conception;
10,000 people have been all this day in the Palais Royal;
a full detail of yesterday's proceedings was brought this
morning, and read by many apparent leaders of little
parties, with comments, to the people." To my surprise,
the king's propositions are received with universal disgust.
He said nothing explicit on the periodical meeting of the
states; he declared all the old feudal rights to be retained as
property. These, and the change in the balance of representation in the provincial assemblies, are the articles that
give the greatest offence. But instead of looking to, or
hoping for further concessions on these points, in order to
make them more consonant to the general wishes; the
people seem, with a sort of phrenzy, to reject all idea of
compromise, and to insist on the necessity of the orders
uniting, that full power may consequently reside in the
commons, to effect what they call the regeneration of the
kingdom, a favourite term, to which they affix no precise
idea, but add the indefinite explanation of the general
reform of all abuses. They are also full of suspicions at

M. Necker's offering to resign, to which circumstance they seem to look more than to much more essential points. It is plain to me, from many conversations and harangues I have been witness to, that the constant meetings at the Palais Royal, which are carried to a degree of licentiousness and fury of liberty, that is scarcely credible, united with the innumerable inflammatory publications that have been hourly appearing since the assembly of the states, have so heated the people's expectations, and given them the idea of such total changes, that nothing the king or court could do, would now satisfy them; consequently it would be idleness itself to make concessions that are not steadily adhered to, not only to be observed by the king, but to be enforced on the people, and good order at the same time restored. But the stumbling-block to this and every plan that can be devised, as the people know and declare in every corner, is the situation of the finances, which cannot possibly be restored but by liberal grants of the states on one hand, or by a bankruptcy on the other. It is well known, that this point has been warmly debated in the council: Mons. Necker has proved to them, that a bankruptcy is inevitable, if they break with the states before the finances are restored; and the dread and terror of taking such a step, which no minister would at present dare to venture on, has been the great difficulty that opposed itself to the projects of the Queen and the count d'Artois. The measure they have taken is a middle one, from which they hope to gain a party among the people, and render the deputies unpopular enough to get rid of them: an expectation, however, in which they will infallibly be mistaken. If, on the side of the people it is urged, that the vices of the old government make a new system necessary, and that it can only be by the firmest measures that the people can be put in possession of the blessings of a free government; it is to be replied, on the other hand, that the personal character of the king is a just foundation for relying that no measures of actual violence can be seriously feared: that the state of the finances, under any possible regimen, whether of faith or bankruptcy, must secure their existence, at least for time sufficient to secure by negociation, what may be hazarded by violence: that by driving things to extremities, they risque an union between all the other orders of the state, with the parliaments, army, and a great body even of the people, who must disapprove of all extremities; and when to this is added the possibility of involving the kingdom in a civil war, now so familiarly talked of, that it is upon the lips of all the world, we must confess, that the commons, if they steadily refuse what is now held out to them, put immense and certain benefits to the chance of fortune, to that hazard which may make posterity curse, instead of bless, their memories as real patriots, who had nothing in view but the happiness of their country. Such an incessant buzz of politics has been in my ears for some days past, that I went to-night to the Italian opera, for relaxation. Nothing could be better calculated for that effect, than the piece performed, *La Villanella Rapita*, by Bianchi, a delicious composition. Can it be believed, that this people, who so lately valued nothing at an opera but the dances, and could hear nothing but a squall,—now attend with feeling to Italian melodies, applaud with taste and rapture, and this without the meretricious aid of a single dance! The music of this piece is charming, elegantly playful, airy, and pleasing, with a duet, between Signora Mandini and Vigagnoni, of the first lustre. The former is a most fascinating singer,—her voice nothing, but her grace, expression, soul, all strung to exquisite sensibility.

The 25th. The criticisms that are made on Mons. Necker's conduct, even by his friends, if above the level of the people, are severe. It is positively asserted, that Abbé Syeyes, Messrs. Mounier, Chapellier,[1] Bernave, Target,[2] Tourette, Rabaud, and other leaders, were almost on their

---

[1] Chapelier (Isaac le), 1754-1794. The upright and eloquent President of the Assemblée Legislative, and at the onset of the Revolution an uncompromising antagonist of the Abbé Maury, and the reactionaries. Later he headed the party in favour of constitutional monarchy, and in consequence was arraigned before the Revolutionary Tribunal.

[2] This brilliant advocate, although a determined opponent of the court, was selected by Louis XVI. to defend him. Target refused the hazardous task, which was at once undertaken by the venerable Malesherbes and young Desèze. He nevertheless published his " Observations sur le procès de Louis XVI.," pointing to an acquittal. He was instrumental in drawing up the Code Civil, and died in 1806.

knees to him, to insist peremptorily on his resignation being accepted, as they were well convinced that his retreat would throw the Queen's party into infinitely greater difficulties and embarrassment than any other circumstance. But his vanity prevailed over all their efforts, to listen to the insidious persuasions of the Queen, who spoke to him in a style of asking a request that would keep the crown on the king's head; at the same time that he yielded to do it, contrary to the interest of the friends of liberty, he courted the huzzas of the mob of Versailles, in a manner that did much mischief. The ministers never go to and from the king's apartment on foot, across the court, which Mons. Necker took this opportunity of doing, though he himself had not done it in quiet times, in order to court the flattery of being called the father of the people, and moving with an immense and shouting multitude at his heels. Nearly at the time that the Queen, in an audience almost private, spoke as above to M. Necker, she received the deputation from the nobility, with the Dauphin in her hand, whom she presented to them, claiming of their honour, the protection of her son's rights; clearly implying that if the step the king had taken, was not steadily asserted, the monarchy would be lost, and the nobility sunk. While M. Necker's mob was heard through every apartment of the chateau, the king passed in his coach to Marly, through a dead and mournful silence,—and that just after having given to his people, and the cause of liberty, more perhaps than ever any monarch had done before. Of such materials are all mobs made,—so impossible is it to satisfy in moments like these, when the heated imagination dresses every visionary project of the brain, in the bewitching colours of liberty. I feel great anxiety to know what will be the result of the deliberations of the commons, after their first protests are over, against the military violence which was so unjustifiably and injudiciously used. Had the king's proposition come after the supplies were granted, and on any inferior question, it would be quite another affair; but to offer this before one shilling is granted, or a step taken, makes all the difference imaginable.——Evening.—The conduct of the court is inexplicable, and without plan: while the late step was taken, to secure the orders sitting separate, a great body of the clergy has been permitted to go to the commons, and the duc d'Orleans, at the head of forty-seven of the nobility, has done the same: and, what is equally a proof of the unsteadiness of the court, the commons are in the common hall of the states, contrary to the express command of the king. The fact is, the *seance royale* was contrary to the personal feelings of the king, and he was brought to it by the council, with much difficulty; and when it afterwards became, as it did every hour, to give new and effective orders to support the system then laid down, it was necessary to have a new battle for every point; and thus the scheme was only opened and not persisted in:—this is the report, and apparently authentic: it is easy to see that that step had better, on a thousand reasons, not have been taken at all, for all vigour and effect of government will be lost, and the people be more assuming than ever. Yesterday at Versailles, the mob was violent,—they insulted, and even attacked all the clergy and nobility that are known to be strenuous for preserving the separation of orders. The bishop of Beauvais [1] had a stone on his head, that almost struck him down.[2] The archbishop of Paris had all his windows broken, and forced to move his lodgings; and the cardinal de la Rochefoucauld hissed and hooted. The confusion is so great, that the court have only the troops to depend on; and it is now said confidently, that if an order is given to the French guards to fire on the people, they will refuse obedience: this astonishes all, except those who know how they have been disgusted by the treatment, conduct, and manœuvres of the duc de Chatelet, their colonel: so wretchedly have the affairs of the court, in every particular, been managed; so miserable its choice of the men in office, even such as are the most intimately connected with its safety, and even existence. What a

[1] If they had knocked him on the head, he would not have been an object of much pity. At a meeting of the society of agriculture in the country, where common farmers were admitted to dine with people of the first rank, this proud fool made difficulties of sitting down in such company.—*Author's note.*

[2] The poor "proud fool" was a victim of the September massacres three years later. The archbishop died in 1790. The cardinal joined the emigrés.

lesson to princes how they allow intriguing courtiers, women, and fools, to interfere, or assume the power that can be lodged, with safety, only in the hands of ability and experience. It is asserted expressly, that these mobs have been excited and instigated by the leaders of the commons, and some of them paid by the duc d'Orleans. The distraction of the ministry is extreme.—At night to the theatre *Francoise*; the Earl of Essex,[1] and the *Maison de Moliere*.

The 26th. Every hour that passes seems to give the people fresh spirit: the meetings at the Palais Royal are more numerous, more violent, and more assured; and in the assembly of electors, at Paris, for sending a deputation to the National Assembly, the language that was talked, by all ranks of people, was nothing less than a revolution in the government, and the establishment of a free constitution. what they mean by a free constitution is easily understood—*a republic*; for the doctrine of the times runs every day more and more to that point; yet they profess, that the kingdom ought to be a monarchy too; or, at least, that there ought to be a king. In the streets one is stunned by the hawkers of seditious pamphlets, and descriptions of pretended events, that all tend to keep the people equally ignorant and alarmed. The supineness, and even stupidity of the court, is without example: the moment demands the greatest decision,—and yesterday, while it was actually a question, whether he should be a doge of Venice, or a king of France, the king went a hunting! The spectacle the Palais Royal presented this night, till eleven o'clock, and, as we afterwards heard, almost till morning, is curious. The croud was prodigious, and fireworks of all sorts were played off, and all the building was illuminated: these were said to be rejoicings on account of the duc d'Orleans and the nobility joining the commons; but united with the excessive freedom, and even licentiousness, of the orators, who harangue the people. With the general movement which before was threatening, all this bustle and noise, which will not leave them a moment tranquil, has a prodigious effect in preparing them for whatever purposes the leaders of the

---

[1] Several French plays bear this name.

commons shall have in view; consequently they are grossly and diametrically opposite to the interests of the court;—but all these are blind and infatuated. It is now understood by everybody, that the king's offers, in the *seance royale*, are out of the question. The moment the commons found a relaxation, even in the trifling point of assembling in the great hall, they disregarded all the rest, and considered the whole as null, and not to be taken notice of, unless enforced in a manner of which there were no signs. They lay it down for a maxim, that they have a right to a great deal more than what the king touched on, but that they will accept of nothing as the concession of power: they will assume and secure all to themselves, as matters of right. Many persons I talk with, seem to think there is nothing extraordinary in this,—but it appears, that such pretensions are equally dangerous and inadmissible, and lead directly to a civil war, which would be the height of madness and folly, when public liberty might certainly be secured, without any such extremity. If the commons are to assume everything as their right, what power is there in the state, short of arms, to prevent them from assuming what is not their right? They instigate the people to the most extensive expectations, and if they are not gratified, all must be confusion; and even the king himself, easy and lethargic as he is, his indifference to power will, by and by, be seriously alarmed, and then he will be ready to listen to measures, to which he will not at present give a moment's attention. All this seems to point strongly to great confusion, and even civil commotions; and to make it apparent, that to have accepted the king's offers, and made them the foundation of future negociation, would have been the wisest conduct, and with that idea I shall leave Paris.

The 27th. The whole business now seems over, and the revolution complete. The king has been frightened by the mobs into overturning his own act of the *seance royale*, by writing to the presidents of the orders of the nobility and clergy, requiring them to join the commons,—full in the teeth of what he had ordained before. It was represented to him, that the want of bread was so great in every part of the kingdom, that there was no extremity to which the people might not be driven: that they were nearly starving, and consequently ready to listen to any suggestions, and on the *qui vive* for all sorts of mischief: that Paris and Versailles would inevitably be burnt; and in a word, that all sorts of misery and confusion would follow his adherence to the system announced in the *seance royale*. His apprehensions, got the better of the party, who had for some days guided him; and he was thus induced to take this step, which is of such importance, that he will never more know where to stop, or what to refuse; or rather he will find, that in the future arrangement of the kingdom, his situation will be very nearly that of Charles I. a spectator, without power, of the effective resolutions of a long parliament. The joy this step occasioned was infinite: the assembly, uniting with the people, all hurried to the chateau. *Vive le Roi* might have been heard at Marly: the king and queen appeared in the balcony, and were received with the loudest shouts of applause; the leaders, who governed these motions, knew the value of the concession much better than those who made it. I have to-day had conversation with many persons on this business; and, to my amazement, there is an idea, and even among many of the nobility, that this union of the orders is only for the verification of their powers, and for *making the constitution*, which is a new term they have adopted; and which they use as if a constitution was a pudding to be made by a receipt. In vain I have asked, where is the power that can separate them hereafter, if the commons insist on remaining together, which may be supposed, as such an arrangement will leave all the power in their own hands? And in vain I appeal to the evidence of the pamphlets written by the leaders of that assembly, in which they hold the English constitution cheap, because the people have not power enough, owing to that of the crown and the house of lords. The event now appears so clear, as not to be difficult to predict: all real power will be henceforward in the commons, having so much inflamed the people in the exercise of it, they will find themselves unable to use it temperately; the court cannot sit to have their hands behind them; the clergy, nobility, parliaments, and army, will, when they find themselves all in danger of annihilation, unite in their mutual defence; but as such an union will demand time, they will find the people armed, and a bloody civil war must be the result. I have more than once declared this as my opinion, but do not find that others unite in it.[1] At all events, however, the tide now runs so strongly in favour of the people, and the conduct of the court seems to be so weak, divided, and blind, that little can happen that will not clearly date from the present moment. Vigour and abilities would have turned every thing on the side of the court; for the great mass of nobility in the kingdom, the higher clergy, the parliaments, and the army, were with the crown; but this desertion of the conduct, that was necessary to secure its power, at a moment so critical, must lead to all sorts of pretensions. At night the fire-works, and illuminations, and mob, and noise, at the Palais Royal increased; the expence must be enormous; and yet nobody knows with certainty from whence it arises: shops there are, however, that for 12f. give as many squibs and serpents as would cost five livres. There is no doubt of it being the duc d'Orleans's money: the people are thus kept in a continual ferment, are for ever assembled, and ready to be in the last degree of commotion whenever called on by the men they have confidence in. Lately a company of Swiss would have crushed all this; a regiment would do it now if led with firmness; but, let it last a fortnight longer, and an army will be wanting.—At the play, Mademoiselle Contá, in the Misanthrope of Moliere, charmed me. She is truly a great actress; ease, grace, person, beauty, wit, and soul. Mola did the misanthrope admirably. I will not take leave of the theatre Francois without once more giving it the preference to all I have ever seen. I shall leave Paris, however, truly rejoiced that the representatives of the people have it undoubtedly in their power so to improve the constitution of their country, as to render all great abuses in future, if not impossible, at least exceedingly

[1] I may remark at present, long after this was written, that, although I was totally mistaken in my prediction, yet, on a revision, I think I was right in it, and that the common course of events would have produced such a civil war, to which every thing tended, from the moment the commons rejected the king's propositions of the *seance royale*, which I now think, more than ever, that they ought, with qualifications, to have accepted. The events that followed were as little to be thought of as of myself being made king of France.—*Author's note.*

difficult, and consequently will establish to all useful purposes an undoubted political liberty; and if they effect this, it cannot be doubted but they will have a thousand opportunities to secure to their fellow-subjects the invaluable blessing of civil liberty also. The state of the finances is such, that the government may easily be kept virtually dependent on the states, and their periodical existence absolutely secured. Such benefits will confer happiness on 25 millions of people; a noble and animating idea, that ought to fill the mind of every citizen of the world, whatever be his country, religion, or pursuit. I will not allow myself to believe for a moment, that the representatives of the people can ever so far forget their duty to the French nation, to humanity, and their own fame, as to suffer any inordinate and impracticable views,—any visionary or theoretic systems,—any frivolous ideas of speculative perfection: much less any ambitious private views, to impede their progress, or turn aside their exertions, from that security which is in their hands, to place on the chance and hazard of public commotion and civil war, the invaluable blessings which are certainly in their power. I will not conceive it possible, that men who have eternal fame within their grasp, will place the rich inheritance on the cast of a die, and, losing the venture, be damned among the worst and most profligate adventurers that ever disgraced humanity.—The duc de Liancourt having made an immense collection of pamphlets, buying every thing that has a relation to the present period; and, among the rest, the cahiers of all the districts and towns of France of the three orders; it was a great object with me to read these, as I was sure of finding in them a representation of the grievances of the three orders, and an explanation of the improvements wished for in the government and administration. These cahiers being instructions given to their deputies, I have now gone through them all, with a pen in hand, to make extracts, and shall therefore leave Paris to-morrow.

The 28th. Having provided myself a light French cabriolet for one horse, or gig Anglois, and a horse, I left Paris, taking leaving of my excellent friend, Mons. Lazowski, whose anxiety for the fate of his country, made me respect his character as much as I had reason to love it for the thousand attentions I was in the daily habit of receiving from him. My kind protectress, the dutchess d'Estissac, had the goodness to make me promise, that I would return to her hospitable hotel, when I had finished the journey I was about to undertake. Of the place I dined at on my road to Nangis,[1] I forget the name, but it is a post-house on the left, at a small distance out of the road. It afforded me a bad room, bare walls, cold raw weather, and no fire; for, when lighted, it smoked too much to be borne;—I was thoroughly out of humour: I had passed some time at Paris amidst the fire, energy, and animation of a great revolution. And for those moments not filled by political events, I had enjoyed the resources of liberal and instructing conversation; the amusements of the first theatre in the world, and the fascinating accents of Mandini, had by turns solaced and charmed the fleeting moments; the change to inns, and those French inns; the ignorance of everybody of those events that were now passing, and which so intimately concerned them; the detestable circumstance of having no newspapers, with a press much freer than the English, altogether formed such a contrast, that my heart sunk with depression. At Guignes,[2] an itinerant dancing-master was fiddling to some children of tradesmen; to relieve my sadness, I became a spectator of their innocent pleasures, and, with great magnificence I gave four 12f. pieces for a cake for the children, which made them dance with fresh animation; but my host, the postmaster, who is a surly pickpocket, thought that if I was so rich, he ought also to receive the benefit, and made me pay 9 liv. 10f. for a miserable tough chicken, a cutlet, a sallad, and a bottle of sorry wine. Such a dirty, pilfering disposition, did not tend to bring me into better humour.—30 miles.

The 29th. To Nangis,[3] the chateau of which belongs to the marquis de Guerchy, who last year at Caen had kindly made me promise to spend a few days here. A house almost full of company, and some of them agreeable, with the eagerness of Mons. de Guerchy for farming, and the

---

[1] (Seine and Marne.)   [2] *Ibid.*
[3] Portions of this château remain in good preservation.

amiable *naiveté* of the marchioness, whether in life, politics, or a farm, were well calculated to bring me into tune again. But I found myself in a circle of politicians, with whom I could agree in hardly any other particular, except the general one of cordially wishing that France might establish an indestructible system of liberty; but for the means of doing it, we were far as the poles asunder. The chaplain of Mons. de Guerchy's regiment, who has a cure here, and I had known at Caen, Mons. l'Abbé de ————, was particularly strenuous for what is called the regeneration of the kingdom, by which it is impossible, from the explanation, to understand any thing more than a theoretic perfection of government; questionable in its origin, hazardous in its progress, and visionary in its end; but always presenting itself under a most suspicious appearance to me, because its advocates, from the pamphlets of the leaders in the National Assembly, to the gentlemen who make its panegyric at present, all affect to hold the constitution of England cheap in respect of liberty : and as that is unquestionably, and by their own admission the best the world ever saw, they profess to appeal from practice to theory, which, in the arrangement of a question of science, might be admitted (though with caution); but, in establishing the complex interests of a great kingdom, in *securing* freedom to 25 millions of people, seems to me the very acmé of imprudence, the very quintessence of insanity. My argument was an appeal to the English constitution; take it at once, which is the business of a single vote ; by your possession of a real and equal representation of the people, you have freed it from its only great objection; in the remaining circumstances, which are but of small importance, improve it—but improve it cautiously ; for surely that ought to be touched with caution, which has given from the moment of its establishment, felicity to a great nation ; which has given greatness to a people designed by nature to be little ; and, from being the humble copiers of every neighbour, has rendered them, in a single century, rivals to the most successful nations in those decorative arts that embellish human life : and the masters of the world in all those that contribute to its convenience. I was commended for my attachment to *what I thought was liberty*; but answered, that the king of France must have no *veto* on the will of the nation; and that the army must be in the hands of the provinces, with an hundred ideas equally impracticable and preposterous. Yet these are the sentiments which the court has done all in its power to spread through the kingdom; for, will posterity believe, that while the press has swarmed with inflammatory productions, that tend to prove the blessings of theoretical confusion, and speculative licentiousness, not one writer of talents has been employed to refute and confound the fashionable doctrines, nor the least care taken to disseminate works of another complexion? By the way, when the court found that the states could not be assembled on the old plan, and that great innovations must accordingly be made, they ought to have taken the constitution of England for their model; in the mode of assembling, they should have thrown the clergy and nobles into one chamber, with a throne for the king, when present. The commons should have assembled in another, and each chamber have, as in England, verified their powers only to themselves. And when the king held a *seance royale*, the commons should have been sent for to the bar of the lords, where seats should have been provided; and the king, in the edict that constituted the states, should have copied from England enough of the rules and orders of proceeding to prevent those preliminary discussions, which in France lost two months, and gave time for heated imaginations to work upon the people too much. By taking such steps, security would have been had, that if changes or events unforeseen arose, they would at least be met with in no such dangerous channel as another form and order of arrangement would permit.—15 miles.

The 30th. My friend's chateau is a considerable one, and much better built than was common in England in the same period, 200 years ago; I believe, however, that this superiority was universal in France, in all the arts. They were, I apprehend, in the reign of Henry IV. far beyond us in towns, houses, streets, roads, and in short, in every thing. We have since, thanks to liberty, contrived to turn the tables on them. Like all the chateaus I have seen in France, it stands close to the town, indeed joining the end of it; but the back *front*, by some very judicious plantations, has entirely the air of the country, without the sight of any buildings. There the present marquis has formed an English lawn, with some agreeable winding walks of gravel, and other decorations, to skirt it. In this lawn they are making hay; and I have had the marquis, Mons. l'Abbé, and some others on the stack to shew them how to make and tread it: such hot politicians!—it is well they did not set the stack on fire. Nangis is near enough to Paris for *the people* to be politicians; the perruquier that dressed me this morning tells me, that every body is determined to pay no taxes, should the National Assembly so ordain. But the soldiers will have something to say. No, Sir, never:—be assured as we are, that the French soldiers will never fire on the people: but, if they should, it is better to be shot than starved. He gave me a frightful account of the misery of the people; whole families in the utmost distress; those that work have a pay insufficient to feed them—and many that find it difficult to get work at all. I enquired of Mons. de Guerchy concerning this, and found it true. By order of the magistrates no person is allowed to buy more than two bushels of wheat at a market, to prevent monopolizing. It is clear to common sense, that all such regulations have a direct tendency to increase the evil, but it is in vain to reason with people whose ideas are immoveably fixed. Being here on a market-day, I attended, and saw the wheat sold out under this regulation, with a party of dragoons drawn up before the market-cross to prevent violence. The people quarrel with the bakers, asserting the prices they demand for bread are beyond the proportion of wheat, and proceeding from words to scuffling, raise a riot, and then run away with bread and wheat for nothing: this has happened at Nangis, and many other markets; the consequence was, that neither farmers nor bakers would supply them till they were in danger of starving, and, when they did come, prices under such circumstances must necessarily rise enormously, which aggravated the mischief, till troops became really necessary to give security to those who supplied the markets. I have been sifting Madame de Guerchy on the expences of living; our friend Mons. l'Abbé joined the conversation, and I collect from it, that to live in a chateau like this, with six men-servants, five maids, eight horses, a garden, and a regular table, with company, but never to go to Paris, might be done for 1000 louis a year. It would in England cost 2000; the mode of living (not the price of things) is therefore cent. per cent. different. —There are gentlemen (noblesse) that live in this country on 6 or 8000 liv. (262l. to 350l.), that keep two men, two maids, three horses, and a cabriolet; there are the same in England, but they are fools. Among the neighbours that visited Nangis was Mons. Trudaine de Montigny, with his new and pretty wife, to return the first visit of ceremony: he has a fine chateau at Montigny,[1] and an estate of 4000 louis a year. This lady was Mademoiselle de Cour Breton, niece to Madame Calonne; she was to have been married to the son of Mons. Lamoignon,[2] but much against her inclinations; finding that common refusals had no avail, she determined on a very uncommon one, which was to go to church, in obedience to her father's orders, and give a solemn NO instead of a *yea*. She was afterwards at Dijon, and never stirred but she was received with huzzas and acclamations by the people for refusing to be allied with la Cour Pleniere; and her firmness was every where spoken of much to her advantage. Mons. la Luzerne was with them, nephew to the French ambassador at London, who, in some broken English, informed me, that he had learned to box of Mendoza.[3] No one can say that he has travelled without making acquisitions. Has the duc d'Orleans learned to box also? The news from Paris is bad: the commotions increase greatly: and such an alarm has spread, that the Queen has called the marechal de Broglio to the king's closet; he has had several conferences: the report is, that

[1] Probably Montigny-Le Roi (Hte. Marne). There are four towns of this name in eastern France.

[2] Lamoignon was associated with Brienne de Loménie in the establishment of the *cour plénière*, a measure which did more than anything else to hasten the Revolution. During the Middle Ages, the name had been applied to assemblages of the king and his vassals on the occasion of fêtes or tourneys. Under an obsolete title, Louis XVI. established a kind of High Court, suspending the provincial parliaments, and investing judicial power in himself, his ministers, and the court. Lamoignon, like Brienne, committed suicide. See H. Martin, vol. xvi. ch. 106.

[3] At the time Arthur Young wrote boxing formed a regular exhibition, and a theatre was opened for it in the Strand. Mendoza opened the Lyceum in 1791.

an army will be collected under him. It may be now necessary; but woeful management to have made it so.

JULY 2. To Meaux¹ Mons. de Guerchy was so kind as to accompany me to Columiers;² I had a letter to Mons. Anveé Dumeé. Pass Rosoy³ to Maupertuis,⁴ through a country chearfully diversified by woods, and scattered with villages; and single farms spread every where as about Nangis. Maupertuis seems to have been the creation of the marquis de Montesquiou, who has here a very fine chateau of his own building; an extensive English garden, made by the count d'Artois' gardener, with the town, has all been of his own forming. I viewed the garden with pleasure; a proper advantage has been taken of a good command of a stream, and many fine springs which rise in the grounds; they are well conducted, and the whole executed with taste. In the kitchen-garden, which is on the slope of a hill, one of these springs has been applied to excellent use: it is made to wind in many doubles through the whole on a paved bed, forming numerous basons for watering the garden, and might, with little trouble, be conducted alternately to every bed as in Spain. This is a hint of real utility to all those who form gardens on the sides of hills; for watering with pots and pails is a miserable, as well as expensive succedaneum to this infinitely more effective method. There is but one fault in this garden, which is its being placed near the house, where there should be nothing but lawn and scattered trees when viewed from the chateau. The road might be hidden by a judicious use of planting. The road to Columiers is admirably formed of broken stone, like gravel, by the marquis of Montesquieu, partly at his own expence. Before I finish with this nobleman, let me observe, that he is commonly esteemed the second family in France, and by some who admit his pretensions, even the first; he claims from the house of Armagnac, which was undoubtedly from Charlemagne: the present king of France, when he signed some paper relative to this family,

---

¹ (Seine and Marne.)
² Coulommiers. There are several places of this name in France, the derivation of the word being *Colombier*, a place for rearing pigeons (Seine and Marne).
³ Rozoy-en-Brie (Seine and Marne) ⁴ Maupertuis (*ibid.*).

that seemed to admit the claim, or refer to it, remarked, that it was declaring one of his subjects to be a better gentleman than himself. But the house of Montmorenci, of which family are the dukes of Luxembourg and Laval, and the prince of Robec, is generally admitted to be the first. Mons. de Montesquieu[1] is a deputy in the states, one of the *quarante* in the French academy, having written several pieces: he is also chief minister to Monsieur the king's brother, an office that is worth 100,000 liv. a year (4,375l.) Dine with Mons. and Madame Dumeé; conversation here, as in every other town of the country, seems more occupied by the dearness of wheat than on any other circumstance; yesterday was market-day, and a riot ensued of the populace, in spite of the troops, that were drawn up as usual to protect the corn: it rises to 46 liv. (2l. 3d.) the septier, or half-quarter,—and some is sold yet higher. To Meaux.—32 miles.

The 3d. Meaux was by no means in my direct road; but its district, Brie,[2] is so highly celebrated for fertility, that it was an object not to omit. I was provided with letters for M. Bernier, a considerable farmer, at Chaucaunin, near Meaux; and for M. Gibert, of Neuf Moutier,[3] a considerable cultivator, whose father and himself had between them made a fortune by agriculture. The former gentleman was not at home; by the latter I was received with great hospitality; and I found in him the strongest desire to give me every information I wished. Mons. Gibert has built a very handsome and commodious house, with farming-offices, on the most ample and solid scale. I was pleased to find his wealth, which is not inconsiderable, to have arisen all from the plough. He did not forget to let me know, that he was noble; and exempted from all tailles; and that he had the honours of the chace, his father having purchased the charge of *Secretaire du Roi*: but he very wisely lives *en fermier*. His wife made ready the table

---

[1] Soldier, politician, littérateur. He separated himself from the court after the flight to Varennes, commanded the victorious Republican army in Savoy, but being accused of monarchical sympathies, retired to Switzerland in 1792. Died 1798.

[2] The Comté de Brie, in Champagne, now forming part of the department of Seine and Marne, famous for its cheeses.

[3] Neufmontier, near Meaux.

for dinner, and his bailiff, with the female domestic, who has the charge of the dairy, &c. both dined with us. This is in a true farming style; it has many conveniencies, and looks like a plan of living, which does not promise, like the foppish modes of little gentlemen, to run through a fortune, from false shame and silly pretensions. I can find no other fault with his system than having built a house enormously beyond his plan of living, which can have no other effect than tempting some successor, less prudent than himself into expences that might dissipate all his and his father's savings. In England that would certainly be the case: the danger, however, is not equal in France.

The 4th. To Chateau Thiery,[1] following the course of the Marne. The country is pleasantly varied, and hilly enough to render it a constant picture, were it inclosed. Thiery is beautifully situated on the same river. I arrived there by five o'clock, and wished, in a period so interesting to France, and indeed to all Europe, to see a newspaper. I asked for a coffee-house, not one in the town. Here are two parishes, and some thousands of inhabitants, and not a newspaper to be seen by a traveller, even in a moment when all ought to be anxiety.—What stupidity, poverty, and want of circulation! This people hardly deserve to be free; and should there be the least attempt with vigour to keep them otherwise, it can hardly fail of succeeding. To those who have been used to travel amidst the energetic and rapid circulation of wealth, animation, and intelligence of England, it is not possible to describe, in words adequate to one's feelings, the dulness and stupidity of France. I have been to day on one of their greatest roads, within thirty miles of Paris, yet I have not seen one diligence, and met but a single gentleman's carriage, nor anything else on the road that looked like a gentleman.—30 miles.

The 5th. To Mareuil.[2] The Marne, about 25 rods broad, flows in an arable vale to the right. The country hilly, and parts of it pleasant; from one elevation there is a noble view of the river. Mareuil is the residence of Mons. Le Blanc, of whose husbandry and improvements, particularly

---

[1] Château-Thierry (Aisne).   [2] Mareuil-sur-Ay (Marne).

in sheep of Spain, and cows of Switzerland, Mons. de Broussonet had spoken very advantageously. This was the gentleman also on whom I depended for information relative to the famous vineyards of Epernay, that produce the fine Champagne. What therefore was my disappointment, when his servants informed me that he was nine leagues off on business. Is Madame Le Blanc at home? *No, she is at Dormans.* My complaining ejaculations were interrupted by the approach of a very pretty young lady, whom I found to be Mademoiselle Le Blanc. *Her mama would return to dinner, her papa at night; and, if I wished to see him, I had better stay.* When persuasion takes so pleasing a form, it is not easy to resist it. There is a manner of doing every thing that either leaves it absolutely indifferent or that interests. The unaffected good humour and simplicity of Mademoiselle Le Blanc entertained me till the return of her mama, and made me say to myself, *you will make a good farmer's wife.* Madame Le Blanc, when she returned, confirmed the native hospitality of her daughter; assured me, that her husband would be at home early in the morning, as she must dispatch a messenger to him on other business. In the evening we supped with Mons. B. in the same village, who married Madame Le Blanc's niece; to pass Mareuil, it has the appearance of a small hamlet of inconsiderable farmers, with the houses of their labourers; and the sentiment that would arise in most bosoms, would be that of picturing the banishment of being condemned to live in it. Who would think that there should be two gentlemen's families in it; and that in one I should find Mademoiselle Le Blanc singing to her systrum, and in the other Madame B. young and handsome, performing on an excellent English piano forte? Compared notes of the expences of living in Champagne and Suffolk;—agreed, that 100 louis d'or a year in Champagne, were as good an income as 180 in England, which I believe true. On his return, Mons. Le Blanc, in the most obliging manner, satisfied all my enquiries, and gave me letters to the most celebrated wine districts.

The 7th. To Epernay,[1] famous for its wines. I had letters

---

[1] (Marne.)

for Mons. Paretilaine, one of the most considerable merchants, who was so obliging as to enter, with two other gentlemen, into a minute disquisition of the produce and profit of the fine vineyards. The *hotel de Rohan* here is a very good inn, where I solaced myself with a bottle of excellent *vin mousseux* for 40*f.* and drank prosperity to *true* liberty in France.—12 miles.

The 8th. To Ay,[1] a village not far out of the road to Rheims, very famous for its wines. I had a letter for Mons. Lasnier, who has 60,000 bottles in his cellar, but unfortunately he was not at home. Mons. Dorse has from 30 to 40,000. All through this country the crop promises miserably, not owing to the great frost, but the cold weather of last week.

To Rheims,[2] through a forest of five miles, on the crown of the hill, which separates the narrow vale of Epernay from the great plain of Rheims. The first view of that city from this hill, just before the descent, at the distance of about four miles, is magnificent. The cathedral makes a great figure, and the church of St. Remy terminates the town proudly. Many times I have had such a view of towns in France, but when you enter them, all is a clutter of narrow, crooked, dark, and dirty lanes. At Rheims it is very different: the streets are almost all broad, straight, and well built, equal in that respect to any I have seen; and the inn, the *hotel de Moulinet*, is so large and well-served as not to check the emotions raised by agreeable objects, by giving an impulse to contrary vibrations in the bosom of the traveller, which at inns in France is too often the case. At dinner they gave me also a bottle of excellent wine. I suppose fixed air is good for the rheumatism; I had some writhes of it before I entered Champagne, but the *vin mousseux* has absolutely banished it. I had letters for Mons. Cadot l'aîné, a considerable manufacturer, and the possessor of a large vineyard, which he cultivates himself; he was therefore a double fund to me. He received me very politely, answered my enquiries, and shewed me his fabric. The cathedral is large, but does not strike me like that of Amiens, yet ornamented, and many painted

[1] (Marne.)   [2] (*Ibid.*)

windows. They showed me the spot where the kings are crowned. You enter and quit Rheims through superb and elegant iron gates : in such public decorations, promenades, &c. French towns are much beyond English ones. Stopped at Sillery,[1] to view the wine press of the marquis de Sillery;[2] he is the greatest wine-farmer in all Champagne, having in his own hands 180 arpents. Till I got to Sillery, I knew not that it belonged to the husband of Madame de Genlis; but I determined, on hearing that it did, to pluck up impudence enough to introduce myself to the marquis, should he be at home : I did not like to pass the door of Madame de Genlis without seeing her : her writings are too celebrated. *La Petite Loge*, where I slept, is bad enough of all conscience, but such a reflection would have made it ten times worse : the absence, however, of both Mons. and Madame quieted both my wishes and anxieties. He is in the states.—28 miles.

The 9th. To Chalons,[3] through a poor country and poor crops. M. de Broussonet had given me a letter to Mons. Sabbatier, secretary to the academy of sciences, but he was absent. A regiment passing to Paris, an officer at the inn addressed me in English :—He had learned, he said, in America, damme!—*He* had taken lord Cornwallis, damme! —Marechal Broglio was appointed to command an army of 50,000 men near Paris—it was necessary—the *tiers état* were running mad—and wanted some wholesome correction ;—they want to establish a republic—absurd! Pray, Sir, what did you fight for in America? To establish a republic. What was so good for the Americans, is it so bad for the French? Aye, damme! that is the way the English want to be revenged. It is, to be sure, no bad opportunity. Can the English follow a better example? He then made many enquiries about what we thought and said upon it in England : and I may remark, that almost every person I meet has the same idea—*The English must be very well contented at our confusion.* They feel pretty pointedly what they deserve.—12½ miles.

[1] (Marne.)
[2] First called the Comte de Genlis ; he was afterwards member of the Convention, guillotined 1793.
[3] Châlons-sur-Marne (Marne).

The 10th. To Ove.¹ Pass Courtisseau,² a small village, with a great church; and though a good stream, not an idea of irrigation. Roofs of houses almost flat, with projecting eaves, resembling those from Pau to Bayonne. At St. Menehoud³ a dreadful tempest, after a burning day, with such a fall of rain, that I could hardly get to Mons. l'Abbé Michel, to whom I had a letter. When I found him, the incessant flashes of lightning would allow me no conversation; for all the females of the house came into the room for the Abbé's protection I suppose, so I took leave. The *vin de Champagne*, which is 40*f.* at Rheims, is 3 liv. at Chalons and here, and execrably bad; so there is an end of my physic for the rheumatism.—25 miles.

The 11th. Pass Islets,⁴ a town (or rather collection of dirt and dung) of new features, that seem to mark, with the faces of the people, a country not French.—25 miles.

The 12th. Walking up a long hill, to ease my mare, I was joined by a poor woman, who complained of the times, and that it was a sad country; demanding her reasons, she said her husband had but a morsel of land, one cow, and a poor little horse, yet they had a *franchar* (42 lb.) of wheat, and three chickens, to pay as a quit-rent to one Seigneur; and four *franchar* of oats, one chicken and 1*f.* to pay to another, besides very heavy tailles and other taxes. She had seven children, and the cow's milk helped to make the soup. But why, instead of a horse, do not you keep another cow? Oh, her husband could not carry his produce so well without a horse; and asses are little used in the country. It was said, at present, that *something was to be done by some great folks for such poor ones, but she did not know who nor how*, but God send us better, *car les tailles & les droits nous ecrasent.*—This woman, at no great distance, might

---

¹ Auve, on the river of that name (Marne).
² Courtisois, a curious Celtic community (Marne).
³ St. Menehould (Marne).
⁴ Les Islettes. This "collection of dirt and dung" is historic. From the neighbouring village of Grandpré, Dumouriez wrote to the Minister of War in September, 1792. "J'attends les Prussiens. Le camp de Grandpré et celui des Islettes sont les Thermopyles de la France; mais je serai plus heureux que Léonidas."—MIGNET. The prophecy was not strictly fulfilled. The Prussians foiled his manœuvres at Grandpré; but a few days later the victory of Valmy saved the Republic.

have been taken for sixty or seventy, her figure was so bent, and her face so furrowed and hardened by labour,—but she said she was only twenty-eight. An Englishman who has not travelled, cannot imagine the figure made by infinitely the greater part of the countrywomen in France; it speaks, at the first sight, hard and severe labour: I am inclined to think, that they work harder than the men, and this, united with the more miserable labour of bringing a new race of slaves into the world, destroys absolutely all symmetry of person and every feminine appearance. To what are we to attribute this difference in the manners of the lower people in the two kingdoms? To GOVERNMENT.—23 miles.

The 13th. Leave Mar-le-Tour[1] at four in the morning: the village herdsman was sounding his horn; and it was droll to see every door vomiting out its hogs or sheep, and some a few goats, the flock collecting as it advances. Very poor sheep, and the pigs with mathematical backs, large segments of small circles. They must have abundance of commons here, but, if I may judge by the report of the animals carcases, dreadfully overstocked. To Metz,[2] one of the strongest places in France; pass three draw-bridges, but the command of water must give a strength equal to its works. The common garrison is 10,000 men, but there are fewer at present. Waited on M. de Payen, secretary of the academy of sciences; he asked my plan, which I explained; he appointed me at four in the afternoon at the academy, as there would be *seance* held; and he promised to introduce me to some persons who could answer my enquiries. I attended accordingly, when I found the academy assembled at one of their weekly meetings. Mons. Payen introduced me to the members, and, before they proceeded to their business, they had the goodness to sit in council on my enquiries, and to resolve many of them. In the "Almanach des Trois Evechés," 1789, this academy is said to have been instituted particularly for agriculture; I turned to the list of their honorary members to see what attention they had paid to the men who, in the present age,

---

[1] Mars-la-Tour (Meurthe and Moselle).
[2] Metz, former chef-lieu of the department of the Moselle, now annexed to Prussia.

have advanced that art. I found an Englishman, Dom Cowley, of London. Who is Dom Cowley?—Dined at the table d'hôte, with seven officers, out of whose mouths, at this important moment, in which conversation is as free as the press, not one word issued for which I would give a straw, nor a subject touched on of more importance, than a coat, or a puppy dog. At table d'hôtes of officers, you have a voluble garniture of bawdry or nonsense; at those of merchants, a mournful and stupid silence. Take the mass of mankind, and you have more good sense in half an hour in England than in half a year in France—Government! Again:—all—all—is government.—15 miles.

The 14th.[1] They have a *cabinet literaire* at Metz, something like that I described at Nantes, but not on so great a plan; and they admit any person to read or go in and out for a day, on paying 4*f*. To this I eagerly resorted, and the news from Paris, both in the public prints, and by the information of a gentleman, I found to be interesting. Versailles and Paris are surrounded by troops: 35,000 men are assembled, and 20,000 more on the road, large trains of artillery collected, and all the preparations of war. The assembling of such a number of troops has added to the scarcity of bread; and the magazines that have been made for their support, are not easily by the people distinguished from those they suspect of being collected by monopolists. This has aggravated their evils almost to madness; so that the confusion and tumult of the capital are extreme. A gentleman of an excellent understanding, and apparently of consideration, from the attention paid him, with whom I had some conversation on the subject, lamented in the most pathetic terms, the situation of his country; he considers a civil war as impossible to be avoided. There is not, he added, a doubt but the court, finding it impossible to bring the National Assembly to terms, will get rid of them; a bankruptcy at the same moment is inevitable; the union of such confusion must be a civil war; and it is now only by torrents of blood that we have any hope of establishing a freer constitution: yet it must be established; for the old government is rivetted to abuses that are insup-

---

[1] Needless perhaps to remind the reader that on this day took place the storming of the Bastile.

portable. He agreed with me entirely, that the propositions of the *seance royale*, though certainly not sufficiently satisfactory, yet, were the ground for a negociation, that would have secured by degrees *all even that the sword can give us, let it be as successful as it will. The purse—the power of the purse is every thing; skilfully managed, with so necessitous a government as ours, it would, one after another, have gained all we wished. As to a war, Heaven knows the event; and if we have success, success itself may ruin us; France may have a Cromwell in its bosom, as well as England.* Metz is, without exception, the cheapest town I have been in. The table d'hôte is 36*f*. a head, plenty of good wine included. We were ten, and had two courses and a dessert of ten dishes each, and those courses plentiful. The supper is the same; I had mine, of a pint of wine and a large plate of chaudiés,[1] in my chamber, for 10*f*. a horse, hay, and corn 25*f*. and nothing for the apartment; my expence was therefore 71*f*. a day, or 2s. 11½d.; and with the table d'hôte for supper, would have been but 97*f*. or 4s. 0½d.—In addition, much civility and good attendance. It is at the *Faisan*. Why are the cheapest inns in France the best?—The country to Pont-a-Mousson[2] is all of bold feature.—The river Moselle, which is considerable, runs in the vale, and the hills on either side are high. Not far from Metz there are the remains of an ancient aqueduct for conducting the waters of a spring across the Moselle: there are many arches left on this side, with the houses of poor people built between them. At Pont-a-Mousson Mons. Pichon, the sub-delegué of the intendant, to whom I had letters, received me politely, satisfied my enquiries, which he was well able to do from his office, and conducted me to see whatever was worth viewing in the town. It does not contain much; the *école militaire*, for the sons of the poor nobility, also the *convent de Premonte*,[3]

---

[1] Echaudé, galette or fritter.
[2] Pont-à-Mousson (Meurthe and Moselle).
[3] Our author was misinformed here. The Prémontrés having resisted alike the authority of the Bishop of Metz, the King and the Pope, had been finally replaced, as a teaching body, by the Jesuits under Louis XIII. The convent of St. Eloi, originally occupied by the Prémontrés, was exchanged by their successors for the more commodious house of des Petits Carmes, in 1635, and it is of this that Arthur Young

which has a very fine library, 107 feet long and 25 broad. I was introduced to the abbot as a person who had some knowledge in agriculture.—17 miles.

The 15th. I went to Nancy,[1] with great expectation, having heard it represented as the prettiest town in France. I think, on the whole, it is not undeserving the character in point of building, direction, and breadth of streets.— Bourdeaux is far more magnificent; Bayonne and Nantes are more lively; but there is more equality in Nancy; it is almost all good; and the public buildings are numerous. The *place royale*, and the adjoining area are superb. Letters from Paris! all confusion! the ministry removed: Mons. Necker ordered to quit the kingdom without noise. The effect on the people of Nancy was considerable.—I was with Mons. Willemet when his letters arrived, and for some time his house was full of enquirers; all agreed, that it was fatal news, and that it would occasion great commotions. *What will be the result at Nancy?* The answer was in effect the same from all I put this question to: *We are a provincial town, we must wait to see what is done at Paris; but every thing is to be feared from the people, because bread is so dear, they are half starved, and are consequently ready for commotion.*—This is the general feeling; they are as nearly concerned as Paris; but they dare not stir; they dare not even have an opinion of their own till they know what Paris thinks; so that if a starving populace were not in question, no one would dream of moving. This confirms what I have often heard remarked, that the *deficit* would not have produced the revolution but in concurrence with the price of bread. Does not this shew the infinite consequence of great cities to the liberty of mankind? Without Paris, I question whether the present revolution, which is fast working in France, could possibly have had an origin. It is not in the villages of Syria or Diarbekir that the Grand Seigneur meets with a murmur against his will;

evidently wrote. The buildings are now appropriated as Caisse d'Epargne and Maison de Piété, and the church as a Public Library and Museum. The library contains many illuminated MSS. The country curés, largely recruited from this order, rendered much service to agriculture. See "L'administration de l'agriculture, 1785-7."

[1] (Meurthe and Moselle.) This department was formed from what remained of the two of that name; the greater part of which was annexed to Germany in 1871.

it is at Constantinople that he is obliged to manage and mix caution even with despotism. Mr. Willemet, who is demonstrator of botany, shewed me the botanical garden, but it is in a condition that speaks the want of better funds. He introduced me to a Mons. Durival, who has written on the vine, and gave me one of his treatises, and two of his own on botanical subjects. He also conducted me to Mons. l'Abbé Grandpére, a gentleman curious in gardening, who, as soon as he knew that I was an Englishman, whimsically took it into his head to introduce me to a lady, my countrywoman, who hired, he said, the greatest part of his house. I remonstrated against the impropriety of this, but all in vain; the Abbé had never travelled, and thought that if he were at the distance of England from France (the French are not commonly good geographers) he should be very glad to see a Frenchman; and that, by parity of reasoning, this lady must be the same to meet a countryman she never saw or heard of. Away he went, and would not rest till I was conducted into her apartment. It was the dowager Lady Douglas; she was unaffected, and good enough not to be offended at such a strange intrusion.—She had been here but a few days; had two fine daughters with her, and a beautiful Kamchatka dog; she was much troubled with the intelligence her friends in the town had just given her, that she would, in all probability, be forced to move again, as the news of Mons. Necker's removal, and the new ministry being appointed, would certainly occasion such dreadful tumults, that a foreign family would probably find it equally dangerous and disagreeable.—18 miles.

The 16th. All the houses at Nancy have tin eave troughs and pipes, which render walking the streets much more easy and agreeable; it is also an additional consumption, which is politically useful. Both this place and Luneville are lighted in the English manner, instead of the lamps being strung across the streets as in other French towns. Before I quit Nancy, let me caution the unwary traveller, if he is not a great lord, with plenty of money that he does not know what to do with, against the *hotel d'Angleterre*; a bad dinner 3 liv. and for the room as much more. A pint of wine, and a plate of chaudié 20*f.* which at Metz was 10*f.* and in addition, I liked so little my treatment, that I changed my quarters to the *hotel de Halle*, where, at the table d'hôte, I had the company of some agreeable officers, two good courses, and a dessert, for 36*f.* with a bottle of wine. The chamber 20*f.*; for building, however, the *hotel d'Angleterre* is much superior, and is the first inn. In the evening to Luneville. The country about Nancy is pleasing.—17 miles.

The 17th. Luneville [1] being the residence of Mons. Lazowski, the father of my much esteemed friend, who was advertised of my journey, I waited on him in the morning; he received me with not politeness only, but hospitality— with a hospitality I began to think was not to be found on this side of the kingdom.—From Mareuil hither, I had really been so unaccustomed to receive any attentions of that sort, that it awakened me to a train of new feelings agreeable enough.—An apartment was ready for me, which I was pressed to occupy, desired to dine, and expected to stay some days: he introduced me to his wife and family, particularly to M. l'Abbé Lazowski, who, with the most obliging alacrity, undertook the office of shewing me whatever was worth seeing.—We examined, in a walk before dinner, the establishment of the orphans; well regulated and conducted. Luneville wants such establishments, for it has no industry, and therefore is very poor; I was assured not less than half the population of the place, or 10,000 persons are poor. Luneville is cheap. A cook's wages two, three, or four louis. A maid's, that dresses hair, three or four louis; a common house-maid, one louis; a common footman, or a house lad, three louis. Rent of a good house sixteen or seventeen louis. Lodgings of four or five rooms, some of them small, nine louis. After dinner, wait on M. Vaux dit Pompone, an intimate acquaintance of my friend's; here mingled hospitality and politeness also received me, and so much pressed to dine with him tomorrow, that I should certainly have staid had it been merely for the pleasure of more conversation with a very sensible and cultivated man, who, though advanced in years, has the talents and good humour to render his com-

---

[1] (Meurthe and Moselle.) Lunéville is now the seat of a flourishing and beautiful faïence manufactory.

pany universally agreeable: I was obliged to refuse it; I was out of order all day. Yesterday's heat was followed, after some lightning, by a cold night, and I laid, without knowing it, with the windows open, and caught cold I suppose, from the information of my bones. I am acquainted with strangers as easily and quickly as any body, a habit that much travelling can scarcely fail to give, but to be ill among them would be *enuyante*, demand too much attention, and incroach on their humanity. This induced me to refuse the obliging wishes of both the Messrs. Lazowski, Mons. Pompone, and also of a pretty and agreeable American lady, I met at the house of the latter. Her history is singular, and yet very natural. She was Miss Blake, of New-York; what carried her to Dominica I know not; but the sun did not spoil her complexion: a French officer, Mons. Tibalié, on taking the island, made her his captive, and himself became her own, fell in love, and married her; brought his prize to France, and settled her in his native town of Luneville. The regiment, of which he is major, being quartered in a distant province, she complained of seeing her husband not more than for six months in two years. She has been four years at Luneville; and having the society of three children, is reconciled to a scene of life new to her. Mons. Pompone, who, she assured me, is one of the best men in the world, has parties every day at his house, not more to his own satisfaction than to her comfort.—This gentleman is another instance, as well as the major, of attachment to the place of nativity; he was born at Luneville; attended King Stanislaus in some respectable office, near his person; has lived much at Paris, and with the great, and had first ministers of state for his intimate friends; but the love of the *natale solum* brought him back to Luneville, where he has lived beloved and respected for many years, surrounded by an elegant collection of books, amongst which the poets are not forgotten, having himself no inconsiderable talents in transfusing agreeable sentiments into pleasing verses. He has some couplets of his own composition, under the portraits of his friends, which are pretty and easy. It would have given me much pleasure to have spent some days at Luneville; an agreeable opening was made for me in two houses, where I should have met with a friendly and agreeable reception: but the misfortunes of travelling are sometimes the accidents that cross the moments prepared for enjoyment; and at others, the system of a journey inconsistent with the plans of destined pleasure.

The 18th. To Haming,[1] through an uninteresting country.—28 miles.

The 19th. To Savern,[2] in Alsace: the country to Phalsbourg,[3] a small fortified town, on the frontiers, is much the same to the eye as hitherto. The women in Alsace all wear straw hats, as large as those worn in England; they shelter the face, and should secure some pretty country girls, but I have seen none yet. Coming out of Phalsbourg, there are some hovels miserable enough, yet have chimnies and windows, but the inhabitants in the lowest poverty. From that town to Savern all a mountain of oak timber, the descent steep, and the road winding. In Savern, I found myself to all appearance veritably in Germany; for two days past much tendency to a change, but here not one person in an hundred has a word of French; the rooms are warmed by stoves; the kitchen-hearth is three or four feet high, and various other trifles shew, that you are among another people. Looking at a map of France, and reading histories of Louis XIV. never threw his conquest or seizure of Alsace into the light which travelling into it did: to cross a great range of mountains; to enter a level plain, inhabited by a people totally distinct and different from France, with manners, language, ideas, prejudices, and habits all different, made an impression of the injustice and ambition of such a conduct, much more forcible than ever reading had done: so much more powerful are things than words.—22 miles.

The 20th. To Strasbourg,[4] through one of the richest scenes of soil and cultivation to be met with in France, and rivalled only by Flanders, which however, exceeds it. I

---

[1] Héming, French; Hemingen, German.

[2] Saverne, French; Zabern, German.

[3] Phalsburg, formerly in the department of Meurthe, now annexed to Germany.

[4] Formerly chef-lieu of the department of Bas Rhin, now annexed to Prussia.

arrived there at a critical moment, which I thought would have broken my neck; a detachment of horse, with their trumpets on one side, a party of infantry, with their drums beating on the other, and a great mob hallooing, frightened my French mare; and I could scarcely keep her from trampling on Messrs. the *tiers etat*. On arriving at the inn, hear the interesting news of the revolt of Paris.—The *Guardes Francoises* joining the people; the little dependence on the rest of the troops; the taking the Bastile; and the institution of the *milice bourgeoise*; in a word, of the absolute overthrow of the old government. Every thing being now decided, and the kingdom absolutely in the hands of the assembly, they have the power to make a new constitution, such as they think proper; and it will be a great spectacle for the world to view, in this enlightened age, the representatives of twenty-five millions of people sitting on the construction of a new and better order and fabric of liberty, than Europe has yet offered. It will now be seen, whether they will copy the constitution of England, freed from its faults, or attempt, from theory, to frame something absolutely speculative: in the former case, they will prove a blessing to their country; in the latter they will probably involve it in inextricable confusions and civil wars, perhaps not in the present period, but certainly at some future one. I hear nothing of their removing from Versailles; if they stay there under the controul of an armed mob, they must make a government that will please the mob; but they will, I suppose, be wise enough to move to some central town Tours, Blois, or Orleans, where their deliberations may be free. But the Parisian spirit of commotion spreads quickly; it is here; the troops that were near breaking my neck, are employed, to keep an eye on the people who shew signs of an intended revolt. They have broken the windows of some magistrates that are no favourites; and a great mob of them is at this moment assembled demanding clamourously to have meat at 5*f.* a pound. They have a cry among them that will conduct them to good lengths,—*Point d'impôt & vivent les etâts.*—Waited on Mons. Herman, professor of natural history in the University here, to whom I had letters; he replied to some of my questions, and introduced me for others to Mons. Zimmer, who having been in some degree a practitioner, had understanding enough of the subject to afford me some information that was valuable. View the public buildings, and cross the Rhine passing for some little distance into Germany, but no new features to mark a change; Alsace is Germany, and the change great on descending the mountains. The exterior of the cathedral is fine, and the tower singularly light and beautiful; it is well known to be one of the highest in Europe; commands a noble and rich plain, through which the Rhine, from the number of its islands, has the appearance of a chain of lakes rather than of a river.—Monument of marechal Saxe, &c. &c. I am puzzled about going to Carlsrhue, the residence of the Margrave of Baden: it was an old intention to do it, if ever I was within an hundred miles; for there are some features in the reputation of that sovereign, which made me wish to be there. He fixed Mr. Taylor, of Bifrons in Kent, whose husbandry I describe in my Eastern Tour, on a large farm; and the *œconomistes*, in their writings, speak much of an experiment he made in their Physiocratical rubbish, which, however erroneous their principles might be, marked much merit in the prince. Mons. Herman tells me also, that he has sent a person into Spain to purchase rams for the improvement of wool, I wish he had fixed on somebody likely to understand a good ram, which a professor of botany is not likely to do too well. This botanist is the only person Mons. Herman knows at Carlsrhue, and therefore can give me no letter thither, and how can I go, unknown to all the world, to the residence of a sovereign prince, for Mr. Taylor has left him, is a difficulty apparently insurmountable.—22½ miles.

The 21st. I have spent some time this morning at the *cabinet literaire*, reading the gazettes and journals that give an account of the transactions at Paris: and I have had some conversation with several sensible and intelligent men on the present revolution. The spirit of revolt is gone forth into various parts of the kingdom; the price of bread has prepared the populace every where for all sorts of violence; at Lyons there have been commotions as furious as at Paris, and the same at a great many other places: Dauphiné is in arms: and Bretagne in absolute rebellion. The idea is, that the people will, from hunger, be driven to revolt; and when once they find any other means of subsistence than that of honest labour, every thing will be to be feared. Of such consequence it is to a country, and indeed to every country, to have a good police of corn; a police that shall by securing a high price to the farmer, encourage his culture enough to secure the people at the same time from famine. My anxiety about Carlsrhue is now at an end; the Margrave is at Spaw; I shall not therefore think of going.——*Night*—I have been witness to a scene curious to a foreigner; but dreadful to Frenchmen that are considerate. Passing through the square of the *hotel de ville*, the mob were breaking the windows with stones, notwithstanding an officer and a detachment of horse was in the square. Perceiving that their numbers not only increased, but that they grew bolder and bolder every moment, I thought it worth staying to see what it would end in, and clambered on to the roof of a row of low stalls opposite the building, against which their malice was directed. Here I beheld the whole commodiously. Perceiving that the troops would not attack them, except in words and menaces, they grew more violent, and furiously attempted to beat the door in pieces with iron crows; placing ladders to the windows. In about a quarter of an hour, which gave time for the assembled magistrates to escape by a back door, they burst all open, and entered like a torrent with a universal shout of the spectators. From that minute a shower of casements, sashes, shutters, chairs, tables, sophas, books, papers, pictures, &c., rained incessantly from all the windows of the house, which is seventy or eighty feet long, and which was then succeeded by tiles, skirting boards, bannisters, frame-work, and every part of the building that force could detach. The troops, both horse and foot, were quiet spectators. They were at first too few to interpose, and, when they became more numerous, the mischief was too far advanced to admit of any other conduct than guarding every avenue around, permitting none to go to the scene of action, but letting every one that pleased retire with his plunder; guards being at the same time placed at the doors of the churches, and all public buildings. I was for two hours a spectator at different places of the scene, secure myself from the falling furniture, but near enough to see a fine lad of about 14 crushed to death by something as he was handing plunder to a woman, I suppose his mother, from the horror pictured in her countenance. I remarked several common soldiers, with their white cockades, among the plunderers, and instigating the mob even in sight of the officers of the detachment. There were amongst them people so decently dressed, that I regarded them with no small surprize:— they destroyed all the public archives; the streets for some way around strewed with papers; this has been a wanton mischief; for it will be the ruin of many families unconnected with the magistrates.

The 22d. To Schelestadt.[1] At Strasbourg, and the country I passed, the lower ranks of women wear their hair in a toupee in front, and behind braided into a circular plait, three inches thick, and is most curiously contrived to convince one that they rarely pass a comb through it. I could not but picture them as the *nidus* of living colonies, that never approach me (they are not burthened with too much beauty,) but I scratched my head from sensations of imaginary itching. The moment you are out of a great town all in this country is German; the inns have one common large room, many tables and cloths ready spread, where every company dines; gentry at some, and the poor at others. Cookery also German: *schnitz*[2] is a dish of bacon and fried pears; has the appearance of a mess for the devil; but I was surprized, on tasting, to find it better than passable. At Schelestadt I had the pleasure of finding the count de la Rochefoucauld, whose regiment (of Champagne), of which he is second major, is quartered here. No attentions could be kinder than what I received from him; they were a renewal of the numerous ones I was in the habit of experiencing from his family; and he introduced me to a good farmer from whom I had the intelligence I wanted.—25 miles.

The 23d. An agreeable quiet day, with the count de la

---

[1] Schleltstadt, German; Schlestadt, French, formerly in the department of Bas Rhin, now annexed to Germany.

[2] Schnitz is a name applied to any fruit cut and dried in the oven.

Rochefoucauld: dine with the officers of the regiment, the count de Loumené, the colonel, nephew to the cardinal de Loumené, present. Sup at my friend's lodgings; an officer of infantry, a Dutch gentleman who has been much in the East Indies, and speaks English there. This has been a refreshing day; the society of well informed people, liberal, polite, and communicative, has been a contrast to the *sombre* stupidity of table d'hôtes.

The 24th. To Isenheim,[1] by Colmar.[2] The country is in general a dead level, with the Voge mountains very near to the right; those of Suabia to the left; and there is another range very distant, that appears in the opening to the south. The news at the table d'hôte at Colmar curious, that the Queen had a plot, nearly on the point of execution, to blow up the National Assembly by a mine, and to march the army instantly to massacre all Paris. A French officer present presumed but to doubt of the truth of it, and was immediately overpowered with numbers of tongues. A deputy had written it; they had seen the letter, and not a hesitation could be admitted: I strenuously contended, that it was folly and nonsense at the first blush, a mere invention to render persons odious who, for what I knew, might deserve to be so, but certainly not by such means; if the angel Gabriel had descended and taken a chair at table to convince them, it would not have shaken their faith. Thus it is in revolutions, one rascal writes, and an hundred thousand fools believe.—25 miles.

The 25th. From Isenheim, the country changes from the dead flat, to pleasant views and inequalities, improving all the way to Befort,[3] but neither scattered houses nor inclosures. Great riots at Befort:—last night a body of mob and peasants demanded of the magistrates the arms in the magazine, to the amount of three or four thousand stand; being refused, they grew riotous and threatened to set fire

---

[1] Ensisheim, now Prussian.
[2] Colmar was formerly chef-lieu of the department of the Haut Rhin, now annexed to Germany.
[3] Belfort, formerly in the department of Haut Rhin, now chef-lieu of the department of the Territoire de Belfort, created in 1871; a fortified place of the first importance, and saved from annexation by the efforts of M. Thiers.

to the town, on which the gates were shut; and to-day the regiment of Bourgogne arrived for their protection. Mons. Necker passed here to-day in his way from Basle to Paris, escorted by 50 bourgeois horsemen, and through the town by the music of all the troops. But the most brilliant period of his life is past; from the moment of his reinstatement in power to the assembling of the states, the fate of France, and of the Bourbons, was then in his hands; and whatever may be the result of the present confusions they will, by posterity, be attributed to his conduct, since he had unquestionably the power of assembling the states in whatever form he pleased: he might have had two chambers, three, or one; he might have given what would unavoidably have slid into the constitution of England; all was, in his hands; he had the greatest opportunity of political architecture that ever was in the power of man: the great legislators of antiquity never possessed such a moment: in my opinion he missed it completely, and threw that to the chance of the winds and waves, to which he might have given impulse, direction, and life. I had letters to Mons. de Bellonde, *commissaire de Guerre*; I found him alone: he asked me to sup, saying he should have some persons to meet me who could give me information. On my returning, he introduced me to Madame de Bellonde, and a circle of a dozen ladies, with three or four young officers, leaving the room himself to attend Madame, the princess of something, who was on her flight to Switzerland. I wished the whole company very cordially at the devil, for I saw, at one glance, what sort of information I should have. There was a little *coterie* in one corner listening to an officer's detail of leaving Paris. This gentleman further informed us, that the count d'Artois, and all the princes of the blood, except Monsieur, and the duke d'Orleans, the whole connection of Polignac, the marechal de Broglio, and an infinite number of the first nobility had fled the kingdom, and were daily followed by others; and lastly, that the King, Queen, and royal family, were in a situation at Versailles really dangerous and alarming, without any dependence on the troops near them, and, in fact, more like prisoners than free. Here is, therefore, a revolution effected by a sort of magic; all powers in the realm are destroyed but that of the commons; and it now will remain to see what sort of architects they are at rebuilding an edifice in the place of that which has been thus marvellously tumbled in ruins. Supper being announced, the company quitted the room, and as I did not push myself forward, I remained at the rear till I was very whimsically alone; I was a little struck at the turn of the moment, and did not advance when I found myself in such an extraordinary situation, in order to see whether it would arrive at the point it did. I then, smiling, took my hat, and walked fairly out of the house. I was, however, overtaken below; but I talked of business—or pleasure—or of something, or nothing—and hurried to the inn. I should not have related this, if it had not been at a moment that carried with it its apology: the anxiety and distraction of the time must fill the head, and occupy the attention of a gentleman;—and, as to ladies, what can French ladies think of a man who travels for the plough?—25 miles.

The 26th. For twenty miles to Lisle sur Daube,[1] the country nearly as before; but after that, to Baume les Dames, it is all mountainous and rock, much wood, and many pleasing scenes of the river flowing beneath. The whole country is in the greatest agitation; at one of the little towns I passed, I was questioned for not having a cockade of the *tiers etat*. They said it was ordained by the *tiers*, and, if I was not a Seigneur, I ought to obey. *But suppose I am a Seigneur, what then, my friends?*—What then? they replied sternly, why, be hanged; for that most likely is what you deserve. It was plain this was no moment for joking, the boys and girls began to gather, whose assembling has every where been the preliminaries of mischief; and if I had not declared myself an Englishman, and ignorant of the ordinance, I had not escaped very well. I immediately bought a cockade, but the hussey pinned it into my hat so loosely, that before I got to Lisle it blew into the river, and I was again in the same danger. My assertion of being English would not do. I was a Seigneur, perhaps in disguise, and without doubt a great rogue. At this moment a priest came into the street with a letter

[1] L'Isle-sur-le-Doubs (Doubs).
[2] Baume-les-Dames amid very picturesque scenery (Doubs).

in his hand: the people immediately collected around him, and he then read aloud a detail from Befort, giving an account of M. Necker's passing, with some general features of news from Paris, and assurances that the condition of the people would be improved. When he had finished, he exhorted them to abstain from all violence; and assured them, they must not indulge themselves with any ideas of impositions being abolished; which he touched on as if he knew that they had got such notions. When he retired, they again surrounded me, who had attended to the letter like others; were very menacing in their manner; and expressed many suspicions: I did not like my situation at all, especially on hearing one of them say that I ought to be secured till somebody would give an account of me. I was on the steps of the inn, and begged they would permit me a few words; I assured them, that I was an English traveller, and to prove it, I desired to explain to them a circumstance in English taxation, which would be a satisfactory comment on what Mons. l'Abbé had told them, to the purport of which I could not agree. He had asserted, that the impositions must be paid as heretofore: that the impositions must be paid was certain, but not as heretofore, as they might be paid as they were in England. Gentlemen, we have a great number of taxes in England, which you know nothing of in France; but the *tiers etat*, the poor do not pay them; they are laid on the rich; every window in a man's house pays; but if he has no more than six windows, he pays nothing; a Seigneur, with a great estate, pays the *vingtiemes* and *tailles*, but the little proprietor of a garden pays nothing; the rich for their horses, their voitures, and their servants, and even for liberty to kill their own partridges, but the poor farmer nothing of all this: and what is more, we have in England a tax paid by the rich for the relief of the poor; hence the assertion of Mons. l'Abbé, that because taxes existed before they must exist again, did not at all prove that they must be levied in the same manner; our English method seemed much better. There was not a word of this discourse, they did not approve of; they seemed to think that I might be an honest fellow, which I confirmed, by crying, *vive le tiers, sans impositions*, when they gave me a bit of a huzza, and

I had no more interruption from them. My miserable French was pretty much on a par with their own *patois*. I got, however, another cockade, which I took care to have so fastened as to lose it no more. I do not half like travelling in such an unquiet and fermenting moment; one is not secure for an hour beforehand.—35 miles.

The 27th. To Besançon;[1] the country mountain, rock, and wood, above the river; some scenes are fine. I had not arrived an hour before I saw a peasant pass the inn on horseback, followed by an officer of the *guard bourgeois*, of which there are 1200 here, and 200 under arms, and his party-coloured detachment, and these by some infantry and cavalry. I asked, why the militia took the *pas* of the king's troops? *For a very good reason*, they replied, *the troops would be attacked and knocked on the head, but the populace will not resist the milice.* This peasant, who is a rich proprietor, applied for a guard to protect his house, in a village where there is much plundering and burning. The mischiefs which have been perpetrated in the country, towards the mountains and Vesoul,[2] are numerous and shocking. Many chateaus have been burnt, others plundered, the seigneurs hunted down like wild beasts, their wives and daughters ravished, their papers and titles burnt, and all their property destroyed: and these abominations not inflicted on marked persons, who were odious for their former conduct or principles, but an indiscriminating blind rage for the love of plunder. Robbers, galley-slaves, and villains of all denominations, have collected and instigated the peasants to commit all sorts of outrages. Some gentlemen at the table d'hôte informed me, that letters were received from the Maconois, the Lyonois, Auvergne, Dauphné, &c. and that similar commotions and mischiefs were perpetrating every where; and that it was expected they would pervade the whole kingdom. The backwardness of France is beyond credibility in every thing that pertains to intelligence. From Strasbourg hither, I have not been able to see a newspaper. Here I asked for the *Cabinet Literaire?* None. The gazettes? At the coffee-house. Very easily replied; but not so easily

---

[1] (Doubs.)   [2] (Haute Saône.)

found. Nothing but the *Gazette de France;* for which at this period, a man of common sense would not give one *sol.* To four other coffee-houses; at some no paper at all, not even the *Mercure;* at the *Caffé Militaire,* the *Courier de l'Europe* a fortnight old; and well dressed people are now talking of the news of two or three weeks past, and plainly by their discourse know nothing of what is passing. The whole town of Besançon has not been able to afford me a sight of the *Journal de Paris,* nor of any paper that gives a detail of the transactions of the states; yet it is the capital of a province, large as half a dozen English counties, and containing 25,000 souls,—with strange to say! the post coming in but three times a week. At this eventful moment, with no licence, nor even the least restraint on the press, not one paper established at Paris for circulation in the provinces, with the necessary steps taken by *affiche,* or *placard,* to inform the people in all the towns of its establishment. For what the country knows to the contrary, their deputies are in the Bastile, instead of the Bastile being razed; so the mob plunder, burn, and destroy, in complete ignorance: and yet, with all these shades of darkness, these clouds of tenebrity, this universal mass of ignorance, there are men every day in the states, who are puffing themselves off for the FIRST NATION IN EUROPE! the GREATEST PEOPLE IN THE UNIVERSE! as if the political juntos, or literary circles of a capital constituted a people; instead of the universal illumination of knowledge, acting by rapid intelligence on minds prepared by habitual energy of reasoning to receive, combine, and comprehend it. That this dreadful ignorance of the mass of the people, of the events that most intimately concern them, is owing to the old government, no one can doubt; it is however curious to remark, that if the nobility of other provinces are hunted like those of Franche Compté, of which there is little reason to doubt, that whole order of men undergo a proscription, suffer like sheep, without making the least effort to resist the attack. This appears marvellous, with a body that have an army of 150,000 men in their hands; for though a part of those troops would certainly disobey their leaders, yet let it be remembered, that out of the 40,000, or possibly 100,000 noblesse of France, they might, if they had intelligence and union amongst themselves, fill half the ranks of more than half the regiments of the kingdom, with men who have fellow-feelings and fellow-sufferings with themselves; but no meetings, no associations among them; no union with military men; no taking refuge in the ranks of regiments to defend or avenge their cause; fortunately for France they fall without a struggle, and die without a blow. That universal circulation of intelligence, which in England transmits the least vibration of feeling or alarm, with electric sensibility, from one end of the kingdom to another, and which unites in bands of connection men of similar interests and situations, has no existence in France. Thus it may be said, perhaps with truth, that the fall of the king, court, lords, nobles, army, church, and parliaments is owing to a want of intelligence being quickly circulated, consequently is owing to the very effects of that thraldom in which they held the people: it is therefore a retribution rather than a punishment.—18 miles.

The 28th. At the table d'hôte last night a person gave an account of being stopped at Salins for want of a passport, and suffering the greatest inconveniencies; I found it necessary, therefore, to demand one for myself, and went accordingly to the *Bureau*; this was the house of a Mons. Bellamy, an attorney; with whom the following dialogue ensued:

Mais, Monsieur, qui me repondra de vous? Est ce que personne vous connoit? Connoissez vous quelqun a Besançon?

Non personne, mon dessein etoit d'aller a Vesoul d'oü j'aurois eu des lettres, mais j'ai changé de route a cause de ces tumultes.

Monsieur je ne vous connois pas, & si vous etes inconnu a Besançon vous ne pouvez avoir de passport.

Mais voici mes lettres j'en ai plusieurs pour d'autres villes en France, il y a en même d'adressées a Vesoul e a Arbois, ouvrez & lisez les, & vous trouverez que je ne suis pas inconnu ailleurs quoique je le sois a Besançon.

N'importe; je ne vous connois pas, il n'y a personne ici qui vous connoisse ainsi vous n'aurez point de passport.

Je vous dit Monsieur que ces lettres vous expliqueront.

Il me faut des gens, et non pas des lettres pour m'expliquer qui vous etes; ces lettres ne me valent rien.

Cette façon d'agir me paroît assez singuliere ; apparaement que vous la croyez tres honnête ; pour moi, Monsieur, j'en pense bien autrement.

Eh Monsieur je ne m'en soucie de ce que vous en pensez.

En verité voici ce qui s'appelle, avoir des manieres gracieuses envers un etranger ; c'est la premiere, fois que j'ai eu a faire avec ces Messieurs du tiers etat, & vous m'avourez qu'il n'y a rien ici qui puisse me donner une haute idée du caracteré de ces Messieurs là.

Monsieur, cela m'est fort égal.

Je donnerai a mon retour en Angleterre le detail de mon voyage au publique, & assurement Monsieur je n'oublirai pas d'enregistrer ce trait de vôtre politesse, il vous fait tant d'honneure, & à ceux pour qui vous agissez.

Monsieur je regarde tout cela avec la derniere indifference.

My gentleman's manner was more offensive than his words ; he walked backward and forward among his parchments, with an air *veritablement d'un commis de bureau.*— These passports are new things from new men, in new power, and show that they do not bear their new honours too meekly. Thus it is impossible for me, without running my head against a wall, to go see the Salins,[1] or to Arbois,[2] where I have a letter from M. de Broussonet, but I must take my chance and get to Dijon as fast as I can, where the president de Virly knows me, having spent some days at Bradfield, unless indeed being a president and a nobleman he has got knocked on the head by the *tiers état*. At night to the play; miserable performers; the theatre, which has not been built many years, is heavy; the arch that parts the stage from the house is like the entrance of a cavern, and the line of the amphitheatre, that of a wounded eel; I do not like the air and manners of the people here—and I would see Besançon swallowed up by an earthquake before I would live in it. The music, and bawling, and squeaking of *l'Epreuve Villageoise* of Gretry, which is wretched, had no power to put me in better humour. I will not take leave of this place, to which I never desire to come again, without saying that they have a fine promenade ; and that Mons. Arthaud, the arpenteur,

---

[1] (Jura.)   [2] (*Ibid.*)

to whom I applied for information, without any letter of recommendation was liberal and polite, and answered my enquiries satisfactorily.

The 29th. To Orechamp¹ the country is bold and rocky, with fine woods, and yet it is not agreeable; it is like many men that have estimable points in their characters, and yet we cannot love them. Poorly cultivated too. Coming out of St. Veté,² a pretty riant landskip of the river doubling through the vale, enlivened by a village and some scattered houses: the most pleasing view I have seen in Franche Compté—23 miles.

The 30th. The mayor of Dole³ is made of as good stuff as the notary of Besançon; he would give no passport; but as he accompanied his refusal with neither airs nor graces, I let him pass. To avoid the centinels, I went round the town. The country to Auxonne⁴ is chearful. Cross the Saone at Auxonne; it is a fine river, through a region of flat meadow of beautiful verdure; commons of great herds of cattle; vastly flooded, and the hay-cocks underwater. To Dijon is a fine country, but wants wood. My passport demanded at the gate: and as I had none, two *bourgeois* musqueteers conducted me to the *hotel de ville*, where I was questioned, but finding that I was known at Dijon, they let me go to my inn. Out of luck: Mons. de Virly, on whom I most depended for Dijon, is at Bourbon les Bains, and Mons. de Morveau,⁵ the celebrated chymist, who I expected would have had letters for me, had none, and though he received me very politely, when I was forced to announce myself as his brother in the royal society of London, yet I felt very awkwardly; however, he desired to see me again next morning. They tell me here,

---

¹ Orcbamps (Doubs).   ² St. Vit (*ibid.*).
³ Dôle (Jura).
⁴ (Côte-d'Or.) This little walled-in town resisted all the attacks of the Germans in 1871.
⁵ Guyton de Morveau, born at Dijon, 1732, died 1813. His house still remains. Distinguished scientist and littérateur. He became a member of the Legislative Assembly, and joined in the regicide vote; on the creation of Ecole Polytechnique, under the Convention he was named director. His services to science, industry, education, and the public health were considerable, and he wrote many works of value in their day.

that the intendant is fled; and that the prince of Condé, who is governor of Burgundy, is in Germany; they positively assert, and with very little ceremony, that they would both be hanged, if they were to come here at present; such ideas do not mark too much authority in the *milice burgeoise*, as they have been instituted to stop and prevent hanging and plundering. They are too weak, however, to keep the peace: the licence and spirit of depredation, of which I heard so much in crossing Franche Compté, has taken place, but not equally in Burgundy. In this inn, *la Ville de Lyon*, there is at present a gentleman, unfortunately a seigneur, his wife, family, three servants, an infant but a few months old, who escaped from their flaming chateau half naked in the night; all their property lost except the land itself; and this family valued and esteemed by the neighbours, with many virtues to command the love of the poor, and no oppressions to provoke their enmity. Such abominable actions must bring the more detestation to the cause from being unnecessary; the kingdom might have been settled in a real system of liberty, without the *regeneration* of fire and sword, plunder, and bloodshed. Three hundred *bourgeois* mount guard every day at Dijon, armed, but not paid at the expence of the town: they have also six pieces of cannon. The noblesse of the place, as the only means of safety, have joined them—so that there are croix de St. Louis in the ranks. The *palais des états* here, is a large and splendid building, but not striking proportionably to the mass and expence. The arms of the prince of Condé are predominant; and the great salon is called the *Salle a manger de Prince*. A Dijon artist has painted the battle of Seniff,[1] and the Grande Condé thrown from his horse, and a cieling, both well executed. Tomb of the duke of Bourgogne, 1404. A picture by Rubens at the Chartreuse.[2] They talk of the house of Mons. de Montigny, but his sister being in it, not shown. Dijon, on the whole is a handsome town;

---

[1] Seneffe, Belgium, a somewhat indecisive battle between the Dutch, under the Prince of Orange, afterwards William III. and the French, led by the great Condé, 11th August, 1674.

[2] Burial place of the Duke of Burgundy, just outside Dijon. Here is still seen the magnificent piece of sculpture called Moses' Well.

the streets, though old built, are wide, and very well paved, with the addition, uncommon in France, of *trotoirs*. —28 miles.

The 31st. Waited on Mons. de Morveau, who has, most fortunately for me, received, only this morning, from Mons. de Virly, a recommendation of me, with four letters from Mons. de Broussonet; but Mons. Vaudrey, of this place, to whom one of them is addressed, is absent. We had some conversation on the interesting topic to all philosophers, phlogiston; Mons. de Morveau contends vehemently for its non-existence; treats Dr. Priestley's last publication as wide of the question; and declared, that he considers the controversy as much decided as the question of liberty is in France. He shewed me part of the article *air* in the New Encyclopædia by him, to be published soon; in which work, he thinks he has, beyond controversy, established the truth of the doctrine of the French chymists of its non-existence. Mons. de Morveau requested me to call on him in the evening to introduce me to a learned and agreeable lady; and engaged me to dine with him tomorrow. On leaving him, I went to search coffee-houses; but will it be credited, that I could find but one in this capital of Burgundy, where I could read the newspapers? —At a poor little one in the square, I read a paper, after waiting an hour to get it. The people I have found every where desirous of reading newspapers; but it is rare that they can gratify themselves: and the general ignorance of what is passing may be collected from this, that I found nobody at Dijon had heard of the riot at the town-house of Strasbourg; I described it to a gentleman, and a party collected around me to hear it; not one of them had heard a syllable of it, yet it is nine days since it happened; had it been nineteen, I question whether they would more than have received the intelligence; but, though they are slow in knowing what has really happened, they are very quick in hearing what is impossible to happen. The current report at present, to which all possible credit is given, is, that the Queen has been convicted of a plot to poison the King and Monsieur, and give the regency to the count d'Artois; to set fire to Paris, and blow up the *Palais Royale* by a mine!—Why do not the several parties in the states cause papers to be printed, that shall transmit only their own sentiments and opinions? In order that no man in the nation, arranged under the same standard of reasoning, may want the facts that are necessary to govern his arguments, and the conclusions that great talents have drawn from those facts. The king has been advised to take several steps of authority against the states, but none of his ministers have advised the establishment of journals, and their speedy circulation, that should undeceive the people in those points his enemies have misrepresented. When numerous papers are published in opposition to each other, the people take pains to sift into and examine the truth; and that inquisitiveness alone—the very act of searching, enlightens them; they become informed, and it is no longer easy to deceive them. At the table d'hôte only three, myself, and two noblemen, driven from their estates, as I conjecture by their conversation, but they did not hint at any thing like their houses being burnt. Their description of the state of that part of the province they come from, in the road from Langres [1] to Gray,[2] is terrible; the number of chateaus burnt not considerable, but three in five plundered, and the possessors driven out of the country, and glad to save their lives. One of these gentlemen is a very sensible well informed man; he considers all rank, and all the rights annexed to rank, as destroyed in fact in France; and that the leaders of the National Assembly having no property, or very little themselves, are determined to attack that also, and attempt an equal division. The expectation is got among many of the people; but whether it takes place or not, he considers France as *absolutely ruined.* That, I replied, was going too far, for the destruction of rank did not imply *ruin.* "I call nothing ruin," he replied, "but a general and confirmed civil war, or dismemberment of the kingdom, in my opinion, both are inevitable; not perhaps this year, or the next, or the year after that, but whatever government is built on the foundation now laying in France, cannot stand any rude shocks; an unsuccessful or a successful war will equally destroy it."—He spoke with great knowledge of his-

---

[1] (Hte. Saône.) [2] (Hte. Marne.)

torical events, and drew his political conclusions with much acumen. I have met very few such men at table d'hôtes. It may be believed, I did not forget M. de Morveau's appointment. He was as good as his word; Madame Picardet is as agreeable in conversation as she is learned in the closet; a very pleasing unaffected woman; she has translated Scheele [1] from the German, and a part of Mr. Kirwan from the English; a treasure to M. de Morveau, for she is able and willing to converse with him on chymical subjects, and on any others that tend either to instruct or please. I accompanied them in their evening's promenade. She told me, that her brother, Mons. de Poule, was a great farmer, who had sowed large quantities of sainfoin, which he used for fattening oxen; she was sorry he was engaged so closely in the municipal business at present, that he could not attend me to his farm.

AUGUST 1. Dined with Mons. de Morveau by appointment; Mons. Professeur Chausée, and Mons. Picardet of the party. It was a rich day to me; the great and just reputation of Mons. de Morveau, for being not only the first chymist of France, but one of the greatest that Europe has to boast, was alone sufficient to render his company interesting; but to find such a man void of affectation; free from those airs of superiority which are sometimes found in celebrated characters, and that reserve which oftener throws a veil over their talents, as well as conceals their deficiencies for which it is intended—was very pleasing. Mons. de Morveau is a lively, conversable, eloquent man, who, in any station of life, would be sought as an agreeable companion. Even in this eventful moment of revolution, the conversation turned almost entirely on chymical subjects. I urged him, as I have done Dr. Priestley more than once, and Mons. La Voisier also, to turn his enquiries a little to the application of his science to agriculture; that there was a fine field for experiments in that line, which could scarcely fail of making discoveries; to which he assented; but added, that he had no time for such enquiries: it is clear, from his conversation, that his views

---

[1] Scheele, Karl, August, 1724-1786. Swedish scientist and discoverer.

are entirely occupied by the non-existence of phlogiston, except a little on the means of establishing and enforcing the new nomenclature. While we were at dinner a proof of the New Encyclopædia was brought him, the chymical part of which work is printed at Dijon, for the convenience of Mons. de Morveau. I took the liberty of telling him, that a man who can devise the experiments which shall be most conclusive in ascertaining the questions of a science, and has talents to draw all the useful conclusions from them, should be entirely employed in experiments, and their register; and if I was king, or minister of France, I would make that employment so profitable to him, that he should do nothing else. He laughed, and asked me, if I was such an advocate for working, and such an enemy to writing what I thought of my friend Dr. Priestley? And he then explained to the two other gentlemen, that great philosopher's attention to metaphysics, and polemic divinity. If an hundred had been at table, the sentiment would have been the same in every bosom. Mons. M. spoke, however, with great regard for the experimental talents of the Doctor, as indeed who in Europe does not?—I afterwards reflected on Mons. de Morveau's not having time to make experiments that should apply chymistry to agriculture, yet have plenty for writing in so voluminous a work as Pankouck's.[1] I lay it down as a maxim, that no man can establish or support a reputation in any branch of experimental philosophy, such as shall really descend to posterity, otherwise than by experiment; and that commonly the more a man works, and the less he writes the better, at least the more valuable will be his reputation. The profit of writing has ruined that of many (those who know Mons. de Morveau will be very sure I am far enough from having him in my eye; his situation in life puts it out of the question); that compression of materials, which is luminous; that brevity which appropriates facts to their destined points, are alike inconsistent with the principles that govern all compilations; there are able and respect-

---

[1] Panckoucke, Charles Joseph, 1736-1798. Celebrated son of the distinguished bookseller of that name, editor with Beaumarchais and others of the "Encyclopédie Méthodique," and many valuable works. His son was a littérateur of some distinction.

able men now in every country for compiling; experimenters of genius should range themselves in another class. If I were a sovereign, and capable consequently of rewarding merit, the moment I heard of a man of real genius engaged in such a work, I would give him double the bookseller's price to let it alone, and to employ himself in paths that did not admit a rival at every door. There are who will think that this opinion comes oddly from one who has published so many books as I have; but I hope it will be admitted, to come naturally at least from one who is writing a work from which he does not expect to make one penny, who, therefore, has stronger motives to brevity than temptations to prolixity. The view of this great chymist's laboratory will show that he is not idle:—it consists of two large rooms, admirably furnished indeed. There are six or seven different furnaces (of which Macquer's is the most powerful), and such a variety and extent of apparatus, as I have seen no where else, with a furniture of specimens from the three kingdoms, as looks truly like business. There are little writing desks, with pens and paper, scattered every where, and in his library also, which is convenient. He has a large course of eudiometrical experiments going on at present, particularly with Fontana's and Volta's eudiometers. He seems to think, eudiometrical trials are to be depended on: keeps his nitrous air in quart bottles, stopped with common corks, but reversed; and that the air is always the same, if made from the same materials. A very simple and elegant method of ascertaining the proportion of vital air, he explained to us, by making the experiment; putting a morsel of phosphorus into a glass retort, confined by water or mercury, and inflaming it, by holding a bougie under it. The diminution of air marks the quantity that was vital on the antiphlogistic doctrine. After one extinction, it will boil, but not enflame. He has a pair of scales made at Paris, which, when loaded with 3000 grains, will turn with the twentieth part of one grain; an air pump, with glass barrels, but one of them broken and repaired; the count de Busson's system of burning lens; an absorber; a respirator, with vital air in a jar on one side, and lime-water in another; and abundance of new and most ingenious inventions for facilitating enquiries in the new philosophy of air. These are so various, and at the same time so well contrived to answer the purpose intended, that this species of invention seems to be one very great and essential part of Mons. de Morveau's merit; I wish he would follow Dr. Priestley's idea of *publishing his tools*, it would add not inconsiderably to his great and well earned reputation, and at the same time promote the enquiries he engages in amongst all other experimenters. M. de Morveau had the goodness to accompany me in the afternoon in the academy of sciences: they have a very handsome salon, ornamented with the busts of Dijon worthies; of such eminent men as this city has produced, Bossuet—Fevret—De Brosses—De Crebillon—Pyron—Bonhier—Rameau—and lastly Buffon;[1] and some future traveller will doubtless see here, that of a man inferior to none of those, Mons. de Morveau, by whom I had now the honour of being conducted. In the evening we repaired again to Madame Picardet, and accompanied her promenade: I was pleased, in conversation on the present disturbances of France, to hear Mons. de Morveau remark, that the outrages committed by the peasants arose from their defects of *lumieres*. In Dijon it had been publicly recommended to the *curés* to enlighten them somewhat politically in their sermons, but all in vain, not one would go out of the usual routine of his preaching.—*Quere*, Would not one newspaper enlighten them more than a score of priests? I asked Mons. de Morveau, how far it was true that the chateaus had been plundered and burnt by the peasants alone; or whether by those troops of *brigands*, reported to be formidable? He assured me, that he has made strict enquiries to ascertain this matter, and is of opinion, that all the violences in this province, that have come to his knowledge, have been committed by the peasants only; much has been reported of *brigands*, but

[1] Concerning the lesser lights in this galaxy of illustrious Dijonnais, here are a few facts. Fevrette de Fontette, archæologist and historic writer, 1710-1772; Chas. de Brosses, 1709-1777, president of the Dijon Parliament, savant and littéraire; Bonhier, Jean, 1673-1746, a writer on philosophy, jurisprudence, history, antiquities, of whom D'Alembert wrote: "Il fit ses preuves dans tous les genres et dans la plupart il fit des œuvres distinguées." His splendid library enriched that of Dijon, Montpellier, and other towns.

nothing proved. At Besançon I heard of 800; but how could a troop of 800 banditti march through a country, and leave their existence the least questionable?—as ridiculous as Mr. Bayes's [1] army *incog.*

The 2d. To Beaune;[2] a range of hills to the right under vines, and a flat plain to the left, all open and too naked. At the little insignificant town of Nuys·[3] forty men mount guard every day, and a large corps at Beaune. I am provided with a passport from the mayor of Dijon, and a flaming cockade of the *tiers état*, and therefore hope to avoid difficulties; though the reports of the riots of the peasants are so formidable, that it seems impossible to travel in safety. Stop at Nuys for intelligence concerning the vineyards of this country, so famous in France, and indeed in all Europe; and examine the *Clos de Veaugeau*,[4] of 100 *journaux*, walled in, and belonging to a convent of Bernardine Monks.—When are we to find these fellows chusing badly? The spots they appropriate shew what a righteous attention they give to things of the spirit.—— 2 miles.

The 3d. Going out of Chagnie,[5] where I quitted the great Lyons road, pass by the canal of Chaulais,[6] which goes on very poorly; it is a truly useful undertaking, and therefore left undone; had it been for boring cannon, or coppering men of war, it would have been finished long ago. To Montcenis[7] a disagreeable country; singular in its features. It is the seat of one Mons. *Weelkainsong*'s establishments for casting and boring cannon: I have already described one near Nantes. The French say, that this active Englishman is brother-in-law of Dr. Priestly, and therefore a friend of mankind; and that he taught them to bore cannon, in order to give liberty to America.

---

[1] Bayes is the hero of the Duke of Buckingham's farce, "The Rehearsal," in which a battle is fought between foot-soldiers and great hobby-horses.
[2] (Côte d'Or.)   [3] Nuits (*ibid.*).
[4] This celebrated vineyard was created by the monks of Citeaux. The abbey and grounds are now used as a juvenile penitentiary and orphanage, under State control.
[5] Chagny (Saône and Loire).
[6] The canal here alluded to is the canal du Centre.
[7] Montchanin (Saône and Loire).

The establishment is very considerable; there are from 500 to 600 men employed, besides colliers; five steam engines are erected for giving the blasts, and for boring; and a new one building. I conversed with an Englishman who works in the glass-house, in the crystal branch; there were once many, but only two are left at present: he complained of the country, saying there was nothing good in it but wine and brandy; of which things I question not but he makes a sufficient use.—25 miles.

The 4th. By a miserable country most of the way, and through hideous roads to Autun.[1] The first seven or eight miles the agriculture quite contemptible. From thence to Autun all, or nearly all, inclosed, and the first so for many miles. From the hill before Autun an immense view down on that town, and the flat country of the Bourbonnois for a great extent.—View at Autun the temple of Janus—the walls—the cathedral—the abbey. The reports here of *brigands*, and burning and plundering, are as numerous as before; and when it was known in the inn that I came from Burgundy and Franche Compté, I had eight or ten people introducing themselves, in order to ask for news. The rumour of *brigands* here had got to 1600 strong. They were much surprized to find, that I gave no credit to the existence of *brigands*, as I was well persuaded, that all the outrages that had been committed, were the work of the peasants only, for the sake of plundering. This they had no conception of, and quoted a list of chateaus burnt by them; but on analysing these reports, they plainly appeared to be ill founded.—20 miles.

The 5th. The extreme heat of yesterday made me feverish; and this morning I waked with a sore throat. I was inclined to waste a day here for the security of my health; but we are all fools in trifling with the things most valuable to us. Loss of time, and vain expence, are always in the head of a man who travels as much *en philosophe* as I am forced to do. To Maison de Bourgogne,[2] I thought myself in a new world; the road is not only excellent, of gravel, but the country is inclosed and wooded. There are many gentle inequalities, and several ponds that

---

[1] (Saône and Loire.)   [2] *Ibid.*

decorate them. The weather, since the commencement of August, has been clear, bright, and burning; too hot to be perfectly agreeable in the middle of the day, but no flies, and therefore I do not regard the heat. This circumstance may, I think, be fixed on as the test. In Languedoc, &c. these heats, as I have experienced, are attended by myriads, and consequently they are tormenting. One had need be sick at this *Maison de Bourgogne;* a healthy stomach would not be easily filled; yet it is the post-house. In the evening to Lusy,[1] another miserable post-house. Note, through all Burgundy the women wear flapped men's hats, which have not nearly so good an effect as the straw ones of Alsace.—22 miles.

The 6th. To escape the heat, out at four in the morning, to Bourbon Lancy,[2] through the same country inclosed, but villainously cultivated, and all amazingly improveable. If I had a large tract in this country, I think I should not be long in making a fortune; climate, prices, roads, inclosures, and every advantage, except government. All from Autun to the Loire is a noble field for improvement, not by expensive operations of manuring and draining, but merely by substituting crops adapted to the soil. When I see such a country thus managed, and in the hands of starving *métayers*, instead of fat farmers,[3] I know not how to pity the seigneurs, great as their present sufferings are. I met one of them, to whom I opened my mind:—he pretended to talk of agriculture, finding I attended to it; and assured me, that he had Abbé Roziere's *corps complete*, and he believed, from his accounts, that this country would not do for any thing but rye. I asked him, whether he or Abbé Roziere knew the right end of a plough? He assured me, that he was *un homme de grand merite, beaucoup d'agriculteur.* Cross the Loire by a ferry; it is here the same nasty scene of shingle, as in Touraine. Enter the Bourbonnois; the same inclosed country, and a beautiful gravel road. At *Chavanne le Roi*,[4] Mons. Joly, the *auber-*

---

[1] Luzy (Nièvre).   [2] (Saône and Loire.)
[3] "Fat farmers" innumerable may now be seen at the September (Autun) fair. Every kind of land tenure exists in this part of France, and métayage has greatly advanced the condition of the peasants.
[4] Chevagnes (Allier).

giste, informed me of three domains (farms) to be sold, adjoining almost to his house, which is new and well built. I was for appropriating his inn at once in my imagination for a farm-house, and had got hard at work on turnips and clover, when he told me, that if I would walk behind his stable, I might see, at a small distance, two of the houses; he said the price would be about 50 or 60,000 liv. (2,625l.), and would altogether make a noble farm. If I were twenty years younger, I should think seriously of such a speculation; but there again is the folly and deficiency of life; twenty years ago, such a thing would, for want of experience, have been my ruin; and, now I have the experience, I am too old for the undertaking.—27 miles.

The 7th. Moulins [1] appears to be but a poor ill built town. I went to the *Belle Image*, but found it so bad that I left it, and went to the *Lyon d'Or*, which is worse. This capital of the Bourbonnois, and on the great post road to Italy, has not an inn equal to the little village of Chavanne. To read the papers, I went to the coffee-house of Madame Bourgeau, the best in the town, where I found near twenty tables set for company, but, as to a newspaper, I might as well have demanded an elephant. Here is a feature of national backwardness, ignorance, stupidity, and poverty: In the capital of a great province, the seat of an intendant, at a moment like the present, with a National Assembly voting a revolution, and not a newspaper to inform the people whether Fayette, Mirabeau, or Louis XVI. is on the throne. Companies at a coffee-house, numerous enough to fill twenty tables, and curiosity not active enough to command one paper. What impudence and folly!—Folly in the customers of such a house not to insist on half a dozen papers, and all the journals of the assembly; and impudence of the woman not to provide them! Could such a people as this ever have made a revolution, or become free? Never, in a thousand centuries: The enlightened mob of Paris, amidst hundreds of papers and publications, have

[1] Moulins (*ibid.*). Here is a different account of Moulins written just twenty-three years later: "Moulins offre aux voyageurs des bains propres, un joli café, une petite salle de spectacle, une riche bibliothèque publique et de charmants promenades."—Vaysse de Villiers, "Description de l'Empire Français," 1813.

done the whole. I demanded why they had no papers? *They are too dear;* but she made me pay 24*f.* for one dish of coffee, with milk, and a piece of butter about the size of a walnut. It is a great pity there is not a camp of *brigands* in your coffee-room, Madame Bourgeau. Among the many letters for which I am indebted to Mons. Broussonet, few have proved more valuable than one I had for Mons. l'Abbé de Barut, principal of the college of Moulins, who entered with intelligence and animation into the object of my journey, and took every step that was possible to get me well informed. He carried me to Mons. le count de Grimau, lieutenant general of the Baillage, and director of the society of agriculture at Moulins, who kept us to dinner. He appears to be a man of considerable fortune, of information, and knowledge, agreeable and polite. He discoursed with me on the state of the Bourbonnois; and assured me, that estates were rather given away than sold: that the *métayers* were so miserably poor, it was impossible for them to cultivate well. I started some observations on the modes which ought to be pursued; but all conversation of that sort is time lost in France. After dinner, M. Grimau carried me to his villa, at a small distance from the town, which is very prettily situated, commanding a view of the vale of the Allier. Letters from Paris, which contain nothing but accounts truly alarming, of the violences committed all over the kingdom, and particularly at and in the neighbourhood of the capital. M. Necker's return, which it was expected would have calmed every thing, has no effect at all; and it is particularly noted in the National Assembly, that there is a violent party evidently bent on driving things to extremity: men who, from the violence and conflicts of the moment, find themselves in a position, and of an importance that results merely from public confusion, will take effectual care to prevent the settlement, order, and peace, which, if established, would be a mortal blow to their consequence: they mount by the storm, and would sink in a calm. Among other persons to whom Mons. l'Abbé Barut introduced me, was the marquis de Goutte, *chef d'escadre* of the French fleet, who was taken by admiral Boscawen at Louisbourg, in 1758, and carried to England, where he learned English, of which he yet retains something. I had mentioned to Mons. l'Abbé Barut, that I had a commission from a person of fortune in England, to look out for a good purchase in France; and knowing that the marquis would sell one of his estates he mentioned it to him. Mons. de Goutte gave me such a description of it, that I thought, though my time was short, that it would be very well worth bestowing one day to view it, as it was no more than eight miles from Moulins, and, proposing to take me to it the next day in his coach, I readily consented. At the time appointed, I attended the marquis, with M. l'Abbé Barut, to his chateau of Riaux,[1] which is in the midst of the estate he would sell on such terms, that I never was more tempted to speculate: I have very little doubt but that the person who gave me a commission to look out for a purchase, is long since sickened of the scheme, which was that of a residence for pleasure, by the disturbances that have broken out here: so that I should clearly have the refusal of it myself. It would be upon the whole a more beneficial purchase than I had any conception of, and confirms Mons. de Grimau's assertion, that estates are here rather given away than sold. The chateau is large and very well built, containing two good rooms, either of which would hold a company of thirty people, with three smaller ones on the ground floor; on the second ten bedchambers, and over them good garrets, some of which are well fitted up; all sorts of offices substantially erected, and on a plan proportioned to a large family, including barns new built, for holding half the corn of the estate in the straw, and granaries to contain it when threshed. Also a wine press and ample cellaring, for keeping the produce of the vineyards in the most plentiful years. The situation is on the side of an agreeable rising, with views not extensive, but pleasing, and all the country round of the same features I have described, being one of the finest provinces in France.[2] Adjoining the chateau is a field of five or six arpents, well walled in, about half of which is in culture as a garden, and thoroughly planted with all sorts of fruits. There are twelve ponds, through a small stream runs,

---

[1] Château de Ryau, at Villeneuve-sur-Allier, now in ruins.
[2] "The Bourbonnais, the sweetest part of France."—STERNE.

sufficient to turn two mills, that let at 1000 liv. (43l. 15s.) a-year. The ponds supply the proprietor's table amply with fine carp, tench, perch, and eels; and besides yield a regular revenue of 1000 liv. There are 20 arpents of vines that yield excellent white and red wine, with houses for the vignerons; woods more than sufficient to supply the chateau with fuel; and lastly, nine domains or farms let to *metayers*, tenants at will, at half produce, producing in cash, 10,500 liv. (459l. 7s. 6d.) consequently, the gross produce, farms, mills, and fish, is 12,500 liv. The quantity of land, I conjecture from viewing it, as well as from notes taken, may be above 3000 arpents or acres, lying all contiguous and near the chateau. The out goings for those taxes paid by the landlord; repairs, *garde de chasse*, game-keeper (for here are all the seigneural rights, *haute justice*, &c.) steward, expences on wine, &c. amount to about 4400 liv. (192l. 10s.) It yields therefore net something more than 8000 liv. (350l.) a year. The price asked is 300,000 liv. (13,125l.); but for this price is given in the furniture complete of the chateau, all the timber, amounting, by valuation of oak only, to 40,000 liv. (1750l.) and all the cattle on the estate, viz. 1000 sheep, 60 cows, 72 oxen, 9 mares, and many hogs. Knowing, as I did, that I could, on the security of this estate, borrow the whole of the purchase-money, I withstood no trifling temptation when I turned my back on it. The finest climate in France, perhaps in Europe; a beautiful and healthy country; excellent roads; a navigation to Paris; wine, game, fish, and every thing that ever appears on a table, except the produce of the tropics; a good house, a fine garden, ready markets for every sort of produce; and, above all the rest, 3000 acres of inclosed land, capable in a very little time of being, without expence, quadrupled in its produce, altogether formed a picture sufficient to tempt a man who had been five-and-twenty years in the constant practice of husbandry adapted to this soil. But the state of government—the possibility that the leaders of the Paris democracy might in their wisdom abolish property as well as rank; and that in buying an estate I might be purchasing my share in a civil war—deterred me from engaging at present, and induced me only to request that the marquis would give me the refusal of it, before he sold it to any body else. When I have to connect with a person for a purchase, I shall wish to deal with such an one as the marquis de Goutte. He has a physiognomy that pleases me; the ease and politeness of his nation is mixed with great probity and honour; and is not rendered less amiable by an appearance of dignity that flows from an ancient and respectable family. To me he seems a man in whom one might, in any transaction, place implicit confidence. I could have spent a month in the Bourbonnois, looking at estates to be sold; adjoining to that of M. de Goutte's is another of 270,000 liv. purchase, Ballain; Mons. l'Abbé Barut having made an appointment with the proprietor, carried me in the afternoon to see the chateau and a part of the lands; all the country is the same soil, and in the same management. It consists of eight farms, stocked with cattle and sheep by the landlords; and here too the ponds yield a regular revenue. Income at present 10,000 liv. (437l. 10s.) a year; price 260,000 liv. (11,375l.) and 10,000 liv. for wood—twenty-five years purchase. Also near St. Poncin [1] another of 400,000 liv. (17,500l.), the woods of which, 450 acres, produce 5000 liv. a year; 80 acres of vines, the wine so good as to be sent to Paris; good land for wheat, and much sown; a modern chateau, *avec toutes les aisances*, &c. And I heard of many others. I conjecture that one of the finest contiguous estates in Europe might at present be laid together in the Bourbonnois. And I am further informed, that there are at present 6000 estates to be sold in France; if things go on as they do at present, it will not be a question of buying estates, but kingdoms, and France itself will be under the hammer. I love a system of policy that inspires such confidence as to give a value to land, and that renders men so comfortable on their estates as to make the sale of them the last of their ideas. Return to Moulins.—30 miles.

The 10th. Took my leave of Moulins, where estates and farming have driven even Maria and the poplar from my head, and left me no room for the tombeau de Montmorenci; having paid extravagantly for the mud walls,

---

[1] St. Pourçain (Allier).

cobweb tapestry, and unsavoury scents of the *Lyon d'Or* I turned my mare towards Chateauneuf,[1] on the road to Auvergne. The accompanyment of the river makes the country pleasant. I found the inn full, busy, and bustling. To St. Poncin.—30 miles.

The 11th. Early to Riom,[2] in Auvergne. Near that town the country is interesting ; a fine wooded vale to the left, every where bounded by mountains ; and those nearer to the right of an interesting outline. Riom, part of which is pretty enough, is all volcanic ; it is built of lava from the quarries of volvic, which are highly curious to a naturalist. The level plain, which I passed in going to Clermont, is the commencement of the famous Limagne of Auvergne, asserted to be the most fertile of all France ; but that is an error, I have seen richer land in both Flanders and Normandy. This plain is as level as a still lake; the mountains are all volcanic, and consequently interesting.—Pass a scene of very fine irrigation, that will strike a farming eye, to Mont Ferrand,[3] and after that to Clermont, Riom, Ferrand, and Clermont, are all built, or rather perched, on the tops of rocks. Clermont is in the midst of a most curious country, all volcanic; and is built and paved with lava : much of it forms one of the worst built, dirtiest, and most stinking places I have met with. There are many streets that can, for blackness, dirt, and ill scents, only be represented by narrow channels cut in a night dunghill. The contention of nauseous savours, with which the air is impregnated, when brisk mountain gales do not ventilate these excrementitious lanes, made me envy the nerves of the good people, who, for what I know, may be happy in them. It is the fair, the town full, and the table d'hôtes crouded.—25 miles.

The 12th. Clermont is partly free from the reproach I throw on Moulins and Besançon, for there is a *salle de lecture* at a Mons. Bovares, a bookseller, where I found several newspapers and journals ; but at the coffee-house, I

[1] Châteauneuf (Puy de Dôme).
[2] (Puy de Dôme.)
[3] Montferrand, formerly a considerable town and fortress, may now be considered a suburb of Clermont-Ferrand, chef-lieu of the department of the Puy de Dôme.

enquired for them in vain:—they tell me also, that the people here are great politicians, and attend the arrival of the courier with impatience. The consequence is, there have been no riots; the most ignorant will always be the readiest for mischief. The great news just arrived from Paris, of the utter abolition of tythes, feudal rights, game, warrens, pidgeons, &c. has been received with the greatest joy by the mass of the people, and by all not immediately interested; and some even of the latter approve highly of the declaration: but I have had much conversation with two or three very sensible people, who complain bitterly of the gross injustice and cruelty of any such declarations of what will be done, but is not effected and regulated at the moment of declaring. Mons. l'Abbé Arbre, to whom Mons. de Broussonet's letter introduced me, had the goodness not only to give me all the information relative to the curious country around Clermont, which particularly depended on his enquiries as a naturalist, but also introduced me to Mons. Chabrol, as a gentleman who has attended much to agriculture, and who answered my enquiries in that line with great readiness.

The 13th. At Roya,[1] near Clermont, a village in the volcanic mountains, which are so curious, and of late years so celebrated, are some springs, reported by philosophical travellers to be the finest and most abundant in France; to view these objects, and more still, a very fine irrigation, said also to be practised there, I engaged a guide. Report, when it speaks of things of which the reporter is ignorant, is sure to magnify; the irrigation is nothing more than a mountain side converted by water to some tolerable meadow, but done coarsely, and not well understood. That in the vale, between Riom and Ferrand, far exceeds it. The springs are curious and powerful: they gush, or rather burst from the rock, in four or five streams, each powerful enough to turn a mill, into a cave a little below the village. About half a league higher there are many others; they are indeed so numerous, that scarcely a projection of the rocks or hills is without them. At the village, I found that my guide, instead of knowing the country perfectly,

---

[1] Royat (Puy de Dôme).

was in reality ignorant; I therefore took a woman to conduct me to the springs higher up the mountain; on my return, she was arrested by a soldier of the *guarde bourgeois* (for even this wretched village is not without its national militia), for having, without permission, become the guide of a stranger. She was conducted to a heap of stones, they call the chateau. They told me they had nothing to do with me; but as to the woman, she should be taught more prudence for the future: as the poor devil was in jeopardy on my account, I determined at once to accompany them for the chance of getting her cleared, by attesting her innocence. We were followed by a mob of all the village, with the woman's children crying bitterly, for fear their mother should be imprisoned. At the castle, we waited some time, and were then shewn into another apartment, where the town committee was assembled; the accusation was heard; and it was wisely remarked by all, that, in such dangerous times as these, when all the world knew that so great and powerful a person as the queen was conspiring against France in the most alarming manner, for a woman to become the conductor of a stranger—and of a stranger who had been making so many suspicious enquiries as I had, was a high offence. It was immediately agreed, that she ought to be imprisoned. I assured them she was perfectly innocent; for it was impossible that any guilty motive should be her inducement; finding me curious to see the springs, having viewed the lower ones, and wanting a guide for seeing those higher in the mountains, she offered herself: that she certainly had no other than the industrious view of getting a few *sols* for her poor family. They then turned their enquiries against myself, that if I wanted to see springs only, what induced me to ask a multitude of questions concerning the price, value, and product of the lands? What had such enquiries to do with springs and volcanoes? I told them, that cultivating some land in England, rendered such things interesting to me personally: and lastly, that if they would send to Clermont, they might know, from several respectable persons, the truth of all I asserted; and therefore I hoped, as it was the woman's first indiscretion, for I could not call it offence, they would dismiss her. This was refused at first, but assented to at last, on my declaring, that if they imprisoned her, they should do the same by me, and answer it as they could. They consented to let her go, with a reprimand, and I departed; *not* marvelling, for I have done with that, at their ignorance, in imagining that the Queen should conspire so dangerously against their rocks and mountains. I found my guide in the midst of the mob, who had been very busy in putting as many questions about me, as I had done about their crops.—There were two opinions, one party thought I was a *commissaire*, come to ascertain the damage done by the hail: the other, that I was an agent of the Queen's, who intended to blow the town up with a mine, and send all that escaped to the gallies. The care that must have been taken to render the character of that princess detested among the people, is incredible; and there seems every where to be no absurdities too gross, nor circumstances too impossible for their faith. In the evening to the theatre, the *Optimist* well acted. Before I leave Clermont, I must remark, that I dined, or supped, five times at the table d'hôte, with from twenty to thirty merchants and tradesmen, officers, &c.; and it is not easy for me to express the insignificance,—the inanity of the conversation. Scarcely any politics, at a moment when every bosom ought to beat with none but political sensations. The ignorance or the stupidity of these people must be absolutely incredible; not a week passes without their country abounding with events that are analyzed and debated by the carpenters and blacksmiths of England. The abolition of tythes, the destruction of the *gabelle*, game made property, and feudal rights destroyed, are French topics, that are translated into English within six days after they happen, and their consequences, combinations, results, and modifications, become the disquisition and entertainment of the grocers, chandlers, drapers, and shoemakers, of all the towns of England; yet the same people in France do not think them worth their conversation, except in private. Why? because conversation in private wants little knowledge; but in public, it demands more, and therefore I suppose, for I confess there are a thousand difficulties attending the solution, they are silent. But how many people, and how many subjects, on which volubility is proportioned to ignorance? Account for the fact as you please, but it is confirmed with me, and admits no doubt.

The 14th. To Izoire,[1] the country all interesting, from the number of conic mountains that rise in every quarter; some are crowned with towns;—on others are Roman castles, and the knowledge that the whole is the work of subterranean fire, though in ages far too remote for any record to announce, keeps the attention perpetually alive. Mons. de l'Arbre had given me a letter to Mons. Brés, doctor of physic, at Izoire: I found him, with all the townsmen, collected at the *hotel de ville*, to hear a newspaper read. He conducted me to the upper end of the room, and seated me by himself: the subject of the paper was the suppression of the religious houses, and the commutation of tythes. I observed that the auditors, among whom were some of the lower class, were very attentive; and the whole company seemed well pleased with whatever concerned the tythes and the monks. Mons. Brés, who is a sensible and intelligent gentleman, walked with me to his farm, about half a league from the town, on a soil of superior richness; like all other farms, this is in the hands of a *métayer*. Supped at his house afterwards, in an agreeable company, with much animated political conversation. We discussed the news of the day; they were inclined to approve of it very warmly; but I contended that the National Assembly did not proceed on any regular well digested system: that they seemed to have a rage for pulling down, but no taste for rebuilding: that if they proceeded much further in such a plan, destroying every thing, but establishing nothing, they would at last bring the kingdom into such confusion, that they would even themselves be without power to restore it to peace and order; and that such a situation would, in its nature, be on the brink of the precipice of bankruptcy and civil war. —I ventured further, to declare it as my idea, that without an upper house, they never could have either a good or a durable constitution. We had a difference of opinion on these points; but I was glad to find, that there could be

---

[1] Issoire (Puy de Dôme).

a fair discussion,—and that, in a company of six or seven gentlemen, two would venture to agree with a system so unfashionable as mine.—17 miles.

The 15th. The country continues interesting to Brioud.[1] On the tops of the mountains of Auvergne are many old castles, and towns, and villages. Pass the river, by a bridge of one great arch, to the village of Lampdes.[2] At that place, wait on Mons. Greyffier de Talairat, *avocat* and *subdelegué*, to whom I had a letter; and who was so obliging as to answer, with attention, all my enquiries into the agriculture of the neighbourhood. He enquired much after lord Bristol; and was not the worst pleased with me, when he heard I came from the same province in England. We drank his lordship's health, in the strong white wine, kept four years in the sun, which lord Bristol had much commended.—18 miles.

The 16th. Early in the morning, to avoid the heat, which has rather incommoded me, to Fix.[3] Cross the river by a ford, near the spot where a bridge is building, and mount gradually into a country, which continues interesting to a naturalist, from its volcanic origin; for all has been either overturned, or formed by fire. Pass Chomet;[4] and descending, remark a heap of basaltic columns by the road, to the right; they are small, but regular sexagons. Poulaget[5] appears in the plain to the left. Stopped at St. George,[6] where I procured mules, and a guide, to see the basaltic columns at Chilliac,[7] which, however, are hardly striking enough to reward the trouble. At Fix, I saw a field of fine clover; a sight that I have not been regaled with, I think, since Alsace. I desired to know to whom it belonged? to Mons. Coffier, doctor of medicine. I went to his house to make enquiries, which he was obliging enough to gratify, and indulged me in a walk over the principal part of his farm. He gave me a bottle

[1] Brioude (Puy de Dôme).
[2] Lempdes, Station (Puy de Dôme).
[3] Fix-Saint-Geneys (Hte. Loire).
[4] Chomette (Hte. Loire). [5] Paulhaguet (Hte. Loire).
[6] St. Georges-d'Aurac (Hte. Loire).
[7] On the railway from Paris to Nismes, travellers alight here to see la Voûte-Chiliac, a picturesque site.

of excellent *vin blanc mousseux*, made in Auvergne. I enquired of him the means of going to the mine of antimony, four leagues from hence; but he said the country was so *enragè* in that part, and had lately been mischievous, that he advised me by all means to give up the project. This country, from climate, as well as pines, must be very high. I have been for three days past melted with heat; but to-day, though the sun is bright, the heat has been quite moderate, like an English summer's day, and I am assured that they never have it hotter; but complain of the winter's cold being very severe,—and that the snow in the last was sixteen inches deep on the level. The interesting circumstance of the whole is the volcanic origin: all buildings and walls are of lava: the roads are mended with lava, pozzuolana, and basalts; and the face of the country everywhere exhibits the origin in subterranean fire. The fertility, however, is not apparent, without reflection. The crops are not extraordinary, and many bad; but then the height is to be considered. In no other country that I have seen are such great mountains as these, cultivated so high; here corn is seen every where, even to their tops, at heights where it is as usual to find rock, wood, or ling (*erica vulgaris*).—42 miles.

The 17th. The whole range of the fifteen miles to Le Puy en Velay, is wonderfully interesting. Nature, in the production of this country, such as we see it at present, must have proceeded by means not common elsewhere. It is all in its form tempestuous as the billowy ocean. Mountain rises beyond mountain, with endless variety: not dark and dreary, like those of equal height in other countries, but spread with cultivation (feeble indeed) to the very tops. Some vales sunk among them, of beautiful verdure, please the eye. Towards Le Puy the scenery is still more striking, from the addition of some of the most singular rocks any where to be seen. The castle of Polignac,[1] from which the duke takes his title, is built on a bold and enormous one, it is almost of a cubical form, and towers perpendicularly above the town, which sur-

---

[1] This striking ruin is now shown to strangers.

rounds it at its foot. The family of Polignac claim an origin of great antiquity; they have pretensions that go back, I forget whether to Hector or Achilles; but I never found any one in conversation inclined to allow them more than being in the first class of French families, which they undoubtedly are. Perhaps there is no where to be met with a castle more formed to give a *local* pride of family than this of Polignac: the man hardly exists that would not feel a certain vanity, at having given his own name, from remote antiquity, to so singular and so commanding a rock; but if, with the name, it belonged to me, I would scarcely sell it for a province. The building is of such antiquity, and the situation so romantic, that all the feudal ages pass in review in one's imagination, by a sort of magic influence; you recognize it for the residence of a lordly baron, who, in an age more distant and more respectable, though perhaps equally barbarous, was the patriot defender of his country against the invasion and tyranny of Rome. In every age, since the horrible combustions of nature which produced it, such a spot would be chosen for security and defence. To have given one's name to a castle, without any lofty pre-eminence or singularity of nature, in the midst, for instance, of a rich plain, is not equally flattering to our feelings; all antiquity of family derives from ages of great barbarity, when civil commotions and wars swept away and confounded the inhabitants of such situations. The Bretons of the plains of England, were driven to Bretagne; but the same people, in the mountains of Wales, stuck secure, and remain there to this day. About a gun-shot from Polignac is another rock, not so large, but equally remarkable; and in the town of Le Puy, another commanding one rises to a vast height; with another more singular for its tower-like form,—on the top of which St. Michael's church is built. Gypsum and lime-stone abound; and the whole country is volcanic; the very meadows are on lava: every thing, in a word, is either the product of fire, or has been disturbed or tossed about by it. At Le Puy, fair day, and a table d'hôte, with ignorance as usual. Many coffee-houses, and even considerable ones, but not a single newspaper to be found in any.—15 miles.

The 18th. Leaving Puy, the hill which the road mounts on the way to Costerous,[1] for four or five miles, commands a view of the town far more picturesque than that of Clermont. The mountain, covered with its conical town, crowned by a vast rock, with those of St. Michael and of Polignac, form a most singular scene. The road is a noble one, formed of lava and pozzuolana. The adjacent declivities have a strong disposition to run into basaltic pentagons and sexagons; the stones put up in the road, by way of posts, are parts of basaltic columns. The inn at Pradelles,[2] kept by three sisters, Pichots, is one of the worst I have met with in France. Contraction, poverty, dirt, and darkness.—20 miles.

The 19th. To Thuytz;[3] pine woods abound; there are saw mills, and with ratchet wheels to bring the tree to the saw, without the constant attention of a man, as in the Pyrenees; a great improvement. Pass by a new and beautiful road, along the side of immense mountains of granite; chesnut trees spread in every quarter, and cover with luxuriance of vegetation rocks apparently so naked, that earth seems a stranger. This beautiful tree is known to delight in volcanic soils and situations: many are very large; I measured one fifteen feet in circumference, at five from the ground; and many are nine to ten feet, and fifty to sixty high. At Maisse[4] the find road ends, and then a rocky, almost natural one for some miles; but for half a mile before Thuytz recover the new one again, which is here equal to the finest to be seen, formed of volcanic materials, forty feet broad, without the least stone, a firm and naturally level cemented surface. They tell me that 1800 toises of it, or about 2½ miles, cost 180,000 liv. (8250l.) It conducts, according to custom, to a miserable inn, but with a large stable; and in every respect Mons. Grenadier excels the Demoiselles Pichots. Here mulberries first appear, and with them flies; for this is the first day I have been incommoded. At Thuytz I had an object which I supposed would demand a whole day: it is within four hours ride of the *Montagne de la coupe au Colet d'Aisa*,[5] of which

[1] Costaros (Hte. Loire).
[2] Pradelles (Hte. Loire).
[3] Thueyts (Ardèche).
[4] Mayres (Ardèche).
[5] La coupe d'Aizac, the most characteristic crater of the Vivarais, is

M. Faujas de St. Fond has given a plate, in his *Researches sur les volcans eteints*, that shews it to be a remarkable object: I began to make enquiries, and arrangements for having a mule and a guide to go thither the next morning; the man and his wife attended me at dinner, and did not seem, from the difficulties they raised at every moment, to approve my plan: having asked them some questions about the price of provisions, and other things, I suppose they regarded me with suspicious eyes, and thought that I had no good intentions. I desired, however, to have the mule —some difficulties were made—I must have two mules— Very well, get me two. Then returning, a man was not to be had; with fresh expressions of surprise, that I should be eager to see mountains that did not concern me. After raising fresh difficulties to everything I said, they at last plainly told me, that I should have neither mule nor man; and this with an air that evidently made the case hopeless. About an hour after, I received a polite message from the marquis Deblou, seigneur of the parish, who hearing that an inquisitive Englishman was at the inn, enquiring after volcanoes, proposed the pleasure of taking a walk with me. I accepted the offer with alacrity, and going directly towards his house met him in the road. I explained to him my motives and my difficulties; he said, the people had got some absurd suspicions of me from my questions, and that the present time was so dangerous and critical to all travellers, that he would advise me by no means to think of any such excursions from the great road, unless I found much readiness in the people to conduct me: that at any other moment than the present, he should be happy to do it himself, but that at present it was impossible for any person to be too cautious. There was no resisting this reasoning, and yet to lose the most curious volcanic remains in the country, for the crater of the mountain is as distinct in the print of Mons. de St. Fond, as if the lava was now running from it, was a mortifying circumstance. The marquis then shewed me his garden and his chateau, amidst the mountains; behind it is that of

best visited from Antraigues-sur-Volane, a picturesque village about eight miles from Aubenas, by way of Vals, the miniature Vichy of the

Gravene,[1] which is an extinguished volcano likewise, but the crater not discernible without difficulty. In conversation with him and another gentleman, on agriculture, particularly the produce of mulberries, they mentioned a small piece of land that produced, by silk only, 120 liv. (5l. 5s.) a year, and being contiguous to the road we walked to it. Appearing very small for such a produce, I stepped it to ascertain the contents, and minuted them in my pocket-book. Soon after, growing dark, I took my leave of the gentlemen, and retired to my inn. What I had done had more witnesses than I dreamt of; for at eleven o'clock at night, a full hour after I had been asleep, the commander of a file of twenty *milice bourgeois*, with their musquets, or swords, or sabres, or pikes, entered my chamber, surrounded my bed, and demanded my passport. A dialogue ensued, too long to minute; I was forced first to give them my passport, and, that not satisfying them, my papers. They told me that I was undoubtedly a conspirator with the Queen, the count d'Artois, and the count d'Entragues (who has property here), who had employed me as an *arpenteur*, to measure their fields, in order to double their taxes. My papers being in English saved me. They had taken it into their heads that I was not an Englishman—only a pretended one; for they speak such a jargon themselves, that their ears were not good enough to discover by my language that I was an undoubted foreigner. Their finding no maps, or plans, nor anything that they could convert by supposition to a *cadastre* of their parish, had its effect, as I could see by their manner, for they conversed entirely in Patois. Perceiving, however, that they were not satisfied, and talked much of the count d'Entragues, I opened a bundle of letters that were sealed—these, gentlemen, are my letters of recommendation to various cities of France and Italy, open which you please, and you will find, for they are written in French, that I am an honest Englishman, and not the rogue you take me for. On this they held a fresh consultation and debate, which ended in my favour; they refused to open the letters, prepared to leave me, saying, that my numerous questions about lands, and

---

[1] La Gravenne, ascended from Thueyts.

measuring a field, while I pretended to come after volcanoes, had raised great suspicions, which they observed were natural at a time when it was known to a certainty that the Queen, the count d'Artois, and the count d'Entragues were in a conspiracy against the Vivarais. And thus, to my entire satisfaction, they wished me good night, and left me to the bugs, which swarmed in the bed like flies in a honey-pot. I had a narrow escape—it would have been a delicate situation to have been kept prisoner probably in some common gaol, or, if not, guarded at my own expence, while they sent a courier to Paris for orders, and me to pay the piper.—20 miles.

The 20th. The same imposing mountain features continue to Villeneuve de Berg.[1] The road, for half a mile, leads under an immense mass of basaltic lava, run into configurations of various forms, and resting on regular columns; this vast range bulges in the centre into a sort of promontory. The height, form, and figures, and the decisive volcanic character the whole mass has taken, render it a most interesting spectacle to the learned and unlearned eye. Just before Aubenas,[2] mistaking the road, which is not half finished, I had to turn; it was on the slope of the declivity, and very rare that any wall or defence is found against the precipices. My French mare has an ill talent of backing too freely when she begins: unfortunately she exercised it at a moment of imminent danger, and backed the chaise, me, and herself down the precipice; by great good luck, there was at the spot a sort of shelf of rock, that made the immediate fall not more than five feet direct. I leaped out of the chaise in a moment, and fell unhurt: the chaise was overthrown and the mare on her side, entangled in the harness, which kept the carriage from tumbling down a precipice of sixty feet. Fortunately she lay quietly, for had she struggled both must have fallen. I called some lime-burners to my assistance, who were with great difficulty brought to submit to directions, and not each pursue his own idea to the certain precipitation of both mare and chaise. We extri-

[1] (Ardèche), full of souvenirs of Oliver de Serres. The house in which the great agriculturist was born still exists.
[2] (Ardèche).

cated her unhurt, secured the chaise, and, then with still greater difficulty, regained the road with both. This was, by far the narrowest escape I have had. A blessed country for a broken limb—confinement for six weeks or two months at the *Cheval Blanc*, at Aubenas, an inn that would have been purgatory to one of my hogs :—alone,—without relation, friend, or servant, and not one person in sixty that speaks French.—Thanks to the good providence that preserved me! What a situation—I shudder at the reflection more than I did falling in the jaws of the precipice. Before I got from the place there were seven men about me, I gave them a 3 liv. piece to drink, which for sometime they refused to accept, thinking, with unaffected modesty, that it was too much. At Aubenas repaired the harness, and leaving that place, viewed the silk mills, which are considerable. Reach Villeneuve de berg. I was immediately hunted out by the *milice bourgeoise*. *Where is your certificate?* Here again the old objection that my features and person were not described.—*Your papers?* The importance of the case, they said, was great: and looked as big as if a marshal's batton was in hand. They tormented me with an hundred questions; and then pronounced that I was a suspicious looking person. They could not conceive why a Suffolk farmer could travel into the Vivarais? Never had they heard of any person travelling for agriculture! They would take my passport to the *hotel de ville*—have the permanent council assembled—and place a centinel at my door. I told them they might do what they pleased, provided they did not prohibit my dinner, as I was hungry; they then departed. In about half an hour a gentleman-like man, a *Croix de St. Louis* came, asked me some questions very politely, and seemed not to conclude that Maria Antonietta and Arthur Young were at this moment in any very dangerous conspiracy. He retired, saying, he hoped I should not meet with any difficulties. In another half hour a soldier came to conduct me to the *hotel de ville*; where I found the council assembled; I had a good many questions asked; and some expressions of surprise that an English farmer should travel so far for agriculture—they had never heard of such a thing;—but all was in a polite liberal manner; and though travelling for agriculture was as new to them, as if it had been like the antient philosopher's tour of the world on a cow's back, and living on the milk,—yet they did not deem any thing in my recital improbable, signed my passport very readily, assured me of every assistance and civility I might want, and dismissed me with the politeness of gentlemen. I described my treatment at Thuytz, which they loudly condemned. I took this opportunity to beg to know where that Pradel[1] was to be found in this country, of which Oliver de Serres was seigneur, the well known French writer on agriculture in the reign of Henry IV. They at once pointed out of the window of the room we were in to the house, which in this town belonged to him, and informed me that Pradel was within a league. As this was an object I had noted before I came to France, the information gave me no slight satisfaction. The mayor, in the course of the examination, presented me to a gentleman who had translated Sterne into French, but who did not speak English; on my return to the auberge I found that this was Mons. de Boissiere, *avocat general* of the parliament of Grenoble. I did not care to leave the place without knowing something more of one who had distinguished himfelf by his attention to English literature; and I wrote him a note, begging permission to have the pleasure of some conversation with a gentleman who had made our inimitable author speak the language of a people he loved so well. Mons. de Boissiere came to me immediately, conducted me to his house, introduced me to his lady and some friends, and as I was much interested concerning Oliver de Serres, he offered to take a walk with me to Pradel. It may easily be supposed that this was too much to my mind to be refused, and few evenings have been more agreeably spent. I regarded the residence of the great parent of French agriculture, and who was undoubtedly one of the first writers on the subject that had then appeared in the world, with that sort of veneration, which those only can feel who have addicted themselves strongly to some predominant pursuit, and find it in such moments indulged in its most exquisite feelings Two

---

[1] Le Pradel, close to Villeneuve de Berg.

hundred years after his exertions, let me do honour to his memory, he was an excellent farmer and a true patriot, and would not have been fixed on by Henry IV. as his chief agent in the great project of introducing the culture of silk in France, if he had not possessed a considerable reputation; a reputation well earned, since posterity has confirmed it. The period of his practice is too remote to gain anything more than a general outline of what may now be supposed to have been his farm. The basis of it is limestone; there is a great oak wood near the chateau, and many vines, with plenty of mulberries, some apparently old enough to have been planted by the hand of the venerable genius that has rendered the ground classic. The estate of Pradel, which is about 5000 liv. (218l. 15s.) a year, belongs at present to the marquis of Mirabel who inherits it in right of his wife, as the descendant of De Serres. I hope it is exempted for ever from all taxes; he whose writings laid the foundation for the improvement of a kingdom, should leave to his posterity some marks of his countrymen's gratitude. When the present bishop of Sisteron was shewn, like me, the farm of De Serres, he remarked, that the nation ought to erect a statue to his memory.[1] The sentiment is not without merit, though no more than common snuff-box chat; but if this bishop has a well cultivated farm in his hands it does him honour. Supped with Mons. and Madame de Boissiere, &c. and had the pleasure of an agreeable and interesting conversation. —21 miles.

The 21st. Mons. de Boissiere, wishing to take my advice in the improvement of a farm, which he had taken into his hands, six or seven miles from Berg, in my road to Viviers, accompanied me thither. I advised him to form one well executed and well improved inclosure every year —to finish as he advances, and to do well what he attempts to do at all; and I cautioned him against the common abuse of that excellent husbandry, paring and burning. I suspect, however, that his *homme d'affaire* will be too potent for the English traveller.—I hope he has received the

---

[1] A statue of de Serres now adorns Villeneuve de Berg, also a pyramidal monument to his memory, and a street and square are named after him.

turnip-seed I sent him. Dine at Viviers,[1] and pass the Rhone. After the wretched inns of the Vivarais, dirt, filth, bugs, and starving, to arrive at the *hotel de Monsieur*, at Montilimart,[2] a great and excellent inn, was something like the arrival in France from Spain: the contrast is striking; and I seemed to hug myself, that I was again in a christian country among the Milor Ninchitreas, and my Ladi Bettis, of Mons. Chabot.—23 miles.

The 22d. Having a letter to Mons. Faujas de St. Fond,[3] the celebrated naturalist, who has favoured the world with many important works on volcanoes, aerostation, and various other branches of natural history, I had the satisfaction, on enquiring, to find that he was at Montilimart; and, waiting on him—to perceive, that a man of distinguished merit was handsomely lodged, with every thing about him that indicated an easy fortune. He received me with the frank politeness inherent in his character; introduced me, on the spot to a Mons. l'Abbé Berenger, who resided near his country-seat, and was, he said, an excellent cultivator; and likewise to another gentleman, whose taste had taken the same good direction. In the evening Mons. Faujas took me to call on a female friend, who was engaged in the same enquiries, Madame Cheinet, whose husband is a member of the National Assembly; if he has the good luck to find at Versailles some other lady as agreeable as her he has left at Montilimart, his mission will not be a barren one; and he may perhaps be better employed than in voting regenerations. This lady accompanied us in a walk for viewing the environs of Montilimart; and it gave me no small pleasure to find, that she was an excellent farmeress, practises considerably, and had the goodness to answer many of my enquiries, particularly in the culture of silk. I was so charmed with the *naiveté* of character, and pleasing conversation of this very agree-

---

[1] (Ardèche), the ancient capital of the Vivarais.
[2] Montélimar (Drôme).
[3] Few of our author's numerous introductory letters brought him a more distinguished acquaintance than this. M. Faujas St. Fond, afterwards his visitor at Bradfield, is known as one of the creators of the science of geology in France. His English and Scotch Travels have been translated. Died 1819.

able lady, that a longer stay here would have been delicious —but the plough!

The 23d. By appointment, accompanied Mons. Faujas to his country-seat and farm at l'Oriol,[1] fifteen miles north of Montilimart, where he is building a good house. I was pleased to find his farm amount to 280 septerés[2] of land: I should have liked it better, had it not been in the hands of a *métayer*. Mons. Faujas pleases me much; the liveliness, vivacity, *phlogiston* of his character, do not run into pertness, foppery, or affectation; he adheres steadily to a subject; and shews, that to clear up any dubious point, by the attrition of different ideas in conversation, gives him pleasure; not through a vain fluency of colloquial powers, but for better understanding a subject. The next day, Mons. l'Abbé Berenger, and another gentlemen, passed it at Mons. Faujas': we walked to the Abbé's farm. He is of the good order of beings, and pleases me much; curé of the parish, and president of the permanent council. He is at present warm on a project of reuniting the protestants to the church; spoke, with great pleasure, of having persuaded them, on occasion of the general thanksgiving for the establishment of liberty, to return thanks to God, and sing the *Te Deum* in the catholic church, in common as brethren, which, from confidence in his character, they did. His is firmly persuaded, that by both parties giving way a little, and softening or retrenching reciprocally somewhat in points that are disagreeable, they may be brought together. The idea is so liberal, that I question it for the multitude, who are never governed by reason, but by trifles and ceremonies,—and who are usually attached to their religion, in proportion to the absurdities it abounds with. I have not the least doubt but the mob in England would be much more scandalized at parting with the creed of St. Athanasius, than the whole bench of bishops, whose illumination would perhaps reflect correctly that of the throne. Mons. l'Abbé Berenger has prepared a memorial, which is ready to be presented to the National Assembly, proposing and explaining this ideal union of the two religions; and

---

[1] Loriol (Drôme).
[2] Setier, ancient measure of land, as much as could be sowed with a setier (156 litres), of corn.

he had the plan of adding a clause, proposing that the clergy should have permission to marry. He was convinced, that it would be for the interest of morals, and much for that of the nation, that the clergy should not be an insulated body, but holding by the same interests and connections as other people. He remarked, that the life of a *curé*, and especially in the country, is melancholy; and, knowing my passion, observed, that a man never could be so good a farmer, on any possession he might have, excluded from being succeeded by his children. He shewed me his memoir, and I was pleased to find that there is at present great harmony between the two religions, owing certainly to such good *curés*. The number of protestants is very considerable in this neighbourhood. I strenuously contended for the insertion of the clause respecting marriage; assured him, that at such a moment as this, it would do all who were concerned in this memorial the greatest credit; and that they ought to consider it as a demand of the rights of humanity, violently, injuriously, and, relative to the nation, impolitically, withheld. Yesterday, in going with Mons. Faujas, we passed a congregation of protestants, assembled, Druid-like,[1] under five or six spreading oaks, to offer their thanksgiving to the great Parent of their happiness and hope.—In such a climate as this, is it not a worthier temple, built by the great hand they revere, than one of brick and mortar?—This was one of the richest days I have enjoyed in France; we had a long and truly farming dinner; drank à l'Anglois success to THE PLOUGH! and had so much agricultural conversation, that I wished for my farming friends in Suffolk to partake my satisfaction. If Mons. Faujus de St. Fond comes to England, as he gives me hope, I shall introduce him to them with pleasure. In the evening return to Montilimart.—30 miles.

The 25th. To Chateau Rochemaur,[2] across the Rhone.

[1] In 1788, Louis XVI. acting on former advice of Turgot, had passed a decree ameliorating the condition of Protestants in France. They were still ineligible for civil appointments, but were permitted to celebrate worship, their marriages were now legal, and their children legitimate before the law. Entire liberty of conscience and civil equality were decreed by the National Assembly a year later.

[2] Rochemaure (Ardèche), one of the most striking objects seen by the traveller steaming from Lyons to Avignon.

It is situated on a basaltic rock, nearly perpendicular, with every columnar proof of its volcanic origin. See Mons. de Faujas' *Recherches*. In the afternoon to Piere Latte,[1] through a country steril, uninteresting, and far inferior to the environs of Montilimart.—22 miles.

The 26th. To Orange,[2] the country not much better; a range of mountains to the left: see nothing of the Rhone. At that town there are remains of a large Roman building, seventy or eighty feet high, called a circus, of a triumphal arch, which, though a good deal decayed, manifests, in its remains, no ordinary decoration, and a pavement in the house of a poor person, which is very perfect and beautiful, but much inferior to that of Nismes. The *vent de bize* has blown strongly for several days, with a clear sky, tempering the heats, which are sometimes sultry and oppressive; it may, for what I know, be wholesome to French constitutions, but it is diabolical to mine; I found myself very indifferent, and as if I was going to be ill, a new and unusual sensation over my whole body: never dreaming of the wind, I knew not what to attribute it to, but my complaint coming at the same time, puts it out of doubt; besides, instinct now, much more than reason, makes me guard as much as I can against it. At four or five in the morning it is so cold that no traveller ventures out. It is more penetratingly drying than I had any conception of; other winds stop the cutaneous perspiration; but this piercing through the body seems, by its sensation, to dessicate all the interior humidity.—20 miles.

The 27th. To Avignon.—Whether it was because I had read much of this town in the history of the middle ages, or because it had been the residence of the Popes, or more probably from the still more interesting memoirs which Petrarch has left concerning it, in poems that will last as long as Italian elegance and human feelings shall exist, I know not—but I approached the place with a sort of interest, attention, and expectancy, that few towns have kindled. Laura's tomb, is in the church of the Cordeliers; it is nothing but a stone in the pavement, with a figure engraven on it partly effaced, surrounded by an inscription in

---

[1] Pierrelatte (Drôme).   [2] (Vaucluse.)

Gothic letters, and another in the wall adjoining, with the armorial of the family of Sade. How incredible is the power of great talents, when employed in delineating passions common to the human race. How many millions of women, fair as Laura, have been beloved as tenderly—but, wanting a Petrarch to illustrate the passion, have lived and died in oblivion! whilst his lines, not written to die, conduct thousands under the impulse of feelings, which genius only can excite, to mingle in idea their melancholy sighs with those of the poet who consecrated these remains to immortality!—There is a monument of the brave Crillon[1] in the same church; and I saw other churches and pictures—but Petrarch and Laura are predominant at Avignon.—19 miles.

The 28th. Wait upon Pere Brouillony, provincial visitor,[2] who, with great politeness, procured me the information I wished, by introducing me to some gentlemen understanding in agriculture. From the rock of the legates palace, there is one of the finest views of the windings of the Rhone that is to be seen: it forms two considerable islands, which, with the rest of the plain, richly watered, cultivated, and covered with mulberries, olives, and fruit-trees, have a fine boundary in the mountains of Provence, Dauphiné, and Languedoc.—The circular road fine. I was struck with the resemblance between the women here and in England. It did not at once occur in what it consisted; but it is their caps; they dress their heads quite different from the French women. A better particularity, is there being no wooden shoes here, nor, as I have seen, in Provence.[3]—I have often complained of the stupid ignorance I met with at table d'hôtes. Here, if possible, it has been worse than common. The politeness of the French is proverbial, but it never could arise

---

[1] A celebrated captain who served Henri IV.

[2] "Le père visiteur" is charged with the inspection of religious houses of his order.

[3] We were, like you, struck with the resemblance of the women at Avignon to those of England, but not for the reason you give; it appeared to us to originate from their complexions being *naturally* so much better than that of the other French women, more than their head-dress, which differs as much from ours, as it does from the French: —*Note by a female friend to Arthur Young.*

from the manners of the classes that frequent these tables. Not one time in forty will a foreigner, as such, receive the least mark of attention. The only political idea here is, that if the English should attack France, they have a million of men in arms to receive them; and their ignorance seems to know no distinction between men in arms in their towns and villages, or in action without the kingdom. They conceive, as Sterne observes, much better than they combine: I put some questions to them, but in vain: I asked, if the union of a rusty firelock and a *bourgeois* made a soldier?—I asked them, in which of their wars they had wanted men? I demanded, whether they had ever felt any other want than that of money? And whether the conversion of a million of men, into the bearers of musquets, would made money more plentiful? I asked, if personal service was not a tax? And whether paying the tax of the service of a million of men increased their faculties of paying other and more useful taxes? I begged them to inform me, if the regeneration of the kingdom, which had put arms into the hands of a million of mob, had rendered industry more productive, internal peace more secure, confidence more enlarged, or credit more stable? And lastly, I assured them, that should the English attack them at present, they would probably make the weakest figure they had done from the foundation of their monarchy: but, gentlemen, the English, in spite of the example you set them in the American war, will disdain such a conduct; they regret the constitution you are forming, because they think it a bad one—but whatever you may establish, you will have no interruption, but many good wishes from your neighbour. It was all in vain; they were well persuaded their government was the best in the world; that it was a monarchy, and no republic, which I contended; and that the English thought it good, because they would unquestionably abolish their house of lords, in the enjoyment of which accurate idea I left them. —In the evening to Lille,[1] a town which has lost its name in the world, in the more splendid fame of Vaucluse. There can hardly be met with a richer, or better cultivated

---

[1] L'Isle, stat. (Vaucluse), on an island surrounded by branches of the Sorgues.

sixteen miles; the irrigation is superb. Lille is most agreeably situated. On coming to the verge of it I found fine plantations of elms, with delicious streams, bubbling over pebbles on either side; well dressed people were enjoying the evening at a spot, I had conceived to be only a mountain village. It was a sort of fairy scene to me. Now, thought I, how detestable to leave this fine wood and water, and enter a nasty, beggarly, walled, hot, stinking town; one of the contrasts most offensive to my feelings. What an agreeable surprise, to find the inn without the town, in the midst of the scenery I had admired! and more, a good and civil inn. I walked on the banks of this classic stream for an hour, with the moon gazing on the waters, that will run for ever in mellifluous poetry: retired to sup on the most exquisite trout and craw fish in the world. To-morrow to the famed origin.—16 miles.

The 29th. I am delighted with the environs of Lille; beautiful roads, well planted, surround and pass off in different directions, as if from a capital town, umbrageous enough to form promenades against a hot sun, and the river splits and divides into so many streams, and is conducted with so much attention that it has a delicious effect, especially to an eye that recognises all the fertility of irrigation. To the fountain of Vaucluse, which is justly said to be as celebrated almost as that of Helicon. Crossing a plain, which is not so beautiful as one's idea of Tempe; the mountain presents an almost perpendicular rock, at the foot of which is an immense and very fine cavern, half filled with a pool of stagnant, but clear water, this is the famous fountain; at other seasons it fills the whole cavern, and boils over in a vast stream among rocks; its bed now marked by vegetation. At present the water gushes out 200 yards lower down, from beneath masses of rock, and in a very small distance forms a considerable river, which almost immediately receives deviations by art for mills and irrigation. On the summit of a rock above the village, but much below the mountain, is a ruin, called, by the poor people here, the chateau of Petrarch—who tell you it was inhabited by Mons. Petrarch and Madame Laura. The scene is sublime; but what renders it truly interesting to our feelings, is the celebrity which great talents have given it. The power of rocks, and water, and mountains, even in their boldest features, to arrest attention, and fill the bosom with sensations that banish the insipid feelings of common life—holds not of inanimate nature. To give energy to such sensations, it must receive animation from the creative touch of a vivid fancy: described by the poet, or connected with the residence, actions, pursuits, or passions of great geniusses; it lives, as it were, personified by talents, and commands the interest that breathes around whatever is consecrated by fame. To Orgon.[1] Quit the Pope's territory, by crossing the Durance; there view the skeleton of the navigation of Boisgelin, the work of the archbishop of Aix, a noble project, and, where finished, perfectly well executed; a hill is pierced by it for a quarter of a mile, a work that rivals the greatest similar exertions. It has, however, stood still many years for want of money. The *vent de bize* gone, and the heat increased, the wind now S.W. my health better to a moment, which proves how pernicious it is, even in August.—20 miles.

The 30th. I forgot to observe that, for a few days past, I have been pestered with all the mob of the country shooting: one would think that every rusty gun in Provence is at work, killing all sorts of birds; the shot has fallen five or six times in my chaise and about my ears. The National Assembly has declared that every man has a right to kill game on his own land; and advancing this maxim so absurd as a declaration, though so wise as a law, without any statute of provision to secure the right of game to the possessor of the soil, according to the tenor of the vote, has, as I am every where informed, filled all the fields of France with sportsmen to an utter nuisance. The same effects have flowed from declarations of right relative to tythes, taxes, feudal rights, &c. In the declarations, conditions and compensations are talked of; but an unruly ungovernable multitude seize the benefit of the abolition, and laugh at the obligations or recompense. Out by daybreak for Salon,[2] in order to view the Crau, one of the most singular districts in France for its soil, or rather want of soil, being apparently a region of sea flints,

---

[1] (Vaucluse.)   [2] (Bouches du Rhône.)

yet feeding great herds of sheep: View the improvement of Monsieur Pasquali, who is doing great things, but roughly: I wished to see and converse with him, but unfortunately he was absent from Salon. At night to St. Canat.[1]—46 miles.

The 31st. To Aix.[2] Many houses without glass windows. The women with men's hats, and no wooden shoes. At Aix waited on Mons. Gibelin, celebrated for his translations of the works of Dr. Priestley, and of the Philosophical Transactions. He received me with that easy and agreeable politeness natural to his character, being apparently a friendly man. He took every method in his power to procure me the information I wanted, and engaged to go with me the next day to Tour D'Aigues[3] to wait on the baron of that name, president of the parliament of Aix, to whom also I had letters; and whose essays, in the *Trimestres* of the Paris society of agriculture, are among the most valuable on rural œconomics in that work.—12 miles.

SEPTEMBER 1st. Tour d'Aigues is twenty miles north of Aix, on the other side of the Durance, which we crossed at a ferry. The country about the chateau is bold and hilly, and swells in four or five miles into rocky mountains. The president received me in a very friendly manner, with a simplicity of manners that gives a dignity to his character, void of affectation; he is very fond of agriculture and planting. The afternoon was passed in viewing his home-farm, and his noble woods, which are uncommon in this naked province. The chateau of Tour d'Aigues, before much of it was accidentally consumed by fire, must have been one of the most considerable in France; but at present a melancholy spectacle is left. The baron is an enormous sufferer by the revolution; a great extent of country, which belonged in absolute right to his ancestors, has been granted for quit rents, *cens*, and other feudal payments, so that there is no comparison between the lands retained and those thus granted by his family. The loss of the *droits honorifiques* is much more than has been

[1] St. Chamas (Bouches du Rhône).
[2] Aix-en-Provence (Bouches du Rhône).
[3] Tour d'Aigues (Bouches du Rhône). The château here spoken of is now a ruin.

apparent, and is an utter loss of all influence; it was natural to look for some plain and simple mode of compensation; but the declaration of the National Assembly allows none; and it is feelingly known in this chateau, that the solid payments which the Assembly have declared to be *rachetable* are every hour falling to nothing, without a shadow of recompense. The people are in arms, and at this moment very unquiet. The situation of the nobility in this country is pitiable; they are under apprehensions that nothing will be left them, but simply such houses as the mob allows to stand unburnt; that the *métayers* will retain their farms without paying the landlord his half of the produce; and that, in case of such a refusal, there is actually neither law nor authority in the country to prevent it. Here is, however, in this house, a large and an agreeable society, and cheerful to a miracle, considering the times, and what such a great baron is losing, who has inherited from his ancestors immense possessions, now frittering to nothing by the revolution. This chateau, splendid even in ruins, the venerable woods, park, and all the ensigns of family and command, with the fortune, and even the lives of the owners at the mercy, and trampled on by an armed rabble. What a spectacle! The baron has a very fine and well filled library, and one part of it totally with books and tracts on agriculture, in all the languages of Europe. His collection of these is nearly as numerous as my own.—20 miles.

The 2d. Mons. Le President dedicated this day for an excursion to his mountain-farm, five miles off, where he has a great range, and one of the finest lakes in Provence, two thousand toises round, and forty feet deep. Directly from it rises a fine mountain, consisting of a mass of shell agglutinated into stone; it is a pity this hill is not planted, as the water wants the immediate accompanyment of wood. Carp rise to 25lb. and eels to 12lb. (Note, there are carp in the lake Bourget, in Savoy, of 60lb.) A neighbouring gentleman, Mons. Jouvent, well acquainted with the agriculture of this country, accompanied us, and spent the rest of the day at the castle. I had much valuable information from the baron de Tour d'Aigues, this gentleman, and from Mons. l'Abbé de ——, I forget his name. In the evening

I had some conversation on housekeeping with one of the ladies, and found among other articles, that the wages of a gardener are 300 liv. (13l. 2s. 6d.); a common man-servant, 150 liv. (7l.); a bourgeois cook, 75 to 90 liv. (90 liv. are 3l. 18s. 9d.); a house-maid, 60 to 70 liv. (3l. 1s. 3d.) Rent of a good house for a Bourgeois 700 or 800 liv. (35l.) —10 miles.

The 3d. Took my leave of Mons. Tour d'Aigues' hospitable chateau, and returned with Mons. Gibelin to Aix.— 20 miles.

The 4th. The country to Marseilles is all mountainous, but much cultivated with vines and olives; it is, however, naked and uninteresting; and much of the road is left in a scandalous condition, for one of the greatest in France, not wide enough, at places, for two carriages to pass with convenience. What a deceiving painter is the imagination! —I had read I know not what lying exaggerations of the *bastides* about Marseilles, being counted not by hundreds, but by thousands, with anecdotes of Louis XIV. adding one to the number of a citadel.—I have seen other towns in France, where they are more numerous; and the environs of Montpellier, without external commerce, are as highly decorated as those of Marseilles; yet Montpellier is not singular. The view of Marseilles, in the approach, is not striking. It is well built in the new quarter, but, like all others, in the old, close, ill built, and dirty; the population, if we may judge from the throng in the streets, is very great; I have met with none that exceeds it in this respect. I went in the evening to the theatre, which is new, but not striking; and not in any respect to be named with that of Bourdeaux, or even Nantes; nor is the general magnificence of the town at all equal to Bourdeaux; the new buildings are neither so extensive, nor so good—the number of ships in the port not to be compared, and the port itself is a horse-pond, compared with the Garonne.— 20 miles.

The 5th. Marseilles is absolutely exempt from the reproaches I have so often cast on others for want of newspapers. I breakfasted at the *Café d'Acajon* amidst many. Deliver my letters, and receive information concerning commerce; but I am disappointed of one I expected for Mons.

l'Abbé Raynal, the celebrated author. At the table d'hôte, the count de Mirabeau, both here and at Aix, a topic of conversation; I expected to have found him more popular, from the extravagancies committed in his favour in Provence and at Marseilles; they consider him merely as a politician of great abilities, whose principles are favourable to theirs: as to his private character, they think they have nothing to do with it; and assert, that they had much rather trust to a rogue of abilities, than put any confidence in an honest man of no talents; not, however, meaning to assert, that Mons. de Mirabeau deserved any such appellation. They say he has an estate in Provence. I observed, that I was glad to hear he had property; for, in such revolutions, it was a necessary hold on a man, that he will not drive every thing to confusion, in order to possess a consequence and importance which cannot attend him in peaceable and quiet times. But to be at Marseilles without seeing Abbé Raynal, one of the undoubted precursors of the present revolution in France, would be mortifying. Having no time to wait longer for letters, I took the resolution to introduce myself. He was at the house of his friend Mons. Bertrand. I told him my situation: and, with that ease and politeness which flows from a man's knowledge of the world, he replied, that he was always happy to be of use to any gentleman of my nation; and, turning to his friend, said, here also is one, Sir, who loves the English, and understands their language. In conversing on agriculture, which I had mentioned as the object of my journey, they both expressed their surprise to find, by accounts apparently authentic, that we imported great quantities of wheat, instead of exporting, as we formerly did; and desired to know, if this was really the case, to what it was owing? and recurring, at the same time, to the *Mercure de France* for a statement of the export and import of corn, he read it as a quotation from Mr. Arthur Young. This gave me the opportunity of saying, that I was the person, and it proved a lucky introduction; for it was not possible to be received with more politeness, or with more offers of service and assistance. I explained, that the change had taken place in consequence of a vast increase of population, a cause still increasing more rapidly than ever.—We had an interesting conversation on the agriculture of France, and on the present situation of affairs, which they both think going on badly; are convinced of the necessity of an upper house in the legislature; and dread nothing more than a mere democratical government, which they think a species of republic, ridiculous for such a kingdom as France. I remarked, that I had often reflected with amazement, that Mons. Necker did not assemble the states in such a form, and under such regulations, as would have naturally led to adopt the constitution of England, free from the few faults which time has discovered in it. On which Mons. Bertrand gave me a pamphlet he had published, addressed to his friend Abbé Raynal, proposing several circumstances in the English constitution to be adopted in that of France. Mons. l'Abbé Raynal remarked, that the American revolution had brought the French one in its train: I observed, that if the result in France should be liberty, that revolution had proved a blessing to the world, but much more so to England than to America. This they both thought such a paradox, that I explained it by remarking, that I believed the prosperity which England had enjoyed since the peace, not only much exceeded that of any other similar period, but also that of any other country, in any period since the establishment of the European monarchies: a fact that was supported by the increase of population, of consumption, of industry, of navigation, shipping, and sailors: by the augmentation and improvement of agriculture, manufactures, and commerce; and in a peculiar mass and aggregate, flowing from the whole, the rising ease and felicity of the people. I mentioned the authentic documents and public registers which supported such a representation; and I remarked, that Abbé Raynal, who attended closely to what I said, had not seen or heard of these circumstances, in which he is not singular, for I have not met with a single person in France acquainted with them; yet they unquestionably form one of the most remarkable and singular experiments in the science of politics that the world has seen; for a people to lose an empire—thirteen provinces, and to GAIN by that *loss*, an increase of wealth, felicity, and power! When will the obvious conclusions, to be drawn from that prodigious event, be adopted? that all transmarine, or distant dominions, are sources of weakness: and that to renounce them would be wisdom. Apply this in France to St. Domingo, in Spain to Peru, or in England to Bengal, and mark the ideas and replies that are excited. I have no doubt, however, of the fact. I complimented him on his generous gift to the society of agriculture at Paris of 1200 liv. for a premium; he said they had thanked him, not in the usual form, by the secretary signing alone, but had every one present signed it. He said, that he should do the same by the academies of sciences and belles lettres; and he has given the same sum to the academy at Marseilles, for a premium relative to their commerce. He said also, that he had formed a plan which he should execute when he has saved money enough, which is to expend, by means of the society of agriculture, 1200 liv. a year in purchasing models of all the useful implements of husbandry to be found in other countries, especially in England, and to spread them over France. The idea is an excellent one, and merits great praise; yet it is to be questioned, whether the effect would answer the expence. Give the tool itself to a farmer, and he will not know how to use it, or will be too much prejudiced to like it; a model he will still less take the trouble to copy. Gentlemen farming every where their own lands, with enthusiasm and passion for the art, would apply and use those models; but I fear that none such are to be found in France. The spirit and pursuits of gentlemen must be changed from their present frivolous turns, before any such thing could be effected. He approved of my recommending turnips and potatoes; but said, that good sorts were wanting; and mentioned a trial he had made himself, a comparison of the English and Provençal potatoes in making bread, and the English produced one-third more flour than the French.—Among other causes of bad husbandry in France, he named the illegality of usury: at present moneyed people in the country locked it up, instead of lending it for improvement. These sentiments of an illustrious writer do him honour; and it was pleasing to me to find, that he gave attention to objects which have almost monopolized mine; and yet more so to find, that this justly celebrated writer, though not young, is in good spirits; and that he may live many years to enlighten the world by the productions of a pen that has never been employed but for the benefit of the human species.

The 8th. The Cuges.[1] For three or four miles the road leads through rows of *bastides* and walls; it is made of powdered white stone, and without exception, the most dusty I ever saw; the vines, for twenty rods on each side, were like a dressed head: the country all mountains of rocks, with poor pines.—Uninteresting and ugly; the plains, of no great breadth, are covered with vines and olives. Meet capers first at Cuges. At Aubagne,[2] I dined on six dishes, not bad, a dessert, and a bottle of wine, for 24*f.* and by myself too, for no table d'hôte. What Mons. Dutens could mean by calling the post-house at Cuges a good *auberge*, is inexplicable; it is a miserable hole, in which I have one of the best rooms, without glass to the windows.—21 miles.

The 9th. The country to Toulon is more interesting; the mountains are bolder; the sea adds to the view; and there is one passage among the rocks, where are sublime features. Nine-tenths are waste mountain, and a wretched country of pines, box, and miserable aromatics, in spite of the climate. Near Toulon, especially at Olioules,[3] there are pomegranates in the hedges, with fruit as large as nonpareils; they have a few oranges also. The bason of Toulon, with ranges of three deckers, and other large men of war, with a quay of life and business, are fine. The town has nothing that deserves description; the great and only thing that is worth seeing, the dock-yard, I could not see, yet I had letters; but the regulation forbidding it, as at Brest, all applications were vain.—25 miles.

The 10th. Lady Craven[4] has sent me upon a wild-goose chase to Hyeres—one would think this country, from her's and many other descriptions, was all a garden; but it has

---

[1] Cujés, a poor-looking town near which the caper is cultivated.
[2] (Bouches du Rhône.)
[3] Ollioules (Var), in the valley of the Reppe, famous for its orange trees and immortelles.
[4] Elizabeth, Lady Craven, who after a Platonic friendship of many years' standing, married the Margrave of Anspach, and was the author of works of travel, and an autobiography.

been praised much beyond its merit. The vale is every where richly cultivated, and planted with olives and vines, with a mixture of some mulberries, figs, and other fruit trees. The hills are either rocks, or spread with a poor vegetation of evergreens, pines, lentiscus, &c. The vale, though scattered with white *bastides* which animate the scene, yet betrays that poverty in the robe of nature, which always offends the eye where olives and fruits form the principal cloathing. Every view is meagre, on comparison with the rich foliage of our northern forests. The only singular features are the orange and lemon trees; they here thrive in the open air, are of a great size, and render every garden interesting to eyes that travel to the south; but last winter's frost has shorn them of their glory. They are all so nearly destroyed as to be cut almost to the root, or to the trunk, but are in general shooting again. I conjecture that these trees, even when in health and foliage, however they may be separately taken, add but little to the general effect of a view. They are all in gardens, mixed with walls and houses, and consequently lose much beauty as the part of a landscape. Lady Craven's Tour sent me to the chapel of *Notre Dame de consolation*,[1] and to the hills leading to Mons. Glapiere de St. Tropes; and I asked for father Laurent, who was however, very little sensible of the honour she had done him. The views from the hills on both sides of the town are moderate. The islands Portecroix, Pourcurolle, and Levant[2] (the nearest joined to the continent by a causeway and saltmarsh, which they call a pond,) the hills, mounts, rocks, all are naked. The pines that spread on some of them have not a much better effect than gorse. The verdure of the vale is hurt by the hue of the olives. There is a fine outline to the views; but for a climate, where vegetation is the chief glory, it is poor and meagre; and does not refresh the imagination with the idea of a thick shade

---

[1] Notre Dame, a favourite pilgrimage.
[2] The Isles d'Hyères or Isles d'Or, viz :—
    1. Porquerolles (300 inhabitants, 5 miles long).
    2. Port Cros.
    3. Levant or Titan, is the largest and most beautiful, and contains a penitentiary for boys.

against the rays of an ardent sun. I can hear of no cotton in Provence, which has been reported in several books; but the date and pistachio succeed: the myrtle is indigenous everywhere, and the *jasminum, commune,* and *fruticans.*[1] In l'Isle de Levant is the *genista candescens,*[2] and the *teucrium herba poma.*[3] Returning from my ride to the *hotel de Necker,* the landlord worried me with a list of English that pass the winter at Hyeres; there are many houses built for letting, from two to six louis a month, including all the furniture, linen, necessary plate, &c. Most of these houses command the prospect of the vale and the sea; and if they do not feel the *vent de bize,* I should suppose it must be a fine winter climate. In December, January, and February perhaps it may not incommode them, but does it not in March and April? There is a table d'hôte, very well served, at the *hotel de Necker* in winter, at 4 liv. a-head each meal. View the King's garden here, which may be 10 or 12 acres, and nobly productive in all the fruits of the climate, its crop of oranges only last year was 21,000 liv. (918l. 15s.) Oranges at Hyeres have produced as far as two louis each tree. Dine with Mons. de St. Cæsaire, who has a pretty new built house, a noble garden walled in, and an estate around it, which he would sell or let. He was so obliging as to give me, with Doctor Battaile, much useful information concerning the agriculture and produce of this country. In the evening return to Toulon.—34 miles.

The 11th. The arrangement of my journey in Italy occupied some attention. I had been often informed, and by men that have travelled much in Italy, that I must not think of going thither with my one-horse chaise. To watch my horse being fed would, they assured me, take up abundantly too much time, and if it was omitted, with respect to hay, as well as oats, both would be equally stolen. There are also parts of Italy where travelling alone, as I did, would be very unsafe, from the number of robbers that infest the roads. Persuaded by the opinions of

---

[1] Jasminium commune fructicans, yellow jasmine.
[2] Genista candicans, hoary genista.
   Teucrium herba rota in other editions; both equally unintelligible.

persons, who I suppose must know much better than myself, I had determined to sell my mare and chaise, and travel in Italy by the *veturini*, who are to be had it seems everywhere, and at a cheap rate. At Aix they offered me for both 20 louis; at Marseilles, 18; so the further I went I expected the price would sink; but to get out of the hands of the *aubergistes*, and the *garçons d'écuries*, who expected everywhere to make a property of me, I had it drawn into the street at Toulon, with a large label, written *a vendre*, and the price 25 louis: they had cost me at Paris 32. My plan took, and I sold them for 22; they had brought me above twelve hundred miles, but yet were a cheap bargain to an officer that was the purchaser. I had next to consider the method to get to Nice; and will it be believed, that from Marseilles with 100,000 souls, and Toulon with 30,000, lying in the great road to Antibes, Nice, and Italy, there is no diligence or regular voiture. A gentleman at the table d'hôte assured me, they asked him 3 louis for a place in a voiture to Antibes, and to wait till some other person would give 3 more for another seat. To a person accustomed to the infinity of machines that fly about England, in all directions, this must appear hardly credible. Such great cities in France have not the hundredth part of connection and communication with each other that much inferior places enjoy with us: a sure proof of their deficiency in consumption, activity, and animation. A gentleman, who knew every part of Provence well, and had been from Nice to Toulon by sea, advised me to take the common barque, for one day, from Toulon, that I might at least pass the isles of Hyeres: I told him I had been at Hyeres, and seen the coast. I had seen nothing, he said, if I had not seen them, and the coast from the sea, which was the finest object in all Provence; that it would be only one day at sea, as I might land at Cavalero, and take mules for Frejus; and that I should lose nothing, as the common route was the same as what I had seen, mountains, vines, and olives. His opinion prevailed, and I spoke to the captain of the barque for my passage to Cavalero.

The 12th. At six in the morning, on board the barque, captain Jassoirs, of Antibes; the weather was delicious;

and the passage, out of the harbour of Toulon, and its great bason, beautiful and interesting. Apparently it is impossible to imagine a harbour more completely secure and land-locked. The inner one, contiguous to the quay, is large, and seems formed by art; a range of mole, which it is built on, separating it from the great bason. Only one ship can enter at a time, but it could contain a fleet. There are now lying, moored, in two ranges, one ship, the Commerce of Marseilles, of 130 guns, the finest ship in the French navy, and seventeen others of 90 guns, each, with several smaller. When in the great bason, which is two or three miles across, you seem absolutely inclosed by high lands, and it is only on the moment of quitting it, that you can guess where the outlet is, by which you are connected with the sea. The town, the shipping, the high mountain, which rises immediately above it, the hills, covered with plantations, and spread every where with *bastides*, unite to form, a striking *coup d'œil*. But as to the Isles of Hyeres and the fine views of the coast, which I was to enjoy, my informant could have no eyes, or absolutely without taste: they are, as well as all the coast, miserably barren rocks and hills, with only pines to give any idea of vegetation. If it was not for a few solitary houses, with here and there a square patch of cultivation to change the colour of the mountains, I should have imagined that this coast must have borne a near resemblance to those of New Zealand, or New Holland—dark, gloomy, and silent;—a savage *sombre* air spread over the whole. The pines, and evergreen shrubs, that cover the greatest part, cover it with more gloom than verdure. Landed at night at Cavalero, which I expected to have found a little town; but it consists only of three houses, and a more wretched place not to be imagined. They spread a mattress on a stone floor for me, for bed they had none; after starving all day, they had nothing but stale eggs, bad bread, and worse wine; and as to the mules which were to take me to Frejus, there was neither horse, ass, nor mule in the place, and only four oxen for ploughing the ground. I was thus in a pretty situation, and must have gone on by sea to Antibes, for which also the wind gave tokens of being contrary, if the captain had not promised me two of his men to carry my baggage to a village two leagues off, where mules were certainly to be had, with which comfort I betook myself to my mattress.—24 miles.

The 13th. The captain sent three sailors;—one a Corsican, another a mongrel Italian, and the third a Provençal: among the three, there was not French enough for half an hour's conversation. We crossed the mountains, and wandered by crooked unknown paths, and beds of torrents, and then found the village of Gassang on the top of a mountain, which, however, was more than a league from that to which we intended to go. Here the sailors refreshed themselves, two with wine, but the third never drank any thing except water. I asked if he had equal strength with the others that drank wine? Yes, they replied, as strong for his size as any other man: I rather think, that I shall not soon find an English sailor who will make the experiment. No milk; I breakfasted on grapes, rye bread, and bad wine. Mules were reported to abound at this village, or rather that which we missed; but the master of the only two we could hear of being absent, I had no other resource, than agreeing with a man to take my baggage on an ass, and myself to walk a league further, to St. Tropes,[1] for which he demanded 3 liv. In two hours reached that town, which is prettily situated, and tolerably well built, on the banks of a noble inlet of the sea. From Cavalero hither, the country is all mountain, eighteen-twentieths of it covered with pines, or a poor wilderness of evergreen shrubs, rocky and miserable. Cross the inlet, which is more than a league wide; the ferrymen had been on board a king's ship, and complained heavily of their treatment—but said, that now they were freemen, they should be well treated; and, in case of a war, they should pay the English by a different account—it would now be man to man; before it was free men fighting with slaves. Land at St. Maxime, and there hire two mules and a guide to Frejus.[2] The country the same mountainous and rocky desert of pines and lentiscus; but, towards Frejus, some arbutus. Very little culture before the plain near Frejus. I passed to-day thirty miles,

---

[1] St. Tropez (Alpes Maritimes).
[2] Fréjus (Var). The river does not enter the department thus named.

of which five are not cultivated. The whole coast of Provence is nearly the same desert; yet the climate would give, on all these mountains, productions valuable for feeding sheep and cattle; but they are incumbered with shrubs absolutely worthless. The effect of liberty had better appear in their cultivation, than on the decks of a man of war.—30 miles.

The 14th. Staid at Frejus to rest myself;—to examine the neighbourhood, which, however, contains nothing—and to arrange my journey to Nice. Here are remains of an amphitheatre and aqueduct. On enquiring for a voiture to go post, I found there was no such thing to be had; so I had no resource but mules. I employed the *garçon d'écurie* (for a postmaster thinks himself of too much consequence to take the least trouble), and he reported, that I should be well served for 12 liv. to Estrelles: this price, for ten miles, on a miserable mule, was a very entertaining idea; I bid him half the money; he assured me he had named the lowest price, and left me, certainly thinking me safe in his clutches. I took a walk round the town, to gather some plants that were in blossom, and, meeting a woman with an ass-load of grapes, I asked her employment; and found, by help of an interpreter, that she carried grapes from vineyards for hire. I proposed loading her ass to Estrelles with my baggage—and demanded her price.—40 *sols*. I will give it. Break of day appointed; and I returned to the inn, at least an œconomist, saving 10 liv. by my walk.

The 15th. Myself, my female, and her ass jogged merrily over the mountains; the only misfortune was, we did not know one word of each others language; I could just discover that she had a husband and three children. I tried to know if he was a good husband, and if she loved him very much; but our language failed in such explanations; —it was no matter; her ass was to do my business, and not her tongue. At Estrelles I took post-horses; it is a single house, and no women with asses to be had, or I should have preferred them. It is not easy for me to describe, how agreeable a walk of ten or fifteen miles is to a man who walks well, after sitting a thousand in a carriage. To-day's journey all through the same bad country, mountain beyond mountain, incumbered with worthless evergreens, and not one mile in twenty cultivated. The only relief is the gardens at Grasse,[1] where very great exertions are made, but of a singular kind. Roses are a great article for the famous *otter*, all of which is commonly supposed to come from Bengal. They say, that 1500 flowers go to a single drop; twenty flowers sell for 1 *fol*, and an ounce of the *otter* 400 liv. (17l. 10s.). Tuberoses, &c. are also cultivated for perfumes in immense quantities, for Paris and London. Rosemary, lavender, bergamot, and oranges, are here capital articles of culture. Half Europe is supplied with essences from hence. Cannes is prettily situated, close on the shore, with the isles of St. Marguerite, where is a detestable state prison, about two miles off, and a distant boundary of the Estrelles mountains, with a bold broken outline. These mountains are barren to excess. At all the villages, since Toulon, at Frejus, Estrelles, &c. I asked for milk, but no such thing to be had, not even of goats or sheep: the cows are all in the higher mountains; and as to butter, the landlord at Estrelles told me, it was a contraband commodity that came from Nice. Good heaven!—what an idea northern people have, like myself, before I knew better, of a fine sun and a delicious climate, as it is called, that gives myrtles, oranges, lemons, pomegranates, jasmines, and aloes, in the hedges; yet are such countries, if irrigation be wanted, the veriest deserts in the world. On the most miserable tracts of our heaths and moors, you will find butter, milk, and cream; give me that which will feed a cow, and let oranges remain to Provence. The fault, however, is in the people more than the climate; and as the people have never any faults (*till they become the masters*) all is the effect of government. The arbutus, laurustinus, cistus, and Spanish broom, are found scattered about the wastes. Nobody in the inn but a merchant of Bourdeaux returning home from Italy; we supped together, and had a good deal of conversation, not uninteresting; he was melancholy to think, he said, what a sad reputation the French revolution has wherever he has been in Italy. Unhappy France! was his frequent ejaculation. He made many enquiries of me, and said, his letters confirmed my

---

[1] (Alpes Maritimes.)

accounts; the Italians seemed all convinced that the rivalry of France and England was at an end, and that the English would now have it in their power amply to revenge the American war, by seizing St. Domingo, and indeed all the possessions the French have out of France itself. I said the idea was a pernicious one, and so contrary to the personal interests of the men who governed England, that it was not to be thought of. He replied, that if we did not do it, we should be marvellously forbearing, and set an example of political purity sufficient to eternize that part of our national character, in which the world thought us most deficient, *moderation.* He complained bitterly of the conduct of certain leaders of the National Assembly, who seemed to be determined on a bankruptcy, and perhaps a civil war.—22 miles.

The 16th. At Cannes, I was quite without a choice; no post-house, carriage, nor horses, nor mules to let; I was therefore forced again to take refuge in a woman and her ass. At five in the morning I walked to Antibes.[1] This line of nine miles is chiefly cultivated, but the mountains rise so immediately, that, in a general idea, all is waste. Antibes being a frontier town, is regularly fortified; the mole is pretty, and the view from it pleasing. Take a post-chaise to Nice: cross the Var, and bid adieu for the present to France. The approach to Nice is pleasing. The first approach to that country so long and justly celebrated that has produced those who have conquered, and those who have decorated the world, fills the bosom with too many throbbing feelings to permit a bush, a stone, a clod to be uninteresting. Our percipient faculties are expanded; we wish to enjoy; and then all is attention, and willingness to be pleased. The approach marks a flourishing town; new buildings, the never-failing mark of prosperity, are numerous. Pass many gardens full of oranges. Arrive in time for dinner at the table d'hôte, *hotel de quatre nations,* and agree with the master of it for my apartment, which is exceedingly good, and dinner and supper at five Piedmontese livres a-day, that is five shillings. Here I am, then, in the midst of another people, language, sovereignty

---

[1] (Alpes Maritimes.)

and country—one of the moments of a man's life that will always be interesting, because all the springs of curiosity and attention are on the stretch. Several Frenchmen, but more Italians, at the table d'hôte; and the French revolution only talked of. The Frenchmen all in favour of it, and the Italians all against it, and absolute victors in the argument.—25 miles.

The 17th. I have no letters for Nice; and therefore, knowing nothing of the insides of the houses, I must be content with what meets the eye. The new part of the town is very well built; the streets straight and broad. The sea-view is fine, and, for enjoying it in greater perfection, they have an admirable contrivance, which I have seen no where else. A row of low houses forming one side of a street, a quarter of a mile long, has flat roofs, which are covered with a stucco floor, forming a noble terrace, opens immediately to the sea, raised above the dirt and annoyance of a street, and equally free from the sand and shingle of a beach. At one end some finely situated lodging-houses open directly on to it. The walk this terrace affords is, in fine weather, delicious. The square is handsome, and the works which form the port are well built, but it is small and difficult to enter, except in favourable weather; admits ships of near three hundred tons; yet, though free, has but an inconsiderable trade.—The number of new streets and houses building at present is an unequivocal proof that the place is flourishing; owing very much to the resort of foreigners, principally English, who pass the winter here, for the benefit and pleasure of the climate. They are dismally alarmed at present, with the news that the disturbances in France will prevent many of the English from coming this winter; but they have some consolation in expecting a great resort of French. Last winter, there were fifty-seven English, and nine French; this winter, they think it will be nine English, and fifty-seven French. At the table d'hôte informed that I must have a passport for travelling in Italy; and that the English consul is the proper person to apply to. I went to Mr. Consul Green, who informed me that it was a mistake, there was no want of any passport; but if I wished to have one, he would very readily give it. My name occurring to him, he took the opportunity to be very polite to me, and offered any thing in his power to assist me. On my telling him the object of my travels, he remarked, that the gardens here, and mixture of half garden half farm, were rather singular, and if I called on him in the evening, he would walk and shew me some. I accepted his obliging invitation, and when I went again, met a Colonel Ross, a gentleman from Scotland, second in command in the king of Sardinia's marine, and at present in chief: having been much in Sardinia, I made some enquiries of him concerning that island, and the circumstances he instanced were curious. The *intemperia* is so prevalent in summer, from the quantity of evaporating water leaving mud exposed to the sun, as to be death to a stranger: but in winter it is a good climate. The soil wonderfully rich and fertile, but vast plains that would produce any thing are uncultivated. He has past one line of fifty miles by thirty, all plain and the land good, yet without one house and mostly a neglected desert. The people are wretched, and deplorably ignorant: there are districts, he has been informed, where there are olives, and the fruit left rotting under the trees, for want of knowing how to make oil. In general, there are no roads, and no inns. When a traveller, or other person, goes into the island, he is recommended from convent to convent, or *curé* to *curé*, some of whom are at their ease; you are sure to be well entertained,—and at no other expence than a trifle to the servants. The plenty of game and wild-fowl great. The horses are small, but excellent; all stallions. One has been known to be rode four-and-twenty hours without drawing bit. I demanded to what could be attributed such a neglected state of the island? to government, I suppose? By no means; government has manifested every disposition to set things on a better footing. It certainly is owing to the feudal rights of the nobility, keeping the people in a state of comparative slavery. They are too wretched to have the inducement to industry. Such is the case at present in many other countries besides Sardinia. When I see and hear of the abominable depredations and enormities committed by the French peasants, I detest the democratical principles; when I see or hear of such wastes as are found in Sardinia,

I abhor the aristocratical ones. Accompany Mr. Green to view some gardens, which have a luxuriance of vegetation, by means of watering, that makes them objects worth attention; but the great product, and a most valuable one it is, are oranges and lemons; chiefly the former, and a few bergamots for curiosity. We examined the garden of a nobleman, some under two acres of land, that produces 30 louis d'or a-year in oranges only, besides all the crops of common vegetables. The great value of these products, such is the perversity of human life, is the exact reason why such gardens would be detestable to me, if under the œconomical management of the gentry of Nice. An acre of garden, forms an object of some consequence in the income of a nobleman who, in point of fortune, is reckoned in good circumstances, if he has 150*l*. to 200*l*. a year. Thus the garden, which with us is an object of pleasure, is here one of œconomy and income, circumstances that are incompatible. It is like a well furnished room in a man's house, which he lets to a lodger.—They sell their oranges so strictly, that they cannot gather one to eat. A certain momentary and careless consumption is a part of the convenience and agreeableness of a garden; a system which thus constrains the consumption, destroys all the pleasure. Oranges may certainly be sold with as much propriety as corn or timber, but then let them grow at a distance from the house; that open apartment of a residence, which we call a garden, should be free from the shackle of a contract, and the scene of pleasure, not profit.

The 18th. Walked to Villa Franche,[1] another little seaport of the king of Sardinia's, on the other side of the mountain, to the east of Nice. Call on Mr. Green, the consul, who has given me letters to Genoa, Alexandria, and Padoua: he has behaved with so friendly an attention, that I cannot omit acknowledging warmly his civilities. Learn this morning from him that lord Bristol is somewhere in Italy, and that lady Erne is probably at Turin, my stars will not be propitious if I do not see them both.

---

[1] Villefranche (Alpes Maritimes). A visit to Villefranche is now one of the most delightful excursions from Nice.

The 19th. I have now waited two days merely for the means of getting away; I can go either by a *felucca* to Genoa, or with a *vetturino* to Turin; and there is so much for and against both schemes, that priority of departure is as good a motive for a preference as any other. If I go by Genoa to Milan, I see Genoa and a part of its territory, which is much, but I lose sixty miles of superb irrigation, from Coni to Turin, and I lose the line of country between Turin and Milan, which I am told is better than that between Genoa and Milan; as to Turin itself, I should see it in my return. But here is Luigi Tonini, a *vetturino*, from Coni, who sets out on Monday morning for Turin, which decides me; so with Mr. Green's kind assistance I have bargained with him to take me thither for seven French crowns. He has got two officers in the Sardinian service, and is not to wait longer for filling the third place. We have every day, at the table d'hôte, a Florentine Abbé, who has been a marvellous traveller—no man names a country in which he has not travelled; and he is singular in never having made a note, making rather a boast that his memory retains every particular he would wish to know, even to numbers correctly. The height and measures of the pyramids of Egypt, of St. Peter's church at Rome, and St. Paul's at London, &c. with the exact length and breadth of every fine street in Europe, he has at his tongue's end. He is a great critic in the beauty of cities; and he classes the four finest in the world thus, 1. Rome.—2. Naples.—3. Venice.—4. London. Being a little inclined to the marvellous, in the idea of an old Piedmontese colonel, a knight of St. Maurice, a plain and unaffected character, and apparently a very worthy man, he pecks at the authority of Signore Abbate, and has afforded some amusement to the company.

The 20th, Sunday. Mr. consul Green continues his friendly attention to the last; I dined, by invitation, with him to-day; and, for the honour of Piedmontese grazing, ate as fine, sweet, and fat a piece of roast beef as I would ever wish to do in England, and such as would not be seen at the table d'hôte at the *quatre nations*, in seven years—if in seven ages. An English master and mistress of the table, with roast beef, plumb pudding, and porter, made me drop for a moment the idea of the formidable distance that separated me from England. Unknown and unrecommended at Nice, I expected nothing but what could be shot flying in any town; but I found in Mr. Green both hospitality, and something too friendly to call politeness. In the evening we had another walk among gardens, and conversed with some of the proprietors on prices, products, &c. The description Mr. Green gives me of the climate of Nice in the winter is the most inviting that can be imagined; a clear blue expanse is constantly over head, and a sun warm enough to be exhilerating, but not hot enough to be disagreeable. *But, Sir, the vent de bize !* We are sheltered from it by the mountains; and as a proof that this climate is vastly more mild than where you have felt that wind, the oranges and lemons which we have in such profusion will not thrive either in Genoa or Provence, except in a very few spots, singularly sheltered like this. He remarked, that Dr. Smollet, in his description, has done great injustice to the climate, and even against the feelings of his own crazy constitution; for he never was so well after he left Nice as he had been at it, and made much interest with Lord Shelburne to be appointed consul, who told him, and not without some foundation, that he would on no account be such an enemy to a man of genius;—that he had libelled the climate of Nice so severely, that if he were to go again thither the Nissards would certainly knock him on the head. Mr. Green has seen hay made, and well made, at Christmas.

* * * * * *

DECEMBER 21st.[1] The shortest day in the year, for one of the expeditions that demand the longest, the passage of Mont Cenis, about which so much has been written. To those who, from reading are full of expectation of something very sublime, it is almost as great a delusion as to be met with in the regions of romance: if travellers are to be believed; the descent *rammassant*[2] on the snow, is made with the velocity of a flash of lightning; I was not fortunate

---

[1] The French diary ends on the 19th Sept., and is resumed on the 21st Dec.

[2] Ramasse (Ital. ramazzo), a sledge pushed by a man down snow-covered mountain slopes.—LITTRÉ.

enough to meet with any thing so wonderful. At the *grand croix* we seated ourselves in machines of four sticks, dignified with the name of *traineau*: a mule draws it, and a conductor, who walks between the machine and the animal, serves chiefly to kick the snow into the face of the rider. When arrived at the precipice, which leads down to Lanebourg,[1] the mule is dismissed, and the *rammassang* begins. The weight of two persons, the guide seating himself in the front, and directing it with his heels in the snow, is sufficient to give it motion. For most of the way he is content to follow very humbly the path of the mules, but now and then crosses to escape a double, and in such spots the motion is rapid enough, for a few seconds, to be agreeable; they might very easily shorten the line one half, and by that means gratify the English with the velocity they admire so much. As it is at present, a good English horse would trot as fast as we *rammassed*. The exaggerations we have read of this business have arisen, perhaps, from travellers passing in summer, and accepting the descriptions of the muleteers. A journey on snow is commonly productive of laughable incidents; the road of the *traineau* is not wider than the machine, and we were always meeting mules, &c. It was sometimes, and with reason, a question who should turn out; for the snow being ten feet deep, the mules had sagacity to consider a moment before they buried themselves. A young Savoyard female, riding her mule, experienced a complete reversal; for, attempting to pass my *traineau*, her beast was a little restive, and tumbling, dismounted his rider: the girl's head pitched in the snow, and sunk deep enough to fix her beauties in the position of a forked post; and the wicked muleteers, instead of assisting her, laughed too heartily to move: if it had been one of the *ballerini*, the attitude would have been nothing distressing to her. These laughable adventures, with the gilding of a bright sun, made the day pass pleasantly; and we were in good humour enough to swallow with chearfulness, a dinner at Lanebourg, that, had we been in England, we should have consigned very readily to the dog-kennel.—20 miles.

[1] Lans-le-Bourg (Savoie).

The 22d. The whole day we were among the high Alps. The villages are apparently poor, the houses ill built, and the people with few comforts about them, except plenty of pine wood, the forests of which harbour wolves and bears. Dine at Modane,[1] and sleep at St. Michel.[2]—25 miles.

The 23d. Pass St. Jean Maurienne,[3] where there is a bishop, and near that place we saw what is much better than a bishop, the prettiest, and indeed the only pretty woman we saw in Savoy; on enquiry, found it was Madame de la Coste, wife of a farmer of tobacco; I should have been better pleased if she had belonged to the plough.—The mountains now relax their terrific features: they recede enough, to offer to the willing industry of the poor inhabitants something like a valley; but the jealous torrent seizes it with the hand of despotism, and like his brother tyrants, reigns but to destroy. On some slopes vines: mulberries begin to appear; villages increase; but still continue rather shapeless heaps of inhabited stones than ranges of houses; yet in these homely cots, beneath the snow-clad hills, where natural light comes with tardy beams, and art seems more sedulous to exclude than admit it, peace and content, the companions of honesty, may reside; and certainly would, were the penury of nature the only evil felt; but the hand of despotism may be more heavy. In several places the view is picturesque and pleasing: inclosures seem hung against the mountain sides, as a picture is suspended to the wall of a room. The people are in general mortally ugly and dwarfish. Dine at La Chambre;[4] sad fare. Sleep at Aguebelle.[5]—30 miles.

The 24th. The country to day, that is, to Chambery, improves greatly; the mountains, though high, recede; the vallies are wide, and the slopes more cultivated; and towards the capital of Savoy, are many country houses, which enliven the scene. Above Mal Taverne[6] is Chateauneuf,[7] the house of the Countess of that name. I was

---

[1] (Savoie.)
[2] (Savoie.)
[3] St. Jean de Maurienne (Savoie), original seat of the Dukes of Savoy.
[4] (Savoie.)
[5] Aiguebelle (Savoie).
[6] Malataverne (Savoie).
[7] (Savoie.)

sorry to see, at the village, a *carcan*, or seigneural stardard, erected, to which a chain and heavy iron collar are fastened, as a mark of the lordly arrogance of the nobility, and the slavery of the people. I asked why it was not burned, with the horror it merited? The question did not excite the surprize I expected, and which it would have done before the French revolution. This led to a conversation, by which I learned, that in the *haut* Savoy, there are no seigneurs, and the people are generally at their ease; possessing little properties, and the land in spite of nature, almost as valuable as in the lower country, where the people are poor, and ill at their ease. I demanded why? *Because there are seigneurs every where.* What a vice is it, and even a curse, that the gentry, instead of being the cherishers and benefactors of their poor neighbours, should thus, by the abomination of feudal rights, prove mere tyrants. Will nothing but revolutions, which cause their *chateaux* to be burnt, induce them to give to reason and humanity, what will be extorted by violence and commotion? We had arranged our journey, to arrive early at Chambery, for an opportunity to see what is most interesting in a place that has but little. It is the winter residence of almost all the nobility of Savoy. The best estate in the dutchy is not more than 60,000 Piedmontese livres a year (3000l.), but for 20,000 liv. they live *en grand seigneur* here. If a country gentleman has 150 louis d'or a year, he will be sure to spend three months in a town; the consequence of which must be, nine uncomfortable ones in the country, in order to make a beggarly figure the other three in town. These idle people are this Christmas disappointed, by the court having refused admittance to the usual company of French comedians;—the government fears importing, among the rough mountaineers, the present spirit of French liberty. Is this weakness or policy? But Chambery had objects to me more interesting. I was eager to view Charmettes, the road, the house of Madame de Warens, the vineyard, the garden, every thing, in a word, that had been described by the inimitable pencil of Rousseau. There was something so deliciously amiable in her character, in spite of her frailties—her constant gaiety and good humour—her tenderness and humanity—her farming speculations—but, above all other circumstances, the love of Rousseau, have written her name amongst the few whose memories are connected with us, by ties more easily felt than described. The house is situated about a mile from Chambery, fronting the rocky road which leads to that city, and the wood of chesnuts in the valley. It is small, and much of the same size as we should suppose, in England, would be found on a farm of one hundred acres, without the least luxury or pretension; and the garden, for shrubs and flowers, is confined, as well as unassuming. The scenery is pleasing, being so near a city, and yet, as he observes, quite sequestered. It could not but interest me, and I viewed it with a degree of emotion; even in the leafless melancholy of December it pleased. I wandered about some hills, which were assuredly the walks he has so agreeably described. I returned to Chambery, with my heart full of Madame de Warens. We had with us a young physician, a Monsieur Bernard, of Modanne en Maurienne, an agreeable man, connected with people at Chambery; I was sorry to find, that he knew nothing more of the matter than that Madame de Warens was certainly dead. With some trouble I procured the following certificate:

Extract from the Mortuary Register of the Parish Church of St. Peter de Lemens.

"The 30th of July, 1762, was buried, in the burying ground of Lemens, Dame Louisa Frances Eleonor de la Tour, widow of the Seignor Baron de Warens, native of Vevay, in the canton of Berne, in Switzerland, who died yesterday, at ten in the evening, like a good Christian, and fortified with her last sacraments, aged about sixty-three years. She abjured the Protestant religion about thirty-six years past; since which time she lived in our religion. She finished her days in the suburb of Nesin, where she had lived for about eight years, in the house of M. Crepine. She lived heretofore at the Rectus, during about four years, in the house of the Marquis d'Alinge. She passed the rest of her life, since her abjuration, in this city.

(Signed)   GAIME, rector of Lemens."

"I, the underwritten, present rector of the said Lemens, certify, that I have extracted this from the mortuary register of the parish church of the said place, without any addition or diminution whatsoever; and, having collated it, have found it conformable to the original. In witness of all which, I have signed the presents, at Chambery, the 24th of December, 1789.

(Signed)   A. SACHOD, rector of Lemens."
23 miles.

The 25th. Left Chambery much dissatisfied, for want of knowing more of it. Rousseau gives a good character[1] of the people, and I wished to know them better. It was the worst day I have known for months past, a cold thaw, of snow and rain; and yet in this dreary season, when nature so rarely has a smile on her countenance, the environs were charming. All hill and dale, tossed about with so much wildness, that the features are bold enough for the irregularity of a forest scene; and yet withal, softened and melted down by culture and habitation, to be eminently beautiful.[2] The country inclosed to the first town in France, Pont Beauvoisin,[3] where we dined and slept. The passage of Echelles, cut in the rock by the sovereign of the country, is a noble and stupendous work. Arrive at Pont Beauvoisin, once more entering this noble kingdom, and meeting with the cockades of liberty, and those arms in the hands of THE PEOPLE, which, it is to be wished, may be used only for their own and Europe's peace.—24 miles.

The 26th. Dine at Tour du Pin,[4] and sleep at Verpiliere.[5] This is the most advantageous entrance into France, in respect of beauty of country. From Spain, England, Flanders, Germany, or Italy by way of Antibes, all are inferior to this. It is really beautiful, and well planted, has many inclosures and mulberries, with some

---

[1] " S'il est une petite ville au monde où l'on goûte la douceur de la vie dans un commerce agréable et sur c'est Chambéry." (Confessions.)

[2] Savoy and the Comté de Nice, were annexed to France in 1860, from which were formed the departments of (1) La Savoie, (2) La Hte. Savoie, (3) Les Alpes Maritimes.

[3] Pont de Beauvoisin (Isère or Savoie).

[4] La Tour du Pin, Stat. (Isère).

[5] La Verpilière (Isère).

vines. There is hardly a bad feature, except the houses; which instead of being well built, and white as in Italy, are ugly thatched mud cabins, without chimnies, the smoke issuing at a hole in the roof, or at the windows. Glass seems unknown; and there is an air of poverty and misery about them quite dissonant to the general aspect of the country. Coming out of Tour du Pin, we see a great common. Pass Bourgoyn,[1] a large town. Reach Verpiliere. This day's journey is a fine variation of hill and dale, well planted with *chateaux*, and farms and cottages spread about it. A mild lovely day of sunshine, threw no slight gilding over the whole. For ten or twelve days past, they have had, on this side of the Alps, fine open warm weather, with sun-shine; but on the Alps themselves, and in the vale of Lombardy, on the other side, we were frozen and buried in snow. At Pont Beauvoisin and Bourgoyn, our passports where demanded by the *milice bourgeoise*, but no where else: they assure us, that the country is perfectly quiet every where, and have no guards mounted in the villages—nor any suspicions of fugitives, as in the summer. Not far from Verpiliere, pass the burnt *chateau* of M. de Veau, in a fine situation, with a noble wood behind it. Mr. Grundy was here in August, and it had then but lately been laid in ashes; and a peasant was hanging on one of the trees of the avenue by the road, one among many who were seized by the *milice bourgeoise* for this attrocious act.—27 miles.

The 27th. The country changes at once; from one of the finest in France, it becomes almost flat and *sombre*. Arrive at Lyons, and there, for the last time see the Alps; on the quay, there is a very fine view of Mont Blanc, which I had not seen before; leaving Italy, and Savoy, and the Alps, probably never to return, has something of a melancholy sensation. For all those circumstances that render that classical country illustrious, the seat of great men—the theatre of the most distinguished actions—the exclusive field in which the elegant and agreeable arts have loved to range—what country can be compared with Italy? to please the eye, to charm the ear, to gratify the

---

[1] Bourgoin (Isère), in 1768, Rousseau resided here.

enquiries of a laudable curiosity, whither would you travel? In every bosom whatever, Italy is the second country in the world—of all others, the surest proof that it is the first. To the theatre; a musical thing, which called all Italy by contrast to my ears! What stuff is French music! the distortions of embodied dissonance. The theatre is not equal to that of Nantes; and very much inferior to that of Bourdeaux.—18 miles.

The 28th. I had letters to Mons. Goudard, a considerable silk merchant, and, waiting on him yesterday, he appointed me to breakfast with him this morning. I tried hard to procure some information relative to the manufactures of Lyons; but in vain: every thing was *selon* and *suivant*. To Mons. l'Abbé Rozier, author of the voluminous dictionary of agriculture, in quarto. I visited him, as a man very much extolled, and not with an idea of receiving information in the plain practical line, which is the object of my enquiries, from the compiler of a dictionary. When Mons. Rozier lived at Beziers, he occupied a considerable farm; but, on becoming the inhabitant of a city, he placed this motto over his door—*Laudato ingentia rura, exiguum colito*,[1] which is but a bad apology for *no farm at all*. I made one or two efforts towards a little *practical* conversation; but he flew off from that centre in such eccentric *radii* of science, that the vanity of the attempt was obvious in the moment. A physician present, remarked to me, that if I wanted to know common practices and products, I should apply to common farmers, indicating, by his air and manner, that such things were beneath the dignity of science. Mons. l'Abbé Rozier is, however, a man of considerable knowledge, though no farmer; in those pursuits, which he has cultivated with inclination, he is justly celebrated—and he merits every elogium, for having set on foot the *Journal de Physique*, which, take it for all and all, is by far the best journal that is to be found in Europe. His house is beautifully situated, commanding a noble prospect; his library is furnished with good books; and every appearance about

---

[1] Virgil, Georgics, iii. v. 113
"Praise great estates, cultivate small ones."

him points out an easy fortune. Waited then on Mons. de Frossard, a protestant minister, who, with great readiness and liberality, gave me much valuable information; and for my further instruction on points with which he was not equally acquainted, introduced me to Mons. Roland la Platière, inspector of the Lyons fabrics. This gentleman had notes upon many subjects which afforded an interesting conversation; and as he communicated freely, I had the pleasure to find, that I should not quit Lyons without a good portion of the knowledge I sought. This gentleman, somewhat advanced in life, has a young and beautiful wife [1]—the lady to whom he addressed his letters, written in Italy, and which have been published in five or six volumes. Mons. Frossard desiring Mons. de la Platerie to dine with him, to meet me, we had a great deal of conversation on agriculture, manufactures and commerce; and differed but little in our opinions, except on the treaty of commerce between England and France, which that gentleman condemned, as I thought, unjustly; and we debated the point. He warmly contended, that silk ought to have been included as a benefit to France; I urged, that the offer was made to the French ministry, and refused; and I ventured to say, that had it been accepted, the advantage would have been on the side of England, instead of France, supposing, according to the vulgar ideas, that the *benefit* and the *balance* of trade are the same things. I begged him to give me a reason for believing that France would buy the silk of Piedmont and of China, and work it up to undersell England; while England buys the French cotton, and works it into fabrics that undersell those of France, even under an accumulation of charges and duties? We discussed these, and similar subjects, with that sort of attention and candour that render them interesting to persons who love a liberal conversation upon important points.—Among the objects at Lyons, that are worthy of a stranger's curiosity, is the point of junction of the two great rivers, the Soane and the Rhone; Lyons would doubtless be much better situated,

---

[1] Madame Roland had travelled in England and entertained a very high notion of the English nation. See her Memoirs.

if it were really at the junction; but there is an unoccupied space sufficient to contain a city half as large as Lyons itself. This space is a modern embankment, that cost six millions, and ruined the undertakers. I prefer even Nantes to Lyons. When a city is built at the junction of two great rivers, the imagination is apt to suppose, that those rivers form a part of the magnificence of the scenery. Without broad, clean, and well built quays, what are rivers to a city but a facility to carry coals or tar-barrels? What, in point of beauty, has London to do with the Thames, except at the terrace of the Adelphi, and the new buildings of Somerset-place, any more than with Fleet ditch, buried as it is, a common shore? I know nothing in which our expectations are so horribly disappointed as in cities, so very few are built with any general idea of beauty or decoration!

The 29th. Early in the morning, with Mons. Frossard, to view a large farm near Lyons. Mons. Frossard is a steady advocate for the new constitution establishing in France. At the same time, all those I have conversed with in the city, represent the state of the manufacture as melancholy to the last degree. Twenty thousand people are fed by charity, and consequently very ill fed; and the mass of distress, in all kinds, among the lower classes, is greater than ever was known,—or than any thing of which they had an idea. The chief cause of the evil felt here, is the stagnation of trade, occasioned by the emigrations of the rich from the kingdom, and the general want of confidence in merchants and manufacturers; whence, of course, bankruptcies are common. At a moment when they are are little able to bear additional burthens, they raise, by voluntary contributions, for the poor, immense sums; so that, including the revenues of the hospitals, and other charitable foundations, there is not paid, at present, for the use of the poor, less than 40,000 louis d'or a year. My fellow traveller, Mr. Grundy, being desirous to get soon to Paris, persuaded me to travel with him in a post-chaise, a mode of travelling which I detest, but the season urged me to it; and a still stronger motive, was the having of more time to pass in that city, for the sake of observing the extraordinary state of things,—of a King, Queen, and

Dauphin of France, actual prisoners; I, therefore, accepted his proposal, and we set off after dinner to-day. In about ten miles come to the mountains. The country dreary; no inclosures, no mulberries, no vines, much waste, and nothing that indicates the vicinity of such a city. At Arnas,[1] sleep at a comfortable inn.—17 miles.

The 30th. Continue early in the morning to Tarar;[2] the mountain of which name is more formidable in reputation than in reality. To St. Syphorien[3] the same features. The buildings increase, both in number and goodness, on approaching the Seine, which we crossed at Roane;[4] it is here a good river, and is navigable many miles higher, and consequently at a vast distance from the sea. There are many flat bottomed barges on it, of a considerable size.—50 miles.

The 31st. Another clear, fine, sunshiny day; rarely do we see any thing like it at this season in England. After Droiturier,[5] the woods of the Bourbonnois commence. At St. Gerund le Puy[6] the country improves, enlivened by white houses and *chateaux*, and all continues fine to Moulins. Sought here my old friend, Mons. l'Abbe Barut, and had another interview with Mons. le Marquis Degouttes, concerning the sale of his *chateaux* and estate of Riaux; I desired still to have the refusal of it, which he promised, and will, I have no doubt, keep his word. Never have I been so tempted, on any occasion, as with the wish of possessing this agreeable situation, in one of the finest parts of France, and in the finest climate of Europe. God grant, that, should he be pleased to protract my life, I may not, in a sad old age, repent of not closing at once with an offer to which prudence calls, and prejudice only forbids! Heaven send me ease and tranquillity, for the close of life, be it passed either in Suffolk, or the Bourbonnois!—38 miles.

JANUARY 1, 1790. Nevers[7] makes a fine appearance, rising proudly from the Loire; but, on the first entrance, it is like a thousand other places. Towns, thus seen, resemble

---

[1] Les Arnas (Rhône).
[2] Tarare (Rhône).
[3] St. Symphorien-de-Laye (Loire).
[4] Roanne (Loire).
[5] (Allier.)
[6] St. Gérand le Puy (Allier).
[7] (Nièvre).

a groupe of women, huddled close together: you see their nodding plumes and sparkling gems, till you fancy that ornament is the herald of beauty; but, on a nearer inspection, the faces are too often but common clay. From the hill that descends to Pougues,[1] is an extensive view to the north; and after Pouilly[2] a fine scenery, with the Loire doubling through it.—75 miles.

The 2d. At Briare,[3] the canal is an object that announces the happy effects of industry. There we quit the Loire. The country all the way diversified; much of it dry, and very pleasant, with rivers, hills, and woods, but almost every where a poor soil. Pass many *chateaux*, some of which are very good. Sleep at Nemours,[4] where we met with an innkeeper, who exceeded, in knavery, all we had met with, either in France or Italy: for supper, we had a *soupe maigre*, a partridge and a chicken roasted, a plate of celery, a small cauliflower, two bottles of poor *vin du Pays*, and a dessert of two biscuits and four apples: here is the bill:—Potage, 1 liv. 10*f.*—Perdrix, 2 liv. 10*f.*—Poulet, 2 liv.—Celeri, 1 liv. 4*f.*—Choufleur, 2 liv.—Pain et dessert, 2 liv.—Feu & apartement, 6 liv.—Total, 19 liv. 8*f.* Against so impudent an extortion, we remonstrated severely, but in vain. We then insisted on his signing the bill, which, after many evasions, he did, *a l'etoile; Foulliare*. But having been carried to the inn, not as the star, but the *écu de France*, we suspected some deceit: and going out to examine the premises, we found the sign to be really the *écu*, and learned, on enquiry, that his own name was *Roux*, instead of *Foulliare:* he was not prepared for this detection, or for the execration we poured on such an infamous conduct; but he ran away, in an instant, and hid himself, till we were gone. In justice to the world, however, such a fellow ought to be marked out.—60 miles.

The 3d. Through the forest of Fontainbleau, to Melun and Paris. The sixty *postes* from Lyons to Paris, making three hundred English miles, cost us, including 3 louis for

---

[1] (Nièvre), now much resorted to for its mineral waters.
[2] Pouilly-sur-Loire (Nièvre).
[3] (Loire.) The canal thus named connects the Loire with the Seine by joining the Canal du Loing at Montargis.
[4] (Seine and Marne.)

the hire of the post-chaise (an old French cabriolet of two wheels), and the charges at the inns, &c. 15l. English; that is to say, 1s. per English miles, or 6d. per head. At Paris, I went to my old quarters, the hotel de la Rochefoucauld; for at Lyons I had received a letter from the duke de Liancourt, who desired me to make his house my home, just as in the time of his mother, my much lamented friend, the dutchess d'Estissac, who died while I was in Italy. I found my friend Lazowski well, and we were à gorge deployée, to converse on the amazing scenes that have taken place in France since since I left Paris.—46 miles.

The 4th. After breakfast, walk in the gardens of the Thuilleries,[1] where there is the most extraordinary sight that either French or English eyes could ever behold at Paris. The king, walking with six grenadiers of the *milice bourgeoise*, with an officer or two of his household, and a page. The doors of the gardens are kept shut in respect to him, in order to exclude every body but deputies, or those who have admission-tickets. When he entered the palace, the doors of the gardens were thrown open for all without distinction, though the Queen was still walking with a lady of her court. She also was attended so closely by the *gardes bourgeoise*, that she could not speak, but in a low voice, without being heard by them. A mob followed her, talking very loud, and paying no other apparent respect than that of taking off their hats wherever she passed, which was indeed more than I expected. Her majesty does not appear to be in health; she seems to be much affected,

---

[1] The ill-judged banquets given to the Flemish troops at Versailles when the people were starving, had mainly brought about the terrible events of October 1-5, the storming of the palace, and the enforced journey of the royal family to Paris. But Louis XVI.'had still a chance, aye, more than one of inaugurating constitutional monarchy. Even after the flight from Varennes, do we not find him warmly welcomed in the Assembly, his conciliatory speech applauded with cries of " Un di-cours à la Henri Quatre! Vive le roi." (See MIGNET.) This estimable, and considering all things, extraordinarily enlightened monarch, fell a victim to his domestic virtues. But for his exaggerated devotion to Marie Antoinette, his over-weening family affections, he would have kept faith with the nation. Again and again he swore the most solemn oaths to maintain the constitution; five minutes' conference with his wife, the mother of his heir, and he was once more plotting to restore the ancien régime by armed force.

and shews it in her face; but the king is as plump as ease can render him. By his orders, there is a little garden railed off, for the Dauphin to amuse himself in, and a small room is built in it to retire to in case of rain; here he was at work with his little hoe and rake, but not without a guard of two grenadiers. He is a very pretty good-natured-looking boy, of five or six years old, with an agreeable countenance; wherever he goes, all hats are taken off to him, which I was glad to observe. All the family being kept thus close prisoners (for such they are in effect) afford, at first view, a shocking spectacle; and is really so, if the act were not absolutely necessary to effect the revolution; this I conceive to be impossible; but if it were necessary, no one can blame the people for taking every measure possible to secure that liberty they had seized in the violence of a revolution. At such a moment, nothing is to be condemned but what endangers the national freedom. I must, however, freely own, that I have my doubts whether this treatment of the royal family can be justly esteemed any security to liberty; or, on the contrary, whether it were not a very dangerous step, that exposes to hazard whatever had been gained. I have spoken with several persons to-day, and have started objections to the present system, stronger even than they appear to me, in order to learn their sentiments; and it is evident, they are at the present moment under an apprehension of an attempt towards a counter revolution. The danger of it very much, if not absolutely results from the violence which has been used towards the royal family. The National Assembly was, before that period, answerable only for the permanent constitutional laws passed for the future: since that moment, it is equally answerable for the whole conduct of the government of the state, executive as well as legislative. This critical situation has made a constant spirit of exertion necessary amongst the Paris militia. The great object of M. la Fayette, and the other military leaders, is to improve their discipline, and to bring them into such a form as to allow a rational dependence on them, in case of their being wanted in the field; but such is the spirit of freedom, that even in the military, there is so little subordination, that a man is an officer to-day, and in the ranks to-morrow; a mode of proceeding, that makes it the more difficult to bring them to the point their leaders see necessary. Eight thousand men in Paris may be called the standing army, paid every day 15*f.* a man; in which number is included the corps of the French guards from Versailles, that deserted to the people: they have also eight hundred horse, at an expence each of 1500 liv. (62*l.* 15s. 6d.) a year, and the officers have double the pay of those in the army.

The 5th. Yesterday's address of the National Assembly [1] to the king has done them credit with everybody. I have heard it mentioned, by people of very different opinions, but all concur in commending it. It was upon the question of naming the annual sum which should be granted for the civil list. They determined to send a deputation to his majesty, requesting him to name the sum himself, and praying him to consult less his spirit of œconomy, than a sense of that dignity, which ought to environ the throne with a becoming splendour. Dine with the duke de Liancourt, at his apartments in the Thuilleries, which, on the removal from Versailles, were assigned to him as grand master of the wardrobe; he gives a great dinner, twice a week, to the deputies, at which from twenty to forty are usually present. Half an hour after three was the hour appointed, but we waited, with some of the deputies that had left the Assembly, till seven, before the duke and the rest of the company came.

There is in the Assembly at present a writer of character,[2] the author of a very able book, which led me to expect

[1] The Assembly had followed the king to Paris and held its sittings, first in the Archbishop's palace, afterwards in the Manége, or riding ground of the Tuilleries gardens, where a temporary building was erected for the purpose.

[2] A learned friend, M. Dugast-Matifeux, of Montaigu (Vendée), sends me the following elucidation of this passage. "Having carefully examined the allusion I am of opinion that it is not Volney, as you suggest, but Sieyès, to whom Arthur Young refers, Sieyès, whom Mirabeau often styled 'Mahomet,' and Robespierre, with his habitual aptness, 'the mole' (la loupe) of the Republic. Moreover, Young had evidently no mere work of description or philosophy in his mind, but a purely political one of the period, in harmony with public opinion and contemporary events. Sieyès had just published his celebrated pamphlet, thereby obtaining enormous popularity."

something much above mediocrity in him; but he is made up of so many pretty littlenesses, that I stared at him with amazement. His voice is that of a feminine whisper, as if his nerves would not permit such a boisterous exertion as that of speaking loud enough to be heard; when he breathes out his ideas, he does it with eyes half closed; waves his head in circles, as if his sentiments were to be received as oracles; and has so much relaxation and pretension to ease and delicacy of manner, with no personal appearance to second these prettinesses, that I wondered by what artificial means such a mass of heterogeneous parts became compounded. How strange that we should read an author's book with great pleasure; that we should say, this man has no stuff in him; all is of consequence; here is a character uncontaminated with that *rubbish* which we see in so many other men—and after this, to meet the garb of so much littleness.

The 6th, 7th, and 8th. The duke of Liancourt having an intention of taking a farm into his own hands, to be conducted on improved principles after the English manner, he desired me to accompany him, and my friend Lazowski, to Liancourt, to give my opinion of the lands, and of the best means towards executing the project, which I very readily complied with. I was here witness to a scene which made me smile: at no great distance from the *chateau* of Liancourt, is a piece of waste land, close to the road, and belonging to the duke. I saw some men very busily at work upon it, hedging it in, in small divisions; levelling, and digging, and bestowing much labour for so poor a spot. I asked the steward if he thought that land worth such an expence? he replied, that the poor people in the town, upon the revolution taking place, declared, that the poor were the nation; that the waste belonged to the nation; and, proceeding from theory to practice, took possession, without any further authority, and began to cultivate; the duke not viewing their industry with any displeasure, would offer no opposition to it. This circumstance shews the universal spirit that is gone forth; and proves, that were it pushed a little farther, it might prove a serious matter for all the property in the kingdom. In this case, however, I cannot but commend it; for if there be one public nuisance greater than another, it is a man preserving the possession of waste land, which he will neither cultivate himself, nor let others cultivate. The miserable people die for want of bread, in sight of wastes that would feed thousands. I think them wise and rational, and philosophical, in seizing such tracks: and I heartily wish there was a law in England for making this action of the French peasants a legal one with us.—72 miles.

The 9th. At breakfast this morning in the Thuilleries. Mons. Desmarets, of the Academy of Sciences, brought a *Memoire presenté par la Societé Royale d'Agriculture, a l'Assemblée Nationale*, on the means of improving the agriculture of France; in which, among other things, they recommend great attention to bees, to panification, and to the obstetrick art. On the establishment of a free and patriotic government, to which the national agriculture might look for new and halcyon days, these were objects doubtless of the first importance. There are some parts of the memoir that really merit attention. Called on my fellow traveller, Mons. Nicolay, and find him a considerable person; a great hotel; many servants; his father a marechal of France, and himself first president of a chamber in the parliament of Paris, having been elected deputy, by the nobility of that city, for the states-general, but declined accepting; he has desired I would dine with him on Sunday, when he promises to have Mons. Decretot, the celebrated manufacturer and deputy, from Louviers. At the National Assembly—The count de Mirabeau, speaking upon the question of the members of the chamber of vacation, in the parliament of Rennes, was truly eloquent, —ardent, lively, energic, and impetuous. At night to the assembly of the Duchess d'Anville; the Marquis and Madame Condorcet[1] there, &c. not a word but politics.

[1] Condorcet (Marquis de), celebrated geometer, philosopher and politician, represented Paris in the National Assembly, and the Aisne in the Convention. His integrity, brilliant talent and moderation gave him a leading place in both bodies. He opposed the execution of the King, and was proscribed after the fall of the Girondins. The story runs that the mathematician to whom tremendous problems were child's play, lost his life because he did not know how many eggs are used in an omelette. The author of the "Progrès de l'Esprit Humain," had fled from the proscriptions of Robespierre, to Auteuil, and entering

The 10th. The chief leaders in the National Assembly, are, Target, Chapellier, Mirabeau, Barnave, Volney [1] the traveller, and, till the attack upon the property of the clergy, l'Abbé Syeyes; but he has been so much disgusted by that step, that he is not near so forward as before. The violent democrats, who have the reputation of being so much republican in principle, that they do not admit any political necessity for having even the name of a king, are called the *enragés*. They have a meeting at the Jacobins, called the revolution club, which assembles every night, in the very room in which the famous league was formed, in the reign of Henry III.; and they are so numerous, that all material business is there decided, before it is discussed by the National Assembly. I called this morning on several persons, all of whom are great democrats; and mentioning this circumstance to them, as one which savoured too much of a Paris junto governing the kingdom, an idea, which must, in the long run, be unpopular and hazardous; I was answered, that the predominancy which Paris assumed, at present, was absolutely necessary, for the safety of the whole nation; for if nothing were done, but by procuring a previous common consent, all great opportunities would be lost, and the National Assembly left constantly exposed to the danger of a counter-revolution. They, however, admitted, that it did create great jealousies, and nowhere more than at Versailles, where some plots (they added) are, without doubt, hatching at this moment, which have the king's person for their object: riots are frequent there, under pretence of the price of bread; and such movements are certainly very dangerous, for they cannot exist so near Paris, without the aristocratical party of the old government endeavouring to take ad-

an auberge demanded an omelette. "How many eggs thereto, citoyen?" asked the housewife. "A dozen," answered the poor philosopher innocently. Such ignorance of domestic economy betrayed the aristocrat in the eyes of the landlady and he was arrested, but eluded the guillotine by means of poison. His wife, the translator of Adam Smith, survived him. She edited her husband's works. Died 1822.

[1] The famous author of the "Voyage en Egypte," represented Anjou in the Tiers Etat, escaped the guillotine by the fall of Robespierre, and was appointed by the Convention professor in the newly established Ecole Normale. He became a count and senator under the Empire.

vantage of them, and to turn them to a very different end, from what was, perhaps, originally intended. I remarked, in all these conversations, that the belief of plots, among the disgusted party, for setting the king at liberty, is general; they seem almost persuaded, that the revolution will not be absolutely finished before some such attempts are made; and it is curious to observe, that the general voice is, that if an attempt were to be made, in such a manner as to have the least appearance of success, it would undoubtedly cost the king his life; and so changed is the national character, not only in point of affection for the person of their prince, but also in that softness and humanity, for which it has been so much admired, that the supposition is made without horror or compunction. In a word, the present devotion to liberty is a sort of rage; it absorbs every other passion, and permits no other object to remain in view, than what promises to confirm it. Dine with a large party, at the duke de la Rochefoucauld's; ladies and gentlemen, and all equally politicians; but I may remark another effect of this revolution, by no means unnatural, which is, that of lessening, or rather reducing to nothing, the enormous influence of the sex: they mixed themselves before in everything, in order to govern everything: I think I see an end to it very clearly. The men in this kingdom were puppets, moved by their wives, who, instead of giving the *ton*, in questions of national debate, must now receive it, and must be content to move in the political sphere of some celebrated leader,—that is to say, they are, in fact, sinking into what nature intended them for; they will become more amiable, and the nation better governed.

The 11th. The riots at Versailles are said to be serious; a plot is talked of, for eight hundred men to march, armed, to Paris, at the instigation of somebody, to join somebody; the intention, to murder La Fayette, Bailly, and Necker; and very wild and improbable reports are propagated every moment. They have been sufficient to induce Mons. La Fayette to issue, yesterday, an order concerning the mode of assembling the militia, in case of any sudden alarm. Two pieces of cannon, and eight hundred men, mount guard at the Thuilleries every day. See some royalists this morning, who assert, that the public opinion in the kingdom is changing apace; that pity for the king, and disgust at some proceedings of the Assembly, have lately done much: they say, that any attempt at present to rescue the king would be absurd, for his present situation is doing more for him than force could effect, at this moment, as the general feelings of the nation are in his favour. They have no scruple in declaring, that a well concerted vigorous effort would place him at the head of a powerful army, which could not fail of being joined by a great, disgusted, and injured body. I remarked, that every honest man must hope no such event would take place; for if a counter-revolution should be effected, it would establish a despotism, much heavier than ever France experienced. This they would not allow; on the contrary, they believed, that no government could, in future, be secure, that did not grant to the people more extensive rights and privileges than they possessed under the old one. Dine with my brother traveller, the count de Nicolay; among the company, as the count had promised me, was Mons. Decretot, the celebrated manufacturer of Louviers, from whom I learned the magnitude of the distresses at present in Normandy. The cotton mills which he had shewn me, last year, at Louviers, have stood still nine months; and so many spinning jennies have been destroyed by the people, under the idea that such machines were contrary to their interests, that the trade is in a deplorable situation. In the evening, accompanied Mons. Lazowski to the Italian opera, *La Berbiera di Seviglia*, by Paiesello, which is one of the most agreeable compositions of that truly great master. Mandini and Raffanelli excellent, and Baletti a sweet voice. There is no such comic opera to be seen in Italy, as this of Paris, and the house is always full: this will work as great a revolution in French music, as ever can be be wrought in French government. What will they think, by and by, of Lully and Rameau? And what a triumph for the manes of Jean Jacques!

The 12th. To the National Assembly:—a debate on the conduct of the chamber of vacation,[1] in the parliament

[1] Chambre des vacations, chambre chargé de rendre la justice pendant la vacation.—LITTRÉ.

of Rennes, continued. Mons. l'Abbé Maury,[1] a zealous royalist, made a long and eloquent speech, which he delivered with great fluency and precision, and without any notes, in defence of the parliament: he replied to what had been urged by the count de Mirabeau, on a former day, and spoke strongly on his unjustifiable call on the people of Bretagne, to a *redoubtable denombrement*. He said, that it would better become the members of such an assembly, to count their own principles and duties, and the fruits of their attention, to the privileges of the subject, than to call for a *denombrement*, that would fill a province with fire and bloodshed. He was interrupted by the noise and confusion of the assembly, and of the audience, six several times; but it had no effect on him; he waited calmly till it subsided, and then proceeded, as if no interruption had been given. The speech was a very able one, and much relished by the royalists; but the *enragés* condemned it, as good for nothing. No other person spoke without notes; the count de Clermont[2] read a speech that had some brilliant passages, but by no means an answer to l'Abbé Maury, as indeed it would have been wonderful if it were, being prepared before he heard the Abbé's oration. It can hardly be conceived how flat this mode of debate renders the transactions of the Assembly. Who would be in the gallery of the English House of Commons, if Mr. Pitt were to bring a written speech, to be delivered on a subject on which Mr. Fox was to speak before him? And in proportion to its being uninteresting to the hearer is another evil, that of lengthening their sittings, since there are ten persons who will read their opinions, to one that is able to deliver an *impromptu*. The want of order, and every kind

---

[1] The Abbé Maury was one of the ablest and least scrupulous defenders of the ancien régime in the States General. "Quoique avec beaucoup de talent, il manquait de ce qui le vivifie, la vérité. Maury ajoutait les erreurs de son esprit à celles qui étaient inséparables de sa cause."—MIGNET. In 1807, Bonaparte made him a cardinal; after the fall of the Empire he quitted France, and died at Rome, 1817.

[2] Count de Clermont-Tonnerre (not to be confounded with the Marquis de Clermont), député of the noblesse at the States General, he warmly espoused the cause of the people, voluntarily surrendered all seigneurial rights, and demanded civil rights for Protestants, Jews, and comedians. Massacred by his own servants in 1792.

of confusion, prevails now almost as much as when the Assembly sat at Versailles. The interruptions given are frequent and long; and speakers, who have no right by the rules to speak, will attempt it. The count de Mirabeau pressed to deliver his opinion after the Abbé Maury; the president put it to the vote, whether he should be allowed to speak a second time, and the whole house rose up to negative it; so that the first orator of the Assembly has not the influence even to be heard to explain—we have no conception of such rules; and yet their great number must make this necessary. I forget to observe, that there is a gallery at each end of the saloon, which is open to all the world; and side ones for admission of the friends of the members by tickets: the audience in these galleries are very noisy: they clap, when any thing pleases them, and they have been known to hiss; an indecorum which is utterly destructive of freedom of debate. I left the house before the whole was finished, and repaired to the duke of Liancourt's apartments in the Thuilleries, to dine with his customary party of deputies; Mess. Chapellier and Demeusniers were there, who had both been presidents, and are still members of considerable distinction; M. Volney, the celebrated traveller, also was present; the prince de Poix, the count de Montmorenci, &c. Waiting for the duke of Liancourt, who did not arrive till half after seven, with the greatest part of the company, the conversation almost entirely turned upon a strong suspicion entertained of the English having made a remittance for the purpose of embroiling matters in the kingdom. The count de Thiard, *cordon blue*, who commands in Bretagne, simply stated the fact, that some regiments at Brest had been regular in their conduct, and as much to be depended on as any in the service; but that, of a sudden, money had found its way among the men in considerable sums, and from that time their behaviour was changed. One of the deputies demanding at what period, he was answered;[1] on which he immediately observed, that it followed the remittance of 1,100,000 liv. (48,125l.) from England, that had occasioned so much conjecture and conversation. This re-

---

[1] It was a late transaction.—*Author's Note.*

mittance, which had been particularly enquired into, was so mysterious and obscure, that the naked fact only could be discovered; but every person present asserted the truth of it. Other gentlemen united the two facts, and were ready to suppose them connected. I remarked, that if England had really interfered, which appeared to me incredible, it was to be presumed, that it would have been either in the line of her supposed interest, or in that of the king's supposed inclination; that these happened to be exactly the same, and if money were remitted from that kingdom, most assuredly it would be to support the falling interest of the crown, and by no means to detach from it any force whatever; in such a case, remittance from England might go to Metz, for keeping troops to their duty, but would never be sent to Brest to corrupt them, the idea of which was grossly absurd. All seemed inclined to admit the justness of this remark, but they adhered to the two facts, in whatever manner they might, or might not, be connected. At this dinner, according to custom, most of the deputies, especially the younger ones, were dressed *au polisson*, many of them without powder in their hair, and some in boots; not above four or five were neatly dressed. How times are changed! When they had nothing better to attend to, the fashionable Parisians were correctness itself, in all that pertained to the *toilette*, and were, therefore, thought a frivolous people; but now they have something of more importance than dress to occupy them; and the light airy character that was usually given them, will have no foundation in truth. Every thing in this world depends on government.

The 13th. A great commotion among the populace late last night, which is said to have arisen on two accounts—one to get at the baron de Besenval,[1] who is in prison, in order to hang him; the other to demand bread at 2*f.* the pound. They eat it at present at the rate of twenty-two millions a-year cheaper than the rest of the kingdom, and yet they demand a further reduction. However, the cur-

[1] The Baron de Besenval with the Marquis de Favras and Monsieur, the King's brother, was accused of plotting against the constitution. Besenval obtained his liberty, but Favras was executed. The scheme was to place the king at the head of an army at Péronne.

rent discourse is, that Favras, an adventurer also in prison, must be hanged to satisfy the people; for as to Besenval, the Swiss cantons have remonstrated so firmly, that they will not dare to execute him. Early in the morning, the guards were doubled, and eight thousand horse and foot are now patrolling the streets. The report of plots, to carry off the king, is in the mouth of every one; and it is said, these movements of the people, as well as those at Versailles, are not what they appear to be, mere mobs, but instigated by the aristocrats; and if permitted to rise to such a height as to entangle the Paris militia, will prove the part only of a conspiracy against the new government. That they have reason to be alert is undoubted; for though there should actually be no plots in existence, yet there is so great a temptation to them, and such a probability of their being formed, that supineness would probably create them. I have met with the lieutenant-colonel of a regiment of horse, who is come from his quarters, and who asserts, that his whole regiment, officers and men, are now at the king's devotion, and would march wherever he called, and would execute whatever he ordered, not contrary to their ancient feelings; but that they would not have been inclined to be so obedient before he was brought to Paris; and from the conversation he has had with the officers of other regiments, he believes that the same spirit pervades their corps also. If any serious plans have been laid for a counter-revolution, or for carrying off the king, and their execution has been, or shall be prevented, posterity will be much more likely to have information of it than this age. Certainly the eyes of all the sovereigns, and of all the great nobility in Europe, are on the French revolution; they look with amazement, and even with terror, upon a situation which may possibly be hereafter their own case; and they must expect, with anxiety, that some attempts will be made to reverse an example, that will not want copies, whenever the period is favourable to make them. Dine at the Palais Royal, with a select party; politicians they must be, if they are Frenchmen. The question was discussed, Are the plots and conspiracies of which we hear so much at present, real, or are they invented by the leaders of the revolution, to keep up the spirits of the militia, in order to enable themselves to secure the government on its new foundation irreversibly?

The 14th. Plots! plots!—the marquis La Fayette, last night, took two hundred prisoners in the *Champs Elysées*, out of eleven hundred that were collected. They had powder and ball, but no musquets. Who? and what are they? is the question; but an answer is not so easily to be had. *Brigands*, according to some accounts, that have collected in Paris for no good purpose; people from Versailles by others; Germans by a third: but every one would make you believe, they are an appendix to a plot laid for a counter-revolution. Reports are so various and contradictory, that no dependence is to be placed on them; nor credit given to one-tenth of what is asserted. It is singular, and has been much commented on, that La Fayette would not trust his standing troops, as they may be called, that is the eight thousand regularly paid, and of whom the French guards form a considerable portion, but he took, for the expedition, the *bourgeoise* only; which has elated the latter as much as it has disgusted the former. The moment seems big with events; there is an anxiety, an expectation, an uncertainty, and suspense that is visible in every eye one meets; and even the best informed people, and the least liable to be led away by popular reports, are not a little alarmed at the apprehension of some unknown attempt that may be made to rescue the king, and overturn the National Assembly. Many persons are of opinion, that it would not be difficult to take the King, Queen, and Dauphin away, without endangering them, for which attempt the Thuilleries is particularly well situated, provided a body of troops, of sufficient force, were in readiness to receive them. In such a case, there would be a civil war, which, perhaps, would end in despotism, whatever party came off victorious; consequently such an attempt, or plan, could not originate in any bosom from true patriotism. If I have a fair opportunity to pass much of my time in good company at Paris, I have also no small trouble in turning over books, MSS. and papers, which I cannot see in England: this employs many hours a day, with what I borrow from the night, in making notes. I have procured also some public records, the copying of which demands time. He who wishes to give a good account of such a kingdom as France, must be indefatigable in the search of materials; for let him collect with all the care possible, yet when he comes to sit down coolly to the examination and arrangement, will find, that much has been put into his hands, of no real consequence, and more, possibly, that is absolutely useless.

The 15th. To the Palais Royal, to view the pictures of the duke of Orleans,[1] which I had tried once or twice before to do in vain. The collection is known to be very rich, in pieces of the Dutch and Flemish masters; some finished with all the exquisite attention which that school gave to minute expression. But it is a *genre* little interesting, when the works of the great Italian artists are at hand: of these the collection is one of the first in the world. Raphael, Hanibal Carracci, Titian, Dominichino, Correggio, and Paul Veronese. The first picture in the collection, and one of the finest that ever came from the easel, is that of the three Maries, and the dead Christ, by H. Carracci; the powers of expression cannot go further. There is the St. John of Raphael, the same picture as those of Florence and Bologna; and an inimitable Virgin and Child, by the same great master. A Venus bathing, and a Magdalen, by Titian, Lucretia, by Andrea del Sarto, Leda, by Paul Veronese, and also by Tintoretto. Mars and Venus, and several others, by Paul Veronese. The naked figure of a woman, by Bonieu, a French painter, now living, a pleasing piece. Some noble pictures, by Poussin and Le Seur. The apartments must disappoint every one :—I did not see one good room, and all inferior to the rank and immense fortune of the possessor, certainly the first subject in Europe. Dine at the duke of Liancourt's: among the company was Mons. de Bougainville,[2] the celebrated circumnavigator, agreeable as well as sensible; the count de Castellane, and the count

---

[1] This rich collection was afterwards dispersed throughout Europe.

[2] Bougainville, Louis Antoine Comte de (1729-1811). The discoverer of the Samoan group, or Navigator's Islands, was as famous in his own country as Cook in our own. His "Description d'un voyage au tour du Monde," was published in 1771-2.

de Montmorenci, two young legislators, as *enragés* as if their names were only Bernave or Rabeau. In some allusions to the constitution of England, I found they hold it very cheap, in regard to political liberty. The ideas of the moment, relative to plots and conspiracies were discussed, but they seemed very generally to agree, that, however the constitution might, by such means, be delayed, it was now absolutely impossible to prevent its taking place. At night to the national circus, as it is called, at the Palais Royal, a building in the gardens, or area, of that palace, the most whimsical and expensive folly that is easily to be imagined: it is a large ball room, sunk half its height under ground; and, as if this circumstance were not sufficiently adapted to make it damp enough, a garden is planted on the roof, and a river is made to flow around it, which, with the addition of some spirting *jets d'eau*, have undoubtedly made it a delicious place, for a winter's entertainment. The expence of this gew-gaw building, the project of some of the duke of Orleau's friends, I suppose, and executed at his expence, would have established an English farm, with all its principles, buildings, live stock, tools, and crops, on a scale that would have done honour to the first sovereign of Europe; for it would have converted five thousand arpents of desert into a garden. As to the result of the mode that *has been* pursued, of investing such a capital, I know no epithet equal to its merits. It is meant to be concert, ball, coffee, and billiard room, with shops, &c. designed to be something in the style of the amusements of our Pantheon. There were music and singing to night, but the room being almost empty, it was, on the whole, equally cold and *sombre*.

The 16th. The idea of plots and conspiracies has come to such a height as greatly to alarm the leaders of the revolution. The disgust that spreads every day at their transactions, arises more from the king's situation than from any other circumstance. They cannot, after the scenes that have passed, venture to set him at liberty before the constitution is finished: and they dread, at the same time, a change working in his favour in the minds of the people: in this dilemma, a plan is laid for persuading his majesty to go suddenly to the National Assembly, and, in a speech, to declare himself perfectly satisfied with their proceedings, and to consider himself as at the head of the revolution, in terms so couched, as to take away all idea or pretence of his being in a state of confinement or coercion. This is at present a favourite plan; the only difficulty will be, to persuade the king to take a step that will apparently preclude him from whatever turn or advantage the general feeling of the provinces may work in his favour; for, after such a measure, he will have reason to expect that his friends will second the views of the democratical party, from an absolute despair of any other principles becoming efficient. It is thought probable, that this scheme will be brought about; and if it is, it will do more to ease their apprehensions of any attempts than any other plan. I have been among the booksellers, with a catalogue in hand to collect publications, which, unfortunately for my purse, I find I must have on various topics, that concern the present state of France.—These are now every day so numerous, especially on the subjects of commerce, colonies, finances, taxation, *deficit*, &c. not to speak of the subject immediately of the revolution itself, that it demands many hours every day to lessen the number to be bought, by reading pen in hand. The collection the duke of Liancourt has made from the very commencement of the revolution, at the first meeting of the notables, is prodigious, and has cost many hundred louis d'ors. It is uncommonly complete, and will hereafter be of the greatest value, to consult on abundance of curious questions.

The 17th. The plan I mentioned yesterday, that was proposed to the king, was urged in vain: his majesty received the proposition in such a manner as does not leave any great hope of the scheme being executed; but the marquis La Fayette is so strenuous for its being brought about, that it will not yet be abandoned; but proposed again at a more favourable moment. The royalists, who know of this plan (for the public have it not), are delighted at the chance of its failing. The refusal is attributed to the Queen. Another circumstance, which gives great disquiet at present to the leaders of the revolution, are the accounts daily received from all parts of the kingdom, of the distress, and even starving condition of the manufacturers, artists,[1] and sailors, which grow more and more serious, and must make the idea of an attempt to overturn the revolution so much the more alarming and dangerous. The only branch of industry in the kingdom, that remains flourishing, is the trade to the sugar-colonies; and the scheme of emancipating the negroes, or at least of putting an end to importing them, which they borrowed from England, has thrown Nantes, Havre, Marseilles, Bourdeaux, and all other places connected secondarily with that commerce, into the utmost agitation. The count de Mirabeau says publicly, that he is sure of carrying the vote to put an end to negro slavery—it is very much the conversation at present, and principally amongst the leaders, who say, that as the revolution was founded on philosophy, and supported by metaphysics, such a plan cannot but be congenial. But surely trade depends on practice much more than on theory; and the planters and merchants, who come to Paris to oppose the scheme, are better prepared to shew the importance of their commerce, than to reason philosophically on the demerits of slavery. Many publications have appeared on the subject—some deserving attention.

The 18th. At the duke of Liancourt's dinner, to-day, meet the marquis de Casaux, the author of the mechanism of societies; notwithstanding all the warmth, and even fire of argument, and vivacity of manner and composition for which his writings are remarkable, he is perfectly mild and placid in conversation, with little of that effervescence one would look for from his books. There was a remarkable assertion made to-day, at table, by the count de Marguerite, before near thirty deputies; speaking of the determination on the Toulon business,[2] he said, it was openly supported by deputies, under the avowal that more insurrections were

---

[1] Our author's use of this word is now obsolete.

"How to build ships and dreadful ordnance cast,
Instruct the artist and reward their haste."
                                        WALLER.

[2] A sedition that broke out Dec. 1, 1789. The Count Albert de Riom, and other officers, were thrown into prison, accused of insulting the Garde Nationale. See *Le Moniteur*, Dec. 11, 1789.

necessary. I looked round the table, expecting some decisive answer to be given to this, and was amazed to find that no one replied a word. Mons. Volney, the traveller, after a pause of some moments, declared, that he thought the people of Toulon had acted right, and were justifiable in what they had done. The history of this Toulon business is known to all the world. This count de Marguerite has a *tetê dure* and a steady conduct—it may be believed that he is not an *enragé*. At dinner, M. Blin, deputy from Spain, mentioning the conduct of the revolution club at the *Jacobins*, said, we have given you a good president; and then asked the count why he did not come among them? He answered, *Je me trouve heureux en verité de n'avoir jamais été d'aucune société politique particulière; je pense que mes fonctions sont publiques, et qu'elles peuvent aisément se remplir sans associations particulières.* He got no reply here.—At night, Mons. Decretot, and Mons. Blin, carried me to the revolution club at the *Jacobins;* the room where they assemble, is that in which the famous league was signed, as it has been observed above. There were above one hundred deputies present, with a president in the chair; I was handed to him, and announced as the author of the *Arithmétique Politique;* the president standing up, repeated my name to the company, and demanded if there were any objections——None; and this is all the ceremony, not merely of an introduction, but an election: for I was told, that now I was free to be present when I pleased, being a foreigner. Ten or a dozen other elections were made. In this club, the business that is to be brought into the National Assembly is regularly debated; the motions are read, that are intended to be made there, and rejected or corrected and approved. When these have been fully agreed to, the whole party are engaged to support them. Plans of conduct are there determined; proper persons nominated for being of committees, and presidents of the Assembly named. And I may add, that such is the majority of numbers, that whatever passes in this club, is almost sure to pass in the Assembly. In the evening at the dutchess d'Anville's, in whose house I never failed of spending my time agreeably.

One of the most amusing circumstances of travelling

into other countries, is the opportunity of remarking the difference of customs amongst different nations in the common occurrences of life. In the art of living, the French have generally been esteemed by the rest of Europe, to have made the greatest proficiency, and their manners have been accordingly more imitated, and their customs more adopted than those of any other nation. Of their cookery, there is but one opinion; for every man in Europe, that can afford a great table, either keeps a French cook, or one instructed in the same manner. That it is far beyond our own, I have no doubt in asserting. We have about half a dozen real English dishes, that exceed any thing, in my opinion, to be met with in France; by English dishes I mean, a turbot and lobster sauce—ham and chicken—turtle—a haunch of venison—a turkey and oysters—and after these, there is an end of an English table. It is an idle prejudice, to class roast beef among them; for there is not better beef in the world than at Paris. Large handsome pieces were almost constantly on the considerable tables I have dined at. The variety given by their cooks, to the same thing, is astonishing; they dress an hundred dishes in an hundred different ways, and most of them excellent; and all sorts of vegetables have a savouriness and flavour, from rich sauces, that are absolutely wanted to our greens boiled in water. This variety is not striking, in the comparison of a great table in France with another in England; but it is manifest in an instant, between the tables of a French and English family of small fortune. The English dinner, of a joint of meat and a pudding, as it is called, or *pot luck*, with a neighbour, is bad luck in England; the same fortune in France gives, by means of cookery only, at least four dishes to one among us, and spreads a small table incomparably better. A regular dessert with us is expected, at a considerable table only, or at a moderate one, when a formal entertainment is given; in France it is as essential to the smallest dinner as to the largest; if it consists only of a bunch of dried grapes, or an apple, it will be as regularly served as the soup. I have met with persons in England, who imagine the sobriety of a French table carried to such a length, that one or two glasses of wine are all that a man can get at dinner; this is an error; your servant mixes the wine and water in what proportion you please; and large bowls of clean glasses are set before the master of the house, and some friends of the family, at different parts of the table, for serving the richer and rarer sorts of wines, which are drunk in this manner freely enough. The whole nation are scrupulously neat in refusing to drink out of glasses used by other people. At the house of a carpenter or blacksmith, a tumbler is set to every cover. This results from the common beverage being wine and water; but if at a large table, as in England, there were porter, beer, cyder, and perry, it would be impossible for three or four tumblers or goblets to stand by every plate; and equally so for the servants to keep such a number separate and distinct. In table-linen, they are, I think, cleaner and wiser than the English: that the change may be incessant, it is every where coarse. The idea of dining without a napkin seems ridiculous to a Frenchman, but in England we dine at the tables of people of tolerable fortune, without them. A journeyman carpenter in France has his napkin as regularly as his fork; and at an inn, the *fille* always lays a clean one to every cover that is spread in the kitchen, for the lowest order of pedestrian travellers. The expence of linen in England is enormous, from its fineness; surely a great change of that which is coarse, would be much more rational. In point of cleanliness, I think the merit of the two nations is divided; the French are cleaner in their persons, and the English in their houses; I speak of the mass of the people, and not of individuals of considerable fortune. A *bidet* in France is as universally in every apartment, as a bason to wash your hands, which is a trait of personal cleanliness I wish more common in England; on the other hand their necessary houses are temples of abomination; and the practice of spitting about a room, which is amongst the highest as well as the lowest ranks, is detestable: I have seen a gentleman spit so near the cloaths of a dutchess, that I have stared at his unconcern. In every thing that concerns the stables, the English far exceed the French; horses, grooms, harness, and change of equipage; in the provinces you see cabriolets undoubtedly of the last century; an

Englishman, however small his fortune may be, will not be seen in a carriage of the fashion of forty years past; if he cannot have another, he will walk on foot. It is not true that there are no complete equipages at Paris, I have seen many; the carriage, horses, harness, and attendance, without fault or blemish;—but the number is certainly very much inferior to what are seen at London. English horses, grooms, and carriages, have been of late years largely imported. In all the articles of the fitting up and furnishing houses, including those of all ranks in the estimate, the English have made advances far beyond their neighbours. Mahogany is scarce in France, but the use of it is profuse in England. Some of the hotels in Paris are immense in size, from a circumstance which would give me a good opinion of the people, if nothing else did, which is the great mixture of families. When the eldest son marries, he brings his wife home to the house of his father, where there is an apartment provided for them; and if a daughter does not wed an eldest son, her husband is also received into the family, in the same way, which makes a joyous number at every table. This cannot altogether be attributed to œconomical motives, though they certainly influence in many cases, because it is found in families possessing the first properties in the kingdom. It does with French manners and customs, but in England it is sure to fail, and equally so amongst all ranks of people: may we not conjecture, with a great probability of truth, that the nation in which it succeeds is therefore better tempered? Nothing but good humour can render such a jumble of families agreeable, or even tolerable. In dress they have given the *ton* to all Europe for more than a century; but this is not among any but the highest rank an object of such expence as in England, where the mass of mankind wear much better things (to use the language of common conversation) than in France: this struck me more amongst ladies who, on an average of all ranks, do not dress at one half of the expence of English women. Volatility and changeableness are attributed to the French as national characteristicks,—but in the case of dress with the grossest exaggeration. Fashions change with ten times more rapidity in England, in form, colour, and assemblage;

the vicissitudes of every part of dress are phantastic with us: I see little of this in France; and to instance the mode of dressing the gentlemens' hair, while it has been varied five times at London, it has remained the same at Paris. Nothing contributes more to make them a happy people, than the chearful and facile pliancy of disposition with which they adapt themselves to the circumstances of life: this they possess much more than the high and volatile spirits which have been attributed to them; one excellent consequence is, a greater exemption from the extravagance of living beyond their fortunes, than is met with in England. In the highest ranks of life, there are instances in all countries; but where one gentleman of small property, in the provinces of France, runs out his fortune, there are ten such in England that do it. In the blended idea I had formed of the French character from reading, I am disappointed from three circumstances, which I expected to find predominant. On comparison with the English, I looked for great talkativeness, volatile spirits, and universal politeness. I think, on the contrary, that they are not so talkative as the English; have not equally good spirits, and are not a jot more polite: nor do I speak of certain classes of people, but of the general mass. I think them, however, incomparably better tempered; and I propose it as a question, whether good temper be not more reasonably expected under an arbitrary, than under a free government?

The 19th. My last day in Paris, and, therefore, employed in waiting on my friends, to take leave; amongst whom, the duke de Liancourt holds the first place; a nobleman, to whose uninterrupted, polite, and friendly offices I owe the agreeable and happy hours which I have passed at Paris, and whose kindness continued so much, to the last, as to require a promise, that if I should return to France, his house, either in town or country, should be my home. I shall not omit observing, that his conduct in the revolution has been direct and manly from the very beginning; his rank, family, fortune, and situation at court, all united to make him one of the first subjects in the kingdom; and upon the public affairs being sufficiently embroiled, to make assemblies of the nobility necessary, his determination to render himself master of the great questions which were then in debate, was seconded by that attention; and application which was necessary in a period, when none but men of business could be of importance in the state. From the first assembling of the States General, he resolved to take the party of freedom; and would have joined the *tiers* at first, if the orders of his constituents had not prevented it; he desired them, however, either to consent to that step or to elect another representative; and, at the same time, with equal liberality, he declared, that if ever the duty he owed his country became incompatible with his office at court, he would resign it; an act that was not only unnecessary, but would have been absurd, after the king himself had become a party in the revolution. By espousing the popular cause, he acted conformably to the principles of all his ancestors, who in the civil wars and confusions of the preceding centuries, uniformly opposed the arbitrary proceedings of the court. The decisive steps which this nobleman took at Versailles, in advising the king, &c. &c. are known to all the world. He is, undoubtedly, to be esteemed one of those who have had a principal share in the revolution, but he has been invariably guided by constitutional motives; for it is certain, that he has been as much averse from unnecessary violence and sanguinary measures, as those who were the most attached to the ancient government.—With my excellent friend Lazowski, I spent my last evening; he endeavouring to persuade me to reside upon a farm in France, and I enticing him to quit French bustle for English tranquillity.

The 20th—25th. By the diligence to London, where I arrived the 25th; though in the most commodious seat, yet languishing for a horse, which, after all, affords the best means of travelling. Passing from the first company of Paris to the rabble which one sometimes meets in diligences is contrast sufficient.—but the idea of returning to England, to my family, and friends, made all things appear smooth. —272 miles.

The 30th. To Bradfield; and here terminate, I hope, my travels. After having surveyed the agriculture and political resources of England and Ireland, to do the same with France, was certainly a great object, the importance of which animated me to the attempt: and however pleasing it may be to hope for the ability of giving a better account of the agriculture of France than has ever been laid before the public, yet the greatest satisfaction I feel, at present, is the prospect of remaining, for the future, on a farm, in that calm and undisturbed retirement, which is suitable to my fortune, and which, I trust, will be agreeable to my disposition.—72 miles.

ON THE REVOLUTION OF FRANCE.

THE gross infamy which attended *lettres de cachet* and the Bastile, during the whole reign of Louis XV. made them esteemed in England, by people not well informed, as the most prominent features of the despotism of France. They were certainly carried to an access hardly credible; to the length of being sold, with blanks, to be filled up with names at the pleasure of the purchaser; who was thus able, in the gratification of private revenge, to tear a man from the bosom of his family, and bury him in a dungeon, where he would exist forgotten, and die unknown![1]—But such excesses could not be common in any

[1] An anecdote, which I have from an authority to be depended on, will explain the profligacy of government, in respect to these arbitrary imprisonments. Lord Albemarle, when ambassador in France, about the year 1753, negotiating the fixing of the limits of the American colonies, which, three years after, produced the war, calling one day on the minister for foreign affairs, was introduced, for a few minutes, into his cabinet, while he finished a short conversation in the apartment in which he usually received those who conferred with him. As his lordship walked backwards and forwards, in a very small room (a French cabinet is never a large one), he could not help seeing a paper lying on the table, written in a large legible hand, and containing a list of the prisoners in the Bastile, in which the first name was Gordon. When the minister entered, lord Albemarle apologized for his involuntarily remarking the paper; the other replied, that it was not of the least consequence, for they made no secret of the names. Lord A. then said, that he had seen the name of Gordon first in the list, and he begged to know, as in all probability the person of this name was a British subject, on what account he had been put into the Bastile. The minister told him, that he knew nothing of the matter, but would make the proper inquiries. The next time he saw lord Albemarle, he informed him, that, on inquiring into the case of Gordon, he could find no person who could give him the least information; on which he had Gordon himself interrogated, who solemnly affirmed, that he had not the smallest knowledge, or even suspicion, of the cause of his imprisonment, but that he had been confined 30 years; however, added the minister, I ordered him

country; and they were reduced almost to nothing, from the accession of the present King. The great mass of the people, by which I mean the lower and middle ranks, could suffer very little from such engines, and as few of them are objects of jealousy, had there been nothing else to complain of, it is not probable they would ever have been brought to take arms. The abuses attending the levy of taxes were heavy and universal. The kingdom was parcelled into generalities, with an intendant at the head of each, into whose hands the whole power of the crown was delegated for every thing except the military authority; but particularly for all affairs of finance. The generalities were subdivided into elections, at the head of which was a *sub-delegué*, appointed by the intendant. The rolls of the *taille, capitation, vingtièmes*, and other taxes, were distributed among districts, parishes, and individuals, at the pleasure of the intendant, who could exempt, change, add, or diminish, at pleasure. Such an enormous power, constantly acting, and from which no man was free, might in the nature of things, degenerate in many cases into absolute tyranny. It must be obvious, that the friends, acquaintances, and dependents of the intendant, and of all his *sub-delegués*, and the friends of these friends, to a long chain of dependence, might be favoured in taxation at the expence of their miserable neighbours; and that noblemen, in favour at court, to whose protection the intendant himself would naturally look up, could find little difficulty in throwing much of the weight of their taxes on others, without a similar support. Instances, and even gross ones, have been reported to me in many parts of the kingdom, that made me shudder at the oppression to which numbers must have been condemned, by the undue favours granted to such crooked influence. But, without recurring to such cases, what must have been the state of the poor people paying heavy taxes, from which the nobility and clergy were exempted? A cruel aggravation of their misery, to see those who could best afford to pay, exempted because able!

to be immediately released, and he is now at large. Such a case wants no comment.[1]

---

[1] These notes are by Arthur Young except when specified.—ED.

—The inrolments for the militia, which the *cahiers* call *an injustice without example*,[1] were another dreadful scourge on the peasantry; and, as married men were exempted from it, occasioned in some degree that mischievous population, which brought beings into the world, in order for little else than to be starved. The *corvées*, or police of the roads, were annually the ruin of many hundreds of farmers; more than 300 were reduced to beggary in filling up one vale in Loraine: all these oppressions fell on the *tiers état* only; the nobility and clergy having been equally exempted from *tailles*, militia, and *corvées*. The penal code of finance makes one shudder at the horrors of punishment inadequate to the crime.[2] A few features will sufficiently characterize the old government of France.

1. Smugglers of salt, armed and assembled to the number of five, in Provence, *a fine of* 500 liv. *and nine years gallies;*—in all the rest of the kingdom, *death.*

2. Smugglers armed, assembled, but in number under five, *a fine of* 300 liv. *and three years gallies.* Second offence, *death.*

3. Smugglers, without arms, but with horses, carts, or boats; *a fine of* 300 liv. *if not paid, three years gallies.* Second offence, 400 liv. *and nine years gallies.*—In Dauphiné, second offence, *gallies for life.* In Provence, *five years gallies.*

4. Smugglers, who carry the salt on their backs, and without arms, *a fine of* 200 liv. *and, if not paid, are flogged and branded.* Second offence, *a fine of* 300 liv. *and six years gallies.*

---

[1] "Nob. Briey," p. 6, &c. &c.
[2] It is calculated by a writer ("Recherches et Consid. par M. le Baron de Cormeré," tom. ii. p. 187) very well informed on every subject of finance, that, upon an average, there were annually taken up and sent to prison or the gallies, Men, 2340. Women, 896. Children, 201. Total, 3437. 300 of these to the gallies (tom. i. p. 112). The salt confiscated from these miserable people amounted to 12,633 quintals, which, at the mean price of 8 liv. are, ... 101,064 liv.
  2772 lb. of salted flesh, at 10*f.* . . 1,386
  1086 horses, at 50 liv. . . . 54,300
  52 carts, at 150 liv. 7,800
  Fines 53,207
  Seized in houses 105,530
           323,287

5. Women, married and single, smugglers, first offence, *a fine of* 100 liv. Second, 300 liv. Third, *flogged, and banished the kingdom for life. Husbands responsible both in fine and body.*

6. Children smugglers, the same as women.—*Fathers and mothers responsible; and for defect of payment flogged.*

7. Nobles, if smugglers, *deprived of their nobility; and their houses rased to the ground.*

8. Any persons in employment (I suppose in the salt-works or the revenue), if smugglers, *death.* And such as assist in the theft of salt in the transport, *hanged.*

9. Soldiers smuggling, with arms, are *hanged;* without arms, *gallies for life.*

10. Buying smuggled salt to resell it, *the same punishments as for smuggling.*

11. Persons in the salt employments, *empowered if two, or one with two witnesses, to enter and examine houses even of the privileged orders.*

12. All families, and persons liable to the *taille*, in the provinces of the *Grandes Gabelles* inrolled, and their consumption of salt for the *pot and saliére* (that is the daily consumption, exclusive of salting meat, &c. &c.) estimated at 7lb. a head per annum, which quantity they are forced to buy whether they want it or not, under the pain of various fines according to the case.

The *Capitaineries* were a dreadful scourge on all the occupiers of land. By this term, is to be understood the paramountship of certain districts, granted by the king, to princes of the blood, by which they were put in possession of the property of all game, even on lands not belonging to them; and, what is very singular, on manors granted long before to individuals; so that the erecting of a district into a *capitainerie*, was an annihilation of all manorial rights to game within it. This was a trifling business, in comparison to other circumstances; for, in speaking of the preservation of the game in these *capitaineries*, it must be observed, that by game it must be understood whole droves of wild boars, and herds of deer not confined by any wall or pale, but wandering, at pleasure, over the whole country, to the destruction of crops; and to the peopling of the gallies by the wretched peasants, who presumed to kill them, in order to save that food which was to support their helpless children. The game in the *capitainerie* of Montceau, in four parishes only, did mischief to the amount of 184,263 liv. per annum.[1] No wonder then that we should find the people asking, "*Nous demandons à grand cris la destruction des capitaineries & celle de toute sorte de gibier.*"[2] And what are we to think of demanding, as a favour, the permission—"*De nettoyer ses grains, de faucher les prés artificiels, & d'enlever ses chaumes sans égard pour la perdrix on tout autre gibier.*"[3] Now, an English reader will scarcely understand it without being told, that there were numerous edicts for preserving the game which prohibited weeding and hoeing, lest the young partridges should be disturbed; steeping seed, lest it should injure the game; manuring with night soil, lest the flavour of the partridges should be injured by feeding on the corn so produced; mowing hay, &c. before a certain time, so late as to spoil many crops; and taking away the stubble, which would deprive the birds of shelter. The tyranny exercised in these *capitaineries*, which extended over 400 leagues of country, was so great, that many *cahiers* demanded the utter suppression of them.[4] Such were the exertions of arbitrary power which the lower orders felt directly from the royal authority; but, heavy as they were, it is a question whether the others, suffered circuitously through the nobility and the clergy, were not yet more oppressive? Nothing can exceed the complaints made in the *cahiers* under this head. They speak of the dispensation of justice in the manorial courts, as comprizing every species of despotism: the districts indeterminate—appeals endless—irreconcileable to liberty and prosperity—and irrevocably proscribed in the opinion of the public[5]—augmenting litigations—favouring every species of chicane—ruining

---

[1] "Cahier du tiers état de Meaux," p. 49.
[2] "De Mantes" and "Meulan," p. 38.
[3] *Ibid.* p. 40.—Also "Nob. & Tiers Etat de Peronne," p. 42. "De Trois ordres de Monfort," p. 28.
[4] "Clergé de Provins & Montereau," p. 35.—"Clergé de Paris," p. 25.—"Clergé de Mantes & Meulan," pp. 45, 46.—"Clergé de Laon," p. 11.—"Nob. de Nemours," p. 17.—"Nob. de Paris," p. 22.—"Nob. d'Arras," p 29.
[5] "Rennes," art. 12.

the parties—not only by enormous expences on the most petty objects, but by a dreadful loss of time. The judges commonly ignorant pretenders, who hold their courts in *cabarets*, and are absolutely dependent on the seigneurs, in consequence of their feudal powers. They are "*vexations qui sont le plus grand fléau des peuples.*'—*Esclavage affligeant.*[2]—*Ce régime desastreuse.*[3]—That the *feodalité* be for ever abolished. The countryman is tyrannically enslaved by it. Fixed and heavy rents; vexatious processes to secure them; appreciated unjustly to augment: rents, *solidaires*, and *revenchables*; rents, *chéantes*, and *levantes*, *fumages*. Fines at every change of the property, in the direct as well as collateral line; feudal redemption (*retraite*); fines on sale, to the 8th and even the 6th penny; redemptions (*rachats*) injurious in their origin, and still more so in their extension; *banalité* of the mill,[5] of the oven, and of the wine and cyder-press; *corveés* by custom; *corveés* by usage of the fief; *corveés* established by unjust decrees; *corveés* arbitrary, and even phantastical; servitudes; *prestations*, extravagant and burthensome: collections by assessments incollectible; *aveux, minus, impunissemens*; litigations ruinous and without end: the rod of seigneural finance for ever shaken over our heads; vexation, ruin, outrage, violence, and destructive servitude, under which the peasants, almost on a level with Polish slaves, can never but be miserable, vile, and oppressed.[6] They demand also, that the use of hand-mills be free; and hope that posterity if possible, may be ignorant that feudal tyranny in Bretagne, armed with the judicial power, has not blushed even in these times, at breaking hand-mills, and at selling annually to the miserable, the faculty of

[1] "Nevernois," art. 43.
[2] "Tiers Etat de Vannes," p. 24.
[3] "T. Etat Clermont Ferrand," p. 52.
[4] "T. Etat Auxerre," art. 6.
[5] By this horrible law, the people are bound to grind their corn at the mill of the seigneur only; to press their grapes at his press only; and to bake their bread in his oven; by which means the bread is often spoiled, and more especially wine, since in Champagne those grapes which, pressed immediately, would make white wine, will, by waiting for the press, which often happens, make red wine only.
Whilst the guest of a Vendean gentleman in 1876, at Montaign (Vendée), I saw one of these seigneurial mills.—Ed.
[6] "Tiers Etat de Rennes," p. 159.

bruising between two stones a measure of buck-wheat or barley.[1] The very terms of these complaints are unknown in England, and consequently untranslatable: they have probably arisen long since the feudal system ceased in this kingdom. What are these tortures of the peasantry in Bretagne, which they call *chevauchés*,[2] *quintaines, soule, saut de poisson, baiser de marieés ;*[3] *chansons; transporte d'œuf sur un charette; silence des grenouilles ;*[4] *corvée à misericorde; milods ; leide; couponage ; cartelage ; barage ;*[5] *fouage ;*[6] *marechaussé ; banvin ;*[7] *ban d'août ; trousses ; gelinage ; civerage; taillabilité; vingtain;*[8] *sterlage; bordelage;*[9] *minage;*[10] *ban de vendanges; droit d'accapte.*[11] In passing through many of the French provinces, I was struck with the various and heavy complaints of the farmers and little proprietors of the feudal grievances, with the weight of which their industry was burthened; but I could not then conceive the multiplicity of the shackles which kept them poor and depressed. I understood it better afterwards, from the conversation and complaints of some grand seigneurs, as the revolution advanced; and I then learned, that the principal rental of many estates consisted in services and feudal tenures; by the baneful influence of which the industry of the people was almost exterminated. In regard to the oppressions of the clergy, as to tythes, I must do

---

[1] "Rennes," p. 57.
[2] *Chevauchés*, obligation substituted for the *corvée* during royal progresses.
[3] See, concerning the horrible privilege of la Marquette, M. Henri Martin's "Histoire de la France," vol. 5, éclaircissemens. The right alluded to by Arthur Young had existed therefore in other parts of France.—ED.
[4] This is a curious article; when the lady of the seigneur lies in, the people are obliged to *beat the waters* in marshy districts, to keep the frogs silent, that she may not be disturbed; this duty, a very oppressive one, is commuted into a pecuniary fine.
[5] *Bardage*, a kind of turnpike duty. [6] Seigneurial tax upon fires.
[7] Seigneurial right of selling wine exclusively in his parish.
[8] *Vingtaine*, seigneurial right to the twentieth of produce. See De Tocqueville's Ancien Régime. Appendix for Feudal Rights
[9] *Bordelage*, seigneurial right of the Nivernais, a kind of legacy duty.
[10] Seigneurial tax upon each mine or half sétier of corn (Littré).
[11] "Resumé des cahiers," tom. iii. pp. 316, 317.

that body a justice, to which a claim cannot be laid in England. Though the ecclesiastical tenth was levied in France more severely than usual in Italy, yet was it never exacted with such horrid greediness as is at present the disgrace of England. When taken in kind, no such thing was known in any part of France, where I made inquiries, as a tenth; it was always a twelfth, or a thirteenth, or even a twentieth of the produce. And in no part of the kingdom did a new article of culture pay any thing; thus turnips, cabbages, clover, chicorée, potatoes, &c. &c. paid nothing. In many parts, meadows were exempted. Silk worms nothing. Olives in some places paid—in more they did not. Cows nothing. Lambs from the 12th to the 21st. Wool nothing.—Such mildness, in the levy of this odious tax, is absolutely unknown in England. But mild as it was, the burthen to people groaning under so many other oppressions, united to render their situation so bad that no change could be for the worse. But these were not all the evils with which the people struggled. The administration of justice was partial, venal, infamous. I have, in conversation with many very sensible men, in different parts of the kingdom, met with something of content with their government, in all other respects than this; but upon the question of expecting justice to be really and fairly administered, every one confessed there was no such thing to be looked for. The conduct of the parliaments was profligate and atrocious. Upon almost every cause that came before them, interest was openly made with the judges: and woe betided the man who, with a cause to support, had no means of conciliating favour, either by the beauty of a handsome wife, or by other methods. It has been said, by many writers, that property was as secure under the old government of France as it is in England; and the assertion might possibly be true, as far as any violence from the King, his ministers, or the great was concerned: but for all that mass of property, which comes in every country to be litigated in courts of justice, there was not even the shadow of security, unless the parties were totally and equally unknown, and totally and equally honest; in every other case, he who had the best interest with the judges, was sure to be the winner. To reflecting minds, the cruelty and abominable practice attending such courts are sufficiently apparent. There was also a circumstance in the constitution of these parliaments, but little known in England, and which, under such a government as that of France, must be considered as very singular. They had the power, and were in the constant practice of issuing decrees, without the consent of the crown, and which had the force of laws through the whole of their jurisdiction; and of all other laws, these were sure to be the best obeyed; for as all infringements of them were brought before sovereign courts, composed of the same persons who had enacted these laws (a horrible system of tyranny!) they were certain of being punished with the last severity. It must appear strange, in a government so despotic in some respects as that of France, to see the parliaments in every part of the kingdom making laws without the King's consent, and even in defiance of his authority. The English, whom I met in France in 1789, were surprized to see some of these bodies issuing arrêts against the export of corn out out of the provinces subject to their jurisdiction, into the neighbouring provinces, at the same time that the King, through the organ of so popular a minister as Mons. Necker, was decreeing an absolutely free transport of corn throughout the kingdom, and even at the requisition of the National Assembly itself. But this was nothing new; it was their common practice. The parliament of Rouen passed an arrêt against killing of calves; it was a preposterous one, and opposed by administration; but it had its full force; and had a butcher dared to offend against it, he would have found, by the rigour of his punishment, who was his master. Innoculation was favoured by the court in Louis XV.'s time; but the parliament of Paris passed an arrêt against it, much more effective in prohibiting, than the favour of the court in encouraging that practice. Instances are innumerable, and I may remark, that the bigotry, ignorance, false principles, and tyranny of these bodies were generally conspicuous; and that the court (taxation excepted), never had a dispute with a parliament, but the parliament was sure to be wrong. Their constitution, in respect to the administration of justice, was so truly rotten, that the members sat as judges, even in causes of private property, in which they were themselves the parties, and have, in this capacity, been guilty of oppressions and cruelties, which the crown has rarely dared to attempt.

It is impossible to justify the excesses of the people on their taking up arms; they were certainly guilty of cruelties; it is idle to deny the facts, for they have been proved too clearly to admit of a doubt. But is it really the people to whom we are to impute the whole?—Or to their oppressors who had kept them so long in a state of bondage? He who chooses to be served by slaves, and by ill-treated slaves, must know that he holds both his property and life by a tenure far different from those who prefer the service of well treated freemen; and he who dines to the music of groaning sufferers, must not, in the moment of insurrection, complain that his daughters are ravished, and then destroyed; and that his sons' throats are cut. When such evils happen, they surely are more imputable to the tyranny of the master, than to the cruelty of the servant. The analogy holds with the French peasants —the murder of a seigneur, or a chateau in flames, is recorded in every newspaper; the rank of the person who suffers, attracts notice; but where do we find the register of that seigneur's oppressions of his peasantry, and his exactions of feudal services, from those whose children were dying around them for want of bread?[1] Where do we find the minutes that assigned these starving wretches to some vile petty-fogger, to be fleeced by impositions, and a mockery of justice, in the seigneural courts? Who gives us the awards of the intendant and his *sub-delegués*, which took off the taxes of a man of fashion, and laid them with accumulated weight, on the poor, who were so unfortunate as to be his neighbours? Who has dwelt sufficiently upon explaining all the ramifications of despotism, regal, aristocratical, and ecclesiastical, pervading the whole mass of the people; reaching, like a circulating fluid, the most distant capillary tubes of poverty and wretchedness? In these cases, the sufferers are too ignoble to be known; and the mass too indiscriminate to be pitied. But should a philo-

---

[1] Compare this passage with Carlyle's, book i. chap. iii. "Such are the shepherds of the people," &c.—ED.

sopher feel and reason thus? should he mistake the cause for the effect? and giving all his pity to the few, feel no compassion for the many, because they suffer in his eyes not individually, but by millions? The excesses of the people cannot, I repeat, be justified; it would undoubtedly have done them credit, both as men and christians, if they had possessed their new acquired power with moderation. But let it be remembered, that the populace in no country ever use power with moderation; excess is inherent in their aggregate constitution: and as every government in the world knows, that violence infallibly attends power in such hands, it is doubly bound in common sense, and for common safety, so to conduct itself, that the people may not find an interest in public confusions. They will always suffer much and long, before they are effectually roused; nothing, therefore, can kindle the flame, but such oppressions of some classes or order in the society, as give able men the opportunity of seconding the general mass; discontent will soon diffuse itself around; and if the government take not warning in time, it is alone answerable for all the burnings, and plunderings, and devastation, and blood that follow. The true judgment to be formed of the French revolution, must surely be gained, from an attentive consideration of the evils of the old government: when these are well understood—and when the extent and universality of the oppression under which the people groaned—oppression which bore upon them from every quarter, it will scarcely be attempted to be urged, that a revolution was not absolutely necessary to the welfare of the kingdom. Not one opposing voice [1] can, with reason, be raised against this assertion:

[1] Many opposing voices have been raised; but so little to their credit, that I leave the passage as it was written long ago. The abuses that are rooted in all the old governments of Europe, give such numbers of men a direct interest in supporting, cherishing, and defending abuses, that no wonder advocates for tyranny, of every species, are found in every country, and almost in every company. What a mass of people, in every part of England, are some way or other interested in the present representation of the people, tythes, charters, corporations, monopolies, and taxation! and not merely to the things themselves, but to all the abuses attending them; and how many are there who derive their profit or their consideration in life, not merely from such institutions, but from the evils they engender! The great mass of the people, however, is free from such influence, and will be enlightened by degrees;

abuses ought certainly to be corrected, and corrected effectually: this could not be done without the establishment of a new form of government; whether the form that has been adopted were the best, is another question absolutely distinct. But that the above-mentioned detail of enormities practised on the people required some great change is sufficiently apparent; and I cannot better conclude such a list of detestable oppressions, than in the words of the *Tiers Etat* of Nivernois, who hailed the approaching day of liberty, with an eloquence worthy of the subject.

"Les plaintes du peuple se sont long-tems perdues dans l'espace immense qui le sépare du trône: cette classe la plus nombreuse & la plus intéressante de la societé; cette classe qui mérite les premiers soins du gouvernement, puisqu' elle alimente toutes les autres; cette classe à laquelle on doit & les arts nécessaires à la vie, & ceux qui en embellissent le cours; cette classe enfin qui en recueillent moins a toujours payé davantage, peut elle apres tant de siècles d'oppression & de misére compter aujourdhui sur un sort plus heureux? Ce seroit pour ainsi dire blasphémer l'autorité tutélaire sous laquelle nous vivons que d'én douter un seul moment. Un respect aveugle pour les abus établis ou par la violence ou par la superstition, une ignorance profonde des conditions du pacte social voilà ce qui a perpétué jusqu' à nous la servitude dans laquelle ont gemi nos pères. Un jour plus pur est près d'éclorre: le roi a manifesté le desir de trouver des sujets capables de lui dire la vérité; une des ses loix, l'edit de création des assemblées provinciales du moi de Juin 1787, annonce que le vœu le plus pressant de son cœur sera toujours celui qui tendra au soulagement & au bonheur de ses peuples: une autre loi qui a retenti du centre du Royaume à ses dernières extrémités, nous a promis la restitution de tous nos droits, dont nous n'avions perdu, & dont nous ne pouvions perdre que l'exercice puisque le fond de ces mêmes droits est inaliénable & imprescriptible. Osons donc secouer le joug

assuredly they will find out, in every country of Europe, that by combinations, on the principles of liberty and property, aimed equally against regal, aristocratical, and mobbish tyranny, they will be able to resist successfully, that variety of combination, which, on principles of plunder and despotism, is every where at work to enslave them.

des anciennes erreurs : osons dire tout ce qui est vrai, tout ce qui est utile; osons réclamer les droits essentiels & primitifs de l'homme : la raison, l'équité, l'opinion générale, la bienfaisance connue de notre auguste souverain tout concours à assurer le succès de nos doléances."

Having seen the propriety, or rather the necessity, of some change in the government, let us next briefly inquire into the effects of the revolution on the principal interests in the kingdom.

In respect to all the honours, power, and profit derived to the nobility from the feudal system, which was of an extent in France beyond any thing known in England since the revolution, or long parliament of 1640, all is laid in the dust, without a rag or remnant being spared:[1] the importance of these, both in influence and revenue, was so great, that the result is all but ruin to numbers. However, as these properties were really tyrannies; as they rendered the possession of one spot of land ruinous to all round it—and equally subversive of agriculture, and the common rights of mankind, the utter destruction brought on all this species of property, does not ill deserve the epithet they are so fond of in France; it is a real regeneration of the people to the privileges of human nature. No man of common feelings can regret the fall of all of that abominable system, which made a whole parish slaves to the lord of the manor. But the effects of the revolution

---

[1] It is to be observed, that the orders of knighthood were at first preserved; when the National Assembly, with a forbearance that did them honour, refused to abolish those orders, because personal, of merit, and not hereditary, they were guilty of one gross error. They ought immediately to have addressed the King, to institute a new order of knighthood—KNIGHTS OF THE PLOUGH. There are doubtless little souls that will smile at this, and think a thistle, a garter, or an eagle more significant, and more honourable; I say nothing of orders, that exceed common sense and common chronology, such as St. Esprit, St. Andrew, and St. Patrick, leaving them to such as venerate most what they least understand. But that prince, who should first institute this order of rural merit, will reap no vulgar honour: Leopold, whose twenty years, of steady and well earned Tuscan fame gives him a good right to do it with propriety, might, as Emperor, institute it with most effect. In him, such an action would have in it nothing of affectation. But I had rather THE PLOUGH had thus been honoured by a free assembly. It would have been a trait, that marked the philosophy of a new age, and a new system.

have gone much farther; and have been attended with consequences not equally justifiable. The rents of land, which are as legal under the new government as they were under the old, are no longer paid with regularity. I have been lately informed (August 1791), on authority not to be doubted, that associations among tenantry, to a great amount and extent, have been formed, even within fifty miles of Paris, for the non-payment of rent; saying, in direct terms, we are strong enough to detain the rent, and you are not strong enough to enforce the payment. In a country where such things are possible, property of every kind it must be allowed, is in a dubious situation. Very evil consequences will result from this; arrears will accumulate too great for landlords to lose, or for the peasants to pay, who will not easily be brought to relish that order and legal government, which must necessarily secure these arrears to their right owners. In addition to all the rest, by the new system of taxation, there is laid a land-tax of 300 millions, or not to exceed 4s. in the pound; but, under the old government, their *vingtiemes* did not amount to the seventh part of such an impost. In whatever light, therefore, the case of French landlords is viewed, it will appear, that they have suffered immensely by the revolution.— That many of them deserved it, cannot, however, be doubted, since we see their *cahiers* demanding steadily, that all their feudal rights should be confirmed: [1] that the carrying of arms should be strictly prohibited to every body but noblemen: [2] that the infamous arrangements of the militia should remain on its old footing: [3] that breaking up wastes, and inclosing commons, should be prohibited: [4] that the nobility alone should be eligible to enter into the army, church, &c.: [5] that *lettres de cachet* should con-

---

[1] "Evreux," p. 32.—"Bourbonnois," p. 14.—"Artois," p. 22.— "Bazas," p. 8.—"Nivernois," p. 7.—"Poitou," p. 13.—"Saintonge," p. 5.—"Orleans," p. 19.—"Chaumont," p. 7.

[2] "Vermandois," p. 41.—"Quesnoy," p. 19.—"Sens," p. 25.— "Evreux," p. 36.—"Sézanne," p. 17.—"Bar sur Seine," p. 6.—"Beauvais," p. 13.—"Bugey," p. 34.—"Clermont Ferand," p. 11.

[3] "Limoges," p. 36.

[4] "Cambray," p. 19.—"Pont à Mousson," p. 38.

[5] "Lyon," p. 13.—"Touraine," p. 32.—"Angoumois," p. 13.— "Auxerre," p. 13. The author of the "Historical Sketch of the French

tinue:[1] that the press should not be free:[2] and, in fine, that there should be no free corn trade.[3]

To the clergy, the revolution has been yet more fatal. One word will dispatch this inquiry. The revolution was a decided benefit to all the lower clergy of the kingdom; but it was destructive of all the rest. It is not easy to know what they lost on the one hand, or what the national account will gain on the other. Mons. Necker calculates their revenue at 130,000,000 liv. of which only 42,500,000 liv. were in the hands of the *curés* of the kingdom. Their wealth has been much exaggerated: a late writer says, they possessed half the kingdom.[4] Their number was as little known as their revenue; one writer makes them 400,000;[5] another 81,400;[6] a third 80,000.[7]

The clergy in France have been supposed, by many persons in England, to merit their fate from their peculiar profligacy. But the idea is not accurate: that so large a body of men, possessed of very great revenues, should be free from vice, would be improbable, or rather impossible; but they preserved, what is not always preserved in England, an exterior decency of behaviour.—One did not find among them poachers or fox-hunters, who, having spent the morning in scampering after hounds, dedicate the evening to the bottle, and reel from inebriety to the pulpit. Such advertisements were never seen in France, as I have heard of in England:—*Wanted a curacy in a good sporting country,*

Revolution," 8vo. 1792, says, p. 68, "the worst enemies of nobility have not yet brought to light any *cahier*, in which the nobles insisted on their exclusive right to military preferments."—In the same page, this gentleman says, it is impossible for any Englishman to study four or five hundred *cahiers*. It is evident, however, from this mistake, how necessary it is to examine them before writing on the revolution.

[1] "Vermandois," p. 23.—"Chalons-sur-Marne," p. 6.—"Gien," p. 9.
[2] "Crépy," p. 10.
[3] "St. Quintin," p. 9.
[4] "De l'Autorité de Montesquieu dans la revolution presente," 8vo. 1789, p. 61.
[5] "Etats Généraux convoqués, par Louis XVI." par M. Target, prem. suite, p. 7.
[6] "Qu'est ce-que le Tiers Etat," 3d edit. par M. l'Abbé Sieyès. 8vo. p. 51.
[7] "Bibliothèque de l'homme publique," par M Condorcet, &c. tom. iii.

where the duty is light and the neighbourhood convivial. The proper exercise for a country clergyman, is the employment of agriculture, which demands strength and activity —and which, vigorously followed, will fatigue enough to give ease its best relish. A sportsman parson may be, as as he often is in England, a good sort of man, and *an honest fellow;* but certainly this pursuit, and the resorting to obscene comedies, and kicking their heels in the jig of an assembly, are not the occupations for which we can suppose tythes are given.[1] Whoever will give any attention to the demands of the clergy in their *cahiers*, will see, that there was, on many topics, an ill spirit in that body. They maintain, for instance, that the liberty of the press ought rather to be restrained than extended:[2] that the laws against it should be renewed and executed:[3] that admission into religious orders should be, as formerly, at sixteen years of age:[4] that *lettres de cachet* are useful, and even necessary.[5] They solicit to prohibit all division of commons;[6]—to revoke the edict allowing inclosures;[7] that the export of corn be not allowed;[6] and that public granaries be established.[8]

The ill effects of the revolution have been felt more severely by the manufacturers of the kingdom, than by any other class of the people. The rivalry of the English fabrics in 1787 and 1788, was strong and successful; and the confusions that followed in all parts of the kingdom, had the effect of lessening the incomes of so many landlords, clergy, and men in public employments; and such numbers fled from the kingdom, that the general mass of the consumption of national fabrics sunk perhaps three-fourths. The men, whose incomes were untouched, lessened their consumption greatly, from an apprehension of the

---

[1] Nothing appears so scandalous to all the clergy of Europe, as their brethren in England dancing at public assemblies; and a bishop's *wife* engaged in the same amusement, seems to them as preposterous as a bishop, in his lawn sleeves, following the same diversion would to us. Probably both are wrong.

[2] " Saintonge," p. 24.—" Limoges," p. 6.

[3] " Lyon," p. 13.—" Dourdon " (Seine and Oise), p. 5.

[4] " Saintonge," p. 26.—" Montargis," p. 10.

[5] " Limoges," p. 22. [6] " Troyes," p. 11. [7] " Metz," p. 11.

[8] " Rouen," p. 24. [9] " Laon," p. 11.—" Dourdon," p. 17.

unsettled state of things: the prospects of a civil war, suggested to every man, that his safety, perhaps his future bread, depended on the money which he could hoard. The inevitable consequence, was turning absolutely out of employment immense numbers of workmen. I have, in the diary of the journey, noticed the misery to which I was a witness at Lyons, Abbeville, Amiens, &c. and by intelligence, I understood that it was still worse at Rouen: the fact could hardly be otherwise. This effect, which was absolute death, by starving many thousands of families, was a result, that, in my opinion, might have been avoided. It flowed only from carrying things to extremities—from driving the nobility out of the kingdom, and seizing, instead of regulating, the whole regal authority. These violences were not necessary to liberty; they even destroyed true liberty, by giving the government of the kingdom, in too great a degree, to Paris, and to the populace of every town.

The effect of the revolution, to the small proprietors of the kingdom, must, according to common nature of events, be, *in the end*, remarkably happy; and had the new government adopted any principles of taxation, except those of the *œconomistes*, establishing at the same time an absolute freedom in the business of inclosure, and in the police of corn, the result would probably have been advantageous, even at this recent period. The committee of imposts[1] mention (and I doubt not their accuracy), the prosperity of agriculture, in the same page in which they lament the depression of every other brance of the national industry. Upon a moderate calculation, there remained, in the hands of the classes depending on land, on the account of taxes in the years 1789 and 1790, at least 300,000,000 liv.; the execution of *corvées* was as lax as the payment of taxes. To this we are to add two years' tythe, which I cannot estimate at less than 300,000,000 liv. more. The abolition of all feudal rents, and payments of every sort during those two years, could not be less than 100,000,000 liv. including services. But all these articles, great as they were, amounting to near 800,000,000 liv. were less than the immense sums that came into the hands of the farmers

[1] "Rapport du 6 Decembre 1790, sur les moyens de pourvoir aux depenses pour 1791," p. 4.

by the high price of corn throughout the year 1789; a price arising almost entirely from Mons. Necker's fine operations in the corn trade, as it has been proved at large; it is true there is a deduction to be made on account of the unavoidable diminution of consumption in every article of land produce, not essentially necessary to life: every object of luxury, or tending to it, is lessened greatly. But after this discount is allowed, the balance, in favour of the little proprietor farmers, must be very great. The benefit of such a sum being added, as it is to the capital of husbandry, needs no explanation. Their agriculture must be invigorated by such wealth—by the freedom enjoyed by its its professors; by the destruction of its innumerable shackles; and even by the distresses of other employments, occasioning new and great investments of capital in land: and these leading facts will appear in a clearer light, when the prodigious division of landed property in France is well considered; probably half, perhaps two-thirds, of the kingdom are in the possession of little proprietors, who paid quit-rents, and feudal duties, for the spots they farmed. Such men are placed at once in comparative affluence; and as ease is thus acquired by at least half the kingdom, it must not be set down as a point of trifling importance. Should France escape a civil war, she will, in the prosperity of these men, find a resource which politicians at a distance do not calculate. With rents the case is certainly different; for, beyond all doubt, landlords will, sooner or later, avail themselves of these circumstances, by advancing their rents; acting in this respect, as in every other country, is common; but they will find it impossible to deprive the tenantry of a vast advantage, necessarily flowing from their emancipation.

The confusion, which has since arisen in the finances, owing almost entirely to the mode of taxation adopted by the assembly, has had the effect of continuing to the present moment (1791), a freedom from all impost to the little proprietors, which, however dreadful its general effects on the national affairs, has tended strongly to enrich this class.

The effects of the revolution, not on any particular class of cultivators, but on agriculture in general, is with me, I must confess, very questionable; I see no benefits flowing, *particularly* to agriculture (liberty applies equally to *all* classes, and is not yet sufficiently established for the protection of *property*), except the case of tythes; but I see the rise of many evils; restrictions and prohibitions on the trade of corn—a varying land-tax—and impeded inclosures, are mischiefs on *principle*, that may have a generative faculty; and will prove infinite drawbacks from the prosperity, which certainly was attainable. It is to be hoped, that the good sense of the assembly will reverse this system by degrees; for, if it is not reversed, AGRICULTURE CANNOT FLOURISH.

The effect of the revolution, on the public revenue, is one great point on which Mons. de Calonne lays considerable stress; and it has been since urged in France, that the ruin of 30,000 families, thrown absolutely out of employment, and consequently out of bread, in the collection of taxes on salt and tobacco only, has had a powerful influence in spreading universal distress and misery. The public revenue sunk, in one year, 175 millions: this was not a *loss* of that sum; the people to whom assignats were paid on that account lost no more than the discount; the loss, therefore, to the people to whom that revenue was paid, could amount to no more than from 5 to 10 per cent.[1] But was it a loss to the miserable subjects who formerly paid those taxes; and who paid them by the sweat of their brows, at the expence of the bread out of their children's mouths, assessed with tyranny, and levied in blood. Do they feel a loss in having 175 millions in their pockets in 1789, more than they had in 1788? and in possessing other 175 millions more in 1790, and the inheritance in future? Is not such a change ease, wealth, life, and animation to those classes, who, while the pens of political satirists slander all innovations, are every moment reviving, by inheriting from that revolution something which the old government assuredly did not give? The revenue of the clergy may be called the revenue of the public:—those to whom the difference between the present payment of one

---

[1] Since this was written, assignats fell in December 1791, and January 1792, to 34 to 38 per cent. paid in silver, and 42 to 50 paid in gold, arising from great emissions; from the quantity of private paper issued; from forged ones being common, and from the prospect of a war.

hundred and forty millions, and the old tythes, are a deduction of all revenue, are, beyond doubt, in great distress; but what say the farmers throughout the kingdom, from whom the detestable burthen of those taxes were extorted? Do not they find their culture lightened, their industry freed, their products their own? Go to the aristocratical politician at Paris, or at London, and you hear only of the ruin of France—go to the cottage of the *métayer*, or the house of the farmer, and demand of him what the result has been—there will be but one voice from Calais to Bayonne. If tythes were to be at one stroke abolished in England,[1] no doubt the clergy would suffer, but would not the agriculture of the kingdom, with every man dependent on it, rise with a vigour never before experienced?

Future Effects.

It would betray no inconsiderable presumption to attempt to predict what will be the event of the revolution now passing in France; I am not so imprudent. But there are considerations that may be offered to the attention of those who love to speculate on future events better than I do. There are three apparent benefits in an aristocracy forming the part of a constitution; first, the fixed, consolidated, and hereditary importance of the great nobility, is, for the most part, a bar to the dangerous pretensions, and illegal views, of a victorious and highly popular king, president, or leader. Assemblies, so elected, as to be swayed absolutely by the opinion of the people, would frequently, under such a prince, be ready to grant him much more than a well constituted aristocratic senate. Secondly, such popular assemblies, as I have just described, are sometimes led to adopt decisions too hastily, and too

[1] It is an error in France to suppose, that the revenue of the church is small in England. The Royal Society of Agriculture at Paris states that revenue at 210,000l.; it cannot be stated at less than five millions sterling. " Mem. presenté par la S. R. d'Ag. a l'Assemblée Nationale," 1789, p. 52.—One of the greatest and wisest men we have in England, persists in asserting it to be *much less* than two millions. From very numerous inquiries, which I am still pursuing, I have reason to believe this opinion to be founded on insufficient data.

imprudently; and particularly in the case of wars with neighbouring nations; in the free countries, we have known the commonalty have been too apt to call lightly for them. An aristocracy, not *unduly* influenced by the crown, stands like a rock against such phrenzies, and hath a direct interest in the encouragement and support of peaceable maxims. The remark is applicable to many other subjects, in which mature deliberation is wanted to ballast the impetuosity of the people. I always suppose the aristocratic body well constituted, upon the basis of a sufficient property, and at the same time no *unlimited* power in the crown, to throw all the property of the kingdom into the same scale, which is the case in England. Thirdly, whatever benefits may arise from the existence of an executive power, distinct from the legislative, must absolutely depend on some intermediate and independent body between the people and the executive power. Every one must grant, that if there be no such body, the people are enabled, when they please, to annihilate the executive authority,—and assign it, as in the case of the long parliament, to committees of their own representatives; or, which is the same thing, they may appear, as they did at Versailles, armed before the King, and insist on his consent to any propositions they bring him: in these cases, the seeming advantages derived from a distinct executive power are lost. And it must be obvious, that in such a constitution as *the present* one of France, the kingly office can be put down as easily, and a readily, as a secretary can be reprimanded for a false entry in the journals. If a constitution be good, all great changes in it should be esteemed a matter of great difficulty and hazard: it is in bad ones only that alterations should not be looked upon in a formidable light.

That these circumstances may prove advantages in an aristocratical portion of a legislature, there is reason to believe; the inquiry is, whether they be counter-balanced by possible or probable evils. May there not come within this description, the danger of an aristocracy uniting with crown against the people? that is to say, influencing by weight of property and power, a great mass of the people dependent—against the rest of the people who are independent? Do we not see this to be very much the case in

England at this moment? To what other part of our constitution is it imputable that we have been infamously involved in perpetual wars, from which none reap any benefit but that tribe of vermin which thrive most when a nation most declines; contractors, victuallers, paymasters, stock-jobbers, and money-scriveners: a set by whom ministers are surrounded; and in favour of whom whole classes amongst the people are beggared and ruined. Those who will assert a constitution can be good[1] which suffers these things, ought at least to agree, that such an one as would not suffer them would be much better.[2]

If an aristocracy have thus its advantages and disadvantages, it is natural to inquire, whether the French nation be likely to establish something of a senate, that shall have the advantages without the evils. If there should be none, no popular representatives will ever be brought, with the consent of their constituents, to give up a power in their own possession and enjoyment. It is experience alone, and long experience, that can satisfy the doubts which every one must entertain on this subject. What can be know, experimentally, of a government which has not stood the brunt of unsuccessful and of successful wars? The English constitution has stood this test, and has been found deficient; or rather, as far as this test can decide any thing, has been proved worthless; since in a single century, it has involved

[1] It ought not to be allowed even tolerable, for this plain reason, such public extravagance engenders taxes to an amount that will sooner or later force the people into resistance, which is always the destruction of a constitution; and surely that must be admitted bad, which carries to the most careless eye the seeds of its own destruction. Two hundred and forty millions of public debt in a century, is in a ratio impossible to be supported; and therefore evidently ruinous.

[2] "The direct power of the king of England," says Mr. Burke, "is considerable. His indirect is great indeed. When was it that a king of England wanted wherewithal to make him respected, courted, or perhaps even feared in every state in Europe?" It is in such passages as these, that this elegant writer lays himself open to the attacks, formidable, because just, of men who have not an hundredth part of his talents. Who questions, or can question, the power of a prince that in less than a century has expended above 1000 millions, and involved his people in a debt of 240! The point in debate is not the *existence* of power, but its *excess*. What is the constitution that generates or allows of such expences? The very mischief complained of is here wrought into a merit, and brought in argument to prove that poison is salutary.

the nation in a debt of so vast[1] a magnitude, that every blessing which might otherwise have been perpetuated is put to the stake; so that if the nation do not make some change in its constitution, it is much to be dreaded that the constitution will ruin the nation. Where practice and experience have so utterly failed, it would be vain to reason from theory: and especially on a subject on which a very able writer has seen his own prediction, so totally erroneous: "In the monarchical states of Europe, it is highly improbable that any form of properly equal government should be established for many ages; the people, in general, and especially in France, being proud of their monarchs, even when they are oppressed by them."[2]

In regard to the future consequences of this singular revolution, as an example to other nations, there can be no doubt but the spirit which has produced it, will, sooner or later, spread throughout Europe, according to the different degrees of illumination amongst the common people; and it will prove either mischievous or beneficial, in proportion to the previous steps taken by governments. It is unquestionably the subject of all others the most interesting to every class, and even to every individual of a modern state; the great line of division, into which the people divides, is, 1st, those that have property; and, 2d, others that have none. The events that have taken place in France, in many respects, have been subversive of property; and have been effected by the lower people, in direct opposition to the nominal legislature; yet their constitution began its establishment with a much greater degree of regularity, by a formal election of representatives, than there is any probability of seeing in other countries. Revolutions will there be blown up from riotous mobs—from the military called out to quell them, but refusing obedience, and joining the insurgents. Such a flame, spreading rapidly through a country, must prove more hostile, and more fatal

[1] This debt, and our enormous taxation, are the best answer the National Assembly gives to those who would have had the English government, with all its faults on its head, adopted in France; nor was it without reason said by a popular writer, that a government, formed like the English, obtains more revenue than it could do, either by direct despotism, or in a full state of freedom.

[2] Dr. Priestly's "Lectures on Hist." 4to. 1788, p. 917.

to property, than any thing that has prevailed in France. The probability of such events, every one must allow to be not inconsiderable; the ruin that must attend them cannot be doubted; for they would tend not to produce, a National Assembly, and a free constitution, but an universal anarchy and confusion. The first attempt towards a democracy in England would be the common people demanding an admission and voice in the vestries, and voting to themselves whatever rates they thought proper to appropriate; which, in fact, would be an agrarian law. Can there be so much supineness in the present governments of Europe, as to suppose that old principles and maxims will avail any longer? Can such ignorance of the human heart, and such blindness to the natural course of events be found, as the plan of rejecting *all* innovations lest they should lead to greater? There is no government to be found, that does not depend, in the last resort, on a military power; and if that fail them, is not the consequence easily seen? A new policy must either be adopted, or all the governments we know will be swept from their very foundations. This policy must consist, first, in making it the interest, as much as possible, of every class in the state, except those absolutely without property,[1] to support the established government; and also to render it as palatable, as the security of property will allow, even to these; farther than this, none can look; for it is so directly the interest of the people, *without property*, to divide with those *who have it*, that no government can be established, which shall give the poor an equal interest in it with the rich;[2]—the visible tangible in-

[1] The representation of mere population is as gross a violation of sense, reason, and theory, as it is found pernicious in practice; it gives to ignorance to govern knowledge; to uncultivated intellect the lead of intelligence; to savage force the guide of law and justice; and to folly the governance of wisdom. Knowledge, intelligence, information, learning, and wisdom ought to govern nations; and these are all found to reside most in the middle classes of mankind; weakened by the habits and prejudices of *the great*, and stifled by the ignorance of the vulgar.

[2] Those who have not attended much to French affairs, might easily mistake the representation of territory and contribution in the French constitution, as something similar to what I contend for—but nothing is more remote; the number chosen is of little consequence, while persons without property are the electors. Yet Mr. Christie says, vol. i. p. 196, that property is a base on which representation ought to be

terest of the poor (if I may use the expressions), and not the ultimate and remote which they will never voluntarily regard, is a *pure* democracy, and a consequent division of property, the sure path to anarchy and despotism. The means of making a government respected and beloved are, in England, obvious; taxes must be immensely reduced; assessments on malt, leather, candles, soap, salt, and windows, must be abolished or lightened; the funding system, the parent of taxation, annihilated for ever, by taxing the interest of the public debt—the constitution that admits a debt, carries in its vitals the seeds of its destruction; tythes[1] and tests abolished; the representation of parliament reformed, and its duration shortened; not to give the people, without property, a predominancy, but to prevent that corruption, in which our debts and taxes have originated; the utter destruction of all monopolies, and, among them, of all charters and corporations; game-made property, and belonging to the possessor of one acre, as much as to him who has a thousand; and, lastly, the laws, both criminal and civil to be thoroughly reformed.—These circumstances include the great evils of the British consti-

founded; and it is plain he thinks that property is represented, though the representatives of the property are elected by men that do not possess a shilling! It is not that the proprietors of property should have voices in the election proportioned to their property, but that men who have a direct interest in the plunder or division of property should be kept at a distance from power. Here lies the great difficulty of modern legislation, to secure property, and at the same time secure freedom to those that have no property. In England there is much of this effected for the small portion of every man's income that is left to him after public plunder is satiated (the poor, the parson, and the king take 50 to 60 per cent. of every man's rent)—but the rest is secure. In America the poor, the parson, and the king take nothing (or next to nothing), and the whole is secure. In France ALL seems to be at the mercy of the populace.

[1] The exaction of tythes is so absurd and tyrannical an attack on the property of mankind, that it is almost impossible for them to continue in any country in the world half a century longer. To pay a man by force 1000*l*. a year, for doing by deputy what would be much better done for 100*l*. is too gross an imposition to be endured. To levy that 1000*l*. in the most pernicious method that can wound both property and liberty, are circumstances congenial to the tenth century, but not to the eighteenth. Italy, France, and America have set noble examples for the imitation of mankind; and those countries that do not follow them, will soon be as inferior in cultivation as they are in policy.

tution; if they be remedied, it may enjoy even a Venetian longevity; but if they be allowed, like cancerous humours to prey on the nobler parts of the political system, this boasted fabric may not exist even twenty years. To guard property effectually, and to give permanency to the new system, the militia laws ought all to be repealed. When we see, as in all the monarchies of Europe, the government only armed, despotism is established. When those who have property alone are armed, how secure the people from oppression?—When those who have no property are armed, how prevent their seizing the property of others?—Perhaps the best method of guarding against these contrary evils, is to embody, in a national militia, all who have property; and, at the same time, to allow arms (unembodied) to all citizens indiscriminately: we see, in the case of Berne, that the people being armed, keeps an aristocracy in such order, that great oppressions are unknown. An army was always dangerous; and, in the probable state of Europe, it may be doubly so; discipline preserved, it cemented despotism; undisciplined, it may unite with the people of no property, and produce anarchy and ruin. There seems to be no sufficient guard upon it, but a national militia, formed of every man that possesses a certain degree of property, rank and file as well as officers.[1] Such a force, in this island, would probably amount to above 100,000 men; and would be amply sufficient for repressing all those riots, whose object might be, immediately or ultimately, the democratic mischief of transferring property.[2] This for a

[1] The late riots at Birmingham [riots against persons commemorating the French Revolution, July, 1791.—ED.] ought to convince every man, who looks to the preservation of peace, that a *militia of property* is absolutely necessary; had it existed at that town, no such infamous transactions could have taken place, to the disgrace of the age and nation. Those riots may convince us how insecure our property really is in England, and how very imperfect that POLITICAL SYSTEM, which could, twice in twelve years, see two of the greatest towns in England at the mercy of a vile mob. The military must, in relation to the greater part of the kingdom, be always at a distance; but a militia is on the spot, and easy to be collected, by previous regulations, at a moment's warning.

[2] The class of writers who wish to spread the taste of revolutions, and make them every where the *order of the day*, affect to confound the governments of France and America, as if established on the same prin-

free government:—despotic ones, that would wish to escape destruction, must emancipate their subjects, because no military conformation can long secure the obedience of ill ciples; if so, it is a remarkable fact that the result should, to appearance, turn out so differently: but a little examination will convince us, that there is scarcely any thing in common between those governments, except the general principle of being free. In France, the populace are electors, and to so low a degree that the exclusions are of little account; and the qualifications for a seat in the provincial assemblies, and in the national one, are so low that the whole chain may be completed, from the first elector to the legislator, without a single link of what merits the name of property. The very reverse is the case in America, there is not a single state in which voters must not have a qualification of property: in Massachussets and New Hampshire, a freehold of 3l. a year, or other estate of 60l. value: Connecticut is a country of substantial freeholders, and the old government remains: In New York, electors of the senate must have a property of 100l. free from debts; and those of the assembly freeholds of 40s. a year, *rated and paying taxes:* in Pensylvania, payment of taxes is necessary: in Maryland, the possession of 50 acres of land, or other estate worth 30l. : in Virginia, 25 cultivated acres, with a house on it: in North Carolina, for the senate 50 acres, and for the assembly payment of taxes: and in all the states there are qualifications much more considerable, necessary for being eligible to be elected. In general it should be remembered, that taxes being so very few, the qualification of paying them excludes vastly more voters than a similar regulation in Europe. In constituting the legislatures also, the states all have two houses, except Pensylvania. And Congress itself meets in the same form. Thus a ready explanation is found of that order and regularity, and security of property, which strikes every eye in America; a contrast to the spectacle which France has exhibited, where confusion of every sort has operated, in which property is very far from safe; in which the populace legislate and then execute, not laws of their representatives, but of their own ambulatory wills; in which, at this moment (March 1792), they are a scene of anarchy, with every sign of a civil war commencing. These two great experiments, as far as they have gone, ought to pour conviction in every mind, that order and property never can be safe if the right of election is personal, instead of being attached to property: and whenever propositions for the reformation of our representation shall be seriously considered, which is certainly necessary, nothing ought to be in contemplation but taking power from the crown and the aristocracy—not to give it to the mob, but to the middle classes of moderate fortune. The proprietor of an estate of 50l. a year is as much interested, in the preservation of order and of property, as the possessor of fifty thousand; but the people without property have a direct and positive interest in public confusion, and the consequent division of that property, of which they are destitute. Hence the necessity, a pressing one in the present moment, of a militia rank and file, of property; the essential counterpoise to assemblies in ale-house kitchens, clubbing their pence to have treated slaves; and while such governments are giving to their people a constitution worth preserving, they should, by an absolute renunciation of all the views of conquest, make a small army as efficient for good purposes, as a large force for ambitious ones: this new-modelled military should consist, rank and file, of men interested in the preservation of property and order: were this army to consist merely of nobility, it would form a military aristocracy, as dangerous to the prince as to the people; it should be composed, indiscriminately, of individuals, drawn from all classes, but possessing a given property.—A good government, thus supported, may be durable; bad ones will be shivered to pieces by the new spirit that ferments in Europe. The candid reader will, I trust, see, that in whatever I have ventured to advance on so critical a subject as this great and unexampled revolution, I have assigned the merit I think due to it, *which is the destruction of the old government*, and not the establishment of the new. All that I saw, and much that I heard, in France, gave me the clearest conviction, that *a change* was necessary for the happiness of the people; a change, that should limit the royal authority; that should restrain the feudal tyranny of the nobility; that should reduce the church to the level of good citizens; that should correct the abuses of finance; that should give purity to the administration of justice; and that should place the people in a state of ease, and give them weight enough to secure this blessing. Thus far I must suppose every friend of mankind agreed. But whether, in order to effect thus much, all France were to be overthrown, ranks annihilated, property attacked, the

---

the *Rights of Man* read to them, by which should be understood (in Europe, not in America) the RIGHT TO PLUNDER. Let the state of France at present be coolly considered, and it will be found to originate absolutely in population, without property being represented: it exhibits scenes such as can never take place in America. See the National Assembly of a great empire, at the crisis of its fate, listening to the harangues of the Paris populace, the female populace of St. Antoine, and the president formally answering and flattering them! Will such spectacles ever be seen in the American Congress? Can that be a well constituted government, in which the most precious moments are so consumed? The place of assembling (Paris) is alone sufficient to endanger the constitution.

monarchy abolished, and the king and royal family trampled upon; and above all the rest, the whole effect of the revolution, good or bad, put on the issue of a conduct which, to speak in the mildest language, made a civil war probable: —this is a question absolutely distinct. In my private opinion, these extremities were not necessary; France might have been free without violence; a necessitous court, a weak ministry, and a timid prince, could have refused nothing to the demands of the states, essential to public happiness. The power of the purse would have done all that ought to have been done. The weight of the commons would have been predominant; but it would have had checks and a controul, without which *power* is not CONSTITUTION, but *tyranny*.—While, however, I thus venture to think that the revolution might have been accomplished upon better principles, because probably more durable ones, I do not therefore assign the first National Assembly in the gross to that total condemnation, they have received from some very intemperate pens, and for this plain reason, because it is certain that they have not done much which was not called for by the people.

Before the revolution is condemned in the gross, it should be considered what extent of liberty was demanded by the three orders in their *cahiers*; and this in particular is necessary, since those very *cahiers* are quoted to show the mischievous proceedings of the National Assembly. Here are a few of the ameliorations demanded; to have the trial by jury, and the *habeas corpus* of England;[1] to deliberate by head, and not by order, demanded *by the nobility themselves*;[2] to declare all taxes illegal and suppressed—but to grant them anew for a year; to establish for ever the capitaineries;[3] to establish a *caisse nationale separée inaccessible à toute influence du pouvoir executiff*;[4] that all the in-

---

[1] "Nob. Auxois," p. 23. "Artois," p. 13. "T. État de Peronne," p. 15. "Nob. Dauphiné," p. 119.
[2] "Nob. Touraine," p. 4. "Nob. Senlis," p. 46. "Nob. Pays de Labour" (Labourd, Pyrenees, ED.), p. 3. "Nob. Quesnoy," p. 6. "Nob. Sens," p. 3. "Nob. Thimerais," p. 3. "Clergé du Bourbonnois," p. 6. "Clergé du Bas Limosin," p. 10.
[3] Too numerous to quote, of both Nobility and Tiers.
[4] Many; Nobility as well as Tiers.

tendants should be suppressed:[1] that no treaties of commerce should be made but with the consent of the states:[2] that the orders of begging monks be suppressed:[3] that *all* monks be suppressed, and their goods and estates sold:[4] that tythes be for ever suppressed:[5] that all feudal right, duties, payments, and services be abolished:[6] that salaries (*traitement pécuniare*), be paid to the deputies:[7] that the permanence of the National Assembly is a necessary part of its existence:[8] that the Bastile be demolished:[9] that the duties of *aides*, on wine, brandy, tobacco, salt, leather, paper, iron, oil, and soap, be suppressed:[10] that the apanages be abolished:[11] that the domains of the king be alienated:[12] that the king's studs (*haras*), be suppressed:[13] that the pay of the soldiers be augmented:[14] that the kingdom be divided into districts, and the elections proportioned to population and to contributions:[15] that all citizens paying a determinate quota of taxes vote in the parochial assemblies:[16] that it is indispensable in the states-general to consult the Rights of Man:[17] that the deputies shall accept of no place, pension, grace, or favour.[18]

[1] "Nob. Sezanne," p. 14. "T. Etat Metz," p. 42. "T. Etat de Auvergne," p. 9. "T. Etat de Riom," p. 23.
[2] "Nob. Nivernois," p. 25. [3] "Nob. Bas Limosin," p. 12.
[4] "T. Etat du Haut Vivarais," p. 18. "Nob. Rheims," p. 16. "Nob. Auxerre," p. 41.
[5] "Nob. Toulon," p. 18. [6] Too many to quote.
[7] "Nob. Nomery en Loraine," p. 10.
[8] "Nob. Mantes & Meulan," p. 16. "Provins & Montereaux," art. 1. "Rennes," art. 19.
[9] "Nob. Paris," p. 14.
[10] "Nob. Vitry le François," MS. "Nob. Lyon," p. 16. "Nob. Bugey," p. 28. "Nob. Paris," p. 22.
[11] "Nob. Ponthieu," p. 32. "Nob. Chartres," p. 19. "Nob. Auxerre," art. 74.
[12] "Nob. Bugey," p. 11. "Nob. Montargis," p. 18. "Nob. Paris," p. 16. "Nob. Bourbonnois," p. 12. "Nob. Nancy," p. 23. "Nob. Angoumois," p. 20. "Nob. Pays de Labour," fol. 9.
[13] "Nob. Beauvois," p. 18. "Nob. Troyes," p. 25.
[14] "Nob. Limoges," p. 31.
[15] "T. Etat de Lyon," p. 7. "Nismes," p. 13. "Cotentin," art. 7.
[16] "T. Etat Rennes," art. 15. [17] "T. Etat Nismes," p. 11.
[18] "T. Etat Pont à Mousson," p. 17. Mr. Burke says, "When the several orders, in their several bailliages, had met in the year 1789, to chuse and instruct their representatives, they were the *people* of France; whilst they were in that state, in no one of their instructions did they

From this detail of the instructions given by the nation, I will not assert that every thing which the National Assembly has decreed is justifiable; but it may be very fairly concluded, that much the greater part of their arrets, and many that have been the most violently arraigned, are here expressly demanded. To reply that these demands are not those of the nation at large, but of particular bodies only, is very wide from the argument; especially as the most virulent enemies of the revolution, and particularly Mess. Burke and De Calonne, have, from these *cahiers*, deduced such conclusions as suited their purpose; and if they are made authority for condemning the transactions in that kingdom, they certainly are equal authority for supporting those transactions. I shall make but one observation on these demands. The assemblies that drew them up, most certainly never demanded, in express terms, the abolition of the monarchy, or the transfer of all the regal authority to the deputies; but let it be coolly considered, what sort of a monarchy must necessarily remain, while an assembly is permanent, with power to abolish tythes; to suppress the intendants; not only to vote, but to keep the public money: to alienate the king's domains; and to suppress his studs: to abolish the *capitaineries*, and destroy the bastile:—the assembly that is called upon to do all this, is plainly meant to be a body *solely* possessing the legislative authority: it is evidently not meant to *petition the king* to do it; because they would have used, in this case, the form of expression so common in other parts of the *cahiers, that his majesty will have the goodness,* &c.

The result of the whole inquiry, cannot but induce temperate men to conclude, that the abolition of tythe, of feudal services and payments, of the *gabelle,* or salt-tax, of that on tobacco, of the *entreés,* of all excises on manufacturers, and of all duties on transit, of the infamous proceedings in the old courts of justice, of the despotic practices of the old monarchy, of the militia regulations, of the monasteries and nunneries, and of numberless other abuses; I say, that temperate men must conclude, that the advantages derived to the nation are of the very first importance,

charge, or even hint at any of those things which have drawn upon the usurping assembly the detestation of the rational part of mankind."

and such as must inevitably secure to it, as long as they continue, an uncommon degree of prosperity. The men who deny the benefit of such events, must have something sinister in their views, or *muddy in their understandings.* On the other hand, the extensive and unnecessary ruin brought on so many thousands of families, of all descriptions, by violence, plunder, terror, and injustice, to an amount that is shewn in the utter want of the precious metals, the stagnation of industry, and the poverty and misery found amongst many, is an evil of too great a magnitude to be palliated. The nourishment of the most pernicious cancer in the state, public credit: the deluge of paper money; the violent and frivolous extinction of rank;[1] the new system of taxation, apparently so hurtful to landed property; and a restricted corn trade; all these are great deductions from public felicity, and weigh the heavier in the scale, because unnecessary to effect the revolution. Of the nature and durableness of the constitution established, prudent men will not be eager to prophesy: it is a new experiment,[2] and cannot be tried or examined on

---

[1] It is so because the inequality remains as great as if titles had remained, but built on its worst basis, wealth. The nobility were bad, but not so bad as Mr. Christie makes them; they did *not* wait till the *Etats Generaux* before they agreed to renounce their pecuniary privileges, "Letters on the Revolution of France," vol. i. p. 74. The first meeting of the states was May 5, 1789; but the nobility assembled at the Louvre, Dec. 20, 1788, addressed the king, declaring that intention.

[2] After all that has been said of late years, on the subject of constitutions and governments by various writers in England, but more especially in France, one circumstance must strike any attentive reader; it is, that none of the writers who have pushed the most forward in favour of new systems, have said any thing to convince the unprejudiced part of mankind, that experiment is not as necessary a means of knowledge in relation to government, as in agriculture, or any other branch of natural philosophy. Much has been said in favour of the American government, and I believe with perfect justice, *reasoning as far as the experiment extends*; but it is fair to consider it as an imperfect experiment, extending no further than the energy of personal virtue, seconded by the moderation attendant on a circulation not remarkably active. We learn, by Mr. Payne, that General Washington accepted no salary as commander of their troops, nor any as president of their legislature —an instance that does honour to their government, their country, and to human nature; but it may be doubted, whether any such instances will occur two hundred years hence? The exports of the United States now amount to 20 millions of dollars; when they amount to 500 mil-

old ideas; but the EFFECTS, good and bad, here arranged, in opposition to each other, are visible to every eye; the advantages are recognized; the evils are felt. On these circumstances we are competent to reason.[1]

1792.

IT may afford the reader some satisfaction to note a few circumstances of the state of France at the opening of 1792, which I draw from the correspondence of some friends, on whose accuracy I can rely.

Agriculture.—Small proprietors, who farm their own lands, are in a very improved and easy situation: renters are proportionally so, to the degree in which their landlords have not been able to acquire in new rents, the payments from which the land has been freed. Owners of meadows, woods, and a variety of articles for which no tythe was paid before, gain much less than others whose property used to be subject to that burthen. In regard to the payment of rent, there is a distinction between the north and south of

lions, when great wealth, vast cities, a rapid circulation, and, by consequence, immense private fortunes are formed, will such spectacles be found? Will their government then be as faultless as it appears at present? It may. Probably it will still be found excellent; but we have no convictions, no proof; it is in the womb of time—THE EXPERIMENT IS NOT MADE. Such remarks, however, ought always to be accompanied with the admission, that the British government has been experimented.—With what result?—Let a debt of 240 millions—let seven wars—let Bengal and Gibraltar—let 30 millions sterling of national burthens, taxes, rates, tythes, and monopolies—let these answer.

[1] The gross abuse which has been thrown on the French nation, and particularly on their assemblies, in certain pamphlets, and without interruption, in several of our newspapers, ought to be deprecated by every man who feels for the future interests of this country. It is in some instances carried to so scandalous an excess, that we must necessarily give extreme disgust to thousands of people, who may hereafter have an ample opportunity to *vote* and *act* under the influence of impressions unfavourable towards a country, that, unprovoked, has loaded them with so much contumely; for a nation groaning under a debt of 240 millions, that deadens the very idea of future energy, this seems, to use the mildest language, to be at least very imprudent.

of the Loire; in the former, rents continue to be paid; but to the south, many landlords have been unable to receive a penny; and here a difference is observable; absentees, who were not beloved, or whose agents are disliked, are in an ill situation; but others, who reside, or who, though absent, are beloved, are paid proportionally to the ability of the *métayer*, which species of tenant is chiefly found south of the Loire. The last crop (of 1791), is said to have been short; in a good year, in Picardy, 40 sheaves gave a *septier* of wheat, of 240 lb.; but now it takes 50 to 60. This circumstance, however, cannot be general, as the price plainly proves; for January 7th 1792, price at Paris of wheat was 22 to 28 liv. with assignats at 36 per cent. discount, a remarkable proof, that the most depreciated paper currency will answer every purpose for objects of physical necessity, and daily consumption. The discount on this paper, is greater than ever was foretold by those who predicted an enormous rise of all the necessaries of life; a proof how new the science of politics is, and how little able the most ingenious men are to foretell the effects of any specified event. The sale of the national estates has been of late very slow, which is a strange circumstance, since the rapidity of their transfer ought to have been proportioned to the discount upon assignats, for an obvious reason; for, while land is to be acquired with money, the more depreciated paper is, the greater the benefit to the purchaser. While the sale of the estates lasted with any degree of briskness, the common price, of such as have come to my knowledge, was 20 to 30, and even more years purchase; at which rate the advantages attending investments may be great.

Commerce and Manufactures.—The result of the vast discount upon assignats has, in relation to the national industry, been almost contrary to what many persons, not ill informed, expected. Early in the confusion of the revolution, nothing suffered so severely as manufactures; but I am now (1792) informed, that there is much more motion and employment in them than some time past, when the general aspect of affairs was less alarming. The very circumstance which, according to common ideas, should have continued their depression, has most unaccountably revived them in some measure; I mean the depreciation of the assignats. Paper currency has been at so low a pitch, that every species of goods has been preferred in payments; master manufacturers paying their workmen, &c. in assignats, by which bread is purchased at a price proportioned to the crop, can sell the product of that labour to such an advantage, as to create demand enough to animate their business: a most curious political combination, which seems to shew, that in circumstances where evils are of the most alarming tendency, there is a re-action, an undercurrent, that works against the apparent tide, and brings relief, even from the very nature of the misfortune. Combine this with the point of depression of England, in all her wars, as explained with such talents by the ingenious Mr. Chalmers, and something of a similarity will strike the reflecting reader. The loss by the depression of assignats has not been by any interior transactions, but by those with foreign powers. In consequence of it, the course of exchange rose at last so high, that the loss to the kingdom has been great, but by no means so great as some have imagined, who supposed the intercourse to be moving in the same ratio as in preceding periods. But this is no light error: the evil of exchange, like all other political evils, corrects itself; when it is very much against a people, they necessarily lessen their consumption of foreign commodities; and on the contrary, foreign nations consume *theirs* very freely, because so easily paid for. Through the month of January 1792, the course of exchange between us and Paris, has been about 18 on an average; reckoning the par at 30 (which, however, is not exact), here is 40 per cent. against France; deduct 36 for the discount on assignats, and this apparent enormity of evil is reduced to 4 per cent. Through the month of January 1791, the course was $25\frac{1}{2}$; this was 15 per cent. disadvantage and deducting 5 for the discount on assignats, the real disadvantage was 10. Thus the exchange in January, 1792 is 6 per cent. more favourable to France than in 1791; a remark, however, which must not be extended to any other case, and touches not on the internal mischiefs of a depreciated currency. It seems to shew, that the evils of their situation, so little understood by the generality of people here, are correcting themselves, relative to foreigners, through the operation of the causes I have mentioned. It is at the same time to be remarked, that while the price of corn, and other things, in which there is no competition by foreigners, rises merely on account of a scarcity, real or apprehensive; at the same time, every thing bought by foreigners, or which can be bought by them, has risen greatly; for instance, the cloth of Abbeville, a French commodity, has risen from 30 liv. to 42 liv. the aulne; and copper, a foreign commodity, has increased, it is asserted, in the petition of the Norman manufactures to the National Assembly, 70 per cent. Such a fabric may suffer; but if their pins fell proportionably with other things, the evil, it must be admitted, tends to correct itself.

Finances.—The prominent feature is the immensity of the debt which, increases every hour. That which bears interest, may be about 5,000,000,000 liv.; and assignats, or the debt not bearing interest, may be grossly estimated at 1,500,000,000 liv.; in all 6,500,000,000 liv. or 284,375,000l. sterling: a debt of such enormity, that nothing but the most regular, and well paid revenue, could enable the kingdom to support it. The annual *deficit* may be reckoned about 250,000,000 liv. *at present*, but improveable by a better collection of the revenue. The following is the account for the month of February 1792.

Recette	20,000,000
Dépenses extraordinaire de 1792 .	12,000,000
Id. pour 1791	2,000,000
Avances au depart. de Paris .	1,000,000
Deficit	43,000,000
	58,000,000

I am afraid that any attempt to support such infinite burthens, must continue to deluge the kingdom with paper, till, like Congress dollars in America, circulation ceases altogether. There seems to be no remedy but a bankruptcy, which is the best, easiest, and most beneficial measure to the nation, that can be embraced; it is also the most just and the most honourable; all shifting expedients are, in fact, more mischievous to the people, and yet leave government as deeply involved, as if no recourse had been made to them. If the *milice bourgeoise* of Paris is so interested in the funds, as to render this too dangerous, there does not appear to be any other rule of conduct, than one great and last appeal to the nation, declaring, that they must either DESTROY PUBLIC CREDIT, OR BE DESTROYED BY IT. If the National Assembly have not virtue and courage enough thus to extricate France, she must at all events, remain, however free, in a state of political debility.

The impossibility of levying the *œconomistes*, land-tax, is found in France to be as great in practice as the principles of it were absurd in theory. I am informed (February 1792), that the confusion arising from this cause, in almost every part of the kingdom, is great. The tax of 300 millions, laid on the *rental* of France, would not be more than 2s. 6d. in the pound; too great a burthen on just political principles, but not a very oppressive one had it been once fairly assessed, and never afterwards varied. But, by pursuing the jargon of the *produit net*, and making it variable, instead of fixed, every species of inconvenience and uncertainty has arisen. The assembly divided the total among the departments; the departments the *quotas* among the districts; the districts among the municipalities; and the municipalities assembled for the assessment of individuals: the same decree that fixed the tax at 300 millions, limited it also not to exceed one-fifth of the *produit net*; every man had therefore a power to reject any assessment that exceeded that proportion; the consequence was, the total assigned to the municipalities, was scarcely any where to be found, but upon large farms, let at a money-rent in the north of France; among the small proprietors of a few acres, which spread over so large a part of the kingdom, they all screened themselves under definitions, of what the *produit net* meant; and the result was, that the month of December, which ought to have produced 40 millions, really produced but 14. So practicable has this visionary nonsense of the *produit net* proved, under the dispensations of a mere democracy, though acting *nominally*[1] by representatives. The fact has been, that this ill-conceived and ill-laid land-tax, which, under a different management, and under the orderly government of the *settled* part of America, might have been effectively productive, has been so contrived, that it never will, and never can produce what it was estimated at in France. The people, without property, have a direct interest in seconding the refusals of others to pay, that are in the lowest classes of property, and who can really ill afford it; one great objection to all land-taxes, where possessions are much divided. With power in such hands, the refusal is effective, and the national treasury is empty. But supposing such enormous difficulties overcome, and these little properties valued and taxed on some practicable plan, from that moment there must be a new valuation every year; for, if one has wealth enough to improve beyond the capacity of the rest, they immediately shift a proportion of their tax on him; and this has accordingly happened, early as it is in the day, and indeed is inherent in the nature of the tax, as promulgated by the assembly.[2] Thus annual assessments, annual confusion, annual quarrels, and heart-burnings, and annual oppression, must be the consequence; and all this because a plain, simple, and practicable mode of assessment was not laid down by the legislature itself, instead of leaving it to be debated and fought through 500 legislatures, on the plan, purely ideal and theoretical, of the *œconomistes!*

Police of corn.—The National Assembly has been of late repeatedly employed in receiving complaints from various departments, relative to the scarcity and high price of corn, and debates on it arise, and votes pass, which are printed, to satisfy the people that all precautions are taken to prevent exportation. Such a conduct shews, that they tread in the steps of Mons. Necker, and that they consequently may

[1] Whether nominally, or really, is not of consequence, if *effective* qualifications of property be not, at every step, the guard, as in the American constitutions.

[2] " Aussitot que les opérations preliminaires seront termineés les officiers municipaux et les commissaires adjoints feront, en leur âme et conscience l'evaluation du revenu net des differentes propriétes foncières de la communante section par section." " Journal des Etats Gen." tom. xvi. p. 510.

expect, with a crop but slightly deficient, to see a famine. In the "Gazette Nationale," of March 6, 1792, I read, in the journal of the Assembly, *Inquiétudes—précautions prises—commissaires envoyés—veiller à la subsistance du peuple—fonds pour acheter des grains chez l'étranger—dix millions*—&c. Now this is precisely the blind and infatuated conduct of Mons. Necker. If these steps ere necessary to be taken (which is impossible), why talk of and print them? Why alarm the people, by shewing yourselves alarmed? Forty-five millions loss, in the hands of M. Necker, purchased not three days corn from France; ten millions will not purchase one day's consumption! but the report and parade of it will do more mischief than the loss of five times the quantity: without being in France, I am clear, and can rely enough upon principles to know, that these measures will RAISE, not sink the price. One of the many instances in legislation, that proves the immense difference (regarding the cases of France and the United States) between a representation of mere population, and one of property! *M—pour prévenir les inquietudes qui pourraient arriver l'année prochaine et les suivantes, l'assemblée doit s'occuper dès ce moment d'un plan general sur les subsistances*—There is but one plan, ABSOLUTE FREEDOM; and you will shew, by accepting or rejecting it, what class of the people it is that you represent. Proclaim a free trade, and from that moment ordain that an inkstand be crammed instantly into the throat of the first member that pronounces the word corn.

Prohibition of the Export of the raw Materials of Manufactures.—The last information I have had from France is a confirmation of the intelligence our newspapers gave, that the National Assembly had ordered a decree to be prepared for this prohibition. It seems that the master manufacturers of various towns, taking advantage of the great decline of the national fabrics, made heavy complaints to the National Assembly; and, among other means of redress, demanded a prohibition of the export of cotton, silk, wool, leather, and, in general, of all raw materials. It was strenuously opposed by a few men, better acquainted than the common mass with political principles, but in vain; and orders were given to prepare the decree, which

I am assured will pass. As I have, in various papers in the "Annals of Agriculture," entered much at large into this question, I shall only mention a few circumstances here, to convince France, if possible, of the mischievous and most pernicious tendency of such a system, which will be attended with events little thought of at present in that kingdom. As it is idle to have recourse to reasoning, when facts are hand, it is only necessary to describe the effect of a similar prohibition in the case of wool in England:—1, The price is sunk by it 50 per cent. below that of all the countries around us, which, as is proved by documents unquestionable, amounts to a land-tax of between three and four millions sterling; being so much taken from land and given to manufactures. 2d, Not to make them flourish; for a second curious fact is, that of all the great fabrics of England that of wool is *least* prosperous, and has been regularly *most* complaining, of which the proofs are before the public; the policy therefore has failed; and because it fails in England, it is going to be adopted in France. The home monopoly of wool gives to the manufacturers so great a profit, that they are not solicitous about any extension of their trade beyond the home product; and to this it is owing that no foreign wool, Spanish alone excepted (which is not produced here), is imported into England. The same thing will happen in France; the home-price will fall; the landed interest will be *robbed*; and the manufacturer, tasting the sweets of monopoly, will no longer import as before: the fabric at large will receive no increase; and all the effect will be, to give the master manufacturer a great profit on a small trade: he will gain, but the nation will lose. 3d, The most flourishing manufacture of England is that of cotton, of which the manufacturer is so far from having a monopoly, the $\frac{18}{20}$ths of the material are imported under a duty, and our own exportable duty free. The next (possibly the first) is that of hardware; English iron is exported duty free, and the import of foreign pays 2l. 16s. 2d. a ton; English coals exported in vast quantities. Glass exhibits the same spectacle; English kelp exportable duty free, and 16s. 6d. a ton on foreign; raw silk pays 3s. a lb. on import; export of British hemp and flax undressed is free, foreign pays a duty on import; British rags, for making paper, exportable duty free; unwrought tin, lead, and copper all exportable either free or under a slight duty. The immense progress made by these manufactures, particularly hardware, cotton, glass, flax, and earthern-ware, another in which no monopoly of material can exist, is known to all Europe; they are among the greatest fabrics in the world, and have risen rapidly; but note (for it merits the attention of France), that wool has experienced no such rise.[1] Our policy in wool stands on fact, therefore convicted of rottenness; and this is precisely the policy which the new government of France copies, and extends to every raw material! 4th, The free trade in raw materials is necessary, like the free trade in corn, not to send those materials abroad, but to secure their production at home; and lowering the price, by giving a monopoly to the buyer, is not the way to encourage farmers to produce. 5th, France imports silk and wool to the amount of 50 and 60 millions a year, and exports none, or next to none; why prohibit an export, which in settled times does not take place? At the present moment, the export either takes place, or it does *not* take place? if the latter, why prohibit a trade which has no existence? If it does take place, it proves that the manufacturers cannot buy it as heretofore: is that a reason why the farmers should not produce it? Your manufacturers cannot buy, and you will not let foreigners; what is that but telling your husbandmen that they shall not produce? Why then do the manufacturers ask this favour? They are cunning: they very well know why; they have the same view as their brethren in England—solely that of SINKING THE PRICE, and thereby putting money in their own pockets, at the expence of the landed interests. 6th, All the towns of France, contain but six millions of people; the manufacturing towns not two millions: why are twenty millions in the country to be cheated out of their property, in order to favour one-tenth of that number in towns? 7th, In various passages of these travels, I have shown the wretched state of French agriculture, for want of more sheep; the new system is a curious way to effect an increase

[1] Exports 1757, 4,758,095l. In 1767, 4,277,462l. In 1777, 3,743,537l. In 1787, 3,687,795l. See this subject fully examined, "Annals of Agriculture," vol. x. p. 235.

—*by lowering the profit of keeping them.* 8th, The French manufacturers, under the *old* system of *freedom*, bought raw materials from other nations, to the amount of several millions, besides working up all the produce of France; if sinking the price be not their object, what is? Can they desire to do more than this? If under the new government their fabrics do not flourish as under the old one, is that a reason for prohibition and restriction, for robbery and plunder of the landed interest, to make good their own losses? And if such a demand is good logic in a manufacturer's counting-house, is that a reason for its being received in a NATIONAL ASSEMBLY!!

One of the most curious inquiries that can be made by a traveller, is to endeavour to ascertain how much per cent. a capital invested in land, and in farming-stock, will return for cultivation in different countries; no person, according to my knowledge, has attempted to explain this very important but difficult problem. The price of land, the interest of money, the wages of labour, the rates of all sorts of products, and the amount of taxes, must be calculated with some degree of precision, in order to analyze this combination. I have for many years attempted to gain information on this curious point, concerning various countries. If a man in England buys land rented at 12s. an acre, at thirty years purchase, and cultivates it himself, making five rents, he will make not more than from $4\frac{1}{2}$ to 5 per cent, and at most 6, speaking of general culture, and not estimating singular spots or circumstances, and including the capital invested in both land and stock. I learn, from the correspondence of the best farmer, and the greatest character the new world has produced, certain circumstances, which enable me to assert, with confidence, that money invested on the same principles, in the middle states of North America, will yield considerably more than double the return in England, and in many instances the treble of it. To compare France with these two cases, is very difficult:—had the National Assembly done for the agriculture of the kingdom what France had a right to expect from FREEDOM, the account would have been advantageous. For buying at 30 years purchase, stocking the same as in England, and reckoning products 6 per cent. lower in price (about the fact), the total capital would have paid from 5½ to 6½ per cent.; land-tax reckoned at 3s. in the pound, which is the proportion of the total tax to the rental of the kingdom.[1] It is true, that the course of exchange would make an enormous difference, for when exchange is at 15, this ratio per cent. instead of 5½ becomes 11, if the capital is remitted from Britain: but as that immense loss (50 per cent.), on the exchange of France, arises from the political state of the kingdom, the same circumstances which cause it, would be estimated at so much hazard and danger. But bring to account the operations of the National Assembly, relating to the non-inclosure of commons: the land-tax, variable with improvements (an article sufficient to stifle the thoughts of such a thing); the export of corn at an end; the transport every where impeded; and your granaries burnt and plundered at the pleasure of the populace, if they do not like the price; and, above all, the prohibition of the export of all materials of manufactures, as wool, &c. and it is sufficiently clear, that America offers a vastly more eligible field for the investment of capital in land than France does; a proof that the measures of the National Assembly have been ill-judged, ill-advised, and unpolitical: I had serious thoughts of settling in that kingdom, in order to farm there; but the two measures adopted, of a variable land-tax, and a prohibition of the export of wool, damped my hopes, ardent as they were, that I might have breathed that fine climate, free from the extortions of a government, stupid in this respect as that of England. It is, however, plain enough, that America is the only country that affords an adequate

[1] But this land-tax is variable, and therefore impossible to estimate accurately; if you remain no better farmers than your French neighbours, *it is so much;* but if you improve, *you are raised, and they are sunk;* all that has, and can be said against tythes, bears with equal force against such a tax. And though this imposition cannot go by the present law beyond 4s. in the pound, it would be very easy to shew, by a plain calculation, that 4s. in the pound, *rising with improvement,* is a tax impossible to be borne *by one who improves;* and consequently, that it is a direct tax on improvement; and it is a tax in the very worst form, since the power to lay and inforce it, is not in the government of the kingdom, but in the municipal government of the parish. Your neighbour, with whom you may be on ill terms, has the power to tax you; no such private heart-burnings and tyranny are found in excises.

profit, and in which a man, who calculates with intelligence and precision, can think of investing his capital. How different would this have been, had the National Assembly conducted themselves on principles directly contrary; had they avoided all land-taxes;[1] had they preserved the free corn-trade, a trade of import more than export; had they been silent upon inclosures; and done nothing in relation to raw materials, the profit of investments would have been higher in France than in America, or any country in the world, and immense capitals would have flowed into the kingdom from every part of Europe: scarcity and famine would not have been heard of, and the national wealth would have been equal to all the exigencies of the period.

* * * * * *

April 26, 1792.

In the last moment which the preparation for publication allows me to use, the intelligence is arrived of a declaration of war on the part of France against the House of Austria;—the gentlemen in whose company I hear it, all announce destruction to France;—*they will be beat;—they want discipline;—they have no subordination;*—and

---

[1] To have avoided land-taxes, might very easily have been made a most popular measure, in a kingdom so divided into little properties as France is. No tax is so heavy upon a small proprietor; and the *œconomistes* might have foreseen what has happened, that such little democratic owners would not pay the tax; but taxes on consumption, laid *as in England,* and not in the infamous methods of the old government of France, would have been paid by them in a light proportion, without knowing it; but the *œconomistes,* to be consistent with their old pernicious doctrines, took every step to make all, except land-taxes, unpopular; and the people were ignorant enough to be deceived into the opinion, that it was better to pay a tax on the bread put into their children's mouths—and, what is worse, on the land which ought, but does not produce that bread, than to pay an excise on tobacco and salt, better to pay a tax which is demanded equally, whether they have or have not the money to pay it, than a duty which, mingled with the price of a luxury, is paid in the easiest mode, and at the most convenient moment. In the writings of the *œconomistes,* you hear of a free corn trade, and free export of every thing being the recompence for a land-tax; but see their actions in power—they impose the burthen, and forget the recompence!

this idea I find general. So cautiously as I have avoided *prophetic* presumption through the preceding pages, I shall scarcely assume it so late in my labours;—but thus much I may venture,—that the expectation of destruction to France has many difficulties to encounter. Give all you please to power of field evolution, depending on the utmost strictness of discipline—you must admit that it bears only on the question of battles. But guarded as France is, by the most important frontier fortresses the world knows, why hazard battles? Undisciplined troops behind walls and within *works*, are known on experience to be effective: and where are the resources to be found that shall attack those strong holds, 700 miles from home? I was at Lisle, Metz, and Strasbourg; and if the military intelligence I had was accurate, it would demand 100,000 men, completely provided with everything for a siege, three months to take either of those towns, supposing them well provided and well defended. We know, on positive experience, what the Austrians and Prussians led by some of the greatest men that have existed, were able to do in sieges, when undertaken at their own doors;—what will they effect against places ten times as strong and 700 miles from home? It is a matter of calculation—of pounds and shillings;—not of discipline and obedience.

But many depend on the deranged state of the French finances; that derangement flows absolutely from a vain attempt at preserving public credit:—the National Assembly will see its futility; misery; ruin; the NATION must be preserved—what on comparison is *public credit?*

The divisions, factions, and internal disturbances, offer to others the hope of a civil war. It ought to be a vain hope. During peace, such difficulties fill the papers, and are dwelt upon, till men are apt to think them terrible; in war they are TREASON, and the gallows sweeps from the world, and the columns of a gazette the actors and the recital.

Oil and vinegar—fire and water—Prussians and Austrians are united to carry war amongst 26 millions of men, arranged behind 100 of the strongest fortresses in the world.—If we are deceived, and Frenchmen are not fond of freedom, but will fight for despotism—something may be done; for then France falls by the power of France: but if united but tolerably, the attack will be full of difficulties in a country where every man, woman, and child is an enemy, that fights for freedom.

But, suppose this idea erroneous—suppose an impression made—and that the German banners were flying at Paris.—Where is the security of the rest of Europe? Is the division of Poland forgotten? Is an unforeseen union of two or three great powers to protrude through Europe a predominancy dangerous to all? Gentlemen, who indulge their wishes for a counter-revolution in France, do not, perhaps, wish to see the Prussian colours at the Tower, nor the Austrian at Amsterdam. Yet success to the cause might plant them there. Should real danger arise to France, which I hold to be problematical, it is the business, and direct interest of her neighbours, to support her.

The revolution, and anti-revolution parties of England, have exhausted themselves on the French question; but there can be none, if that people should be in danger:— WE hold at present the balance of the world; and have but to speak, and it is secure.

INDEX.

Abbé de —, 118.
Abbeville, 8, 151, 348.
Achillæa syberica, 162.
Agen, 65.
Agriculture in France, 345; and politics, 131.
Aiguebelle, 278.
Aigues, tour d', 257.
Aiguillon, Duc de, 7, 65, 77; town of, 65.
Aire, 64.
Aire sur la Lys, 111.
Aix, Archbishop of, 159.
Aix-en-Provence, 257, 259.
Aizac, le coupe d', 242.
Alençon, 141.
Allier, valley of the, 228, 230.
Alsace, 205, 207.
Ambigu Comique, l', 100.
Amboise, 77.
America, and France, 338; government of, 344.
America, North, farming in, 354.
Ami, l', des hommes, 85.
Amiens, 8, 112.
Ancenis, 135.
Angoulême, 70, 71.
Anjou, 135.
Annals of Agriculture, 1, 6, 42, 352.
Anspan, 62.
Antibes, 271.
Anville, Duchess D', 305.
Arbois, 217.

Argenson, Count d', 73.
Argenton, 20.
Arnas, les, 284.
Arpajon, 17.
Arras, 111.
Artois, Count d', 9, 14, 19, 171, 177, 211, 220.
Aubagne, 263.
Aubenas, 245.
Auch, 63, 64.
Auge, pays d', 116.
Aulus, 56.
Aumale, 112.
Auray, 128.
Austria, declaration of war against, by France, 1792, 356.
Autun, 227.
Auve, 197.
Auvergnac (Lauvergnac), 130.
Auxonne, 218.
Avignon, 252.
Ay, 195.

Bagnères de Bigorre, 59.
Bagnères de Luchon. *See* Luchon.
Bailly, J. S., 165, 173, 294.
Barbézieux, 70.
Barentin, 114.
Barnave. *See* Bernarve.
Barré, Du (Dubarry), Mme., 32, 100.
Barsac, 66.
Barut, l'abbé, 286.
Bassies (Bassines), 21.

360   INDEX.

Bastille, prisoners of, 134, 313; storming of, 199, 206; and the *lettres de cachet*, 313.
Baume-les-Dames, 212.
Bayes, Mr., his army, 226.
Bayonne, 59, 62, 63.
Béarn, 61.
Bears in the Pyrenees, 41.
Beaucaire, fair of, 50.
Beauce, la, 17.
Beaumont sur Sarthe, 141.
Beaune, 226.
Beauvais, 90.
Beauvais, Bishop of, 180.
Beauvoisin, Pont de, 279.
Bédarieux, 55.
Befort (Belfort), 210, 211.
Belle Angloise (Bellenglise), 105.
Belle-île-en-Mer, 130.
Belleisle (Belle-Isle-Bégard), 126.
Belloy, De, 69.
Berchtold, Count de, 150.
Bernarve (Barnave), Mons., 165, 178, 293.
Bernay (Eure), 141.
Bernay (Pas de Calais), 7.
Berri, Duc de, 14.
Berri, le, 20.
Besançon, 214, 215.
Besenval, Baron de, 298.
Béthune, 111.
Béziers, 46, 47, 48, 55.
Birmingham, the Priestley riots at, 338.
Bissy (Bizy), Château de, 144.
Blois, 77.
Blois, Bishop of, 159.
Bolbec, 114.
Bon, 117.
Bonbrie (Pont de Brique), 6.
Bonhier, Jean, 225.
Bordeaux, 66, 67, 68, 69.
Bossuet, 225.
Bouchaine (Bouchain), 107.
Bougainville, Comte de. 301.
Bouillon, Duc de, 64, 70.
Boulogne, 5.
Bourbon, Lancy, 228.
Bourges, 19.
Bourgoyn (Bourgoin), 282.
Brasseuse, 88.

Brest, 126.
Breteuil, 9.
Brézé, Marquis de, 170, 175.
Briare, Canal de, 287.
Brie, 192.
Brien (Canal de Brienne), 32.
Brienne, Loménie de, 32, 97.
Brioude, 239.
Brittany, 123.
Brive, 25, 26.
Broglio (Broglie, and Count de), 72; Château de, 141; Maréchal Duc de, 210.
Broons, 125.
Brosses, Chas. de, 225.
Broussonet, P. A., 91, 100, 101, 102, 105, 161, 170, 217, 220.
Brown, Robert, 101.
Buffon, 225.
Burney, Dr. and Miss, 150.

Caen, 116.
Café Foy, 155.
Cahors, 28.
Calais, 5, 13, 16, 28, 43, 109, 110, 148, 150.
Calonne, Mons. de, 97, 331.
Cambray, 106.
Camelford, Lord, 159.
Campan, Valley of, 59.
Cannes, 271.
Capestan, 55.
Capitaineries, the, 316.
Carcassonne, 55, 56.
Carentan, 118, 122.
Cassel, 108.
Castres, 66.
Catnoir (Catenoy), 88.
Caudec, 72.
Caussade, 29.
Cavalero, 266.
Cavignac, 70.
Chabert, M. de, 99.
Chagny, 226.
Chalmers, Mr., on war and trade, 347.
Chalons-sur-Marne, 196.
Chambers, Sir W., 101.
Chambéry, 278, 279.
Chambord, 78, 79.
Chambre la, 278.

INDEX. 361

Champagne, province of, 194, 195.
Chanteloup, 76, 77.
Chantilly, 10, 82, 86.
Chapelier, Isaac le, 178, 293, 297.
Charente, la, 70, 71.
Charenton, 98.
Chartreuse, la (Dijon), 219.
Chateaulandrin, 126.
Chateaulin, 128.
Châteauneuf, 234.
Chateaurault (Châtellerault), 73.
Châteauroux, 20.
Château-Thiery, 193.
Chaunay, 72.
Chaussée (Chausey), isles of, 123.
Chavanne le Roi (Chevagne), 228.
Cher, le, 19.
Cherbourg, 119, 120, 121.
Chiliac, 239.
Chinese hemp, 162.
Choiseul, Duc de, 76, 77.
Chomet (Chomettes), 239.
Cierp, 35.
Clergy of France and the Revolution, 327.
Clermont, Ferrand, 234, 235, 236, 237.
Clermont (Oise), 9, 85.
Clermont-Tonnerre, Comte de, 296.
Colmar, 210.
Columiers (Coulommiers), 191.
Combourg, 123.
Comédie Française, 94, 96.
Comédie Italienne, 94.
Commerce and manufactures and the Revolution, 346, 351.
Commercial Treaty, 1786, 8, 69.
Condé, Prince de, 11, 87.
Condorcet, Marquis de, 23, 292.
Coni, 275.
Conversation, Society, &c., in France, 37.
Cookery, food, &c., French, 39, 306.
Corbon, Valley of, 116.
Corday, Charlotte, 157.
Cordeliers, Church of the, 31.
Corn, price of, 350.
Costaros, 242.

Coucy, 105.
Cour Plenière, la, 190.
Courtisseau (Courtisois), 197.
Coutances, 122.
Crau, le, 256.
Craven, Lady, 263.
Crébillon, 225.
Cujes, the (Cujés), 263.

Dammartin, 105.
D'Armentières, 108.
Darnetal, 142.
Dax, 63.
Degouttes, Marquis, 286.
Denainvilliers, 80.
Dicquemare, the Abbé, 115.
Dieppe, 147.
Dijon, 218, 219, 220, 221, 223.
Dol, 123.
Dôle, 218.
Donzenac, 25.
Dordogne, la, 27, 70.
Dress, fashions, &c., in France, 308.
Dubarry, Mme. de, 32, 100.
Dugny, 105, 166.
Duhamel, M. de, 80.
Dunkirk, 108.
Droiturier, 286.
Duretal (Durtal), Château de, 136.

Ecole Militaire, 100.
Ecole Vetérinarie, 98.
Elbœuf, 142.
England, agriculture in, 131.
Epernay, 194.
Ermenonville, 86.
Estrelles, 269.
Etampes, 17.
Exchange, course of, and the Revolution, 347.
Exports, French and English, 351, 353.
Eyre, Sir James, 159.

Falaise, 116, 117.
Farming, profits of, 354.
Faujas, de Saint-Fond, B., 243, 249.
Faujeaux, 55.
Favras, Marquis de, 298.
Fère, la, 136.
Ferté-la-Lowendahl, 18.

Fevret de Fontette, C. M., 225.
Fix, Saint-Geneys, 239.
Flèche, la, 136.
Fleurance, 65.
Flixcourt, 8.
Fontainebleau, 81.
Fox, C. J., 112.
Foy, Café, de, 155.
France, the old government of, 315; in 1792, 345; its debt and the Revolution, 348.
France and America, 338.
Francis I., 81.
Free trade, 351, 353, 356.
Fréjus, 269.
Frontignan, 49.

Gacé, 141.
Game laws in France, 316.
Ganges (Hérault), 54.
Gardening, 101.
Garonne, la, 32, 34.
Genlis, Mme. de, 196.
Germany and France, 356-358.
Gibelin, Mons., 257.
Girardon, (Girardin) Marquis de, 87.
Gobelins, les, 98.
Gordon, an English prisoner in the Bastile, 313.
Gouzat, cascade of, 40.
Grandval (Granville), 123.
Gravelines, 109.
Gravenne, la, 244.
Grasse, 270.
Gray (Haute Marne), 221.
Grisolles, 30.
Grundy, Mr., 285.
Guerces (La Guierche), 141.
Guerchy, Marquis de, 116.
Guibray, 116, 117.
Guienne, la, 26.
Guingamp, 125.
Guignes, 186.
Guillon, 144.
Guyton-Morveau. *See* Morveau.

Haming (Hemingen), 205.
Harcourt, Château d', 118.
Harfleur, 114.
Harwich, 6.

Hasparren, 62.
Hatsell's "Precedents," 166.
Havre, le, 114.
Hédé, 123.
Hemp, Chinese, 162.
Hennebont, 129.
Henri IV., 18, 60, 61.
Hyères, Isles de, 264.

Indret, 134.
Innkeeper, knavery of one, 287.
Inns, 56.
Ireland, 25, 122.
Ireland, Tour in, 3.
Isenheim (Ensisheim), 210.
Isigny, 118.
Islets (les Islettes), 197.
Issoire, 238.
Italian agriculture, 1.

Jacobins Club, 305.
Jeu de Paume, 164, 171, 173.
Jeux Floraux, 31.
Jonquiera, 42.

Kames, Lord, 10.
Kirwan, Richard, 94, 222.

La Chambre, 278.
La Fayette, 294, 300, 301.
La Fére, 105.
La Flèche, 136.
La Loge, 19.
Lamballe, 125.
Lamoignon, Mons., 190.
Land and farming, 354.
Land tax in France, 349, 355, 356.
Landernau (Landerneau), 127.
Landervisier (Landivisiau), 127
Langon, 66.
Langres, 221.
Languedoc, canal of, 32, 45, 46, 55; province of, 45, 48, 58.
Lans-le-Bourg (Savoie), 277.
Larboust, 40.
La Rochefoucauld, Count de, 12, 16.
La Rochefoucauld, Duke de, and counts of, 14, 36, 37, 43, 71, 159, 209.

INDEX.

La Roche Guyon, 143.
Larrive, M., 68.
La Tour du Pin, 281.
Lauresse (Loures), 34.
Lauvergnac, 130.
Lave, la, 19.
La Ville au Brun, 21.
Lavoisier, 93, 94, 95, 222.
Lazowski, M. de, 12, 13, 16, 36, 43, 86, 163, 185.
Lectoure, 65.
Lettres de cachet and the Bastile, 313.
Le Mans, 141.
Lempdes, 239.
Léonnais, le, 127.
Le Puy, 241, 242, 243.
Les Islettes, 197.
Les Ormes, 73.
Levant, L'isle de, 264.
Leyrac, 65.
Liancourt, duc de, and château, 10, 12, 13, 14, 15, 16, 82, 88, 89, 166, 172, 173, 174, 185, 288, 291, 303, 304, 309.
Libourne, 27.
Lille (L'isle, Vaucluse), 254.
Lilliers, 111.
Limoges, 22.
Limousin, le, 24, 26, 31.
Lisle (Lille, Nord), 107, 357.
L'Isle sur le Doubs, 210.
Lodève, 55.
Loire, the, 17, 18, 72, 73, 74, 75, 76, 78, 79, 82, 83, 130, 135, 286, 347.
Loménie de Brienne, 32, 97.
Lomond, M., 96.
Londrins fabric, 55.
L'orient, 128.
L'Oriol (Loriol), 250.
Louis d'or, the, 18.
Louis XI., 74, 78.
Louis XIV., 8, 46, 70, 102, 108.
Louis XV., 32, 79, 100.
Louis XVI., 14, 97, 106, 171, 180, 181, 182, 211, 288, 290.
Lourdes, 60.
Louviers, 144, 145.
Luchon, Bagnères de, 14, 35, 40, 41, 42, 43, 46, 59, 64.

Lunéville, 203.
Lusienne (Lucienne), 100.
Luzarches, 11.
Luzy, 228.
Lyons, 282-285.

Macartney, Lord, 23.
Madières, 54.
Maisse (Mayres), 242.
Malataverne, 278.
Malsherbs (Malesherbes), 97; château de, 81.
Marche, la, 21.
Mareuil, 193.
Marie Antoinette, 15, 16, 159, 168, 171, 177, 178, 179, 183, 210, 211, 220, 236, 244, 288, 298, 300.
Marseilles, 259, 260, 261.
Mars-la-Tour, 198.
Maupertuis, 191.
Maury, l'Abbé, 296.
Meaux, 191.
Mendoza and boxing, 190.
Métayage, system, 18.
Metz, 199, 357.
Meulan (Melun), 82.
Meusnier, M. de, 119.
Mignianne (La Meignanne), 135.
Militaire, Ecole, 100.
Millau, 53.
Militia grievance of the French Peasantry, 315.
Mills' "Husbandry," 138.
Mirabeau, Marquis de, 85.
Mirabeau, Marquis de, (the Tribune), 164, 168, 176, 260, 296.
Mirepoix, 55, 56.
Modane, 276.
Mondardier, 54.
Monein, 61.
Montauban, 29, 30, 33.
Montauban, cascade of, 40.
Montauban de Bretagne, 125.
Montbazin, 49.
Mont Cassel, 108.
Montchanin, 226.
Montesquieu, Marquis de, 191.
Montferrand, 234.
Montgeron, 82.
Montigny, 190.

364   INDEX.

Montilimart (Montélimar), 249.
Montmorin, Count de, 174.
Montpellier, 48, 49, 51.
Montreuil sur Mer, 7.
Morefontaine (Mortefontaine), 86.
Morlaix, 126.
Morveau-Guyton, Mons.,218, 220, 222, 223, 225.
Motte, de la, Madame, 168.
Moulins, 229.
Mounier, J. J., 164, 178.
Musiliac (Muzillac), 130.

Nancy, 201.
Nangis, 186, 187, 188.
Nantes 131, 132, 133.
Nanteuil, (Nanteuil le Hardouin), 105.
Narbonne, 44, 45.
National Assembly, 199, 206, 290, 295, 305, 341, 349, 351, 354.
Navarrenx, 62.
Necker, Mons., 85, 159, 160, 168, 172, 173, 175, 176, 177, 179, 201, 202, 211, 230, 294, 321, 350.
Nemours, 287.
Neste, the, 35.
Neuf Montier (Neufmontier), 192.
Neuilié (Neuilly), 100.
Nevers, 286.
Newbury, 7.
Newchatel (Neufchâtel), 112.
Nice, 270, 271, 274.
Nîmes, 50, 52.
Noailles, château de, 26.
Nobility of France, 325, 344.
Nouans (Sarthe), 141.
Nouant le Fuzelier, 19.
Nuys (Nuits), 226.

Ollioules, 263.
Opera, the, 91.
Opéra Comique, **94.**
Orange, 252.
Orchees (Orchies), 107.
Orechamp, (Orchamps), 218.
Orgon, 256.
Orleans, 16, 80.
Orleans, Duke of, 158, 173, 174, 179, 180, 190.

Ormes, Les, 73.
Ove (Auve), 197.

Paine, Thomas, 344; his " Rights of Man," 340.
Pamiers, 56, 57.
Panckoucke, C. J., 223.
Paper currency and the Revolution, 347.
Paris, 11, 13, 16, 90-105, 151, 152, 153, 154, 155, 156, 157, 158, 159, 161, 166, 176-186, 285 to end of vol.
Parliaments, the, of Louis XVI., 321.
Parmentier, 103.
Pau, 60, 61.
Payrac, 27.
Peasantry, the, of France, 315.
Penthievre, Duc de, 158.
Perges, 29.
Perpignan, 43.
Petivier (Pithiviers), 80.
Pézenas, 48.
Phalsbourg, 205.
Pia, 43.
Picardy, 346; canal of, 105.
Picquigny, 9.
Pierrebussière, 24.
Pierrelatte, 252.
Pignan, 49.
Place du Peyrou, 49.
Plessis lès Tours, 74.
Poitiers, 72.
Polignac, château de, 241.
Poliguac, Duc and Duchesse de, 160, 211.
Pompadour, 24.
Pompignon, 30.
Pont (Pont St. Maixence), 88.
Pont à Mousson, 200.
Pont de l'Arche, 144.
Pont de Beauvoisin, 281.
Pont de Brique, 6.
Pont du Gard, 51.
Pont de Rode, 28.
Pontoise, 90.
Pontorsin (Pontorson), 123.
Porquerolles, 264.
Port Cros, 264.
Potato, the, in France, 103.

INDEX.

Pougues, 287.
Pouilly, 287.
Poulaget (Paulhaguet), 239.
Pradel, le, 247.
Pradelles, 242.
Premontrés, les, 200.
Priestly, Dr., 220, 222, 223, 335; riots at Birmingham. 338.
Protestants at worship, 251.
Prouille, 55.
Puy. *See* Le Puy.
Pyrenees, 16, 29, 30, 37, 40, 42, 43, 50, 55, 59.

Quercy, 26.
Quimper, 128.
Quimperlé, 128.

Raynal, l'Abbé, 155, 157, 261.
Rennes, 124.
Revolution, the French, 199, 201, 206, 207, 313-358; effects of, 328, 332.
Rheims, 195.
Riaux (Ryau), château de, 231.
Richelieu, Tomb of, 94.
Riom, 234, 304.
Rivesaltes, 44.
Roanne, 286.
Robais, Van, 8.
Robespierre, 290.
Robine, la, 45.
Rochefoucauld, Cardinal de la, 180.
Roche la Guyon, 143.
Rochemaure, 251.
Rochon, l'Abbé, 145.
Rodez, 53.
Roland, Monsieur and Madame, 284.
Rosoy (Rozoy-en-Brie), 191.
Rossendal (Rosendael, Le), 109.
Rouen, 112, 142.
Rouergue, la, 53.
Rousseau, 84, 283; his tomb, 87, 280.
Roussillon, le, 43, 45.
Roya (Royat), 235.
Rozier, l'Abbé, 47, 228, 283.
Ruffec, 72.

Sabatier, château, de, 52.
Sablonville, 170.
St. Bertrand, 34.
St. Brieux, 125.
St. Canat (St. Chamas), 257.
St. Cloud, 16.
St. Etienne, Rabaut, 164, 173, 174, 179.
St. Gaudens, 34.
St. George, 25.
St. Georges D'Aurac, 239.
St. Georges-sur-Loire, 135.
St. Germains, 92. 101.
St. Germain-les-Belles, 25.
St. Gérund le Puy, 286.
St. Girons, 57.
St. Gobin (St. Gobain), 105.
St. Hippolyte du Fort, 53.
St. Jean de Maurienne, 278.
St. Jory, 31.
St. Laurence, 54.
St. Louis, Church of, 173.
St. Martino, 34.
St. Martory, 58.
St. Maurice, 54.
St. Maxime, 268.
St. Menehould, 197.
St. Michel, 278.
St. Nazaire, 131.
St. Omer, 111.
St. Palais, 62.
St. Poncin (St. Pourçain), 233.
St. Pourçain, 233.
St. Priest, M. de, 174.
St. Quintin, 106.
St. Severe (St. Sever), 64.
St. Symphorien-de-Laye, 286.
St. Tropez, 268.
St. Veté (St. Vit.), 218.
Salins, 216.
Salon, 256.
Samer, 7.
Sancerre, 20.
Sardinia, 273.
Sauve, 52.
Savanal (Savenay), 132.
Saverne (Zabern), 205.
Scenery, 40.
Scheele, Karl, 222.
Schelestadt (Schlestadt), 209.
Senár (Sénart, forest of), 82.

Seneffe, battle of, 219.
Senlis, 105.
Serres, Olivier de, 247, 248.
Seve (Sèvres), 101.
Sieyès, l'abbé, 155, 162, 163, 166, 168, 173, 178, 288, 290.
Sijean, 44.
Sillery, 196.
Soissons, 105.
Sologne, La, 18.
Souillac, 26, 27.
States-General, 151.
Strasburg, 205, 357.
Suffrein, Admiral, 15.
Symonds, Professor, 1.

Target, 178.
Taxes in France, 314. *See also* Land tax, &c.
Thabor, le, 124.
Theatres, at Bourdeaux, 68; at Paris, 94, 95, 96, 184.
Thuillieries, gardens, 288.
Thuytz (Thueyts), 242, 243, 244.
Tonnance (Tonneins), 66.
Tote (Tôtes), 147.
Toulon, 263.
Toulon, affair of, 304.
Toulouse, 31, 32, 33.
Tourbilly (Turbilly), 137, 138, 139.
Tour d'Aigues, château de, 257.
Tour du Pin, la, 281.
Tours, 74, 75.
Toury, 17.
Trade, depression of, 347. *See also* Free Trade.
Traguer (Tréguier), 128.
Trianon, La Petite, 101.
Tull, Jethro, 66.
Turbarries, 7.
Turbilly, 137.
Turgot, 23, 97, 117.
Turnips, 157.
Tythes, 337.

Uzerche, 25.

Valenciennes, 107.
Valognes, 119.
Vannes, 129.
Van Robais cloth, 8.
Var (Vaast, St.), 111.
Vatan, 20.
Vaucluse, 252, 254.
Vaucusson, Mons., 162.
Ventaillac, 29.
Vermont, l'Abbé de, 160.
Vernon, 144.
Verpilière, la, 281.
Versailles, 13, 14, 15, 100, 101, 102, 171, 172, 173, 174, 175, 288.
Verteuil, 71.
Vesoul, 214.
Vic-Bigorre, 64.
Viella, 42.
Vierzon, 19.
Vigan, le, 53.
Villefranche, 274.
Villeneuve de Berg, 245, 246.
Villeneuve St. Georges, 82.
Villers-Cotterets, 105.
Viviers, 249.
Volney, 288, 290, 293, 305.
Vologues (Valognes), 119.
Volta's eudiometers, 224.
Voltaire, 8.

Warens, Madame de, 279.
Watt, Mr., of Birmingham, 162.
Women in France, 84, 253.
Wool, exports of, French and English, 352.

Yvetot, 114.

Zabern, 205.

London, October 1896.

A CLASSIFIED CATALOGUE
OF
SELECTED WORKS
PUBLISHED BY
GEORGE BELL AND SONS.

CONTENTS.

POETRY	1	ROYAL NAVY HANDBOOKS	18
THE ALDINE POETS	5	BOTANY	18
BIOGRAPHY AND HISTORY	6	ECONOMICS AND FINANCE	19
STANDARD BOOKS	10	SPORTS AND GAMES	19
DICTIONARIES AND BOOKS OF REFERENCE	13	ALL-ENGLAND & CLUB SERIES	21
		FICTION	22
ART AND ARCHÆOLOGY	14	BOOKS FOR THE YOUNG	23

** *Theological Books are not included in this Catalogue, but a separate list will be sent on application. Messrs. Bell will be glad to send their Complete Catalogue, Catalogue of Bohn's Libraries, or Educational Catalogue, to any address, post free.*

POETRY.

Aidé (Hamilton). Songs without Music. 3rd edition. With additional Pieces. Fcap. 8vo. 5s.

Barry Cornwall. English Songs and Lyrics. 2nd edition. Fcap. 8vo. 6s.

Bridges (R.) Shorter Poems. 4th edition. Fcap. 8vo. 5s. net.

——— A Series of Plays. Fcap. 4to. printed on hand-made paper, double columns, paper wrappers, each 2s. 6d. net (except No. 8). The eight Plays are paged consecutively, and are intended to form a Volume:—
    1. NERO. The First Part. History of the first five years of Nero's reign. with the Murder of Britannicus to the Death of Agrippina.
                                                                                    [*Out of print at present.*
    2. PALICIO. A Romantic Drama in Five Acts, in the Elizabethan manner.
    3. THE RETURN OF ULYSSES. A Drama in Five Acts, in a mixed manner.
    4. THE CHRISTIAN CAPTIVES. A Tragedy in Five Acts, in a mixed manner, without change of scene.
    5. ACHILLES IN SCYROS. A Drama in Five Acts, in a mixed manner, without change of scene.
    6. THE HUMOURS OF THE COURT. A Comedy in Three Acts, in the Spanish manner.
    7. THE FEAST OF BACCHUS. A Comedy in Five Acts, in the Latin manner, without change of scene.
    8. NERO. The Second Part. In Five Acts: comprising the Conspiracy of Piso to the Death of Seneca, in the Elizabethan manner. 3s. net, with general title-page, &c., for the volume.

Bridges (R.) Eros and Psyche: A Poem in Twelve Measures. The Story done into English from the Latin of Apuleius. 2nd edition revised. Fcap. 8vo. 5s. net.

———— **Prometheus the Firegiver.** *[Out of print.*

———— **Achilles in Scyros.** New Edition. Fcp. 8vo. 2s. 6d. net.

———— **Eden.** A Cantata in Three Acts, set to music by C. Villiers Stanford. Words only, by Robert Bridges. 2s. net.

Browning's Strafford. With Notes by E. H. Hickey, and an Introduction by S. R. Gardiner, LL.D. 2nd edition. Crown 8vo. 2s. 6d.

  Handbook to Robert Browning's Works. By Mrs. Sutherland Orr. 6th edition, with additions and full bibliography. Fcap. 8vo. 6s.

  Stories from Robert Browning. By Frederic M. Holland. With an Introduction by Mrs. Sutherland Orr. Wide fcap. 4s. 6d.

Calverley (C. S.) Works by the late C. S. Calverley, M.A., late Fellow of Christ's College, Cambridge.

  New and Cheaper uniform Edition in 4 vols. Crown 8vo. 5s. each.

 Vol. I. LITERARY REMAINS, with Portrait and Memoir. Edited by Sir Walter J. Sendall, K.C.M.G.
 Vol. II. VERSES AND FLY LEAVES.
 Vol. III. TRANSLATIONS into English and Latin.
 Vol. IV. THEOCRITUS, in English Verse.

    Original Editions.
FLY LEAVES. 17th edition. Fcap. 8vo. 3s. 6d.
VERSES AND TRANSLATIONS. 15th edition. Fcap. 8vo. 5s.

De Vere (Sir Aubrey). Mary Tudor: an Historical Drama, in Two Parts. By the late Sir Aubrey De Vere. New edition. Fcap. 8vo. 5s.

De Vere (Sir Stephen). Translations from Horace. By Sir Stephen E. De Vere, Bart. 3rd edition enlarged. Imperial 16mo. 7s. 6d. net.

Fanshawe (R.) Two Lives. A Poem. By Reginald Fanshawe, M.A. 4s. 6d. net.

Ferguson (Sir S.) Congal: A Poem in Five Books. By the late Sir Samuel Ferguson, Knt., Q.C., LL.D., P.R.I.A. Fcap. 8vo. 2s.

———— **Poems.** Demy 8vo. 7s. 6d.

Field (Michael). Underneath the Bough. A Book of Verses. 2nd edition. Royal 16mo. 4s. 6d. net.

———— **Callirrhoë, Fair Rosamund.** 2nd edition. Crown 8vo. parchment cover, 6s.

———— **Canute the Great; a Cup of Water.** Two Plays. Crown 8vo. 7s. 6d.

———— **The Father's Tragedy; William Rufus; Loyalty or Love?** Crown 8vo. parchment cover, 7s. 6d.

———— **The Tragic Mary.** On hand-made paper, bound in brown boards, with Design by Selwyn Image, imperial 16mo. 7s. 6d. net.

  Large-paper Edition, on Whatman's paper, bound in vellum, with design in gold, 60 copies only (numbered), fcap. 4to. 21s. net.

Lang (Andrew). Helen of Troy. A Poem. 5th edition. Wide fcap. 8vo. cloth, 2s. 6d. net.

Patmore (Coventry). Poems. Collective Edition in 2 vols. 5th edition. Fcap. 8vo. 9s.

―――― The Unknown Eros, and other Poems. 3rd edition. Fcap. 8vo. 2s. 6d.

―――― The Angel in the House. 7th edition. Fcap. 8vo. 3s. 6d.

Procter (A. A.) Legends and Lyrics. By Adelaide Anne Procter. With Introduction by Charles Dickens. New edition, printed on hand-made paper. 2 vols. pott 8vo., extra binding, 10s.

ORIGINAL EDITION. First Series. 69th thousand. 2s. 6d. Second Series. 61st thousand. 2s. 6d.

CROWN 8vo EDITION. New Issue, with additional Poems, and 10 Illustrations by Ida Lovering. 19th thousand. Post 8vo. cloth, gilt edges, 5s.

CHEAP EDITION, with 18 Illustrations, double columns. 2 Series. 30th thousand. Fcap, 4to. paper cover, 1s. each; or in 1 vol. cloth, 3s.

The Procter Birthday Book. Demy 16mo. 1s. 6d.

Rickards (M. S. C.) Lyrics and Elegiacs. By Marcus S. C. Rickards. Crown 8vo. 4s. net.

―――― Poems of Life and Death. Crown 8vo. 4s. 6d. net.

―――― The Exiles: A Romance of Life. Crown 8vo. 4s. 6d. net.

Sweetman (E.) The Footsteps of the Gods, and other Poems. Crown 8vo. 6s. net.

Tennyson (Lord). A Key to Tennyson's 'In Memoriam.' By Alfred Gatty. D.D., Vicar of Ecclesfield and Sub-Dean of York. Fourth edition, with Portrait of Arthur Hallam, 3s. 6d.

Handbook to Lord Tennyson's Works. By Morton Luce. With Bibliography. Fcap. 8vo. 6s.

Trevelyan (Sir G. O.) The Ladies in Parliament, and other Pieces. Republished, with Additions and Annotations. By Sir George Otto Trevelyan. Crown 8vo. 1s. 6d.

Waddington (S.) A Century of Sonnets. Fcap. 4to. 4s. 6d.

―――― Poems. Fcap. 8vo.

Beaumont and Fletcher, their finest Scenes, Lyrics, and other Beauties (selected), with Notes and Introduction by Leigh Hunt. Small post 8vo. 3s. 6d.

Butler's Hudibras, with Variorum Notes, a Biography, and a General Index, a Portrait of Butler, and 28 Illustrations. Small post 8vo. 5s.

Chaucer's Poetical Works. With Poems formerly printed with his or attributed to him. Edited, with a Memoir, Introduction, Notes, and a Glossary, by Robert Bell. Revised, with a Preliminary Essay by Rev. Prof. Skeat, M.A. With Portrait. 4 vols. small post 8vo. 3s. 6d. each.

Greene, Marlowe, and Ben Jonson, Poems of. Edited, with Critical and Historical Notes and Memoirs, by Robert Bell. Small post 8vo. 3s. 6d.

Milton's Poetical Works. With a Memoir and Critical Remarks by James Montgomery, an Index to Paradise Lost, Todd's Verbal Index to all the Poems, and a Selection of Explanatory Notes by Henry G. Bohn. Illustrated with 120 Wood Engravings by Thompson, Williams, O. Smith, and Linton, from Drawings by W. Harvey. 2 vols. small post 8vo. 3s. 6d. each.

Pope's Poetical Works. Edited, with copious Notes, by Robert Carruthers. 2 vols. with numerous Illustrations, small post 8vo. 10s.

——— **Homer's Iliad and Odyssey.** With Introduction and Notes by the Rev. J. S. Watson, M.A. Illustrated by the entire Series of Flaxman's Designs. 2 vols. small post 8vo. 5s. each.

Sheridan's Dramatic Works. Complete. With Life by G. G. S., and Portrait, after Reynolds. Small post 8vo. 3s. 6d.

Shakespeare. Dramatic Works. Edited by S. W. Singer. With a Life of Shakespeare by W. W. Lloyd. Uniform with the Aldine Edition of the Poets. In 10 vols. fcap. 8vo. cloth, 2s. 6d. each.

——— **Plays and Poems.** With Notes and Life by Charles Knight. Royal 8vo. 10s. 6d.

——— **Pocket Volume Edition.** Comprising all his Plays and Poems. Edited from the First Folio Edition by T. Keightley. 13 vols. royal 32mo. in a cloth box, price 21s.

Critical Essays on the Plays. By W. W. Lloyd. Uniform with Singer's Edition of Shakespeare, 2s. 6d.

Lectures on Shakespeare. By Bernhard ten Brink. Translated by Julia Franklin. Small post 8vo. 3s. 6d.

Shakespeare's Dramatic Art. The History and Character of Shakespeare's Plays. By Dr. Hermann Ulrici. Translated by L. Dora Schmitz. 2 vols. sm. post 8vo. 3s. 6d. each.

Shakespeare: A Literary Biography by Karl Elze, Ph.D., LL.D. Translated by L. Dora Schmitz. Sm. post 8vo. 5s.

Coleridge's Lectures on Shakespeare, &c. Edited by T. Ashe. Sm. post 8vo. 3s. 6d.

Hazlitt's Lectures on the Characters of Shakespeare's Plays. Sm. post 8vo. 1s.

Jameson's Shakespeare's Heroines. Sm. post 8vo. 3s. 6d.

Lamb's Specimens of English Dramatic Poets of the Time of Elizabeth. With Notes, together with the Extracts from the Garrick Plays. Sm. post 8vo. 3s. 6d.

Ballads and Songs of the Peasantry of England, taken down from oral recitation, and transcribed from private manuscripts, rare broadsides, and scarce publications. Edited by Robert Bell. Sm. post 8vo. 3s. 6d.

Percy's Reliques of Ancient English Poetry. Collected by Thomas Percy, Lord Bishop of Dromore. With an Essay on Ancient Minstrels, and a Glossary. A new edition by J. V. Prichard, A.M. 2 vols. Sm. post 8vo. 7s.

English Sonnets by Living Writers. Selected and arranged, with a Note on the History of the Sonnet, by S. Waddington. 2nd edition, enlarged. Fcap. 8vo. 2s. 6d.

English Sonnets by Poets of the Past. Selected and arranged by S. Waddington. Fcap. 8vo. 2s. 6d.

Who Wrote It? A Dictionary of Common Poetical Quotations in the English Language. 4th edition. Fcap. 8vo. 2s. 6d.

Bohn's Dictionary of Quotations from the English Poets, arranged according to subjects. 4th edition. Post 8vo. 6s.

A Classified Catalogue of Selected Works. 5

New Editions, fcap. 8vo. 2s. 6d. each net.
THE ALDINE EDITION
OF THE
BRITISH POETS.

'This excellent edition of the English classics, with their complete texts and scholarly introductions, are something very different from the cheap volumes of extracts which are just now so much too common.'—*St. James's Gazette.*
'An excellent series. Small, handy, and complete.'—*Saturday Review.*

Akenside. Edited by Rev. A. Dyce.
Beattie. Edited by Rev. A. Dyce.
*Blake. Edited by W. M. Rossetti.
*Burns. Edited by G. A. Aitken. 3 vols.
Butler. Edited by R. B. Johnson. 2 vols.
Campbell. Edited by His Son-in-law, the Rev. A. W. Hill. With Memoir by W. Allingham.
Chatterton. Edited by the Rev. W. W. Skeat, M.A. 2 vols.
Chaucer. Edited by Dr. R. Morris, with Memoir by Sir H. Nicolas. 6 vols.
Churchill. Edited by Jas. Hannay. 2 vols.
*Coleridge. Edited by T. Ashe, B.A. 2 vols.
Collins. Edited by W. Moy Thomas.
Cowper. Edited by John Bruce, F.S.A. 3 vols.
Dryden. Edited by the Rev. R. Hooper, M.A. 5 vols.
Falconer. Edited by the Rev. J. Mitford.
Goldsmith. Edited by Austin Dobson.
*Gray. Edited by J. Bradshaw, LL.D.
Herbert. Edited by the Rev. A. B. Grosart.
*Herrick. Edited by George Saintsbury. 2 vols.
*Keats. Edited by the late Lord Houghton.

Kirke White. Edited by J. Potter Briscoe.
Milton. Edited by Dr. Bradshaw. 3 vols.
Parnell. Edited by G. A. Aitken.
Pope. Edited by G. R. Dennis. With Memoir by John Dennis. 3 vols.
Prior. Edited by R. B. Johnson. 2 vols.
Raleigh and Wotton. With Selections from the Writings of other COURTLY POETS from 1540 to 1650. Edited by Ven. Archdeacon Hannah, D.C.L.
Rogers. Edited by Edward Bell, M.A.
Scott. Edited by John Dennis. 5 vols.
Shakespeare's Poems. Edited by Rev. A. Dyce.
Shelley. Edited by H. Buxton Forman. 5 vols.
Spenser. Edited by J. Payne Collier. 5 vols.
Surrey. Edited by J. Yeowell.
Swift. Edited by the Rev. J. Mitford. 3 vols.
Thomson. Edited by the Rev. D. C. Toovey. 2 vols.
Vaughan. Sacred Poems and Pious Ejaculations. Edited by the Rev. H. Lyte.
Wordsworth. Edited by Prof. Dowden. 7 vols.
Wyatt. Edited by J. Yeowell.
Young. 2 vols. Edited by the Rev. J. Mitford.

* These volumes may also be had bound in Irish linen, with design in gold on side and back by Gleeson White, and gilt top, 3s. 6d. each net.

BIOGRAPHY AND HISTORY.

Memoir of Edward Craven Hawtrey, D.D., Headmaster, and afterwards Provost, of Eton. By F. St. John Thackeray, M.A. With Portrait and 3 Coloured Illustrations. Small crown 8vo. 7s. 6d.

Memorials of the Hon. Ion Keith-Falconer, late Lord Almoner's Professor of Arabic in the University of Cambridge, and Missionary to the Mohammedans of Southern Arabia. By the Rev. Robert Sinker, D.D. With new Portrait. 6th edition. Crown 8vo. 2s. 6d.

A Memoir of Edward Steere, Third Missionary Bishop in Central Africa. By the Rev. R. M. Heanley, M.A. With Portrait, Four Illustrations, and Map. 2nd edition, revised. Crown 8vo. 5s.

François Severin Marceau. A Biography. By Captain T. G. Johnson. With Portraits and Maps. Crown 8vo. 5s.

Robert Schumann. His Life and Works. By August Reissmann. Translated by A. L. Alger. Sm. post 8vo. 3s. 6d.

Schumann's Early Letters. Translated by May Herbert. With a Preface by Sir George Grove, D.C.L. Sm. post 8vo. 3s. 6d.

William Shakespeare. A Literary Biography by Karl Elze, Ph.D., LL.D. Translated by L. Dora Schmitz. Sm. post 8vo. 5s.

Boswell's Life of Johnson, with the Tour in the Hebrides, and Johnsoniana. New edition, with Notes and Appendices by the late Rev. Alexander Napier, M.A., Trinity College, Cambridge, Vicar of Holkham, Editor of the Cambridge Edition of the 'Theological Works of Barrow.' With Steel Engravings. 5 vols. Demy 8vo. 3l.; or in 6 vols. sm. post 8vo. 3s. 6d. each.

Johnson's Lives of the Poets. Edited, with Notes, by Mrs. Alexander Napier, and an Introduction by Professor J. W. Hales, M.A. 3 vols. Sm. post 8vo. 3s. 6d. each.

North's Lives of the Norths: Right Hon. Francis North, Baron Guildford, the Hon. Sir Dudley North, and the Hon. and Rev. Dr. John North. Edited by A. Jessopp, D.D. With 3 Portraits. 3 vols. Sm. post 8vo. 3s. 6d. each.

Vasari's Lives of the most Eminent Painters, Sculptors, and Architects. Translated by Mrs. J. Foster, with Notes. 6 vols. Sm. post 8vo. 3s. 6d. each.

Walton's Lives of Donne, Hooker, &c. New edition, revised by A. H. Bullen. With numerous illustrations. Sm. post 8vo. 5s.

Helps (Sir Arthur). The Life and Labours of the late Thomas Brassey. 7th edition. Sm. post 8vo. 1s. 6d.

—— **The Life of Hernando Cortes, and the Conquest of Mexico,** Dedicated to Thomas Carlyle. 2 vols. Small post 8vo. 3s. 6d. each.

—— **The Life of Christopher Columbus, the Discoverer of America.** 10th edition. Small post 8vo. 3s. 6d.

—— **The Life of Pizarro.** With some Account of his Associates in the Conquest of Peru. 3rd edition. Small post 8vo. 3s. 6d.

—— **The Life of Las Casas, the Apostle of the Indies.** 5th edition. Small post 8vo. 3s. 6d.

Irving (Washington). Life of Oliver Goldsmith. 1s.

——— Life and Voyages of Columbus and his Companions. 2 vols. With Portraits. 3s. 6d. each.

——— Life of Mahomet and His Successors. With Portrait. 3s. 6d.

——— Life of George Washington. With Portrait. 4 vols. 3s. 6d. each.

Life and Letters of Washington Irving. By his nephew, Pierre E. Irving. With Portrait. 2 vols. 3s. 6d. each.

Lockhart's Life of Burns. Revised and corrected with Notes and Appendices, by William Scott Douglas. With Portrait. Sm. post 8vo. 3s. 6d.

Southey's Life of Nelson. With Additional Notes, Index, Portraits, Plans, and upwards of 50 Engravings. Sm. post 8vo. 5s.

——— Life of Wesley, and the Rise and Progress of Methodism. With Portrait. Sm. post 8vo. 5s.

Life of Wellington. By 'An Old Soldier.' From the materials of Maxwell. With 18 Steel Engravings. Sm. post. 8vo. 5s.

Life of Burke. By Sir James Prior. With Portrait. Sm. post 8vo. 3s. 6d.

Life and Letters of Locke. By Lord King. Sm. post 8vo. 3s. 6d.

Life of Pope. By Robert Carruthers. Illustrated. Sm. post. 8vo. 5s.

Cellini's Memoirs. Translated by T. Roscoe. With Portrait. Sm. post 8vo. 3s. 6d.

Memoirs of the Life of Colonel Hutchinson. By his Widow. With Portrait. Sm. post 8vo. 3s. 6d.

Memorials and Letters of Charles Lamb. Talfourd's edition, revised. By W. Carew Hazlitt. 2 vols. Sm. post 8vo. 3s. 6d. each.

Robert Southey: The Story of his Life Written in his Letters. With an Introduction. Edited by John Dennis. Small post 8vo. 3s. 6d.

Letters and Works of Lady Mary Wortley Montagu. Edited, with Memoir, by W. Moy Thomas. Revised edition, with 5 Portraits. 2 vols. small post 8vo. 5s. each.

Memoirs of Philip de Commines. Translated by A. R. Scoble. With Portraits. 2 vols. small post 8vo. 3s. 6d. each.

The Diary of Samuel Pepys. Transcribed from the Shorthand MS. by the Rev. Mynors Bright, M.A. With Lord Braybrooke's Notes. Edited, with Additions, by Henry B. Wheatley, F.S.A. 9 vols. demy 8vo. with Portraits and other Illustrations, 10s. 6d. each.
*** The only complete edition.

Evelyn's Diary and Correspondence, with the Private Correspondence of Charles I. and Sir Edward Nicholas, and between Sir Edward Hyde (Earl of Clarendon) and Sir Richard Browne. Edited from the Original MSS. by W. Bray, F.A.S. With 45 Engravings. 4 vols. small post 8vo. 20s.

Pepys' Diary and Correspondence. With Life and Notes by Lord Braybrooke, and 31 Engravings. 4 vols. small post 8vo. 20s.

The Early Diary of Frances Burney, 1768-1778. With a Selection from her Correspondence and from the Journals of her Sisters, Susan and Charlotte Burney. Edited by Annie Raine Ellis. 2 vols. demy 8vo. 32s.

The Diary and Letters of Madame D'Arblay. As edited by her Niece, Charlotte Barrett. With Portraits. 4 vols. demy 8vo. 30s.

Handbooks of English Literature. Edited by J. W. Hales, M.A., Fellow of Christ's College, Cambridge, Professor of English Literature at King's College, London. Crown 8vo. 3s. 6d. each.

    The Age of Pope. By John Dennis.

    The Age of Dryden. By R. Garnett, LL.D.

    The Age of Milton. By J. Bass Mullinger, M.A., and the Rev. J. H. B. Masterman.

    The Age of Wordsworth. By Prof. C. H. Herford, Litt.D.

        PREPARING.

    The Age of Chaucer. By Professor Hales.

    The Age of Shakespeare. By Professor Hales.

    The Age of Johnson. By Thomas Seccombe.

    The Age of Tennyson. By Professor Hugh Walker.

Ten Brink's History of English Literature. Vol. I.—Early English Literature (to Wiclif). Translated into English by Horace M. Kennedy, Professor of German Literature in the Brooklyn Collegiate Institute. 3s. 6d. Vol. II.—(Wiclif, Chaucer, Earliest Drama, Renaissance). Translated by W. Clarke Robinson, Ph.D. 3s. 6d. Vol III.—(To the Death of Surrey). Edited by Professor Alois Brandl. Translated by L. Dora Schmitz. Small post 8vo. 3s. 6d.

The British Fleet: the Growth, Achievements, and Duties of the Navy of the Empire. By Commander Charles N. Robinson, R.N. With 150 Illustrations. Cheaper edition. Crown 8vo. 6s.

Achievements of Cavalry. By General Sir Evelyn Wood, V.C., G.C.B., G.C.M.G. Crown 8vo. with Maps and Plans. [In the press.

The Campaign of Sedan: The Downfall of the Second Empire, August-September 1870. By George Hooper. With General Map and Six Plans of Battles. Demy 8vo. 14s.

Waterloo: The Downfall of the First Napoleon. A History of the Campaign of 1815. By George Hooper. With Maps and Plans. New edition, revised. Small post 8vo. 3s. 6d.

History of the Irish Rebellion in 1798. By W. H. Maxwell. Illustrated by George Cruikshank. 13th edition. 7s. 6d.

The War of the Succession in Spain during the Reign of Queen Anne, 1702-1711. Based on Original Manuscripts and Contemporary Records. By Col. the Hon. Arthur Parnell, R.E. Demy 8vo. 14s. With Map, &c.

The Revolutionary Movements of 1848-9 in Italy, Austria, Hungary, and Germany. With some Examination of the previous Thirty-three Years. By C. Edmund Maurice. With Illustrations. Demy 8vo. 16s.

History of Germany in the Middle Ages. By E. F. Henderson, Ph.D. Crown 8vo. 7s. 6d. net.

England in the Fifteenth Century. By the late Rev. W. Denton, M.A., Worcester College, Oxford. Demy 8vo. 12s.

History of Modern Europe, from the Taking of Constantinople to the Establishment of the German Empire, A.D. 1453-1871. By the late Dr. T. H. Dyer. A new edition. 5 vols. 2l. 12s. 6d.

Lives of the Queens of England. From the Norman Conquest to the reign of Queen Anne. By Agnes Strickland. Library edition. With Portraits, Autographs, and Vignettes. 8 vols. demy 8vo. 7s. 6d. each. Also a Cheaper Edition in 6 vols. with 6 Portraits, small post 8vo. 30s.

Life of Mary Queen of Scots. By Agnes Strickland. With Index and 2 Portraits of Mary. 2 vols. small post 8vo. 10s.

Lives of the Tudor and Stuart Princesses. By Agnes Strickland. With Portraits. Small post 8vo. 5s.

The Works of Flavius Josephus. Whiston's Translation. Thoroughly revised by Rev. A. R. Shilleto, M.A. With Topographical and Geographical Notes by Sir C. W. Wilson, K.C.B. 5 vols. small post 8vo. 17s. 6d.

Coxe's Memoirs of the Duke of Marlborough. 3 vols. With Portraits. Small post 8vo. 3s. 6d. each.

_{*} ATLAS OF THE PLANS OF MARLBOROUGH'S CAMPAIGNS. 4to. 10s. 6d.

—— History of the House of Austria. 4 vols. With Portraits. Small post 8vo. 3s. 6d. each.

Draper's History of the Intellectual Development of Europe. 2 vols. Small post 8vo. 3s. 6d. each.

Falckenberg's History of Modern Philosophy. Translated by Professor A. C. Armstrong. Demy 8vo. 16s.

Gibbon's Decline and Fall of the Roman Empire. Complete and Unabridged, with Variorum Notes. With Index, Maps, and Portrait. 7 vols. Small post 8vo. 3s. 6d. each.

Gregorovius's History of the City of Rome in the Middle Ages. Translated by Annie Hamilton. Crown 8vo. Vols. I., II., and III., each 6s. net. Vol. IV., in 2 parts, each 4s. 6d. net.

Guizot's History of Civilisation. Translated by W. Hazlitt. 3 vols. With Portraits. Small post 8vo. 3s. 6d. each.

Lamartine's History of the Girondists. 3 vols. With Portraits. Small post 8vo. 3s. 6d. each.

Machiavelli's History of Florence, the Prince, and other Works. With Portrait. Small post 8vo. 3s. 6d.

Martineau's (Harriet) History of England, from 1800-1815. Sm. post 8vo. 3s. 6d.

—— History of the Thirty Years' Peace, A.D. 1815-46. 4 vols. Small post 8vo. 3s. 6d. each.

Menzel's History of Germany. With Portraits. 3 vols. Small post 8vo. 3s. 6d. each.

Michelet's Luther's Autobiography. Translated by William Hazlitt. Small post 8vo. 3s. 6d.

—— **History of the French Revolution** from its earliest indications to the flight of the King in 1791. Small post 8vo. 3s. 6d.

Mignet's History of the French Revolution, from 1789 to 1814. With Portrait of Napoleon as First Consul. Small post 8vo. 3s. 6d.

Motley's Rise of the Dutch Republic. A new Edition, with Introduction by Moncure D. Conway. 3 vols. Small post 8vo. 3s. 6d. each.

Ranke's History of the Popes. Translated by E. Foster. 3 vols. With Portraits. Small post 8vo. 3s. 6d. each.

STANDARD BOOKS.

(See also ' Biography and History,' ' Poetry,' ' Fiction,' &c.)

Addison's Works. With the Notes of Bishop Hurd. Edited by H. G. Bohn. 6 vols. With Portrait and Plates. Small post 8vo. 3s. 6d. each.

Bacon's Essays, and Moral and Historical Works. Edited by J. Devey. With Portrait. Small post 8vo. 3s. 6d.

Bede's Ecclesiastical History, and the Anglo-Saxon Chronicle. Edited by Rev. Dr. Giles. With Map. Small post 8vo. 5s.

Browne's (Sir Thomas) Works. 3 vols. With Portrait. Small post 8vo. 3s. 6d. each.

Burke's Works and Speeches. 8 vols. Sm. post 8vo. 3s. 6d. each.

Burton's Anatomy of Melancholy. Edited, with Notes, by the Rev. A. R. Shilleto, M.A., and an Introduction by A. H. Bullen. 3 vols. Demy 8vo. with binding designed by Gleeson White, 31s. 6d. net. Also a Cheap Edition, in 3 vols. Small post 8vo. 3s. 6d. each.

Coleridge's Prose Works. Edited by T. Ashe. 6 vols. With Portrait. Small post 8vo. 3s. 6d. each.

Defoe's Novels and Miscellaneous Works. 7 vols. With Portrait. Small post 8vo. 3s. 6d. each.

Dunlop's History of Prose Fiction. Revised by Henry Wilson. 2 vols. Small post 8vo. 5s. each.

Emerson's Works. 3 vols. Small post 8vo. 3s. 6d. each.

Goldsmith's (O.) Works. Edited by J. W. M. Gibbs. 5 vols. With Portrait. Small post 8vo. 3s. 6d. each.

Gray's Letters. New Edition, by the Rev. D. C. Tovey, M.A.
[*In the press.*

Hazlitt (William). Lectures and Essays. 7 vols. Small post 8vo. 3s. 6d. each.

Irving (Washington). Complete Works. 15 vols. With Portraits, &c. Small post 8vo. 3s. 6d. each.

A Classified Catalogue of Selected Works. 11

Lamb's Essays of Elia and Eliana. With Portrait. Small post 8vo. 3s. 6d.

Locke (John). Philosophical Works. Edited by J. A. St. John. 2 vols. With Portrait. Small post 8vo. 3s. 6d. each.

Mill (John Stuart). Essays. Collected from various sources by J. W. M. Gibbs. Small post 8vo. 3s. 6d.

Milton's Prose Works. Edited by J. A. St. John. 5 vols. With Portraits. Small post 8vo. 3s. 6d. each.

Prout's (Father) Reliques. By Rev. F. Mahony. Copyright edition. With Etchings by Maclise. Small post 8vo. 5s.

Swift (Jonathan). Prose Works. With Introduction by W. E. H. Lecky, M.P. Vol. I. Small post 8vo. 3s. 6d.

Walton's (Izaak) Angler. Edited by Edward Jesse. With 229 Engravings on Wood and Steel. Small post 8vo. 5s.

White's Natural History of Selborne. Edited by Edward Jesse. With 40 Portraits and Coloured Plates. Small post 8vo. 5s.

Young (Arthur). Travels in France during the Years 1787-89. Edited by M. Betham-Edwards. With Portrait. Small post 8vo. 3s. 6d.

——— Tour in Ireland during the years 1776-9. Edited by A. W. Hutton, Librarian, National Liberal Club. With Bibliography by J. P. Anderson. Index and Map. 2 vols. Small post 8vo., 3s. 6d. each.

Comte's Positive Philosophy. Translated and Condensed by Harriet Martineau. New edition, with Introduction by Frederic Harrison. 3 vols. Small post 8vo. 5s. each.

Hegel's Philosophy of Right (Grundlinien der Philosophie des Rechts). Translated by Samuel W. Dyde, M.A., D.Sc., Professor of Mental Philosophy in Queen's University, Kingston, Canada. Crown 8vo. 7s. 6d.

——— Philosophy of the Sciences, being an Exposition of the Principles of the 'Cours de Philosophie Positive.' By G. H. Lewes. With Index. Small post 8vo. 5s.

Hugo (Victor). Dramatic Works. Hernani—Ruy Blas—The King's Diversion. Translated by Mrs. Newton Crosland and F. L. Slous. Small post 8vo. 3s. 6d.

——— Poems, chiefly Lyrical. Translated by various Writers, collected by J. H. L. Williams. With Portrait. Small post 8vo. 3s. 6d.

Molière's Dramatic Works. Translated by C. H. Wall. 3 vols. With Portrait. Small post 8vo. 3s. 6d. each.

Montaigne's Essays. Cotton's Translation. Edited by W. C. Hazlitt. 3 vols. Small post 8vo. 3s. 6d. each.

Montesquieu's Spirit of Laws. Translated by Dr. Nugent. Revised by J. V. Prichard. 2 vols. With Portrait. Small post 8vo. 3s. 6d. each.

Pascal's Thoughts. Translated by C. Kegan Paul. Small post 8vo. 3s. 6d.

Racine's Tragedies. Translated by R. Bruce Boswell. 2 vols. With Portrait. Small post 8vo. 3s. 6d. each.

Goethe's Works. Including his Autobiography and Annals, Dramatic Works, Poems and Ballads, Novels and Tales, Wilhelm Meister's Apprenticeship and Travels, Tour in Italy, Miscellaneous Travels, Early and Miscellaneous Letters, Correspondence with Schiller and Zelter, and Conversations with Eckermann and Soret. Translated by J. Oxenford, Anna Swanwick, R. D. Boylan, E. A. Bowring, Sir Walter Scott, Edward Bell, L. Dora Schmitz, A. D. Coleridge, and A. Rogers. 16 vols. With Portraits. Small post 8vo. 3s. 6d. each.

────── **Faust.** German Text with Hayward's Prose Translation and Notes. Revised with Introduction by Dr. C. A. Buchheim. Sm. post 8vo. 5s.

Heine's Poems. Translated by E. A. Bowring. Sm. post 8vo. 3s. 6d.

────── **Travel-Pictures.** Translated by Francis Storr. With Map. Small post 8vo. 3s. 6d.

Lessing's Dramatic Works. Edited by Ernest Bell. 2 vols. With Portrait. Small post 8vo. 3s. 6d. each.

────── **Laokoon, Dramatic Notes, &c.** Translated by E. C. Beesley and Helen Zimmern. Edited by Edward Bell. With Frontispiece. Small post 8vo. 3s. 6d.

Richter (Jean Paul). Levana. Translated. Sm. post 8vo. 3s. 6d.

────── **Flower, Fruit, and Thorn Pieces (Siebenkäs).** Translated by Lieut.-Col. A. Ewing. Small post 8vo. 3s. 6d.

Schiller's Works. Including the History of the Seven Years' War, Revolt in the Netherlands, &c., Dramatic and Poetical Works, and Aesthetical and Philosophical Essays. Translated by Rev. A. J. W. Morrison, A. Lodge, E. A. Bowring, J. Churchill, S. T. Coleridge, Sir Theodore Martin, and others. 7 vols. With Portraits. Small post 8vo. 3s. 6d. each.

F. Schlegel's Lectures, and other Works. 5 vols. Small post 8vo. 3s. 6d. each.

A. W. Schlegel's Lectures on Dramatic Art and Literature. Translated by the Rev. A. J. W. Morrison. Small post 8vo. 3s. 6d.

Schopenhauer. On the Fourfold Root of the Principle of Sufficient Reason, and on the Will in Nature. Small post 8vo. 5s.

────── **Essays.** Selected and Translated by E. Belfort Bax. Small post 8vo. 5s.

Alfieri's Tragedies. Translated by E. A. Bowring. 2 vols. Small post 8vo. 3s. 6d. each.

Ariosto's Orlando Furioso, &c. Translated by W. S. Rose. 2 vols. With Portrait and 24 Steel Engravings. Small post 8vo. 5s. each.

Dante. Translated by Rev. H. F. Cary. With Portrait. Small post 8vo. 3s. 6d.

────── Translated by I. C. Wright. With Flaxman's Illustrations. Small post 8vo. 5s.

────── The Italian Text, with English Translation. The Inferno. By Dr. Carlyle. The Purgatorio. By W. S. Dugdale. Sm. post 8vo. 5s. each.

Petrarch's Sonnets, and other Poems. Translated by various hands. With Life by Thomas Campbell, and Portrait and 15 Steel Engravings. Small post 8vo. 5s.

Tasso's Jerusalem Delivered. Translated into English Spenserian Verse by J. H. Wiffen. With Woodcuts and 8 Steel Engravings. Small post 8vo. 5s.

Camoëns' Lusiad. Mickle's Translation revised by E. R. Hodges. Small post 8vo. 3s. 6d.

Antoninus (Marcus Aurelius). The Thoughts of. Translated literally, with Notes, Biographical Sketch, Introductory Essay on the Philosophy, and Index. By George Long, M.A. New edition. Printed at the Chiswick Press, on hand-made paper, and bound in buckram. Pott 8vo. 6s. (Or in Bohn's *Classical Library*, 3s. 6d.)

Epictetus. The Discourses of, with the Encheiridion and Fragments. Translated, with Notes and Introduction, by George Long, M.A. New edition, printed at the Chiswick Press, on hand-made paper, and bound in buckram. 2 vols. Pott 8vo. 10s. 6d. (Or in *Bohn's Classical Library*, 1 vol., 5s.

Plato's Dialogues, referring to the Trial and Death of Socrates, Euthyphro, The Apology, Crito and Phædo. Translated by the late William Whewell, D.D. Printed at the Chiswick Press on hand-made paper, and bound in buckram. Pott 8vo., 4s. 6d.

Plotinus, Select Works of. Translated by Thomas Taylor. Edited by G. R. S. Mead, B.A., M.R.A.S. Small post 8vo. 5s.

Horace. The Odes and Carmen Saeculare. Translated into English Verse by the late John Conington, M.A. 11th edition. Fcap. 8vo. 3s. 6d.

—— The Satires and Epistles. Translated into English Verse by John Conington, M.A. 8th edition. 3s. 6d.

Dictionaries and Books of Reference.

Webster's International Dictionary of the English Language, being the authentic edition of Webster's Unabridged Dictionary, comprising the issues of 1847, 1864, and 1880, now thoroughly revised and enlarged under the supervision of Noah Porter, D.D., LL.D., of Yale University, with Valuable Literary Appendices. Medium 4to. 2118 pages, 3500 Woodcuts. Cloth, 1l. 11s. 6d.; half calf, 2l. 2s.; half russia, 2l. 5s.; full calf, 2l. 8s. Also in 2 vols. cloth, 1l. 14s.

The Standard in the Postal Telegraph Department of the British Isles.
The Standard in the United States Government Printing Office.
Prospectuses with specimen pages sent free on application.

Webster's Brief International Dictionary. A Pronouncing Dictionary of the English Language. Abridged from Webster's International Dictionary. With 800 Illustrations. Demy 8vo. 3s.

A Biographical and Critical Dictionary of Painters and Engravers. With a List of Ciphers, Monograms, and Marks. By Michael Bryan. Imperial 8vo. New edition, thoroughly revised and enlarged by R. E. Graves (of the British Museum) and Walter Armstrong. 2 vols. Imperial 8vo. buckram, 3l. 3s.

A Biographical Dictionary. Containing Concise Notices (upwards of 15,000) of Eminent Persons of all Ages and Countries, and more particularly of Distinguished Natives of Great Britain and Ireland. By Thompson Cooper, F.S.A. With a new Supplement, bringing the work down to 1883. 2 vols. Crown 8vo. 5s. each.

Kluge's Etymological Dictionary of the German Language. Translated by J. F. Davis, D.Lit., M.A. Cheap Edition. Crown 4to. 7s. 6d.

Grimm's Teutonic Mythology. Translated from the 4th edition, with Notes and Appendix, by James Stephen Stallybrass. Demy 8vo. 4 Vols. 3*l*. 3s.; Vols. I. to III. 15s. each; Vol. IV. (containing Additional Notes and References, and completing the Work), 18s.

French and English Dictionary. By F. E. A. Gasc. 6th edition. 8vo. cloth, 10s. 6d.
   A Pocket Dictionary. 16mo. 52nd Thousand. 2s. 6d.

Synonyms and Antonyms of the English Language. Collected and Contrasted. By the late Ven. C. J. Smith, M.A. Small post 8vo. 5s.

Synonyms Discriminated. A Dictionary of Synonymous Words in the English Language, showing the accurate signification of words of similar meaning. Illustrated with Quotations from Standard Writers. By Ven. C. J. Smith, M.A. Edited by the Rev. H. Percy Smith, M.A., of Balliol College, Oxford. Demy 8vo. 14s.

A History of Roman Literature. By Professor W. S. Teuffel. 5th edition, revised, with considerable Additions, by Professor L. Schwabe. Translated by G. C. W. Warr, M.A., Professor of Classical Literature at King's College, London. 2 vols. Medium 8vo. 15s. each.

Corpus Poetarum Latinorum, a se aliisque denuo recognitorum et brevi lectionum varietate instructorum, edidit Johannes Percival Postgate. Vol. I. Large post 4to. 21s. net. Or in 2 parts, paper wrappers, 9s. each net.
                                                         [*Vol. II. preparing.*

Lowndes' Bibliographer's Manual of English Literature. Enlarged edition, by H. G. Bohn. 6 vols. Small post 8vo. 5s. each; or 4 vols., half morocco, 2*l*. 2s.

A Dictionary of Roman Coins, Republican and Imperial. Commenced by the late Seth W. Stevenson, F.S.A., revised in part by C. Roach Smith, F.S.A., and completed by F. W. Madden, M.R.A.S. With upwards of 700 engravings on wood, chiefly executed by the late F. W. Fairholt, F.S.A. 8vo. 2*l*. 2s.

Henfrey's Guide to English Coins, from the Conquest to the present time. New and revised edition. By C. F. Keary, M.A., F.S.A. With an Historical Introduction by the Editor. Small post 8vo. 6s.

Humphreys' Coin Collector's Manual, or Guide to the Numismatic Student in the Formation of a Cabinet of Coins. By H. N. Humphreys. With Index and upwards of 140 Illustrations on Wood and Steel. 2 vols. Small post 8vo. 5s. each.

Clark's Introduction to Heraldry. 18th edition. Revised and Enlarged by J. R. Planché, Rouge Croix. With nearly 1000 Illustrations. Small post 8vo. 5s.; or with the Illustrations Coloured, half-morocco, roxburgh, 15s.

ART AND ARCHÆOLOGY.

Sir Edward Burne-Jones, Bart. A Record and Review. By Malcolm Bell. Illustrated with over 100 Reproductions of the most popular pictures by the Artist; including many paintings and drawings hitherto unpublished, and a representative selection of his designs for stained glass, tapestry, &c. With full and complete lists of his finished works and of his cartoons. 3rd edition, with binding designed by Gleeson White. Small Colombier 8vo. 21s. net.

Albert Moore: his Life and Works. By A. Lys Baldry. Illustrated with 10 Photogravures and about 70 other Reproductions. Small Colombier 8vo. with binding by Gleeson White, 21s. net.

A Classified Catalogue of Selected Works. 15

Sir Frederic Leighton, Bart., P.R.A. An Illustrated Chronicle. By Ernest Rhys. With Introduction by F. G. Stephens. Illustrated with 15 Photogravures and 100 other Reproductions. Super royal 4to. 3*l.* 3*s.*

The Art of Velasquez. A Critical Study. By R. A. M. Stevenson. With 20 Photogravures and 50 other Illustrations. Small royal 4to. 2*l.* 5*s.* net.

Raphael's Madonnas, and other Great Pictures. Reproduced from the Original Paintings. With a Life of Raphael, and an Account of his Chief Works. By Karl Károly. With 54 Illustrations, including 9 Photogravures. Small Colombier 8vo. 21*s.* net.

Masterpieces of the Great Artists A.D. 1400-1700. By Mrs. Arthur Bell (N. D'Anvers). With 43 full-page Illustrations, including 8 Photogravures. Small Colombier 8vo. 21*s.* net.

Men and Women of the Century. Being a Collection of Portraits and Sketches by Mr. Rudolf Lehmann. Edited, with Introduction and Biographical Notices, by H. C. Marillier, B.A. With 12 Photogravures and 70 facsimile reproductions in Half-tone, some printed in Colour, and all executed and printed by the Swan Electric Engraving Co. Medium 4to. 3*l.* 3*s.*

Richard Cosway, R.A., and his Companions. With numerous Illustrations. By George C. Williamson, Lit.D. Small Colombier 8vo.

Bell (Sir C.) The Anatomy and Philosophy of Expression as Connected with the Fine Arts. By Sir Charles Bell, K.H. 7th edition, revised. Small post 8vo. 5*s.*

Bloxam (M. H.) The Principles of Gothic Ecclesiastical Architecture. By M. H. Bloxam. With numerous Woodcuts by Jewitt. 11th edition. Crown 8vo. 2 vols. 15*s.* Companion Volume on CHURCH VESTMENTS. 7*s.* 6*d.*

Bryan's Biographical and Critical Dictionary of Painters and Engravers. With a List of Cyphers, Monograms, and Marks. By Michael Bryan. New edition, thoroughly revised and enlarged by R. E. Graves, of the British Museum, and Walter Armstrong, R.A. 2 vols. imperial 8vo. buckram, 3*l.* 3*s.*

Burn (R.) Ancient Rome and its Neighbourhood. An Illustrated Handbook to the Ruins in the City and the Campagna. By Robert Burn, M.A., Fellow of Trinity College, Cambridge, Author of 'Rome and the Campagna,' &c. With numerous Illustrations. 7*s.* 6*d.*
*** This volume is also issued in limp red cloth, with Map Pocket, for the convenience of Travellers.

Cunningham's Lives of the Most Eminent British Painters. A new edition, with Notes and Sixteen fresh Lives. By Mrs. Heaton. 3 vols. small post 8vo. 3*s.* 6*d.* each.

Delamotte (P. H.) The Art of Sketching from Nature. By P. H. Delamotte. Illustrated by 24 Woodcuts and 20 Coloured Plates, arranged progressively, from Water-colour Drawings by Prout, E. W. Cooke, R.A., Girtin, Varley, De Wint, and the Author. New edition. Royal 4to. 21*s.*

Demmin's Illustrated History of Arms and Armour, from the Earliest Period. By Auguste Demmin. Translated by C. C. Black, M.A., Assistant Keeper, South Kensington Museum. With nearly 2000 Illustrations. Small post 8vo. 7*s.* 6*d.*

Didron's Christian Iconography. A History of Christian Art in the Middle Ages. Translated from the French, with additions, &c., by Margaret Stokes. 2 vols. small post 8vo. 5*s.* each.

Ex-Libris Series. Edited by Gleeson White.

    English Book-Plates (Ancient and Modern). By Egerton Castle, M.A., F.S.A. With more than 200 Illustrations. 3rd edition. 10s. 6d. net.

    French Book-Plates. By Walter Hamilton. With nearly 200 Illustrations. 2nd edition, revised and enlarged. 8s. 6d. net.

    German Book-Plates. By Dr. Heinrich Pallmann and G. Ravenscroft Dennis. With numerous Illustrations. [*Preparing.*

    American Book-Plates. By Charles Dexter Allen. With Bibliography by Eben Newell Hewins, and numerous Illustrations. 12s. 6d. net.

    Ladies' Book-Plates. By Norna Labouchere. With numerous Illustrations. 8s. 6d. net.

    Printers' Marks. By W. Roberts, Editor of the 'Bookworm,' &c. With about 250 Examples. 7s. 6d. net.

    The Decorative Illustration of Books. By Walter Crane. With numerous Illustrations. 10s. 6d. net.

    Modern Book Illustration. By Joseph Pennell. With 150 Illustrations. 10s. 6d. net.

    Bookbindings, Old and New. By Brander Matthews. With numerous Illustrations. 7s. 6d. net.

    Decorative Heraldry. By G. W. Eve. [*Preparing.*

    Durer's Little Passion. Printed from stereotypes taken from the original wood-blocks. With Introduction by Austin Dobson, and Photogravure Portrait of Dürer, by himself. 5s. net.

Fairholt's Costume in England. A History of Dress to the end of the Eighteenth Century. 3rd edition. Revised by the Hon. H. A. Dillon, F.S.A. Illustrated with above 700 Engravings. 2 vols. sm. post 8vo. 5s. each.

Flaxman's Classical Compositions, reprinted in a cheap form for the use of Art Students. Oblong demy, paper cover, 2s. 6d. each.
    THE ILIAD OF HOMER, 39 Designs. THE ODYSSEY OF HOMER, 34 Designs. THE TRAGEDIES OF AESCHYLUS, 36 Designs. THE WORKS AND DAYS AND THEOGONY OF HESIOD, 37 Designs. SELECT COMPOSITIONS FROM DANTE'S DIVINE DRAMA. 37 Designs. Oblong, paper cover, 2s. 6d.

Flaxman. Lectures on Sculpture, as delivered before the President and Members of the Royal Academy. By J. Flaxman, R.A. With 53 Plates. New edition. Small post 8vo. 6s.

Gatty (Mrs.) The Book of Sun-dials. Collected by Mrs. Alfred Gatty, Author of 'Parables from Nature,' &c. Edited by Horatio K. F. Eden and Eleanor Lloyd. With numerous Illustrations. 3rd edition. Fcap. 4to. 15s.

Heaton (Mrs.) A Concise History of Painting. By Mrs. Charles Heaton. New edition, revised, by Cosmo Monkhouse. Small post 8vo. 5s.

Hiatt (C. T. J.) Picture Posters. A Handbook on the History of the Illustrated Placard. With numerous Reproductions of the most artistic examples of all countries. By C. T. J. Hiatt. 8vo. 12s. 6d. net.

Lanzi's History of Painting in Italy, from the Period of the Revival of the Fine Arts to the End of the Eighteenth Century. With a Biographical Notice of the Author, Indexes, and Portraits. Translated by Thomas Roscoe. 3 vols. small post 8vo. 3s. 6d. each.

Law (E.) The History of Hampton Court Palace. Profusely Illustrated with Copper-plates, Autotypes, Etchings, Engravings, Maps, and Plans. By Ernest Law, B.A. In 3 vols. fcap. 4to. Vol. I.—IN TUDOR TIMES, 21s.; Vol. II.—IN STUART TIMES, 21s.; Vol. III.—IN ORANGE AND GUELPH TIMES, 31s. 6d.

Leonardo da Vinci's Treatise on Painting. With a Life of Leonardo. New edition, revised, with numerous Plates. Small post 8vo. 5s.

Moody (F. W.) Lectures and Lessons on Art. By the late F. W Moody, Instructor in Decorative Art at South Kensington Museum. With Diagrams to illustrate Composition and other matters. 5th edition. Demy 8vo. sewed, 4s. 6d.

Patmore (C.) Principle in Art. By Coventry Patmore. 2nd edition. Fcap. 8vo. 5s.

Petit (J. T.) Architectural Studies in France. By the late Rev. J. T. Petit, F.S.A. New edition, revised by Edward Bell, M.A., F.S.A. Fcap. 4to. with 260 Illustrations, 15s. net.

Planché's History of British Costume, from the Earliest Time to the close of the Eighteenth Century. By J. R. Planché, Somerset Herald. With Index and upwards of 400 Illustrations. Small post 8vo. 5s.

Renton (E.) Intaglio Engraving, Past and Present. By Edward Renton. With numerous Illustrations from Gems and Seals. Fcap. 8vo.

Roberts (W.) Memorials of Christie's. By W. Roberts. With 64 Collotype Reproductions and Coloured Frontispiece. 2 vols. 8vo. 25s. net.

Stokes (Margaret). Three Months in the Forests of France. A Pilgrimage in Search of Vestiges of the Irish Saints in France. With numerous Illustrations of the Architecture, Sculptures, Paintings, and Personal Relics connected with them. By Margaret Stokes, Hon. M.R.I.A., Author of 'Six Months in the Apennines,' 'Early Christian Architecture in Ireland,' &c. Fcap. 4to. 12s. net.

Strange (E. F.) Japanese Illustration. A History of the Arts of Woodcutting and Colour Printing in Japan. By Edward F. Strange, M.J.S. With 8 Coloured Plates and 80 other Illustrations. Demy 8vo. 12s. 6d. net.

—— **Alphabets.** A Handbook of Lettering. With 200 Illus. 5s.

Vasari's Lives of the Most Eminent Painters, Sculptors, and Architects. Translated by Mrs. J. Foster, with Notes, Index, and Portrait. 6 vols. small post 8vo. 3s. 6d. each.

Watson (R. M.) The Art of the House. By Rosamond Marriott Watson. Illustrated. Demy 8vo.

Way (T. R.) Lithographs of Old London. By T. R. Way. With Introduction and Explanatory Letterpress by H. B. Wheatley, F.S.A. Small 4to. 21s. net.

Wedmore (F.) Etching in England. By Frederick Wedmore. With numerous Illustrations. Small 4to. 8s. 6d. net.

Wheatley (H. B.) English Historical Portraits. By H. B. Wheatley, F.S.A. With numerous Reproductions. Demy 8vo.

White (Gleeson). Practical Designing. A Handbook on the Preparation of Working Drawings, showing the Technical Methods employed in preparing them for the Manufacture, and the Limits imposed on the Design by the Mechanism of Reproduction and the materials employed. Freely Illustrated. Edited by Gleeson White. 2nd edition. 6s. net.
  CONTENTS: Carpets, by A. Millar—Drawing for Reproduction, by the Editor—Pottery, by W. P. Rix—Metal Work, by R. Ll. Rathbone—Stained Glass, by Selwyn Image—Bookbinding, by H. Orrinsmith—Tiles, by Owen Carter—Woven Fabrics, Printed Fabrics, and Floorcloths, by Arthur Silver—Wall Papers, by G. C. Haite.

ROYAL NAVY HANDBOOKS.

Edited by Commander CHARLES N. ROBINSON, R.N.

'The series of Naval Handbooks edited by Commander Robinson has made a most hopeful beginning, and may be counted upon to supply the growing popular demand for information in regard to the Navy, on which the national existence depends '—*Times*.

Crown 8vo. Illustrated, 5s. each.

Naval Administration: the Constitution, Character, and Functions of the Board of Admiralty and of the Civil Departments it Directs. By Admiral Sir R. Vesey Hamilton, G.C.B., late First Sea Lord of the Admiralty.

The Mechanism of Men-of-War: being a Description of the Machinery to be found in Modern Fighting Ships. By Fleet Engineer Reginald C. Oldknow, R.N.

Torpedoes and Torpedo-Vessels. With a Chapter on the Effects of Torpedo Warfare, by one who was present at the Yalu and Weiheiwei. By Lieutenant G. E. Armstrong, late R.N.

Naval Ordnance and Small Arms. With the Methods of Mounting Guns on Board Modern Men-of-War. By Captain H. Garbett, R.N.

Other Volumes in Preparation.

BOTANY.

By J. G. BAKER, F.R.S., F.L.S., Keeper of the Herbarium of the Royal Gardens, Kew.

A Flora of the English Lake District. Demy 8vo. 7s. 6d.

Handbook of the Fern Allies. A Synopsis of the Genera and Species of the Natural Orders, Equisetaceae, Lycopodiaceae, Selaginellaceae, Rhizocarpeae. Demy 8vo. 5s.

Handbook of the Amaryllideae, including the Alstroemerieae and Agaveae. Demy 8vo. 5s.

Handbook of the Bromeliaceae. Demy 8vo. 5s.

Handbook of the Irideæ. Demy 8vo. 5s.

English Botany. Containing a Description and Life-size Drawing of every British Plant. Edited by T. BOSWELL (formerly SYME), LL.D., F.L.S., &c. The Figures by J. C. Sowerby, F.L.S., J. De C. Sowerby F.L.S., J. W. Salter, A.L.S., F.G.S., and J. E. SOWERBY. 3rd edition, entirely, revised, with descriptions of all the species by the Editor, and 1937 full-page Coloured Plates. In 12 vols. 24l. 3s. cloth ; 27l. 15s. half morocco ; and 31l. 13s. whole morocco. Also in 89 parts, 5s. each, except part 89, containing an Index to the whole work, 7s. 6d. Volumes sold separately.

*** A Supplement to the third edition is now in preparation. Vol. I. (Vol. XIII. of the complete work) containing orders I. to XL., by N. E. Brown, of the Royal Herbarium, Kew, now ready, 17s. Or in three parts, 5s. each.

Johnson's Gardener's Dictionary. Describing the Plants, Fruits, and Vegetables desirable for the Garden, and explaining the Terms and Operations employed in their cultivation. New edition (1893-4), revised by C. H. Wright, F.R.M.S., and D. Dewar, Curator of the Botanic Gardens, Glasgow. Demy 8vo. 9s. net.

British Fungus-Flora. A Classified Text-book of Mycology. By George Massee. With numerous Illustrations. 4 vols. Post 8vo. 7s. 6d. each.

Botanist's Pocket-Book. By W. R. Hayward. Containing the botanical name, common name, soil or situation, colour, growth, and time of flowering of all plants, arranged in a tabulated form. 8th edition, revised, with a new Appendix. Fcap. 8vo. 4s. 6d.

Index of British Plants, according to the London Catalogue (8th edition), including the Synonyms used by the principal authors, an alphabetical list of English names; also references to the illustrations of Syme's 'English Botany' and Bentham's 'British Flora.' By Robert Turnbull. Paper, 2s. 6d.; cloth, 3s.

The London Catalogue of British Plants. Part I., containing the British Phaenogamia, Filices, Equisetaceae, Lycopodiaceae, Selaginellaceae, Marsileaceae, and Characeae. 9th edition. Demy 8vo. 6d.; interleaved, in limp cloth, 1s.

ECONOMICS AND FINANCE.

The Case against Bimetallism. By Robert Giffen, C.B., LL.D. 4th edition. Crown 8vo. 7s. 6d.

The Growth of Capital. By the same author. Demy 8vo. 7s. 6d.

Ricardo on the Principles of Political Economy and Taxation. Edited by E. C. K. Gonner, M.A., Lecturer, University College, Liverpool. Sm. post 8vo. 5s.

Smith (Adam). The Wealth of Nations. Edited by E. Belfort Bax. 2 vols. Sm. post 8vo. 7s.

The History, Principles, and Practice of Banking. By the late J. W. Gilbart, F.R.S., formerly Director and General Manager of the London and Westminster Bank. New edition, revised by A. S. Michie, of the Royal Bank of Scotland, Glasgow. 2 vols. small post 8vo. 10s.

SPORTS AND GAMES.

Bohn's Handbooks of Athletic Sports. In 8 vols. Sm. post 8vo. 6d. each.

Vol. I.—Cricket, by Hon. and Rev. E. Lyttelton. Lawn Tennis, by H. W. W. Wilberforce. Tennis, Rackets, and Fives, by Julian Marshall, Major Spens, and Rev. J. A. Tait. Golf, by W. T. Linskill. Hockey, by F. S. Creswell.

Vol. II.—Rowing and Sculling, by W. B. Woodgate. Sailing, by E. F. Knight. Swimming, by M. and J. R. Cobbett.

Vol. III.—Boxing, by R. G. Allanson-Winn. Broadsword and Single Stick, with chapters on Quarterstaff, Bayonet, Cudgel, Shillalah, Walking-Stick, and Umbrella, by R. G. Allanson-Winn and C. Phillipps-Wolley. Wrestling, by Walter Armstrong. Fencing, by H. A. Colmore Dunn.

Vol. IV.—Rugby Football, by Harry Vassall. Association Football, by C. W. Alcock. Baseball, by Newton Crane. Rounders, Bowls, Quoits, Curling, Skittles, &c., by C. C. Mott and J. M. Walker.

Vol. V.—Cycling and Athletics, by H. H. Griffin. Skating, by Douglas Adams.

Vol. VI.—Practical Horsemanship, including Riding for Ladies, by W. A. Kerr, V.C.

Vol. VII.—Camping Out, by A. A. Macdonald. Canoeing, by Dr. J. D. Hayward.

Vol. VIII.—Gymnastics, by A. F. Jenkin. Clubs, by G. T. B. Cobbett and A. F. Jenkin.

Bohn's Handbooks of Games. New edition. In 2 vols. Small post 8vo. 3s. 6d. each.

    Vol. I.—TABLE GAMES: Billiards, with Pool, Pyramids, and Snooker, by Major-General A. W. Drayson, F.R.A.S., with a preface by W. J. Peall. Bagatelle, by 'Berkeley.' Chess, by R. F. Green. Draughts, Backgammon, Dominoes, Solitaire, Reversi, Go-Bang, Rouge et Noir, Roulette, E.O., Hazard, Faro, by 'Berkeley.'

    Vol. II.—CARD GAMES: Whist, by Dr. William Pole, F.R.S., Author of 'The Philosophy of Whist,' &c. Solo Whist, by R. F. Green. Piquet, Ecarté, Euchre, Bézique, and Cribbage, by 'Berkeley.' Poker, Loo, Vingt-et-un, Napoleon, Newmarket, Pope Joan, Speculation, &c. &c., by Baxter-Wray.

Morphy's Games of Chess, being the Matches and best Games played by the American Champion, with explanatory and analytical Notes by J. Löwenthal. With short Memoir and Portrait of Morphy. Sm. post 8vo. 5s.

Staunton's Chess-Player's Handbook. A Popular and Scientific Introduction to the Game. With numerous diagrams. 5s.

———— Chess Praxis. A Supplement to the Chess-player's Handbook. Containing the most important modern improvements in the Openings; Code of Chess Laws; and a Selection of Morphy's Games. Small post 8vo. 5s.

———— Chess-Player's Companion. Comprising a Treatise on Odds, Collection of Match Games, and a Selection of Original Problems. With coloured Frontispiece. Small post 8vo. 5s.

Chess Studies and End-Games. In Two Parts. Part I. Chess Studies. Part II. Miscellaneous End-Games. By B. Horwitz and J. Kling. 2nd edition, revised by the Rev. W. Wayte, M.A. Demy 8vo. 7s. 6d.

Hints on Billiards. By J. P. Buchanan. Illustrated with 36 Diagrams. Crown 8vo. 3s. 6d. net.

Sturges's Guide to the Game of Draughts. With Critical Situations. Revised, with Additional Play on the Modern Openings, by J. A. Kear, Editor of 'The International Draught Magazine.' Crown 8vo. 3s. 6d. net.

Hints on Driving. By Captain C. Morley Knight, R.A. Illustrated by G. H. A. White, Royal Artillery. 2nd edition, revised and enlarged. Crown 8vo. 3s. 6d. net.

Hints on Golfing. By H. S. C. Everard, St. Andrew's. With 21 Illustrations. Crown 8vo.

Half-Hours with an Old Golfer; a Pot-pourri for Golfers. By Calamo Currente. With 40 Illustrations and 4 Coloured Plates by G. A. Laundy. Crown 8vo. gilt extra, 5s.

Schools and Masters of Fence, from the Middle Ages to the Eighteenth Century. With a Sketch of the Development of the Art of Fencing with the Rapier and the Small Sword, and a Bibliography of the Fencing Art during that Period. By Egerton Castle, M.A. With numerous Illustrations. 2nd edition. Small post 8vo. 6s.

Oars and Sculls, and How to Use them. By W. B. Woodgate, M.A., Brasenose College, Oxford. Crown 8vo. 2s. 6d.

Dancing as an Art and Pastime. With 40 full-page illustrations from life. By Edward Scott. Crown 8vo. 6s.

THE ALL-ENGLAND SERIES.
HANDBOOKS OF ATHLETIC GAMES.
The only Series issued at a moderate price, by Writers who are in the first rank in their respective departments.

'The best instruction on games and sports by the best authorities, at the lowest prices.'—*Oxford Magazine*.

Small 8vo. cloth, Illustrated. Price 1s. each.

Cricket. By the Hon. and Rev. E. LYTTELTON.
Lawn Tennis. By H. W. W. WILBERFORCE. With a Chapter for Ladies, by Mrs. HILLYARD.
Tennis and Rackets and Fives. By JULIAN MARSHALL, Major J. SPENS, and Rev. J. A. ARNAN TAIT.
Golf. By W. T. LINSKILL.
Rowing and Sculling. By W. B. WOODGATE.
Sailing. By E. F. KNIGHT, dbl. vol. 2s.
Swimming. By MARTIN and J. RACSTER COBBETT.
Camping out. By A. A. MACDONELL. Double vol. 2s.
Canoeing. By Dr. J. D. HAYWARD. Double vol. 2s.
Mountaineering. By Dr. CLAUDE WILSON. Double vol. 2s.
Athletics. By H. H. GRIFFIN. With contributions by E. H. Pelling, H. C. L. Tindall, J. L. Greig, T. Jennings, C. F. Daft, J. Kibblewhite, Tom Ray, Sid Thomas, and the Rev. W. Pollock-Hill.
Riding. By W. A. KERR, V.C. Double vol. 2s.
Ladies' Riding. By W. A. KERR, V.C.
Boxing. By R. G. ALLANSON-WINN. With Prefatory Note by Bat Mullins.

Cycling. By H. H. GRIFFIN, L.A.C., N.C.U., C.T.C. With a Chapter for Ladies, by Miss L. C. DAVIDSON.
Wrestling. By WALTER ARMSTRONG ('Cross-buttocker').
Fencing. By H. A. COLMORE DUNN.
Broadsword and Singlestick. By R. G. ALLANSON-WINN and C. PHILLIPPS-WOLLEY.
Gymnastics. By A. F. JENKIN. Double vol. 2s.
Indian Clubs. By G. T. B. COBBETT and A. F. JENKIN.
Football — Rugby Game. By HARRY VASSALL.
Football—Association Game. By C. W. ALCOCK.
Hockey. By F. S. CRESWELL. (In Paper Cover, 6d.)
Skating. By DOUGLAS ADAMS. With a Chapter for Ladies, by Miss L. CHEETHAM, and a Chapter on Speed Skating, by a Fen Skater. Dbl. vol. 2s.
Baseball. By NEWTON CRANE.
Rounders, Fieldball, Bowls, Quoits, Curling, Skittles, &c. By J. M. WALKER and C. C. MOTT.
Dancing. By EDWARD SCOTT. Double vol. 2s.

THE CLUB SERIES OF CARD AND TABLE GAMES.
'No well-regulated club or country house should be without this useful series of books.' —*Globe*.

Small 8vo. cloth, Illustrated. Price 1s. each.

Whist. By Dr. WM. POLE, F.R.S.
Solo Whist. By ROBERT F. GREEN.
Billiards. The Art of Practical Billiards for Amateurs, with chapters on Pool, Pyramids, and Snooker. By Major-Gen. A. W. DRAYSON, F.R.A.S. With a Preface by W. J. Peall.
Chess. By ROBERT F. GREEN, Editor of the 'British Chess Magazine.'
The Two-Move Chess Problem. By B. G. LAWS.
Chess Openings. By I. GUNSBERG.
Draughts and Backgammon. By 'BERKELEY.'
Reversi and Go Bang. By 'BERKELEY.'

Dominoes and Solitaire. By 'BERKELEY.'
Bézique and Cribbage. By 'BERKELEY.'
Écarté and Euchre. By 'BERKELEY.'
Piquet and Rubicon Piquet. By 'BERKELEY.'
Skat. By LOUIS DIEHL.
⁎ A Skat Scoring-book. 1s.
Round Games, including Poker, Napoleon, Loo, Vingt-et-un, Newmarket, Commerce, Pope Joan, Speculation, Spin, Snip-Snap-Snorum, Jig Cassino, My Bird Sings. Spoil-Five and Lot By BAXTER WRAY.

FICTION.
(See also 'Standard Books.')

Björnson's Arne and the Fisher Lassie. Translated from the Norse with an Introduction by W. H. Low, M.A. Small post 8vo. 3s. 6d.

Burney's Evelina; or, The History of a Young Lady's Entrance into the World. By Frances Burney (Mme. D'Arblay). With an Introduction and Notes by A. R. Ellis. Small post 8vo. 3s. 6d.

────── **Cecilia.** 2 vols. small post 8vo. 3s. 6d. each.

Cervantes' Galatea. A Pastoral Romance. Translated from the Spanish by G. W. J. Gyll. Small post 8vo. 3s. 6d.

────── **Exemplary Novels.** Translated from the Spanish by Walter K. Kelly. Small post 8vo. 3s. 6d.

────── **Don Quixote de la Mancha.** Motteux's Translation, revised. With Lockhart's Life and Notes. 2 vols. small post 8vo. 3s. 6d. each.

Classic Tales, containing Rasselas, Vicar of Wakefield, Gulliver's Travels, and The Sentimental Journey. Small post 8vo. 3s. 6d.

De Staël's Corinne or Italy. By Madame de Staël. Translated by Emily Baldwin and Paulina Driver. Small post 8vo. 3s. 6d.

Ebers' Egyptian Princess. An Historical Novel. By George Ebers. Translated by E. S. Buchheim. Small post 8vo. 3s. 6d.

Edmonds (Mrs.) Amygdala. A Story of the French Revolution. 2s. 6d. net.

Fielding's Adventures of Joseph Andrews and His Friend Mr. Abraham Adams. With Cruikshank's Illustrations. 3s. 6d.

────── **History of Tom Jones, a Foundling.** Roscoe's Edition, with George Cruikshank's Illustrations. 2 vols. small post 8vo. 3s. 6d. each.

────── **Amelia.** Illustrated by George Cruikshank. 5s.

Gift (Theo.) Dishonoured. 6s.

Gil Blas, the Adventures of. Translated by Smollett. Illustrated by Smirke and Cruikshank. Small post 8vo. 6s.

Hauff's Tales. The Caravan—The Sheik of Alexandria—The Inn in the Spessart. Translated by S. Mendel. Small post 8vo. 3s. 6d.

Hawthorne's Tales. 4 vols. Small post 8vo. 3s. 6d. each.

Hoffmann's Tales. The Serapion Brethren. Translated by Lieut.-Col. Ewing. 2 vols. Small post 8vo. 3s. 6d. each.

Holnut (W. S.) Olympia's Journal. Crown 8vo. 3s. 6d.

Manzoni. The Betrothed. By Alessandro Manzoni. With numerous Woodcut Illustrations Small post 8vo. 5s.

Poushkin's Prose Tales. Translated from the Russian by T. Keane. Small post 8vo. 3s. 6d.

Smollett's Roderick Random. With Cruikshank's Illustrations and Bibliography. Small post 8vo. 3s. 6d.

────── **Peregrine Pickle.** With Cruikshank's Illustrations. 2 vols. Small post 8vo. 3s. 6d. each.

────── **Humphry Clinker.** With Cruikshank's Illustrations. Small post 8vo. 3s. 6d.

Steele (Mrs. A. C.) Lesbia. A Study in one volume. 6s.

Stinde (J.) The Buchholz Family. Sketches of Berlin Life. By Julius Stinde. Translated from the 49th edition of the German by L. Dora Schmitz. Popular edition, picture boards, 2s.

Stinde (J.) The Buchholz Family. Second Part. Popular edition. Picture boards, 2s.

—— The Buchholzes in Italy. Translated from the 37th edition of the original by Harriet F. Powell. Crown 8vo. cloth, 3s.

—— Frau Wilhelmine. Being the Conclusion of 'The Buchholz Family.' Translated by Harriet F. Powell. Crown 8vo. cloth, 3s.

BOOKS FOR THE YOUNG.

Andersen (Hans Christian). Fairy Tales and Sketches. Translated by C. C. Peachey, H. Ward, A. Plesner, &c. With numerous Illustrations by Otto Speckter and others. 7th thousand. Crown 8vo. 3s. 6d.

—— Tales for Children. With 48 full-page Illustrations by Wehnert, and 57 small Engravings on Wood by W. Thomas. 13th thousand. Crown 8vo. 3s. 6d.

—— Danish Legends and Fairy Tales. Translated from the Original by Caroline Peachey. With a Short Life of the Author, and 120 Wood Engravings, chiefly by Foreign Artists. Small post 8vo. 5s.

Edgeworth's Stories for Children. With 8 Illustrations by L. Speed. Small post 8vo. 3s. 6d.

Ford (Mrs. Gerard). Master Rex. By Mrs. Gerard Ford. Illustrated by James Cadenhead, Florence M. Cooper, and Louise S. Sweet. 2nd edition. Crown 8vo. 3s.

—— Pixie; and the Hill-House Farm. Illustrated by James Cadenhead and Florence M. Cooper. 2nd edition. Crown 8vo. 3s.

Gatty's Parables from Nature. With Notes on the Natural History, and numerous full-page Illustrations by W. Holman Hunt, E. Burne Jones, J. Tenniel, J. Wolf, and other eminent artists. Complete edition with short Memoir by J. H. Ewing. Crown 8vo. 5s.
POCKET VOLUME EDITION. 2 vols. Imp. 32mo. 5s.
CHEAP EDITION. Illustrated. 2 vols. Fcap. 4to. paper covers, 1s. each; or bound in 1 vol cloth, 3s.

Grimm's Gammer Grethel; or, German Fairy Tales and Popular Stories, containing 42 Fairy Tales. Translated by Edgar Taylor. With numerous Woodcuts after George Cruikshank and Ludwig Grimm. 3s. 6d.

—— Tales. With the Notes of the Original. Translated by Mrs. A. Hunt. With Introduction by Andrew Lang, M.A. 2 vols. 3s. 6d. each.

Harald the Viking. A Book for Boys. By Capt. Charles Young. With Illustrations by J. Williamson. Crown 8vo. 5s.

Stowe's Uncle Tom's Cabin; or, Life among the Lowly. With Introductory Remarks by Rev. J. Sherman. With 8 full-page Illustrations. Small post 8vo. 3s. 6d.

The Wide, Wide World. A Story. By Elizabeth Wetherell. Sm. post 8vo. 3s. 6d.

Uncle Peter's Riddle. By Ella K. Sanders. Illustrated by Florence M. Cooper. 3s. 6d.

CAPT. MARRYAT'S BOOKS FOR BOYS.

Uniform Illustrated Edition. Small post 8vo. 3s. 6d. each.

Poor Jack.
The Mission; or, Scenes in Africa.
The Pirate, and Three Cutters.
Peter Simple.
The Settlers in Canada.
The Privateersman.
Masterman Ready.
Midshipman Easy.

MRS. EWING'S BOOKS.

Uniform Edition, in 9 vols.

We and The World. A Story for Boys. By the late Juliana Horatio Ewing. With 7 Illustrations by W. L. Jones. 4th edition. 3s.

A Flat Iron for a Farthing; or, Some Passages in the Life of an Only Son. With 12 Illustrations by H. Allingham. 16th edition. 3s.

Mrs. Overtheway's Remembrances. Illustrated with 9 fine full-page Engravings by Pasquier, and Frontispiece by Wolf. 5th edition. 3s.

Six to Sixteen: A Story for Girls. With 10 Illustrations by Mrs. Allingham. 8th edition. 3s.

Jan of the Windmill: a Story of the Plains. With 11 Illustrations by Mrs. Allingham. 5th edition. 3s.

A Great Emergency. A very Ill-tempered Family—Our Field—Madame Liberality. With 4 Illustrations. 3rd edition. 3s.

Melchior's Dream. The Blackbird's Nest—Friedrich's Ballad—A Bit of Green—Monsieur the Viscount's Friend—The Yew Lane Ghosts—A Bad Habit—A Happy Family. With 8 Illustrations by Gordon Browne. 7th edition. 3s.

Lob-Lie-by-the-Fire, or the Luck of Lingborough; and other Tales. With 3 Illustrations by George Cruikshank. 4th edition. Imp. 16mo. 3s. 6d.

The Brownies. The Land of Lost Toys—Three Christmas-trees—An Idyl of the Wood—Christmas Crackers—Amelia and the Dwarfs—Timothy's Shoes—Benjy in Beastland. Illustrated by George Cruikshank. 7th edition. Imp. 16mo. 3. 6.

THE SHILLING SERIES.

Fcap. 4to. double columns, Illustrated, 1s. each.

Mrs. Ewing's Melchior's Dream, and other Tales.

—— A Flat Iron for a Farthing.

—— Six to Sixteen.

—— We and the World.

—— Mrs. Overtheway's Remembrances.

—— Jan of the Windmill.

—— A Great Emergency, and other Tales.

—— The Brownies, and other Tales.

Mrs. Gatty's Parables from Nature. Two Series, each 1s.

Miss Procter's Legends and Lyrics. Two Series, each 1s.

Hector. A Story for Young People. With 12 Illustrations by W. J. Hennessey. By Flora Shaw, Author of 'Castle Blair.'

Andersen's Tales. Translated by Caroline Peachey.

London: GEORGE BELL & SONS, York Street, Covent Garden.

www.ingramcontent.com/pod-product-compliance
Lightning Source LLC
Chambersburg PA
CBHW020524300426
44111CB00008B/537